For Marjorie

Contents

Acknowledgments

A more primitive version of this book was accepted as a doctoral thesis by the University of Toronto in 1966 and I am grateful both to Professor J. M. S. Careless for his attentive supervision of a project which began as a study in the concept of loyalty in Old Ontario and developed, or degenerated, into something quite different, and to Professor D. G. Creighton for his helpful comments on certain aspects of it. I owe a special debt to Ramsay Cook, now of York University, who drew references to my attention and brought his enthusiasm and judgment to bear on so many occasions. And I am also obligated to H. C. Pentland of the University of Manitoba, whose seminar on economic thought first aroused my interest in intellectual history, and to Kenneth McNaught whose course on the American progressive tradition sustained it. Though these individuals have had a hand in whatever merits this book might have, I alone am responsible for its shortcomings and deficiencies.

The research for this study was made possible by a Woodrow Wilson Doctoral Dissertation Fellowship and grants from the Canada Council and the Social Science Research Committee of the University of Toronto, and it was made pleasurable by the efficient staffs of the Public Archives of Canada, the National Library, the Ontario Archives, the Douglas Library at Queen's University, the Toronto Public Library, and the University of Toronto Library.

This book has been published with the help of a grant from the Social Science Research Council of Canada, using funds provided by the Canada Council. The editing process was made as painless as possible by Rik Davidson and Gerry Hallowell of the University of Toronto Press.

To my wife, who simultaneously kept our daughter peaceably disposed, maintained control of our unruly Basset hound (now, alas, departed), and typed these pages many times, I owe more than any hackneyed appreciation can ever suggest.

C. B.

NOTE ON ABBREVIATIONS AND USE OF TITLES

All manuscript collections referred to in the footnotes are held by the Public Archives of Canada, Ottawa, with the exception of those preceded by the following letters: TPL (Baldwin Room, Toronto Public Library); QUL (Douglas Library, Queen's University); OA (Archives of the Province of Ontario); UT (Thomas Fisher Rare Book Library, University of Toronto).

In referring to those Canadians who received honours during the period under discussion, I have mentioned them by title only once and refer to them throughout by their common names. In a study which moves backwards and forwards over half a century such a procedure was the only one compatible with clarity.

Introduction to the Second Edition

It has been more than forty years since *Sense of Power* was first published. In the interim many, many academic and scholarly works of solid quality have appeared, run their course, and faded into the obscurity of time. It is therefore a signal recognition that University of Toronto Press is reissuing this volume with the original text intact. This republication is an acknowledgment not only of the text's quality but also of the fact that the work has become a historical document in its own right. Carl Berger's choice of topic, his methodology, and the impact of the resulting book on subsequent works all reflect a particular era in Canadian scholarship. Thus, this new edition can be read as an excellent piece of historical writing and seen through a perspective some forty years distant as a transformative work in Canadian historiography.

That transformation is unequivocal and multilayered. It is unequivocal in Berger's conclusion that "imperialism was one form of Canadian nationalism" (259). This is widely accepted now, but as Ramsay Cook noted, it "is as revisionist a sentence as any Canadian historian has ever written."[1] Until *Sense of Power* the overwhelming assumption of Canadian historical writing was that imperialism and nationalism were divergent, perhaps even antithetical concepts. The fact that the one could be seen as a subset of the other was nearly incomprehensible much less acceptable. Berger made it not only comprehensible but pretty much the standard interpretation of the way in which Canadian nationalism evolved.

This shift of perspective, however, depended on a work that was complex and subtle in its presentation. Indeed, such a revisionist argument succeeded only because of two preconditions. First, the book was a tremendous piece of research and writing. Second, it fit well into the era in which it was written. To put it another way, it was good but it also resonated with the attitude of the times in topic, approach, and method.

My task is simple: to try and put the book into the historiographic context that gave it such impact. I do so with some trepidation in that I am

---

1 Ramsay Cook, "Carl Berger: Ironic Man as Historian," in Gerald Friesen and Doug Owram, *Thinkers and Dreamers: Historical Essays in Honour of Carl Berger* (Toronto: University of Toronto Press, 2011), 13–32, 14.

essentially undertaking a historiographic interpretation of a work by the person who, in his *Writing of Canadian History* (1976, 2nd edition 1986) established himself as Canada's master historiographer. Indeed, there is something peculiar in citing Berger's *Writing of Canadian History* to help establish the place of his *Sense of Power*. Nonetheless, as I hope to show, *Sense of Power* was indeed a product of its time. The nature of Canada, the nature of the academic community, and the nature of the University of Toronto all shaped Berger's approach.

I

Sense of Power was Carl Berger's first book and was originally researched and written as a doctoral dissertation. *Visions of Grandeur: Studies in the Idea of Canadian Imperialism* was formally accepted by the University of Toronto in, appropriately, Canada's centennial year, 1967. Though *Sense of Power* was a more refined and tightened version of the thesis, the basis of his work was nonetheless the product of graduate school. This book, therefore, is a product not only of the time but of the context in which he, as a graduate student, came to the topic, the methodology, and the perspective that led to the thesis.

This is especially important because the years between which Berger began graduate studies in 1962 and the publication of *Sense of Power* in 1970 were anything but typical, either for academia as a whole or for Canadian history in particular. The years when Carl Berger entered the doctoral program at the University of Toronto and then moved on to the faculty were an age of unusual expansion and opportunity, even affluence, for academics, historians, and especially those who wanted to write about Canada. These years saw some of the most rapid growth of universities in Canadian history. Changing expectations on the job market, combined with the front edge of the baby boom, created unprecedented demand for a university education. What had previously been an experience reserved for the especially privileged or especially intellectually inclined became more and more of a necessity for the middle class. As a result the decade between the late 1950s and early 1970s saw the number of undergraduates in Canadian universities nearly triple. New universities sprang up while older universities expanded beyond recognition.

Such rapid undergraduate growth created a dilemma. Who was going to teach in all those new universities and expanded classes? Expansion of graduate programs thus followed the undergraduate demand more or less immediately. Both federal and provincial governments had to create policies to deal with the demand. Though education was a provincial matter under the British North America Act, the federal government increasingly moved into the post-secondary sphere in the years after the Second World War. The creation of national granting councils and the implementation of direct funding to universities in the name of research both bolstered expensive graduate programs and provided expanded access to scholarships for those who would pursue education through to the doctoral level.[2] In Ontario the need for growth in graduate studies was made explicit when a commission, chaired by John Deutsch, concluded in 1963 that Ontario would need to quadruple the number of faculty positions by the mid 1970s. The government responded with a new set of graduate fellowships and university funding to manage the growth.[3]

This expansion made a decision to pursue a career as an academic extremely attractive. Indeed, while faculty positions have always had an allure for those committed to ideas, in most eras both salaries (low) and job prospects (unlikely) have worked to curb excess enthusiasm for spending years in graduate school. From the late 1950s through the early 1970s, however, the number of faculty positions grew rapidly, indeed at a faster rate than students; the number of full-time university professors increased fourfold in Canada.[4] History was no exception. As the *Canadian Historical Review* commented in 1964, "The expansion of the profession, evident in recent years, continued and even quickened last year with nearly every department adding new members." This was certainly the case at the University of Toronto, where expansion that year meant that eleven new appointments were made in the history department with only one departure.[5]

Two other circumstances might be added to this mix against which the origins of *Sense of Power* should be set. First, while the 1960s would see an expansion of doctoral programs across the country, there was no doubt that, for the time being, the University of Toronto was the pre-eminent doctoral school in the nation, and the University of Toronto history department the pre-eminent place to go for graduate studies in that discipline. As of 1960 few Canadian history departments had doctoral programs, and of these Toronto was by far the largest.[6] Second, Canadian history was at the centre of

2 Donald Fisher, *The Social Sciences in Canada: Fifty Years of National Activity* (Waterloo: Wilfrid Laurier Press, 1991), 44–50.

3 Martin Friedland, *The University of Toronto: A History* (Toronto: University of Toronto Press), 468.

4 F. H. Leacy, ed., *Historical Statistics of Canada*, 2nd ed. (Ottawa: Supply and Services, 1983), W475–485.

5 "Notes and Comments," *Canadian Historical Review*, 45.4 (Dec. 1964), 274–5. Robert Bothwell, *Laying the Foundation: A Century of History at the University of Toronto* (Toronto: Department of History, 1991), 141. Between 1959 and 1970 the department increased by 45 faculty members, a number augmented by the addition of the Erindale and Scarborough campuses.

6 The graduate program appears to have grown to pre-eminence in a department obsessed by its undergraduate honours program. See Bothwell, *Laying the Foundation*, 145–50.

the growth in the discipline. With the advantage of hindsight, something historians enjoy, it is now apparent just how a remarkable number of events came together to shape what might be termed a golden age in the development of the field of Canadian history. Underlying this was a mixture of national awareness and national concern. National awareness came in the sense of pride for our role in the Second World War, through our presence in the forming of the United Nations, and through the famous Nobel Peace Prize won by Lester Pearson. National pride would be fed by economic growth and culminate in 1967 with Montreal's Expo. Canada seemed to have come of age as a nation.

The new attention to Canadian history also had a defensive side. With one breath Canadians felt that their nation was making great strides, while with the next they lamented its fall. The fall could take various forms depending on one's political orientation. The first in time and probably the dominant danger until the later 1960s lay in the great American juggernaut. This had been the central message of the 1951 report of the Royal Commission on the Arts, Letters and Sciences (the Massey Commission), in which the spectre of a failure of Canadian culture in the face of the commercialized forces emanating from the United States had been raised. Reinforced by the Royal Commission on Canada's Economic Prospects (the Gordon Commission) in the mid fifties, the angst reached new heights with the release of philosopher George Grant's *Lament for a Nation* in 1964. Taking up these fears and doing so with increasing vehemence was Canada's pre-eminent historian of the period, Donald Creighton of, significantly, the University of Toronto.[7] The very Canadian identity which had emerged from the shadow of Britain now seemed about to be overwhelmed by the rising power and influence of the United States.

Through the 1960s and into the 1970s these fears were augmented by the disruptions faced in American society. The civil rights movement, the Vietnam War, the repeated assassinations of political leaders, and a general discordance in American life made the predictions of a continentalist destiny all the more disturbing. At least from the turbulent 1963 federal election in Canada through the formation of the radical, nationalist Waffle movement and its battle for the NDP leadership at the 1971 convention, this anxiety about the American presence very much reinforced attention to Canada's own identity, or lack of it, and shaped the nature of Canadian historical writing.

Though fear of continentalism was a pervasive theme through this era there was a second concern that was both part of a long tradition in Cana-

7 On Creighton's views in these years, see Philip Massolin, *Canadian Intellectuals, The Tory Tradition, and the Challenge of Modernity, 1939–1970* (Toronto: University of Toronto Press, 2001), chs. 6–7.

dian writing and one that emerging circumstances would revivify. Canadian identity had somehow to bridge the cultural and linguistic gap between
French and English. From the beginning the "British" nature of Canada had
made this a challenge. In spite of the best arguments and rationalizations,
the reality was that to the degree Canada was British it was not a place
where those of French ancestry would feel they fully belonged. Thus, one
of the bulwarks against rampant continentalism, our adherence to a British
identity, became a potential obstacle to our survival as a united nation.

The sense of urgency around the national unity debate ebbed and flowed
depending on circumstances. Both world wars had converted concern into
crisis, torn apart political parties, and threatened to do the same to the
country. After the Second World War the tension eased somewhat under a
French-Canadian Prime Minister, Louis St Laurent, and a growing debate
within Quebec focused on internal issues of clerical influence, political corruption, and modernization. It was not long, however, before these dynam-
ics turned to the question of Quebec's place in Canada.

The election in Quebec of Jean Lesage's Liberal government in 1960
reflected monumental shifts in Quebec's social and economic structure and
unleashed a set of political forces that led in unfamiliar and often surprising directions. The Quiet Revolution, as it was termed, created a whole
new set of expectations for Quebeckers within their own province and
resurrected the long-term discussion about Quebec's place within Canada.
English-Canadian enthusiasm for the modernization of Quebec soon gave
way to growing concern about a new assertiveness on the part of Franco-
Quebeckers as to the nature of Canada. The opposite side of the coin to
the Massey Commission or *Lament for a Nation* therefore was the creation of the Royal Commission on Bilingualism and Biculturalism in 1963.
Throughout the rest of the decade and well beyond, the place of Quebec in
Canada would preoccupy politicians, journalists, and academics. This was
especially the case because, until the 1960s, the idea of Quebec separation
had always remained on the distant margins of discussion. As the decade
progressed, however, the margins began to move to the centre. The FLQ
crisis of 1970 and election of the Parti Quebecois in 1976 ensured that "the
Quebec issue" continued to remain at the forefront of discussion.

American dominance on one side and fear of national disunity along
linguistic lines on the other were not always reconcilable and led to some
strong and occasionally vitriolic debates among academics, politicians, and
popular writers through the sixties and seventies. No Canadian historian
was more pessimistic, even dyspeptic, than the grand figure of the Toronto
history department Donald Creighton. *Canada's First Century* was published in 1970, the same year as *Sense of Power*, and it did not predict an optimistic future for Canada. Indeed, in many ways it repeated George Grant's

lament and warned of the impending end of Canadian history. "Continentalism," he said, "had divorced Canadians from their history, crippled their creative capacity, and left them without the power to fashion a new future for themselves ... The problem of a separatist Quebec had come to obsess and monopolize the minds of both English Canadians and French Canadians. It had distracted them from other and more vital national tasks." The result, he concluded, "was certain to bring continentalism one long stage further towards its final triumph."[8]

Creighton's pessimistic comments about history notwithstanding, two things stand out about the nature of Canadian historical writing in these years. First, the concerns about national identity, whether fuelled by fear of the United States or fear of French-English discord, meant that historical writing was focused on the national experience. This tended to reinforce attention on political elites, events that shaped the "national consciousness," or national development. Richard Saunders, president of the Canadian Historical Association, argued that there were two underlying principles for a nation's historians in his 1967 presidential address. First, a nation is "a community of people living together over such a period of time that common interests and experiences, common feelings and sympathies all merge into a body of mutual understanding and desired association." Second, this means that a nation's historians have a special role as the "keeper[s] of the national experience."[9] Both assumptions would soon be challenged as regional identity and "history from the bottom up" redefined the nature of Canadian historical writing. Nonetheless, Saunders accurately reflected the fact that the very search for national identity gave historical writing in these years energy and focus.

Second, though Creighton lamented the loss of creative capacity, Canadian history was exceptionally vigorous in these years. The growth of the universities and graduate schools, combined with the debates on Canadian identity and, indeed, Canada's future, opened the way for a fundamental transformation of the profession in the years beginning in the early sixties. As Carl Berger himself noted in a later work, growth in numbers, an increased emphasis on research, and changes in the social, ethnic, and gender composition of graduate students all had an impact.[10]

Until the 1960s the Canadian historical profession was small and the published output, though often of high quality, tended at any given time to be fairly narrow in method if not in conclusions. A focus on constitu-

---

8 Donald Creighton, *Canada's First Century, 1867–1967* (Toronto, 1970), 355, 356.
9 Richard Saunders, "Presidential Address," Canadian Historical Association, *Historical Papers*, vol. 2.1 (1967), 1–9.
10 Carl Berger, *The Writing of Canadian History: Aspects of Canadian Historical Writing since 1900*, 2nd ed. (Toronto: University of Toronto Press, 1986), 262–4.

tional history in the 1910s and '20s was succeeded by economic history in the 1930s and then, as we will see, by a fascination with biography after the Second World War. In part this was due to the nature of the profession where a "small, gentlemanly community of historians" was dominated by a "few outstanding individuals."[11] It might be added that with a few notable exceptions those outstanding individuals spent their careers in the University of Toronto's history department. As testament to this, between 1950 and 1965 five governor general's awards for non-fiction went to the history department of the University of Toronto. A sixth award might be added if Frank Underhill, former University of Toronto history professor, is to be included. No other university, much less a single department, received more than one in the same period.[12]

When Carl Berger came to the University of Toronto history department in 1962 from the University of Manitoba, he was thus moving to the centre of historical writing in Canada. He was also doing so in a time when the "small community" was beginning a period of momentous change. By the early 1960s the profession, the department, and the approach to Canadian history were all in transition.

Change was also coming to the way in which historians wrote. By the time Berger entered graduate studies the dominance of biography was being challenged by new approaches, though the shift would take time. As indicated above, since the Second World War Canadian historians, as with many in other countries, had been preoccupied with history as biography, especially biographies of politicians. As the centre of historical writing in Canada, the University of Toronto history department had been the exemplar of the historical biography, including Creighton's monumental two-volume study of John A. Macdonald, Kenneth McNaught's study of J. S. Woodsworth, and Ramsay Cook's soon-to-be-published study of John W. Dafoe. J. M. S. Careless, Berger's supervisor, was about to publish the second volume of his masterful study of George Brown.[13]

Biography has many advantages for the historian. It emphasizes the importance of individual decisions on the evolution of the past and thus the

11 Berger, *Writing of Canadian History*, 262.
12 This was about to change. In the next fifteen years the University of Toronto history department would receive only one governor general's award, awarded to Carl Berger for *Writing of Canadian History* in 1976.
13 Donald Creighton, *John A. Macdonald: The Young Politician* (Toronto: Macmillan, 1952) and *John A. Macdonald: The Old Chieftain* (Toronto: Macmillan, 1955); K. W. McNaught, *A Prophet in Politics: A Biography of J. S. Woodsworth* (Toronto: University of Toronto Press, 1959); G. R. Cook, *The Politics of John W. Dafoe and the Free Press* (Toronto: University of Toronto Press, 1963); J. M. S. Careless, *Brown of the Globe. Volume 1: The Voice of Upper Canada 1818–1859* (Toronto: Macmillan, 1959) and *Volume 2: Statesman of Confederation 1860–1880* (Toronto: Macmillan, 1963).

fact that history recognizes a uniqueness to the past that is often brushed over by other disciplines. It brought history to life and brought Canadian history forward in a form that appeals to the non-specialist. There may never have been a time when academic history was so connected to the public as in the post-war years and the heyday of biography.[14]

The biographical choices and the interpretations of the authors were shaped by Canada's emergence over the past generation as an independent nation. In one way or another, biographers in the forties and fifties picked their subjects with an eye to their place in the development of Canada. Again, both Creighton's *Macdonald* and Careless's *Brown*, as biographies of the fathers of Confederation, are obvious examples. Other leading politicians chronicled in these years included Wilfrid Laurier, William Lyon Mackenzie King, and his grandfather William Lyon Mackenzie.[15] Thus, biography in Canadian history in the fifties and early sixties tended to mean political biography with an eye to nation building. Few historians ventured beyond the world of politics, though the occasional French explorer made it into the mix.

If biography was the favoured approach, the interpretive framework was built around the expansion of central Canadian influence outward in an eastern and western direction. The "Laurentian thesis," as it was known, dated back to the 1930s and was in some way an academic version of John A. Macdonald's national policy. East-west trade axes, reinforced by government policies and far-seeing statesmen, it was argued, had created Canada as a transcontinental nation.

Thus, in spite of the often vehement debates around national unity and American influence, English-Canadian historical interpretation was actually fairly unified in these years. An emphasis on political leaders, often framed by biography and on east-west policies that these elites developed, told the story of Canada's emergence as a nation.

One additional point might be mentioned. Relative to the rapid expansion of published works that would come over the next generation, the scholarly literature on Canadian history was still relatively small. Aspiring graduate students could, in contrast to American or British history, be expected to study more or less the entire list in preparation for the doctorate. Even if they did there would still be huge gaps in their knowledge – especially in fields outside of political or economic areas. The opportunity to do some-

14 Once again, Berger noted this in *Writing of Canadian History*, 222.
15 Joseph Schull, *Laurier: The First Canadian* (Toronto: Macmillan, 1965); R. MacGregor Dawson, *William Lyon Mackenzie King: A Political Biography* (Toronto: University of Toronto Press, 1958); William Kilbourn, *The Firebrand: William Lyon Mackenzie and the Rebellion in Upper Canada* (Toronto: Clarke Irwin, 1956); Dale Thomson, *Alexander Mackenzie: Clear Grit* (Toronto: Macmillan, 1960).

thing new and original was there for those who could see the possibilities in these gaps.

II

This was the context in which Carl Berger went through his university years. Berger was born and raised in the small town of The Pas, Manitoba (population 4671 according to the 1961 census). He then took the natural step for a Manitoban who wanted to go to university: he journeyed south to Winnipeg and entered the University of Manitoba. Though a major shift from a small northern town, the transition was probably made easier as universities had not yet begun the years of rapid growth that would come in the 1960s, and the University of Manitoba had fewer than 6000 students. Moreover, Berger began his studies at United College, which was a small downtown institution with fewer than 2000 students.[16]

As might be expected, given his future career, two things stand out about Berger's undergraduate years. First, he was an excellent student and one for whom the university experience was an important intellectual journey. Classes mattered, which is not to say that all were greeted with equal enthusiasm, as did the exposure to new ideas and new knowledge outside the classroom. Used bookstores provided the young student with a trove of cheap and wide-ranging readings that supplemented his formal education. Second, the undergraduate years brought a torrent of new ideas that, in some eclectic but also inchoate manner, would help shape work at the graduate level.

Manitoba had considerable strength in Canadian areas at this time. Berger's studies led him to well-known figures like A. L. Burt, W. L. Morton, Walter Young, and others. Outside of Canada, courses in British and American history were also extremely important in that they introduced him to approaches in social and intellectual history that were much more developed than in Canadian writing. In both Canadian and American history Berger read on issues of economic history and the writings of Charles Beard, Harold Innis, and the teachings of Clare Pentland gave him an appreciation of the ways in which economic and social forces interacted. Indeed, by the time he graduated, he thought that economic history might be the focus of his graduate work. As with many others proceeding from undergraduate to graduate years, things would change.[17]

16 United College would evolve into the University of Winnipeg. See A. G. Bedford, *The University of Winnipeg: A History of the Founding Colleges* (Toronto: University of Toronto Press, 1976). On the University of Manitoba, see J. W. Bumsted, *The University of Manitoba: An Illustrated History* (Winnipeg: University of Manitoba Press, 2001).

17 My thanks to Carl Berger for information on his student years at both Manitoba and Toronto.

Carl Berger was not some late bloomer who struggled to find his way into a graduate school only to prove himself later on. His work at Manitoba gained him recognition as a student with real promise. He received the Gold Medal for the highest standing in the honours course and was the recipient of a Woodrow Wilson Fellowship to support graduate study. Thus, he had both the financial support and the academic record that opened up a wide range of graduate schools. That he chose the University of Toronto is further testimony to the power of that department at the time. It was also a choice that determined his career. He would remain in the department as graduate student and professor for the next forty years.

During his graduate years courses from K. W. McNaught (recently transplanted from United College), J. M. S. Careless, and economic historians W. H. Easterbrook and J. H. Dales supplemented his undergraduate work and refined his historical interests. While historians like to see clear and rational patterns in the way in which the past evolves the reality is that there is also a degree of randomness or, if one prefers, serendipity in the way things work out. As the graduate course in economic history hints, Carl Berger had maintained his undergraduate interest in the area. In fact his initial idea for a thesis topic was a history of the Hudson Bay Railway. Though there is no doubt it would have been very well done, it is probably fortunate for the discipline, for Canadian history, and for Carl Berger that the history had already been written. With that avenue closed and with exposure to J. M. S. Careless, whose writings and teaching recognized the importance of ideas, Berger's interests began to shift.

Expansion of graduate programs, the growth of an emphasis on research, and greater opportunity allowed new ideas to flow in from the historical traditions of other countries. Biography would remain an important staple of Canadian historical writing in coming years, but exciting currents in social, labour, and intellectual history were emerging that would, over the next generation, dramatically change the nature of Canadian historical writing. Most important for Carl Berger's directions as a graduate student was the post-war emergence of intellectual history as a distinct sub-discipline.

In its most general sense, intellectual history is simply the study of the role of ideas in history. Defined so broadly, intellectual history was, to one degree or another, a sub-discipline of historical writing throughout the twentieth century. Especially in European history, the study of major intellectual thinkers or significant ideological or cultural ideas had been common. Often these studies overlapped with other disciplines as writers sought to explain political or social theory. More formally, the role of intellectual history emerged in the interwar years, when American historian Arthur Lovejoy developed the concept of the history of ideas and as other historians began to seek a more complete understanding of the "whys" of history as opposed to the rigidly factual approach of the nineteenth-century German school. Intellectual history, however, could take different directions, and the lines often blurred. One line of enquiry, occasionally described as an internalist approach, emphasized the development of "great ideas."[18] A study of Darwin's or Marx's writings could look at the evolution of a person's thinking and its relationship to previous ideas or schools. The social implications of an idea were likely consequential but were not the primary purpose of this type of study. Likewise, the presumption was that the thoughts or individual being studied were of consequence on a world stage and creatively significant in their own right. The popular, ephemeral, or derivative courses of thought lay outside the realm of the history of ideas.

A parallel current of intellectual history started from a different premise. Ideas were interesting in their own right, of course, but their study became especially relevant as they were linked directly to political or social change. It was no longer the "greatness" of the idea but the impact of the idea on society that made it worthy of study. The thought behind popular movements or political upheavals might be superficial or even silly, but they were important. Bigotry, propaganda, and popular culture all became legitimate subjects, though this in no way excluded the subtle, articulate, or great ideas – the basis on which ideas were chosen for study in intellectual history was somewhat different from how they were chosen in the pure history of ideas.

The study of ideas as a means of explaining social or political movements had multiple sources of inspiration and appeared in many countries. However, the most clear-cut expression of the study of ideas probably came from the United States, beginning in the interwar years and exploding in popularity in the later 1940s through the 1960s.

Underlying this was a long-standing tendency in American historical writing to try to explain the unique sense of mission that seemed to run through the American experience. The new world nation and "first democracy," with its unabashed sense of manifest destiny and its successful rise to a world power, seemed to call for some explanation that looked to collective values and currents of thought. From the 1920s onward historians like Vernon Parrington, Merle Curti, and Louis Hartz published works that sought to analyse the sources of this exceptionalism.[19] Aside from such broad syntheses, intellectual history in the United States saw some extremely influential works on specific issues in the inter- and post-war years. Some, like Perry

---

18 Terry Cook, "Nailing Jelly to the Wall: Possibilities in Intellectual History," *Archivaria*, 11 (Winter 1980–1), 205–13, 207.

19 Vernon Parrington, *Main Currents in American Thought* (New York: Harcourt Brace, 1927); Merle Curti, *The Growth of American Thought* (New York: Harper and Row, 1943); Louis Hartz, *The Liberal Tradition in America: An Interpretation of American Political Thought since the Revolution* (New York: Harcourt Brace, 1955).

Miller's monumental two-volume study *New England Mind* (1939, 1953), chose their topic from the perspective of the history of an idea. Others, such as C. Vann Woodward's *Strange Career of Jim Crow* (1955), looked at a political issue (segregation) but did so with a keen eye to the role of ideas and popular prejudice.[20] Richard Hofstadter's contributions through the 1950s and 1960s were groundbreaking in their attempt to understand the role of ideas on both social movements and policy. One essay of his in particular, on American imperialism in 1898, had a direct influence on Berger's thinking.[21] It is instructive that both Miller and Hofstadter, as was the case with many American intellectual studies scholars, were ultimately interested in the way ideas affected collective belief and social and political organization.

This approach to intellectual history was extremely important in the way in which the Canadian discipline evolved. So long as the history of ideas was thought to be a study of the great breakthroughs in thought or of ideas that had had a major world impact, the Canadian sense of inferiority came into play. What Canadian ideas could be studied under these conditions? However, the study of ideas as background to popular assumptions or policies opened up new horizons. Now it was possible to study Canadian ideas without being defensive as to whether those ideas were unique or derivative, sophisticated or superficial. By the late 1950s individual Canadian historians were looking at the ideas of political parties, a natural extension of the emphasis on nation and on biography as a method. By the early to mid 1960s people like S. F. Wise and Ramsay Cook had taken up intellectual history in a series of pioneering essays on aspects of ideas in Canadian history.[22]

The historian's increasing use of ideas to explain social movements had three recurring themes. First, ideas were believed to be crucial in defining historical trends and movements, though they were not presumed to be autonomous. Second, these historians gathered multiple expressions of certain ideas or themes to try to understand collective beliefs. Third, this methodology required a leap of faith – or of assumption – that the sources or individuals cited were indeed representative of something wider. At the extreme, such intellectual history veered close to a Fernand Braudel–style "mentali-

---

20 Perry Miller, *The New England Mind: The Seventeenth Century* and *The New England Mind: From Colony to Province* (Cambridge: Harvard University Press, 1939, 1953); C. Vann Woodward, *The Strange Career of Jim Crow* (Oxford: Oxford University Press, 1955).

21 Richard Hofstadter, *Social Darwinism in American Thought, 1860–1915* (London: Oxford University Press, 1948), *The Age of Reform: From Bryan to F. D. R.* (New York: Vintage, 1955), *Anti-Intellectualism in American Life* (New York: Alfred Knopf, 1963).

22 S. F. Wise, "Sermon Literature and Canadian Intellectual History," *The Bulletin*, 18 (1965); G. R. Cook, *Canada and the French Canadian Question* (Toronto: Macmillan, 1966).

té" approach. More often, though, the collective mind was more narrow, defined around a specific political grouping or idea. Thus, for example, in an influential piece, Wise used correspondence, sermons, newspapers, and other published sources to study anti-Americanism in British North America. His belief that this range of sources from "the politically effective minority" could be extended to the "inarticulate majority" was central to the effectiveness of his argument.[23] Implicitly or explicitly the same was true of most who took this approach to intellectual history. Though Berger was very careful to say that his work was "selective in approach," there is no doubt that his study made the leap, at least in readers' minds, to a broader set of attitudes and beliefs that affected broad parts of the public in late Victorian Canada.

III

One of the reasons that *Sense of Power* has become a landmark in Canadian historical writing is the complex manner in which, in topic, structure, and methodology, it took hold of issues that Canadian history thought important and did so in a way that blended recognizable historical forms with new approaches.

First, the topic itself reflected the concerns of the 1960s as much as those of the late nineteenth century. As the subtitle declares, the book is a study in the ideas of Canadian imperialism from Confederation until the First World War. In choosing this topic Berger looked back to an era when "deep and almost unbridgeable fissures in the foundations of Confederation" led to fear of division or of absorption into the great power to the south (4). It is easy to see not just the general parallel between Confederation and the 1960s but to see, in the rhetoric of Goldwin Smith, a pro-continental version of George Grant's *Lament for a Nation* or, in the alarmist rhetoric of the imperialists, a nineteenth-century precursor to Donald Creighton's sense of impending doom.

As a means of organizing his study, Berger focuses on three key individuals: George Denison of Toronto, military officer and man of many opinions; George M. Grant of Kingston, principal of Queen's University; and George Parkin of New Brunswick, eventual head of the Rhodes Trust. Key secondary figures in the book include the poet and expansionist Charles Mair, humorist and economist Stephen Leacock, as well as McGill professor Andrew McPhail. However, though the book is framed around this

---

23 S. F. Wise, "Colonial Attitudes from the Era of the War of 1812 to the Rebellions of 1837," in S. F. Wise and R. C. Brown, *Canada Views the United States: Nineteenth Century Political Attitudes* (Toronto: Macmillan, 1967), 16.

central group, Berger draws in as many other individuals and writings as necessary.

He then follows these individuals as they wrestle with the immediate aftermath of Confederation and the often vague and contradictory desire of individuals to "instil a Canadian patriotism" (66) that would make the Confederation of 1867 a true nation-building exercise rather than a mere federation of British colonies. Such a grouping to some extent reflects the tendency to biography current in these years. Indeed, his first chapter is essentially a series of brief biographies of his key actors. This is much more than a nod to convention. As Ramsay Cook has noted, Carl Berger's approach to history "always insisted that both individual biographical details and general sociocultural context were necessary to a full understanding of the ideology."[24] Denison's fiery rhetoric or Grant's liberal thoughtfulness cannot be really comprehended unless they are brought alive as people and not just a series of quotes. Finally, for the reader, the foibles and flaws of the individuals bring the era to life and make *Sense of Power* all the more enjoyable.

Yet, the first couple of chapters are fairly conventional in their organizational structure. Then Berger undertakes a significant and somewhat risky shift in approach. Subsequent chapters are organized not around people or events but around ideas. Though the key individuals remain prominent, the rest of the book, as the chapter titles indicate, gives pride of place not to a person but to those themes which Berger sees as making up the core of imperialist thinking. Being fully aware of Carl Berger's resistance to over-reaching the evidence, I will not put too much significance on the fact that structurally the book proceeds from an older and standard historical tradition – biography and chronology – to the newer trends in intellectual history and thereby represents some of the broader shifts taking place in Canadian historical writing in the 1960s. At the very least, though, his decision to undertake such a structural shift and his success in doing so was important to the impact of *Sense of Power*.

There were several reasons that made this reorganization important. As mentioned above, the use of intellectual history to get at popular trends or beliefs of the age requires a successful leap from individuals and individual sources to an acceptance by the reader that the ideas represent something more general in the outlook of the times. Carl Berger is careful to note that the individuals who fully accepted the imperialist platform "would always remain a very small number" (263). Nonetheless, as he runs though themes of moral reform, progress, and so on, he is able to extend his analysis beyond the small number of individuals who are the core of the study. The

24 Ramsay Cook, "Carl Berger: Ironic Man as Historian," 13.

use of ideas as an organizing principle allows him to bring in other sources, ones that reinforce and extend the arguments of his central figures. Doing this in turn allows the reader to understand that what is being discussed here is much broader than that of a few quixotic imperialists. While full acceptance of imperialist ideology may indeed have been limited, the movement had power and influence precisely because so many of its beliefs, myths, and prejudices reflected a widespread current of thought in late Victorian Canada. In reading about the imperialists we therefore learn much about late nineteenth-century attitudes.

Berger's wide-ranging research and the convincing way in which he bridged from the ideas of a few to the outlook of many redefined both imperialism and nationalism in the Canadian context. Many Canadians of the era shared in the pride of an Empire on which the sun never set and in the "sense of power" that affiliation with the greatest power on earth created. They also felt protected behind a British and monarchical bulwark which helped keep American manifest destiny at bay. What Berger did in reconciling nationalism and imperialism, though, went much further. He demonstrated convincingly that imperialism had at least two elements. The first, of course, was a continued membership in the Empire. If that were all there was to it, though, imperialism would have been at best colonialism dressed up by a small group whose identification with the mother country was greater than their identification with Canada.

The second element to Canadian imperialism completed the picture and was integral to the argument that Berger was presenting. Yes, the involvement in a great empire was satisfying and yes, the rhetoric of worldwide influence, the all red route, white man's burden, and so on was present. The heart of imperialism for Canadians, though, was essentially based on Canada's future and Canada's interests as they perceived them. To understand this, it is essential to read the book in full. However, as a simplified introductory comment, the logic of the imperialists went something as follows. Canada, in Confederation and in the annexation of the west, was no longer a colony, nor were its people content to be colonials. Yet, true independence was both undesirable and impossible. Undesirable because the long-term evolution of British freedom, progress, and morality was a legacy that should never be forsaken. Douglas Cole captured this in citing a contemporary of the imperialists, W. H. Withrow: "In all the heroic tradition of the mother land we have a share."[25] That was one of the central messages of the loyalist tradition as well. Independence was undesirable but at any rate it was also impossible, as Berger emphasizes: "One of the commonplaces of

25 Cole, "Canada's 'Nationalistic' Imperialists," *Journal of Canadian Studies*, 5.3 (Aug. 1970), 44–9, 46.

the day was that independence was virtually identical with absorption into the republic" (82).

The only option, then, was to manage a transformation of Canada from colony to nation within the folds of the Empire. Canada, over time, had to become an equal partner with Britain. This was essential not just for Canada but for the sake of the whole future of the Empire. These pro-British imperialists were often surprisingly critical of the rigidity and weaknesses of the mother country. Indeed, elements of Canadian imperialist writing were surprisingly close in tone to a deeply embedded American theme of the new world as energetic and progressive compared to the rigidity and historical burdens of the old. If Canadians (and the British) would only recognize the potential of this new Dominion, the route between colonialism and annexation would create a great Canadian nation that, in turn, would help preserve the greatest empire the world had ever seen. This was the dream that linked nationalism and imperialism. It was probably always unrealistic, and it was certainly doomed when the costs of imperial membership became manifest as Europe's burden of militarism and secret alliances engulfed the Dominion. Notwithstanding its failure, though, imperialism in the Canadian variation was indeed a form of nationalism.

IV

When *Sense of Power* appeared in 1970 it received considerable attention. Reviews appeared that went beyond the discipline, in places like the *Canadian Journal of Political Science*, and beyond Canada, in both Great Britain and the United States. The only omission was perhaps surprising. It appears that for unexplained reasons the book was never reviewed in Canada's flagship historical journal, *The Canadian Historical Review*! This was made up for by the *Journal of Canadian Studies*, which recognized the importance of the publication with two significant review essays.[26]

It is hardly surprising, given the long-term impact of the book, to note that the reviews were generally very positive. David Bell noted that Berger "has propelled the discipline in exciting new directions." In the *American Historical Review* Richard Preston commented that it was "a sensitive and stimulating analysis of an important segment of Canadian thought." Leading Quebec historian Michel Brunet echoed this conclusion, saying that this original work opened "des voies nouvelles a l'historiographie canadienne."[27]

26 R. J. D. Page, "Carl Berger and the Intellectual Origins of Canadian Imperialist Thought," *Journal of Canadian Studies*, 5.3 (Aug. 1970), 39–43; and Douglas Cole, "Canada's 'Nationalistic' Imperialists," 44–9.
27 David Bell, "Review," *Canadian Journal of Political Science* (1972), 322; Richard Preston,

There were some quibbles of course, but often these were the result of reviewers bringing forward their own obsessions or wishing that a different book had been written. Richard Preston's joint review of Berger's *Sense of Power* and Desmond Morton's *Ministers and Generals* devoted the majority of space to Morton's book, something closer to Preston's own interests. A. F. Madden, writing in the *English Historical Review*, complained that the British obsession with imperialism wasn't nearly as great as Berger seemed to imply. An assessment of this issue, he admitted, was "beyond Dr. Berger's brief." It was there because it reflected Madden's own interests. He was using the review to, in effect, restate his perspective on a debate among English historians of the Empire. Indeed, as recent British historical writing would imply, the issue remains far from a settled question even today.[28]

If there was a more consistent challenge to the approach it was that the brand of imperialism described in *Sense of Power* was not unique to Canada. Madden noted this in passing. Douglas Cole's review essay in the *Journal of Canadian Studies* dealt with the question in detail, arguing that "imperialism was not a Canadian phenomenon; it was a Britannic movement."[29] While a reasonable point, the lack of comparative perspective in no way undermined the primary thesis of the book or the validity of the arguments within. Indeed, subsequent attempts to bridge national perspectives and give a true "empire-wide" perspective have hinted that there are real dangers of losing nuance in the attempt to bridge national historical and historiographic traditions.

The initial and positive reaction to *Sense of Power* grew rather than diminished in subsequent years for at least two reasons. First, in spite of the occasional foray against it, the basic thesis Berger set out became a standard part of Canadian historical interpretation. It remains so today. Second, *Sense of Power*, as one reviewer correctly noted, laid the foundation for "intellectual history as a serious study in Canada."[30] Even more specifically, Berger had brought together an assessment of a Victorian strain of thought,

"Review of *Sense of Power* by Carl Berger and *Ministers and Generals* by Desmond Morton," *American Historical Review*, 77.2 (Apr. 1972), 599–600; Michel Brunet, "Review of *Sense of Power* by Carl Berger," *International Journal*, 26.1 (Winter, 1970/1), 280–1.

28 See, for example, John Mackenzie, *Imperialism and Popular Culture*, and Bernard Porter, *The Absent Minded Imperialists: Empire, Society and Culture in Great Britain* (Oxford: Oxford University Press, 2004). Some of the themes of the ongoing debate are set out in John Mackenzie, "Comfort and Conviction: A Response to Bernard Porter," *Journal of Imperial and Commonwealth History*, 36.4 (Dec. 2008), 659–68.

29 Cole, "Canada's 'Nationalistic' Imperialists," 48. For Cole's views on this issue, see Douglas Cole, "The Problem of 'Nationalism' and 'Imperialism' in British Settlement Colonies," *Journal of British Studies*, 10 (May 1971), 160–82.

30 Robert J. D. Page, "Carl Berger and the Intellectual Origins of Canadian Imperialist Thought," 39.

the issue of nationalism, and the importance of ideas in his study. There was obviously something about the mixture that seemed to hold real promise. Over the next fifteen years several books would appear that, in one way or another, expanded upon or further explored some or all these themes.[31]

Thus, *Sense of Power*, along with works by Cook, Wise, and others, made intellectual history a prominent part of Canadian historical writing. Indeed, at the very time when intellectual history was beginning to lose its lustre south of the border it flourished in Canada. As it did it branched out with works that returned to the history of ideas, opened up the previously neglected field of religious history, and influenced writings in other sub-disciplines. Though it is no longer as influential as in the past as an explicit sub-discipline, intellectual history remains active in its own right and, perhaps more importantly, has made the study of ideas an important component of other areas, including the all-devouring area of social history.[32]

Some forty years later, *Sense of Power*'s place in the development of Canadian historical writing remains impressive. No doubt if Carl Berger were writing it today, some of the approaches and details would be different. It is unlikely, though, that the basic thesis would change for the simple reason that it remains convincing. The arguments and evidence presented in *Sense of Power* are a product of the age in which the book was written but have also survived the passage of time. That is ultimately why it is gratifying to see it reissued in a new century and made available to a new generation of readers.

Doug Owram
University of British Columbia, January 2013

---

31 See, for example, A. B. McKillop, *A Disciplined Intelligence: Critical Inquiry and Canadian Thought in the Victorian Era* (Montreal and Kingston: McGill-Queen's University Press, 1979); Doug Owram, *Promise of Eden: The Canadian Expansionist Movement and the Idea of the West, 1856–1900* (Toronto: University of Toronto Press, 1980); Carl Berger, *Science, God, and Nature in Victorian Canada* (Toronto: University of Toronto Press, 1983); Ramsay Cook, *The Regenerators: Social Criticism in Late Victorian English Canada* (Toronto: University of Toronto Press, 1985); David Mills, *The Idea of Loyalty in Upper Canada, 1784–1850* (Montreal and Kingston: McGill-Queen's University Press, 1988); Suzanne Zeller, *Inventing Canada: Early Victorian Science and the Idea of a Transcontinental Nation* (Toronto: University of Toronto Press, 1987); David Marshall, *Secularizing the Faith: Canadian Protestant Clergy and the Crisis of Belief, 1850–1940* (Toronto: University of Toronto Press, 1992); Jane Errington, *The Lion, the Eagle and Upper Canada: A Developing Colonial Ideology* (Montreal and Kingston: McGill-Queen's University Press, 1994).

32 For a critique of the current role of intellectual history, see Michael Gauvreau, "Beyond the Search for Intellectuals: On the Paucity of Paradigms in The Writing of Canadian Intellectual History," in Friesen and Owram, *Thinkers and Dreamers*, 53–92.

The Sense of Power

STUDIES IN THE IDEAS OF
CANADIAN IMPERIALISM
1867–1914

SECOND EDITION

Introduction

This book is a study in Canadian nationalist thought. It is an examination of the ideas and beliefs of a group of men in the late nineteenth and early twentieth centuries, who called their cause imperial unity, their movement imperial federation, and themselves imperialists. The word imperialism crept into the Canadian political vocabulary only in the later years of the last century and for many Canadians it perhaps still connotes a rather distasteful urge to dominate and exploit the underdeveloped areas of the earth and is associated with the tough-minded and domineering behaviour of the great powers in the age of *Realpolitik*. But in the context of Canadian history imperialism means that movement for the closer union of the British Empire through economic and military co-operation and through political changes which would give the dominions influence over imperial policy. Though British North Americans had traditionally taken pride in their connection with the Empire and though the movement for imperial unity drew upon sentiments and traditions which had originated in the distant past, organized efforts to prevent the dissolution of the imperial tie, to strengthen and transform it, began with the formation of the Imperial Federation League in London in 1884 and the subsequent appearance of its branches in Canada. Why its Canadian supporters believed imperial unity compatible with Canadian nationality depended on the way they conceived of that nationality, and how they interpreted Canadian history, character, and destiny. This study seeks to establish and explain their concept of Canada.

Imperialism revived in England and was born in Canada in an atmosphere of pessimism and gloom. Those Englishmen associated with the Royal Colonial Institute, which had been founded in 1869 in order to stem the tide of imperial disengagement, had by the mid-1880s become overburdened with the apprehension that the revolution in the balance of power in Europe and the industrialization of the United States and Germany threatened England's safety and her economic primacy. The rediscovery of the importance of the Empire arose in large part from this feeling of relative decline. By the 1890s the whole cult of empire was pervaded by a fear of impending doom.

Imperialism appeared in Canada at a time when economic depression and antagonism between French and English Canadians revealed deep and almost unbridgeable fissures in the foundations of Confederation. To men who lived through it, the union of 1867 did not appear to be an accomplishment ringing with finality or conclusiveness. Union opened up, but did not guarantee, the prospect that the various regions and communities would one day form in fact what everyone called a "new nationality." Sir John A. Macdonald's nation-building policies – the protective tariff, the transcontinental railway, and the settlement of the west – were calculated to impart solidity and substance to a flimsy political entity and to make it an auxiliary kingdom within the Empire.

Twenty years after Confederation, there was a good deal of concrete evidence in support of those who predicted Canada's collapse; there was only faith on the side of those who defended it. The cultural conflict triggered by the execution of Louis Riel and the long depression which had lasted intermittently since 1873, underlay the general mood of despondency. The depression also proved that the national policy had not worked and this led the Liberal party to commit itself to a policy of freer trade with the United States. Unrestricted reciprocity, or the elimination of tariff barriers between the two countries, imparted by way of reaction the initial impulse to the campaign for imperial unity. Those who repudiated reciprocity did not treat it as an innocuous commercial proposition, nor did they rest their case against it upon the grounds of economic profitability alone. They equated it with continentalism, the gradual assimilation of Canada to the United States, and ultimate political absorption. This spectre of annexation forced them into a defence of Canada, forced them, that is, to say exactly why it was worth preserving Canada at all. That is why the three major spokesmen of imperial unity in Canada – Colonel George Taylor Denison of Toronto, Principal George Monro Grant of Queen's University, and Sir George Robert Parkin, teacher and writer – dealt not only with the relative economic merits of alternate commercial policies, but with history, tradition, power, and religion. In retrospect, it is clear that this debate was inflated, that the threat of continental union was exaggerated, and that Macdonald's narrow victory in the election of 1891 was affected by many other factors. But the net effect of this challenge was to galvanize the defenders of Canada and the British connection into action, and bring out into the open the ideas and sentiments, tradition and hopes, that constituted their sense of nationality.

While it was conceived in a period of doubt and uncertainty the cause of imperial unity did not evaporate with the restoration of self-confidence after the mid-1890s. Indeed, it gathered strength and new adherents, broadened its appeal, and reaffirmed its principles. Its most fervent supporters came from the older areas of Ontario and the Maritimes, particularly from among the descendants of the United Empire Loyalists. By all accounts Toronto was the most imperialistic city in the country. Imperial unity found no favour with the farmers or the working classes, and in French Canada it encountered indifference and hostility. But though the Imperial Federation League in Canada and the British Empire League, which succeeded it in 1896, counted their membership in hundreds, that cause had a far broader appeal. Successful politicians like Sir Wilfrid Laurier were never so unwise, at least not until 1911, as to underestimate the strength of imperialism in English Canada. He capitalized on its popularity by lowering the tariff against British manufactured commodities in 1897 and reluctantly bowed to its pressures in 1899 and dispatched Canadian troops to fight in the Boer War, a move which in itself was a sure indication of the growth of imperial sentiment since 1885 when Macdonald dismissed suggestions for Canadian military involvement in the Sudan with a quip. An incautious optimism was fostered by Canada's exertions in the South African conflict and by the momentum of her material growth during the opening decade of this century, when factories multiplied in Ontario and Quebec, settlers occupied the prairies, and the population increased by over thirty per cent to seven million in 1911.

These developments whetted the appetites of those who hankered for a more influential and less subordinate place within the Empire and grew ever more determined to remove the last vestiges, psychological as well as legal, of colonialism and dependence. Where Canadians were once asked to preserve and defend the connection, they were now summoned to take up the imperial mission and behave like the citizens of the major power their country had already become. The campaign for imperial unity attained a few of its objectives, but the oceanic cables, penny postage, and periodic colonial and imperial conferences seem meagre and disappointing in light of the hopes that were placed in them. These were only devices intended to secure a meaningful and co-operative alliance between Canada and Britain, and, in this, its central ambition, imperialism failed. It was a victim of its own zeal; in another sense, it was a casualty of the First World War.

This fact of failure has been the main influence in shaping the interpretations and characterizations of Canadian imperialism in historical literature. Had the movement for the union of the British North American colonies miscarried in the 1860s, its history would read somewhat like the story of the struggle for imperial unity. Historians would discover ineluctable tides of opinion and material factors working against it, and they would doubtless also conclude that a proposed union of settlements separated by great geographical obstacles was predestined to fail, and that Confederation ran against regional sentiments, or, in the case of the French Canadians, a distinct sense of nationality. The defenders of the independence of the Maritime colonies would probably be looked upon as statesmen jealous of local control of local affairs instead of parochial and unscrupulous politicians. Since Confederation did succeed, historians have not been mainly concerned with the forces that operated against it; since imperial federation did not prevail, they have been interested in little other than the causes of its failure. There is nothing illegitimate about this, except that our knowledge of the outcome makes it difficult to enter into the minds of men who lived in another age and who did not know that they worked in vain for a cause that would never be realized. It also precludes us from seeing the past in all its unpredictability and complexity. As the American literary historian, Vernon Parrington, remarked, time is not always a just winnower and history is partial to success. Lost causes "have a way of shrinking in importance in the memory of later generations" and it is necessary for the historian to "go back to the days before their overthrow and view them in light of their hopes."

Like some other lost causes, the imperial movement in Canada came to be known to posterity largely through the writings of its enemies. Until very recently the treatment of imperialism in Canadian historical writing has been little more than an amplification of the arguments of its opponents, arguments which originally found expression in such works as Goldwin Smith's *In the Court of History: An Apology for Canadians who were Opposed to the South African War* (1902), John S. Ewart's *The Kingdom of Canada* (1908) and *The Kingdom Papers* (1912), Henri Bourassa's *Great Britain and Canada* (1902) and many other pamphlets, and O. D. Skelton's *Life and Letters of Sir Wilfrid Laurier* (1921). These critics wrote much and they wrote persuasively, and though they rejected imperialism for varied and sometimes conflicting reasons, they all tended to identify it with two characteristics which have dominated subsequent discussions of it. The first of these was that the motive force of imperialism was economic; the second was that its objectives and the entire cast of thought upon which it rested were completely antithetical to "Canadian nationalism." These two generalizations require some preliminary comment for they have been long-lived and have impeded a dispassionate understanding of imperial thought.

In locating the mainspring of imperialism in economic conditions these writers were applying a line of argument originally established by the English anti-imperialist, John Hobson, who contended in *Imperialism: A Study* (1902) that the most important factor behind British and American interest in empire was financial capitalism. Though Hobson himself was fully aware of the psychological, religious, and idealistic elements that entered into that impulse, his book did more than any other work, with the possible exception of Lenin's *Imperialism: The Highest Stage of Capitalism* (1917), to popularize the economic interpretation of imperialism. Now no one can deny that late nineteenth-century imperialism in Great Britain and the United States was ultimately tied to a sense of uneasiness and insecurity which was at bottom economic in nature, or that it sprung in part from an urge to seek out sources of raw materials, markets for manufactured goods, and areas of profitable investment. Nor can it be doubted that the depression in Canada and the threat of unrestricted reciprocity enhanced the appeal of imperial federation in general and activated the campaign for imperial preferential trade as an antidote to continental free trade. The literature of imperialism was filled with justifications of the profitability of an intra-imperial trading system, and, indeed, one of the favourite analogies of the more hard-headed imperialists was the comparison of the Empire to a business outfit – "the firm of John Bull and Sons." Because of its obvious peculiarities, however, no one has suggested that imperialism in Canada was the result of the intention of financial interests to exploit overseas territories, but it has been said often enough that the slogans of imperial unity were merely insincere rationalizations concealing less admirable motives.

Without denying that the economic interpretation of history has been an extremely fruitful hypothesis, it should be borne in mind that it has also functioned as a weapon of criticism and reform. This is certainly how it was enlisted in the battle against imperialism. The anti-imperialist critique ran far beyond the point of mentioning how prominently preferential trade figured in the agenda of that movement. Goldwin Smith, for example, once attempted to deflate Canadian enthusiasm for the British cause in the South African War by charging that the Boer War was instigated on behalf of Jewish financiers who sat in the Capetown hotels sipping wine while Canadians were being sacrificed to enhance their speculations. During the debate after 1909 over the question of how Canada could best make provisions for naval defence, imperialists were frequently told that the arms race was a conspiracy of armament manufacturers and that Canada should enter into no agreements for the defence of the Empire because she would only be drawn into an interminable series of wars which were of no concern to her because they were the results of imperialistic economic rivalries.

The search for the economic causes and the pecuniary associations of imperialism stemmed from a desire to discredit as much as the determination to understand. There was hardly a better way in which the inflated and idealistic rhetoric characteristic of that faith could be punctured than by saying that it was only camouflage disguising the "real" carnal and unseemly motives. This is how the economic interpretation of affairs was used by the intellectuals associated with the progressive movement in the United States in the years after 1900. Progressivism thrived on the exposé and was predicated on the belief that certain sinister and hidden powers manipulated things, that the real forces behind events were usually vested interests operating through conspiracy. Just as Charles Beard in his famous study of the American constitution sought to undermine the conservative and legalistic view of that document by showing how prominently property interests figured in the motives of those who had framed it, so too anti-imperialists attempted to throw imperialism into disrepute by claiming that what really mattered were not the exhortations to religious mission or nationality but pecuniary circumstance.

One need not go to the other extreme and paint imperialism as a singularly selfless creed in order to see that the insistence upon its economic nature originated in the heat of the debate it provoked, that these charges were drawn up by those who deliberately set out to destroy it, and that consequently such characterizations should not be taken as proven conclusions about the Canadian imperialist mentality. And if these descriptions are suspect because of their sources, they are made even more so because of the unsubtle and simplistic reading of human nature upon which they are based.

The second characterization of Canadian imperialism which also originated with its critics was the idea that it ran against the rising tide of Canadian national feeling, and that it was a reactionary remnant of the past vainly struggling to prevent the triumph of "Canadian nationalism." According to this critique, imperialism did not grow out of the Canadian soil, but was imposed from outside by an overly zealous British Colonial Office. With a handful of exceptions, its only support within Canada came from misguided colonials who showed an obsequious deference to everything British and disparaged native things, and from recent immigrants who thought of England, not Canada, as their home. It was even suggested that their uncritical and slavish admiration for English culture was accountable for the poor showing of

Canadian literature and art. The intrusion of imperialism into Canada not only embittered the divisions between native Canadians and set race against race, but it was also held that the drive for an economically self-contained Empire was nothing less than a reversion to the mercantilistic structure which had been destroyed in the 1840s. Similarly, proposals for military and naval defence smacked of contributions to a master and testified to a willingness to sacrifice Canadians for the safety of England. Imperialists were constantly reminded that there must always come a time when children grow up and leave the parental home, or, more pointedly, when every boy must learn to stop sleeping with his mother. So too it should be with nations. The conflict between imperialism and nationalism added up to a struggle between the past and the future, the desire to remain a colony and the wish to be a free nation. Once this framework was accepted, it was easy to account for the failure of imperialism: it succumbed to Canadian nationalism.

The main outlines of this interpretation survived largely because of the great influence of O. D. Skelton's biography of Laurier and because of the long dominance of a particular school of Canadian historiography of which it was the finest expression. This so-called liberal nationalist school has lately come under some penetrating scrutiny, its insufficiencies have been exposed and its continued relevance questioned. Naturally, its interpretation of imperialism has also been found wanting, at least by implication. In *Canada and Imperialism, 1896–1899* (1965), Norman Penlington laid to rest the myth that imperialism was imposed from without and demonstrated how substantial were the pressures from within Canada for participation in the Boer War.

Canadian imperialism was one variety of Canadian nationalism – a type of awareness of nationality which rested upon a certain understanding of history, the national character, and the national mission. When critics belaboured imperialism because of its hostility to "Canadian nationalism" what they really meant was that they believed it incompatible with that kind of nationalism which they endorsed. There have been many varieties of Canadian nationalism, and, while they have all been inspired by the same nation, the manner in which the character and interests of Canada have been interpreted vary enormously. Obviously, both O. D. Skelton and G. M. Grant were Canadian nationalists, but no historian can with assurance conclude that either one or the other represented a truer, more legitimate, and superior form of it, unless, of course, he possesses some absolute standard against which they can be measured. Since history itself provides no such standard, the only way in which an account of Canadian nationalist thought can be written is by inquiring into the ideas and ideals which men in the past read into their interpretations of Canada and by exploring the relationship between these conceptions and the environment in which they circulated. Those who require more than this ask more of history than it can ever give.

This study deals with the intellectual contents of Canadian imperialism rather than its workings at the political level. It attempts to analyse the convictions which lay behind the political, military, and economic programme of the movement and to see that body of thought in relation to the intellectual background out of which it grew, against the historical context in which it lived, and in terms of some of the personalities for whom it was a living reality. These assumptions have been searched out in the letters and speeches, books and essays, of those Canadians who were representative and articulate spokesmen for imperial unity. While the main emphasis is accorded to Denison, Grant, and Parkin, who made the fundamentals of that creed explicit at an early date, I have tried to suggest the discontinuities and changes in emphasis in imperialist thought by considering the ideas of the humorist and social critic, Stephen Leacock, and Sir Andrew Macphail, editor of the *University Magazine*, who belonged to a different generation and were more deeply affected by the special circumstances of the decade preceding the First World War. From these five central figures the discussion is broadened to include the ideas of about a dozen other men who elaborated on certain special aspects of imperialism. Imperialism was neither a tidy and symmetrical ideology nor a fixed abstraction and I have not tried to make it so. This book does not claim to be a definitive and comprehensive survey of the movement for imperial unity in Canada, nor does it propose an intellectualist interpretation of it. It is selective in approach, intended to investigate one unexplored dimension of that phenomenon, and concerned with making its ideological framework plain and explicit.

Each of the following chapters, with the exception of the first two, focuses upon a recurrent idea or theme of Canadian imperialism – the idealization of the United Empire Loyalist legacy; the conception of history as the expansion of liberty and self-government; the view of the unique features of the Canadian national character and the place of the French Canadians within it; the critique of the United States; social criticism and reform; the élitist conception of political leadership; the sense of religious mission; and militarism, or the admiration of the martial virtues. The first chapter concentrates upon the five main individuals for whom these ideas were fused into a compelling nationalism. The second examines the Canada First movement of 1869–75.

While most accounts of imperialism justifiably begin in the 1880s, Canada First was taken as the starting point in this study both because of the direct, personal continuity between it and the later organizations of imperial unity, and because in their responses to problems confronting the new Dominion its founding members anticipated reactions and broached solutions that were to become permanent fixtures in the imperialist mentality.

1

Men

Imperialism was a sentiment and an outlook before it became a policy. Individuals were disposed to accept the values and perspectives it embodied because these appeared meaningful in terms of their own experiences and convictions. Different men chose to emphasize certain elements of that concept over others with the result that it exhibited a bewildering variety of meanings. "Imperialism," said an adherent, "may be what any advocate of that idea chooses to define it. It is not fixed. It is in a state of flux."[1] What imperialism signified can therefore only be understood in relation to the characters who espoused it and who came to personify it.

I

When the hosts of imperial unity gathered in Toronto to engage the treasonous foes of Canada and the Empire in the late 1880s, at their head was Colonel George Taylor Denison, a man fitted by tradition, temperament, and training for exactly that role in history. The friendly press described him as the sheet-anchor in the Dominion of all those who professed and called themselves imperialists, a straight-talking soldier who was, in effect, a third political party. Those with a sharper critical capacity and sense of humour said that he was Canada's St George who went forth to slay that dragon from the south who had come ravening for our beloved country, or a Don Quixote, who noisily but fruitlessly tilted at windmills in defence of a belief as dead as feudal chivalry. He was a military writer of major stature, leader of the Canada First movement, the moving force of the Imperial Federation League and the British Empire League in Canada, and the chief spokesman of those who were the most devoted imperialists, the descendants of the United Empire Loyalists.

Denison was born into the landed aristocracy of Upper Canada in

1 George E. Foster, "Preferential Trade," *Empire Club Speeches: Being Addresses Delivered Before the Empire Club of Canada During its Session 1903–04* (Toronto, 1904), 20.

1839. His great-grandfather, John Denison, a brewer by trade, had migrated to British America from Heydon, Yorkshire, in the 1790s, and through a fortunate friendship with Peter Russell, administrator of the colony after Lieutenant-Governor Simcoe's departure, he acquired thousands of acres of land in the vicinity of the town of York and in the eastern district. John's son, George Taylor Denison, both extended these holdings and established the family's respectability by marrying Esther Borden Lippincott, the daughter of a United Empire Loyalist. Service, as well as land and descent, underpinned the family's social status. During the War of 1812, George Denison served as an ensign with the York Volunteers and was captured in a futile attempt to sink the British vessels anchored in the bay to prevent their capture by the Americans. In 1822 he organized a private volunteer cavalry troop, "Denison's Horse," which, like some feudal dignitary, he regarded as a symbol of personal devotion to the Crown. Though he was defeated as a "farmers' candidate" in an election for the assembly, he sat as alderman for St Patrick's ward for a decade. By the 1830s, George Taylor Denison had over a hundred tenants on his estates, converted some land on the banks of the Humber into an endowment for an ecclesiastical living, and had the family portraits painted by Berthon. Not for nothing was he considered "the very embodiment of the English country squire of the times of Addison and Goldsmith";[2] it is not on record, however, that he rode to hounds. When he died in 1853 he left the largest estate ever devised up to that time in Upper Canada.

By 1880 the progeny of John Denison numbered over a hundred. George Taylor Denison I had six sons from four marriages; one of them, George Taylor Denison II, had seven sons, five of whom became soldiers of the Empire on land and sea: Frederick served as an orderly officer to Wolseley on the Red River expedition, and commanded the Canadian *voyageurs* on the Nile in 1884–85; Egerton too saw service on the Nile; Clarence served during the Fenian raids and in the North-West Rebellion of 1885; John rose to the rank of admiral in the Royal Navy. The martial traditions of the "Fighting Denisons" seemed to reach their apogee, as well as their ultimate parody, in the seventh son, who carried the resounding appellation of Septimus Julius Augustus Denison – a perpetual adolescent whose exploits were largely confined to ceremonials and the dispersion of civil rioters, and who, in a moment of complete candour, summed up his life's ambition: "just as the sun had risen above the horizon," he wrote of one happy morning during the Boer War, "I heard the first gun ... and thanked God that I had

2 Samuel Thompson, "Reminiscences of a Canadian Pioneer," *Rose-Belford's Canadian Monthly and National Review*, VII (Nov. 1881), 517.

found at last what I had been searching for for twenty-three years, viz., an enemy."[3]

It would have required a very independent spirit to remain indifferent to the multifarious martial enterprises of this family. George Taylor Denison – the third – gloried in them. He was made a cornet in the active militia at sixteen, a major at twenty-three; the movement of the horses and the accoutrements of the officers attracted him much more than did a career in the law for which his education prepared him. He won no prizes at Upper Canada College, that school for moulding character and training gentlemen, to which he and his brothers were sent. His masters in the fifth form thought the sixteen-year-old's progress "slow," "fair," or "unsatisfactory"; his conduct ranged from "troublesome to very good"; in most subjects he ranked ninth or tenth, except in writing, in which he stood fourth out of a class of fourteen, and in architectural drawing, second.[4] Young men like Denison who were, as the phrase went, "embarking on the ship of life" in that high noon of Victorian improvement and self-help, were enjoined to undertake a rigorous appraisal of their faculties and discover the strength of their character in order the better to determine their calling. For many this meant consultation with the practitioners of phrenology, those nineteenth-century psychologists who read character in the configurations of the cranium.

One day in the autumn of 1859 Denison underwent such an analysis by the New York "Professor of Phrenology," L. N. Fowler. You belong, the analyst told him, "to the executive class of men who cannot very well live a quiet stable life"; you are industrious and ambitious, wilful, and generous, "decidedly fond of argument and litigation." "You have the spirit of Young America"; "you will ... gain your reputation by hard labor and you are a strong friend and partizan, and a whole-hearted man in everything." But the professor said that Denison needed more "Self-Esteem," more of that self-reliance that allows one to be made the subject of jokes and ridicule. "You are prompt in deciding, and a little too firm and stubborn in carrying out your position & opinions, ... You are never in your element so much as when you are overcoming obstacles, clearing your way, and encountering your enemies. You have a romantic class of mind, and your plans are exalted." "Your real spirit," he added, "is that of a soldier, and you would be more in your element if you could be the commanding officer on the battle field, than pleading a case before a court or Jury."[5] Professor Fowler's methods

3 Brigadier General S. J. A. Denison, *Memoirs* (Toronto, 1927), 58.
4 TPL, G. T. Denison Papers, package #4, report, Feb. 28, 1855.
5 G. T. Denison Papers, vol. 17, "Phrenological Character of Mr. George T. Denison given at Fowler and Well's Phrenological Cabinet ... by L. N. Fowler Professor of Phrenology Nov. 1st, 1859."

might be questioned; his assessment of Denison's personality cannot really be challenged. At the age of nineteen, Denison was expelled from Trinity College for what was called "insolent and insubordinate conduct to the College authorities,"[6] and though he received a law degree from the University of Toronto and was called to the bar in 1861, his legal career was fitful and boring. He had no interest in unravelling legal puzzles and weighing conflicting evidence: his heart was with the cavalry.

With the outbreak of the Civil War in the United States in 1861 and the development of an apprehensiveness in certain quarters in Canada, Denison found his element and issued, anonymously, an agitated and alarmist pamphlet entitled *Canada: is she Prepared for War?* Denison did not think so and he pointed to the lessons of history to justify his argument. When nations lose their martial virtues, he wrote, when they become too concerned with materialism, and sacrifice the love for military glory, they must sooner or later succumb to a more warlike power.[7] A few months later, in another tract, he announced that, contrary to those preachers of perpetual peace, "the era of war has not yet passed away," and he warned that when peace was re-established in the United States after the independence of the Confederacy had been recognized, a large body of men would be thrown out of employment and might be used to undertake filibustering expeditions against British America. In proposing the manner in which this contingency might be met, Denison anticipated those doctrines which were to give him a secure place in the history of military thought. The best defensive force for Canada was mounted infantry, equipped with rifles, trained to fight on foot, and dependent upon the horse chiefly for rapid mobility. Expressing a great distaste for the merchant and manufacturer, Denison specified that the agricultural population would make the best soldiers and all inducements should be given to encourage them to join the volunteer cavalry troops. "The farmers," he said, "have horses of their own, and know how to ride them; they have a greater interest in the country than any other class, and when drilled they would remain in the Province, and always be useful in case of war or invasion."[8]

Denison's sympathy for the Southern cause in the Civil War was instinctual and rooted in the loyalist tradition of his family. He adhered to the same values that legend and propaganda had attached to the plantation life and the Confederacy – the martial values and chivalric

6 *Trinity College Conducted As A Mere Boys' School, Not As A College* (Toronto, 1858), 13. This pamphlet reprints letters exchanged between Denison's father and the college officials and was published by the former.
7 "A Native Canadian," *Canada: is she Prepared for War? or a few remarks on The State of her Defences* (Toronto, 1861).
8 G. T. Denison, *The National Defences: or, Observations on the Best Defensive Force for Canada* (Toronto, 1861).

code of honour; the adulation of conservative, landed society; and the detestation of capitalistic business. Bathed in the pastoral imagery of romance, the South seemed to represent the hierarchical order for which the Family Compact had also stood. The homes of the Denison family in Toronto became places of refuge for exiled Confederates, like General Jubal A. Early, during the last two years of the war. Denison conspired with them to use the propeller boat *Georgian* for a raid from Collingwood to free the prisoners on Johnson's Island, and when the St Alban's Raiders arrived in Toronto in April 1865, after being freed on a technicality by a Montreal magistrate, Denison met them at the docks and offered a twenty thousand dollar bond for General Bennett H. Young, the leader of the group. When Jefferson Davis was released from captivity in 1867, he called at the Denison home.[9]

Denison and the Southerners were kindred spirits. He shared their explanations of defeat just as he had expected their victory. "The practical utilitarian spirit of this age," Jubal A. Early told him in 1868, "has asserted itself in no more conspicuous manner, than in the wonderful revolution it has produced in regard to the estimate of deeds of heroism." Because of the revolution in technology, "we have ceased to estimate as the Ancients did, deeds of personal prowess, valour, and self-sacrifice." The hero of this new age was Grant, whose only military conception was never to fight unless the enemy was outnumbered three to one.[10] Denison came to believe that all the heroes had been on the Southern side. Grant, he wrote long after the war, "is very over-rated as a general": the trouble was that, with some, "success is genius, heroism, patriotism, everything, and in a utilitarian age, and among a utilitarian people perhaps it is the only test they know how to apply."[11] It was materialism, not "character," that had defeated the South. History would remember Grant only because he happened to be in command when Lee was defeated. During the war, Denison had sheltered Fitzhugh Lee, the general's nephew and later governor of Virginia, and in March 1870 he visited the great hero himself at Richmond. "I had watched his campaigns with the closest care; had sympathized with his cause from the beginning; had rejoiced at his victories ... He was one of those men that made the ancients believe in demi-gods."[12] Lee became, along with Garibaldi and Bismarck, one in the trilogy of Denison's heroes.

Even the mythology of the Lost Cause struck a responsive chord

9 Denison Papers, Diary, April 6, 1865, May 30, and June 4, 1867.
10 *Ibid.*, MS enclosed in J. A. Early to Denison, Oct. 27, 1868.
11 *Ibid.*, Scrapbook, 1877–1915, clipping from the *Week*, Feb. 7, 1884.
12 G. T. Denison, "A Visit to General Robert E. Lee," *Canadian Monthly*, I (March 1872), 231–7.

in Denison's heritage. The Lost Cause of the Confederacy and the United Empire Loyalist tradition both centred upon defeat suffered at the hands of the "materialistic North." In both traditions, an aristocratic people were bludgeoned into submission by what Denison came to call "the descendants of convicts." In the Southern legend, the poor people who fought for their independence paid the awful penalty of disfranchisement and corrupt Negro rule, just as a century before the United Empire Loyalists had their property confiscated and their children exiled.

From his contacts with Confederate officers, his own experience during the repulse of the Fenian raid of 1866, and his association with Colonel Garnet Wolseley and Major Henry Havelock, who replaced Wolseley in 1869 as assistant quartermaster general of Canada, Denison grew more convinced than ever that his ideas on cavalry represented a new form of warfare and defence. In *Modern Cavalry: its Organization, Armament, and Employment in War* (1868), he restated the case for mounted riflemen in more detail and with frequent references to Civil War engagements. But though his book was translated into Russian and German, Denison exaggerated when he said that his suggestions heavily influenced the German use of cavalry in 1870.[13] Those who thought Denison's propositions sound remained, like him, military mavericks for many years. He succeeded his uncle as colonel of the 1st Troop York Cavalry, which in 1866 had been named "The Governor-General's Body Guard for Upper Canada," but his hopes for a permanent command remained unfulfilled. His involvement with the Canada First movement, a futile attempt to enter Parliament in 1872, and a trip to England as an emigration commissioner, diverted his attention from military writings, but he returned to them in 1874 when he learned that the Czar of Russia was offering three cash prizes for the best books on cavalry. The competition was open to writers in all countries, and Denison, conscious of the disadvantages under which he laboured, perhaps afraid of appearing ridiculous, prepared his book secretively. During the winter of 1875–6, which was so mild that the horsechestnuts budded in January, he rose at four in the morning to read and write; he spent over a thousand dollars for military works, did research at the British Museum and at St. Petersburg, and hired a Russian lady in New York to translate his manuscript into the language of the Czar. *A History of Cavalry from the Earliest Times With Lessons for the*

13 Jay Luvaas, *The Military Legacy of the Civil War: The European Inheritance* (Chicago, 1959), 125. Denison's own thoughts on the influence of his book, as well as an account of its composition, are given in his *Soldiering in Canada: Recollections and Experiences* (Toronto, 1900).

Future (1877) won Denison the first prize, and it quickly became, and still remains,[14] a standard and definitive work. A military position, however, still eluded him. He grew overly defensive about this and was apt to blame the politicians for pandering to the English officers in making appointments. "I would like to see," he more than once confessed, "a Canadian at the head of our Force."[15]

Not even his work as police magistrate of Toronto, a post he filled from 1877 to 1923, could absorb his energy and ambition. Temperamentally unfitted for the role of lawyer, Denison was hardly the picture of the conventional, judicious magistrate. "He wears a helmet in court," joked a friend, "and sits with spurs on."[16] Like the cavalry charge, his justice was swift. On one occasion, he tried one hundred and eighty cases in a hectic three hours, an average of one a minute. His deportment on the bench was invariably compared to the procedure of a court martial, and he became a favourite of the local newspaper reporters who advertised him as a tourist attraction along with Niagara Falls, with the result that on some occasions there were more curious visitors in the court than prisoners. Denison prided himself on his proverbial promptness. In season and out he walked the three or four miles from his home to the court. His features were clear-cut, his moustache iron-grey. So erect was his stance, so military in bearing, that during the First World War, when he was in his seventies, he was approached on a Toronto street as a likely recruit. Arriving at the court, he would hide until the clock struck ten, and then with a bound he mounted the throne of justice. He dispatched all cases of drunkenness first. A British journalist who visited the magistrate's court reported all was typically American hustle. "I had a seat on the bench one morning alongside Colonel Denison ... He called out the names of the prisoners himself, and administered the oath himself to save time ... I was a little breathless at the slapdash manner in which he disposed of forty cases in exactly forty minutes." When asked why he proceeded so quickly when points of law were raised, the Colonel retorted: "I never allow a point of law to be raised. This is a court of justice, not a court of law."[17]

Denison was an impulsive man. In describing the way in which cavalry operated, he revealed something of himself: "infantry perform their duty quietly and collectively; the cavalry, impelled by excitement,

14 Theodore Ropp, *War in the Modern World* (New York, 1962), 33, refers to it as "the best book on cavalry."
15 QUL, Charles Mair Papers, Denison to Mair, Dec. 31, 1882.
16 *Ibid.*, William Foster to Mair, April 29, 1878.
17 John Foster Fraser, *Canada as it is* (London, 1905), 50–1; Denison described his experiences on the bench in *Recollections of a Police Magistrate* (Toronto, 1920).

boldly, rashly and impetuously."[18] You are at your best, the phrenologist had told him, when charging your enemies. The cavalry must lead, Fitzhugh Lee had observed, with boldness, even recklessness. Denison turned the technique of the cavalry charge into a mode of politics and the Imperial Federation League in Toronto bore this unmistakable imprint in its rhetoric and style. There was no subtlety in him, no hesitation before obstacles. His political decisions, while not always predictable, were as swift as the sentences he delivered in court at an average rate of eighty each morning. In one instance, in 1898, after informing Laurier that any Canadian politician who supported a treaty which allowed American warships to reach the sea through the St Lawrence should be locked up in an asylum, the Colonel had second thoughts and was at a loss for heroic remedies. "To tell the truth," he confessed to the Prime Minister, "... the questions are all of a very complicated and intricate kind, and require a judicial mind capable of weighing pros and cons, impartially and laboriously, to come to a fair decision. In most cases that come before me," he explained, "and I try thousands, I make my mind up in almost all with great promptness, but once, perhaps in [every] three months, I get one that troubles and bothers me, and I hesitate and adjourn, and look for fresh evidence before deciding. This Treaty business has been like that to me, so I will not go down to Ottawa, or bother you, but will trust that you will do the best."[19]

That he did not like Americans he never took any pains to conceal: he once informed a friend that Chicago "is filled with disease, bad water, and ruffians."[20] When it was proposed that a statue of George Washington be erected in Westminster Abbey to celebrate the century of Anglo-Saxon concord, he said he would have to go there in order to spit on it. His inability to endure opposition patiently and his tendency to dwell upon history and the trials of his ancestors in the American Revolution made him a wonderful object of satire and humour in newspapers which did not carry comic strips. One cartoon of 1910 showed him with the inevitable bowed legs and pill-box hat, chagrined, puzzled, with tears in his eyes, standing before a picture of Washington: "There was," he is saying, "George the Third, George Washington and George Denison, and there's only one of us left."[21] Denison regaled his family with such jibes and clipped them for his scrapbooks. Those who learned of him only through such reports knew only one side of his character; others who saw him at home understood him better and

18 Denison, *The National Defences*, 6.
19 Sir Wilfrid Laurier Papers, vol. 95, Denison to Laurier, Dec. 28, 1898.
20 Mair Papers, Denison to Mair, Feb. 16, 1892.
21 Denison Papers, Scrapbook, 1877–1915, clipping from the Toronto *Telegram*, Feb. 24, 1910.

glimpsed that sense of humour and sheer delight in incongruous situations so often hidden beneath the stern exterior he showed to the public.[22]

If the character of an individual is reflected in his home, few habitations were more loaded with meaning than Denison's Heydon Villa, a large square building of red brick built in the western section of the city in 1880. The lofty entrance hall was carpeted in red, and just inside the doorway to the left hung a great genealogical chart displaying Denison's loyalist ancestry. Over the door leading to the dining room loomed the head of a buffalo – presented by the poet Charles Mair; across the hall stood a stuffed pelican in a glass case. Once an astonished visitor moved past these items into the drawing room, spacious and uncluttered with those *objets d'art* so beloved by Victorians, he encountered the portraits of the martial Denisons of the past, and the pictures of two of the Colonel's heroes – General Robert E. Lee and Wolseley. At the rear of the house was the Colonel's study, lined on three sides from floor to ceiling with military books. On the wall hung a portrait of one of Denison's Canada First friends, William Foster, along with an Indian bowcase and a quiver of arrows apparently used at the massacre of Custer, a Zulu spear, and a Yankee sword the Colonel had found at Ridgway and which he contemptuously employed in stirring the fire.[23] The house was situated on a slight elevation and was surrounded by trees which had grown there since Denison's ancestors had first come to America. There were shady walks, roses, miniature bridges, and seats from which he observed the birds through binoculars. This man whose library contained one of the finest collections of military books in Canada, and whose public speeches were laced with combative, bellicose language, found his greatest pleasures in watching birds and playing with little children.

To Heydon Villa came a steady stream of visitors, like the English imperialists Joseph Chamberlain, Alfred Milner, and Rudyard Kipling, and Denison's more intimate Canadian friends. He preferred the company of writers and scholars with whom he associated in the Royal Society of Canada, the poets Charles Mair and William Kirby, or the historian and clerk of the House of Commons, Sir John George Bourinot, or Maurice Hutton, classicist and principal of University College, an academic who disdained intellectuality and preached the life of action. Sir John S. Willison, editor-in-chief of the *Globe* until he left it in 1902 to take charge of the more independent Toronto *News*, was a

22 Denison's obituary in the *Times*, London, June 8, 1925, by J. S. Willison.
23 Denison Papers, Scrapbook, 1877–1915, clipping from the Toronto *Daily News*, Aug. 30, 1890.

frequent caller and was one of the few who could gently tease the Colonel in public by saying that he saved us from our enemies even when we did not realize that we were threatened. Always conscious of his own social background, Denison was exclusive in his invitations. One of his associates in the Imperial Federation League was its secretary, John Castell Hopkins, who had been born on a humble Iowa farm and brought to Canada as a child. Hopkins was a prodigious writer and editor, a master of nervous prose, and a historian of some accomplishment, though a severe academic once patronizingly said of one of his books that its sole usefulness was "to lend an air of refinement to the parlours of many farmhouses throughout the countryside."[24] Hopkins saw Denison often and was known to the Colonel's children as "Castile Soapkins," but he was never asked to dine with those of high estate and title. Denison's friendship with Mair was severely tested when the Colonel married for the second time and did not invite Mair to the wedding even though the bride was the poet's niece from Perth.

The source of Denison's imperialism was the United Empire Loyalist tradition and his main contribution to that movement was defensive, sometimes negative. He was a soldier by temperament and in the late 1880s and early 1890s he worked to preserve traditions, guard the British connection, and keep the road open for imperial unity. As late as 1921, four years before his death, he judged the success of imperialism by the fact that there "are practically no annexationists about now."[25] In 1890 he was over fifty and during the three following decades he displayed little ability to adapt to new circumstances: his rhetoric and the burden of his thought never quite shook off the concerns which had shaped it in the late 1880s. In reissuing his history of cavalry in 1913 he saw no reason to change a single sentence in a book published in 1877, and a similar rigidity affected his imperialism. His political memoirs, entitled *The Struggle for Imperial Unity* (1909), were not recollected in tranquility, despite the picture of the aged and mellowed warrior in civilian clothes on the frontispiece. They were intended to expose the resurgent, treasonous conspiracy for free trade with the United States, engineered by the same old clique of 1891. Denison's conception of the Empire was limited. He tended to see it almost exclusively in terms of Canada and Great Britain and he hardly mentioned India or Africa unless by way of warning of impending war. He was oblivious to the sense of religious mission which was the driving

---

24 W. S. Wallace, "Canadian History and Biography," *The Year Book of Canadian Art, 1913, compiled by the Arts & Letters Club of Toronto* (Toronto, n.d.), 20.
25 Sir George Parkin Papers, Denison to Parkin, Dec. 20, 1921.

force of the imperialism of Parkin and Grant. Military considerations dominated his outlook, as indeed they dominated the movement for imperial unity. When an American journalist called Denison "The Roosevelt of Canada"[26] he hit upon an apt comparison. Like the colonel who led the Rough Riders up the San Juan Hill in the Spanish-American War and who praised Denison's book as "the best I have read on the subject,"[27] Denison also admired the strenuous and athletic life and praised military preparedness as the foundation of national character.

Those who liked the Colonel and those who did not were equally struck by his robustness and annoyed by his egoism. Of all the public figures of his generation he alone left behind three volumes of auto-biography. One reviewer scarcely exaggerated when he wrote that *The Struggle for Imperial Unity* should have been called "How I Saved the Empire," unless, of course, that title had been pre-empted by Sam Hughes whose self-esteem verged on megalomania.[28] G. M. Grant, a man of gentle judgment, said of Denison that he is "too hot-headed, & fancies that on all military matters he is infallible."[29] "Such restless energy I never saw in any man before as in Col. D.," Parkin told his wife during a stay at Heydon Villa in 1892. "He would be in my room discussing questions before I was up, and would sit up till any hour of the night." "I have no mental rest with the colonel, except when I shut myself up in my room."[30] The most arresting aspect of Denison's career was the discrepancy between his estimation of his own abilities – and on military matters these were formidable – and his failure to enter Parliament or attain a permanent military command. It was perhaps the resulting sense of bitterness that Parkin noticed when, after remarking on his friend's "concentrated prejudice" and the "profound egoism which sometimes appears," he said that "I cannot help thinking that he is in a way a disappointed man, and as he grows older this shows it-self."[31] But even while they chided him in private, his friends also mentioned Denison's sincerity and integrity of mind. He was, said one, always absolutely "straight."[32] And he displayed in a lucid way that emotional commitment to Canada as he understood it and to the Empire as he hoped it would become. It is in view of this quality of his mind that he must bulk large in any history of that emotion.

26 Denison Papers, Scrapbook, 1909–25, clipping from the *Dearborn Independent*, Dec. 27, 1919.
27 *Ibid.*, clipping from the *Canadian Courier*, Nov. 7, 1912.
28 *Ibid.*, clipping from the Winnipeg *Free Press*, April 19, 1909.
29 Sir John S. Willison Papers, Grant to Willison, Dec. 5, 1898.
30 Parkin Papers, Parkin to Nan, Oct. 16 and Nov. 27, 1892 (copies).
31 *Ibid.*, Parkin to Nan, Feb. 18, 1900 (copy).
32 Denison Papers, Parkin to Denison, May 14, 1902.

II

The Maritime provinces supplied a disproportionate number of Canadian imperialists. George Grant was born at Albion Mines, Nova Scotia, in 1835, and George Parkin in 1846 at Salisbury, a village in Westmoreland County, New Brunswick. John G. Bourinot traced his roots to Sydney, Cape Breton, and Andrew Macphail to Orwell, Prince Edward Island. Grant's son, William, remembered sitting on a dock at Halifax watching the ships come and go, and, like most of those who tried to explain why the seaboard produced men sympathetic to the imperial idea, he said that the ocean put those who dwelt beside it in contact with all the nations and broadened their minds. Life in Toronto had the opposite effect – it was cramped and parochial.[33] Parkin had an almost mystical reverence for the ocean. "Whenever I am near the sea," he wrote late in life, "I am more and more convinced that its influence on the character of races reared in its vicinity is immense." The outward look toward the horizon of the ocean "strangely stirs the imagination, and keeps one's thoughts in touch with all the world." He had lost, he said, his facility with the pen; "perhaps the sea will bring it back."[34]

The hardy Nova Scotian sense of independence, self-confidence, and the consciousness of belonging to an imperial partnership was born in the late eighteenth and early nineteenth centuries out of the realization that while the inland colonies were dependent upon Britain for protection, Nova Scotia was indispensable to the strength of the Empire in the North Atlantic. When in 1854 Joseph Howe confessed that as he entered Westminster Abbey or Greenwich Hospital and saw the memorials of his forebears "I feel that I have a property in these two noble piles which our common ancestors built and bequeathed, quite equal to that of any gentleman in London," he spoke as the authentic voice of that region's loyalism,[35] an attitude which invariably stressed equality of possession and place rather than dependence. This pride, this feeling that Nova Scotians were second to no others in the Empire, expressed itself in the durable belief that while Ontario and Quebec were larger and more wealthy, the Maritimes were far richer in masterful men. "Like the State of Massachusetts, in the American Republic," declared Bourinot, "Nova Scotia has won for herself a pre-eminent position among British American dependencies through the energy and talent

33 Willison Papers, W. L. Grant to Willison, Feb. 3, 1927; W. L. Grant, 'Nation of Prophets, of Sages, and of Worthies': A Speech Delivered on 18th December 1917 ... On His Installation as Headmaster of Upper Canada College (n.p., n.d.), 6.
34 William L. Grant Papers, Parkin to W. L. Grant, Jan. 1921.
35 J. M. Beck, ed., Joseph Howe: Voice of Nova Scotia (Toronto, 1964), 157.

of the men born on her soil."[36] Those like G. M. Grant who supported Confederation with the argument that the kind of manhood produced in New Brunswick and Nova Scotia would ensure that the Maritimers would dominate the union, were not likely to take very seriously those objectors to imperial federation who warned that Canadians would be outnumbered. Just as New England exerted an influence in the political and cultural life of the United States far out of proportion to her population, so too would the Maritimes rule the Dominion, and in time, Canada would likewise prevail within the Empire. Though Maritime imperialists held to these beliefs, they were not oblivious to the less commendable aspects of their native provinces – the slow adaptability to economic change, the low tone of political life, and the perpetuation of bitter sectarianism in religious life. While their imperialism was inspired by cherished traditions, they were also moved by the very shortcomings they knew so well. Of few was this more true than G. M. Grant.

According to family tradition, when "Geordie" Grant mangled his right hand in a mechanical haycutter at the age of eight, it was decided that since he was obviously lost as a farm worker he should find a career in teaching and preaching. He attended the Pictou Academy and then entered Glasgow University with the aid of a scholarship in 1853. Grant's academic performance was superb though his friends recollected that in his college days he was never a studious bookworm. He "appreciated beer, but was a non-smoker. He was anything but abstemious." Once he was involved in so violent a brawl that the police arrested him for stabbing his adversary, a charge from which he was acquitted.[37] He excelled at football and debating, joined the Conservative Club, and helped found the Literary and Philosophical Society. He steeped himself in the writings of the romantics – Coleridge, Wordsworth, and Carlyle – and filled his notebooks with their epigrams. Like them, he was repelled by the cold, austere rationalism of the enlightenment: "In all spiritual things," he once wrote, "there has hardly been so barren a century as the eighteenth."[38] His idolization of that prophet of strenuousness and work, Thomas Carlyle, was life-long and intense; equally lasting was the impress left by one of his teachers, Dr John Caird, who stressed the social results of Christianity. Ordained as a minister of the Church of Scotland in 1860, Grant worked for three years as a missionary in his native Pictou County and in Prince Edward Island, and in 1863 was called to St Matthew's Church in Halifax.

36 J. G. Bourinot, "The Late Judge Marshall," *Canadian Monthly*, IV (May 1880), 516.
37 George M. Grant Papers, vol. 15, MS "Recollections of G. M. Grant, by J. D. Everett," n.d., 2.
38 W. L. Grant and F. Hamilton, *Principal Grant* (Toronto, 1904), 83.

During the summer of 1872 he accompanied his parishioner and personal friend, the engineer Sandford Fleming, across Canada on a survey of a route for the proposed transcontinental railway to the Pacific and described the expedition in a book, *Ocean to Ocean* (1873), which exulted in the discovery of the west and the huge resources of the new Dominion. "Since that journey," he remarked thirty years later, "I have never doubted the future of Canada."[39]

When Grant was named principal of Queen's in 1877, that thirty-six-year-old institution was not in a flourishing financial state. The government had withdrawn its subsidy and the Presbyterian Church assumed responsibility only for the Theological Faculty. Burdened by the cares of administration and lecturing, he conducted an endowment campaign, the first of many, the year after his appointment. Overwork, the wakeful nights spent sitting in coach cars in order to avoid the expenses of a Pullman berth, the vexations that came to one who took a personal interest even in the kind of blinds used in Convocation Hall, permanently undermined his health. The work, he told Fleming, who had been knighted in 1877 and chosen chancellor of Queen's in 1880, "all but killed me." Though Grant looked forward to the time when he would be free from petty financing so that "I may devote myself to that scholarly & literary work that I ought to do,"[40] the day for calm, scholarly repose never came. Hardly had the university been revived than Grant had to fight to prevent it from being moved to the provincial capital and made into an affiliate of the University of Toronto. His justifications for the independence of Queen's included more than loyalty to a region or a denomination. Believing that in intellectual life "uniformity is not desirable in itself" and that it could only be purchased by "cast-iron methods that are injurious to mental freedom," he thought that higher education in Ontario could be enriched by having two different universities – Toronto modelled on London, and Queen's on Edinburgh. There was not a single instance, he said in his inaugural address, of the best results following from the "monopolization of all higher educational work in one institution."[41]

Grant was far more than a university figure. In the two decades after 1880 he attained the stature of a Christian statesman and moral guardian by speaking out on public questions. While his admirers said that he wielded an influence comparable to that of Henry Ward Beecher

39 G. M. Grant, "Thanksgiving and Retrospect," *Queen's Quarterly*, IX (Jan. 1902), 227.
40 Sir Sandford Fleming Papers, Grant to Fleming, March 17, 1886.
41 *Ibid.*, Grant to Fleming, vol. 18, n.d.; *Principal Grant's Inaugural Address Delivered at Queen's University, Kingston, on University Day* (Toronto, 1885), 10.

in the United States, Grant himself interpreted the role of the ministry in terms of what he had seen in Scotland during his student days when the pulpits were occupied by what he called "the real leaders of the Scottish people."[42] He saw the university and the church as vital forces in national development, not refuges shielding scholars from the world, and he defined the work of intellectuals as leaders of democracy and general educators setting forth and clarifying large questions which politicians were too timid to treat. Imperialism was one such topic, and Grant and Fleming, out of whose mind came so many proposals for strengthening the Empire through improved communications, quickly joined the Imperial Federation League. Grant was president of its branch in Kingston. But his imperialism was only an outgrowth of his religious fervour and his position as a leader of Protestant opinion. There are many ways of suggesting his rank, including his presence at the Congress of Religions held in conjunction with the Columbian Exposition at Chicago in 1893 where he appeared as a major spokesman of Canadian Protestantism, but perhaps the best indication is a letter written to him by a troubled farmer. Of uncertain grammar, it dealt with transgressions and vagaries of the flesh. The young man believed that he had made a girl pregnant and he explained that since "she was the first girl that I had ever had sexual intercourse with in my life I considered it my moral duty to offer her marriage, although she did not suit me in every respect." When he discovered, however, that his brother was really responsible he did not know what course to pursue and was therefore consulting "an ablier [sic] mind than my own." Grant's advice cannot be found, but what is so interesting is that on such a "delicate subject" the youth consulted him because "I have read and heard so much of your superiority among the clergy of Ontario."[43]

All the agitations and struggles of the 1890s came into the ambit of Grant's column on "Current Events" in *Queen's Quarterly,* a journal which he helped found in 1893, and the leading feature of his commentaries was the constant striving to place events into a religious perspective and to measure men and actions in relation to Christian precepts. His conclusions frequently occasioned some surprise, as when he supported Catholic separate schools in Manitoba; often they evoked hostility and dispraise from elements within his own communion.

The standard from which he judged social issues and the manner in which his mind worked were exemplified by his reaction to two such popular causes – the campaign for prohibition and the restriction of

42 G. M. Grant, "The Pulpit in Scotland as it is, and as it was Forty Years Ago," *Queen's Quarterly,* vii (Jan. 1900), 195.
43 G. M. Grant Papers, Stephen Sawden to Grant, Feb. 16, 1894.

Chinese immigration. Largely in response to the demands of temperance groups, especially the Methodists, the Liberal party committed itself in 1893 to submit the issue to a plebiscite and when the announcement was made that the vote would be taken in 1897 Grant declared against prohibition in the *Globe*. He neither believed that intemperance was the source of all social evils, as some prohibitionists seemed to think, nor did he agree that compulsion was desirable. But he sided with the forces of "Liquor and Liberty" mainly because he foresaw that restriction would encourage evasion and coercion would produce hypocrisy. "If restriction is pressed so far as to unduly interfere with individual liberty," he wrote in 1902, "the law will be evaded by many, produce a recoil or be flouted by others, band together in a league against the law all who have invested their property in a legal business which has been destroyed without compensation, and stimulate a weak religiosity or sanctimoniousness in those who identify ecclesiastical rules with the eternal obligations of spiritual religion."[44] Though Denison concurred with this argument and jocularly said that he gathered from his own experience that prohibition "keeps liquor away from those whom it would benefit" while not preventing those who should not have it from falling subject to delirium tremens, Grant was barraged by charges that he was championing the liquor interests and "advocating principles diametrically opposed to His Kingdom."[45]

Grant's criticism of those who wanted to exclude Chinese from Canada no more endeared him to organized labour than did his repudiation of prohibition gain him popularity with those whose reading of scripture was more assured than his own. The Chinese had been brought into Canada to build the Canadian Pacific Railway and pressures for either total exclusion or restriction were greeted with indifference by the Dominion government. John A. Macdonald told the House of Commons in 1882 that he shared the objections to "Mongolians becoming permanent settlers" but that nothing could be done until the railway was completed. Once these temporary exigencies were overcome, he promised that he would "be quite ready to join to a reasonable extent in preventing a permanent settlement in the country of Mongolian or Chinese emigrants." True to his word, a royal commission investigated the subject in 1884 and in 1886 Parliament passed a law which required vessels landing in Canada to carry no more than

44 G. M. Grant, "Canada," in Rev. W. D. Grant, ed., *Christendom Anno Domini MDCCCCI: A Presentation of Christian Conditions and Activities in Every Country of the World at the Beginning of the Twentieth Century by more than sixty Competent Contributors* (Toronto, 1902), i, 94.
45 G. M. Grant Papers, Denison to Grant, Dec. 18, 1897; G. G. Scott to Grant, Dec. 17, 1897.

one Chinese for every fifty tons of cargo, and compelled these immigrants, except those in certain specified classes such as governmental representatives and students, to pay a fifty dollar entrance fee. The chief reason Chinese immigration was not prohibited altogether, Macdonald told an assembly of workingmen, was that "One of the advantages we are going to secure from the construction of the Canadian Pacific Railway is ... a GREAT TRADE WITH CHINA, and if we adopted a distinctly hostile policy it might be the means of killing future business relations with that country."[46]

When in the early 1890s the Toronto Trades and Labour Council petitioned the government for total exclusion on the broad grounds that the Chinese were driving down the moral and economic status of white workers, Grant convinced the General Assembly of the Church that it should not only oppose the demands of organized labour but also request Parliament to remove all discriminatory legislation already on the statute books. In his appeal to the Assembly he reassured his listeners that an overwhelmingly large number of Chinese would never come to Canada, and in *Queen's Quarterly* he sympathized with those who wanted British Columbia to be of "the Caucasian not the Mongolian type." But he warned that Canada's legislation endangered Britain's friendly relations with China and he did not think it wise that the Dominion should brutally repudiate the consequences of a policy which she had inaugurated. He could not see that labour would benefit in the long run by drawing up invidious "distinctions based upon race, colour, creed, or sex," and, above all, he held that discriminatory legislation was "contrary to the spirit of Christianity," inconsistent with the sending of Christian missionaries to the Orient, and unfaithful to "Our mission ... to Christianize the world."[47]

Uppermost in Grant's views on social and political questions, including imperialism, was his fervent belief in the inseparability of the spiritual and the temporal and the insistence that religion must penetrate every nook and cranny of national existence. Before the churches could perform their mission, however, they themselves had to be purified and tempered. For Grant this required the co-operation of all Protestant denominations as a preliminary step towards nothing less than the union of all the Canadian churches. He was one of the small band of

46 *Speech of Sir John Macdonald to the Workingmen's Liberal Conservative Association of Ottawa and Le Cercle Lafontaine, delivered in Ottawa on the 8th October, 1886* (n.p., n.d.), 19–20.
47 G. M. Grant, "Current Events," *Queen's Quarterly*, IV (Oct. 1896), 158; G. M. Grant Papers, vol. 9, MS "Report of the Committee on Chinese Immigration" and MS "Résumé of the Action Taken by Our Government with Reference to Chinese Immigration," n.d.

religious leaders who ever since mid-century had grown increasingly impatient with the perpetuation within Canada of the divisions and sub-divisions of Scottish Presbyterianism. In his youth the conflicts between the sects were so intense that on one occasion the snow on the streets of Pictou town was splattered with blood. Grant would undoubtedly have endorsed the sentiments of one missionary, William Proudfoot, who said that the Scottish feuds were a hindrance to the faith in the new world.[48] In a sermon of 1866 Grant lamented the existence of "multitudinous sects, a many-coloured array of beliefs and superstitions, a valley full of the dry-bones of dogma and creeds," and enjoined that no pet doctrines, institutions, or catechisms should stand in the way of "honest work for and with God in Christ."[49] He always tended to emphasize the common Christian tradition of the various denominations and churches rather than the organizational and doctrinal differences which separated them, and in the introduction to his comparative study of the great faiths, *Religions of the World in Relation to Christianity* (1894), he stressed what the founders of Buddhism, Mohammedanism, and Christianity shared. Temperamentally, he was able to transcend the religious divisions which embittered Canadian life. Much to the annoyance of some of his parishioners, one of his closest friends in Halifax was the Roman Catholic Archbishop, Thomas Connolly, and, while principal of Queen's University, he once presided over a meeting called to raise funds to build a synagogue in Kingston. He admired the commodiousness of the Anglican Church and its ability to contain within one communion men of varied outlooks, although he was also aware of the liabilities of such comprehensiveness. He invariably judged the other churches not by the extent to which their organizations or doctrines departed from his own, but by the standard of their moral impact upon society. Unstinting in his admiration for the missionary efforts of the Methodist and Anglican churches in the Canadian west, he was also full of praise for the Catholic Church's work in lifting the soul of the *habitant* "so far above the self-sufficient materialism of lower class Protestantism."[50]

Grant played a major role in bringing about the union of the four Presbyterian denominations into the Presbyterian Church in Canada in 1875, and the union of the Methodists in 1883 inspired him "to hope for triumphs much more signal, and even to dream the dream of faith

48 Neil Gregor Smith, "Nationalism in the Canadian Churches," *Canadian Journal of Theology*, IX, no. 2 (1963), 120.
49 G. M. Grant, *Sermon Preached Before the Synod of Nova Scotia and Prince Edward Island in Connection with the Church of Scotland, on June 26th, 1866* (Halifax, 1866), 13, 18.
50 Grant and Hamilton, *Principal Grant*, 80.

that all things are possible."[51] There would someday be an amalgama-
tion of the Presbyterian and Methodist Churches, he believed, and this
in turn would be a step toward the formation of a national church including Anglicans and Catholics. He believed that behind the tendency
toward organic union of the churches were the forces of social evolution. In an article on the religious prospects of the twentieth century,
Grant argued that the growth of Canadian society was changing the
Protestant denominations by grinding down those abrasive and incidental characteristics which had kept them separate and apart. That
intensity of faith which moved the original Scottish settlers "to divide
on petty issues, ... which had no meaning in Canada, however necessary
it might be to fight them out in Scotland," had been rechannelled by
the young Canadian-born who had promoted the union of 1875. The
further Canada moved away from the frontier stages of development,
the more the Methodist Church would shed the excessively rigid morality, anti-intellectualism, and reliance upon "warm-hearted but ignorant" preachers, which had been its strengths in disciplining a pioneer
people. It was only natural, he added, that a primitive community
should be distrustful of the hierarchical orders of the Anglican Church,
but when society became more complicated, and when wealth increased,
differences of station would be developed and universally acknowledged, "and a corresponding change in the organization of the church
is felt to be proper."[52]

Social development would wear down the sectarianism of the colonial
past, Grant thought, and this was desirable because denominationalism
was "inconsistent with the fundamental position of Protestantism."
The essence of Protestantism was the appeal to the authority of scripture rather than to the authority of the church, and the meaning of
scripture was, within limits, changing. Its contents were being progressively revealed through new knowledge and new thought. To claim
that one denomination possessed the authority to enforce conformity
to its particular creed and faith was therefore to deny the whole basis
of Protestantism itself. Grant believed that the "higher criticism," the
application of historical technique to explain and interpret scripture,
was valuable because it undermined the basis of extreme denominationalism. "The Bible," he told the students at Queen's, "is a history and
a complete though condensed literature; and the special gift of God to
our century is a truer interpretation of ancient history and ancient literatures." He who is opposed to the new criticism "shows that he has more

51 G. M. Grant, "Organic Union of Churches: How Far Should it Go?" *Canadian Methodist Magazine*, xx (Sept. 1884), 244.
52 Grant, "Canada," 88, 91, 95.

faith in Jewish Scribes and Rabbis, whose successors crucified Christ, than he has in the human mind or the Word of God."[53] One of the many functions of the university in fact, was to aid the church in reconciling itself "with all that is best in modern thought,"[54] by which he meant economics and sociology as well as the higher criticism and the theory of evolution. Though Grant doubted that literature, art, or science "can touch the conscience or save it from sin," he thought that the enlightenment of science was necessary to temper the dogmatism of piety. "How often has authoritative religious teaching been invoked in favour of the most horrible crimes, or made to cover the selfishness, pride, perfidy, and general deviltry of priests?" he asked. Even love needs light; piety requires enlightenment.[55]

Against debilitating denominational rivalries Grant placed the idea of practical Christianity. To emphasize the practical and social role of religion was by implication to relegate organizational differences to a level of secondary importance. His practical religion was expressed in two interrelated forms: the first was missionary enterprise. There was work enough for all the churches in the task of making the Canadian west a law-abiding and Christian place, guaranteeing social order, and ministering to the immigrants. So gigantic was the burden that the individual denominations could not handle it alone: co-operation and ultimately union was required.[56] The second related expression of practical Christianity was the social gospel, or the effort to infuse the spirit of the faith into industrial conduct. He had realized long before that the workingmen were losing interest in the church partly because of the social irrelevance of a religion devitalized by sterile feuds. His interest in the social gospel ran back to his mission to the labourers of Glasgow, was strengthened by the parallel movement in the United States, and was, as will be seen, at the heart of his imperialism.

That Canada would lead the way by the formation of a national church which would stand as a model for the reunification of all the churches in Christendom was Grant's most profound conviction. The co-operation in missionary work in western Canada and in carrying the gospel to the dark places of the earth, the rediscovery of the social role of religion, the decreased emphasis upon inherited forms which overwhelmed the spirit, and the efforts of men of good will – all these

53 G. M. Grant, "Christ is Divided," *Sunday Afternoon Addresses in Convocation Hall, Queen's University, Kingston, Ont., Session 1893, Published by the Students* (n.p., n.d.), 92–3.
54 Fleming Papers, Grant to Fleming, March 17, 1886.
55 Martin Griffin Papers, Grant to Griffin, March 8, 1891.
56 G. M. Grant, "Churches and Schools in the North-West," in John Macoun, ed., *Manitoba and the Great North-West* (Guelph, 1882), 523–39.

would restore Christian unity. With this expectation and his efforts to obliterate the artificial demarkation between the spirit and the flesh, his imperialism was intertwined. Imperial unity and church unity were, in Grant's mind, not merely analogous processes – they were both products of identical causes and directed to the same end. Just as the union of the churches was the precondition for the Christianization of the social order, so too the unity of the Empire was necessary to maintain a political power making for righteousness on earth. Both Christianity and imperialism called men to self-sacrifice and service; both required the allegiance to ideals and the denigration of the material and the flesh.

Indicative of both Grant's independence of mind and his sincere effort to uphold moral as opposed to economic imperialism was the fact that he was one of the last Canadian imperialists to support the British government against the Boers. He had little sympathy for those Europeans, the Uitlanders, in the Transvaal who complained that the Boers taxed them unfairly and refused to accord them political rights, and still less feeling for the business imperialism of Cecil Rhodes who dreamed of annexing the Boer republics to South Africa. "It is idle to say," he wrote in 1896 after the Jameson raid had attempted to foment insurrection in the Transvaal, "that the Boers are dirty; ignorant; bigoted; conceited; inhospitable; unsound on the slavery question, and above all that they do not like the English!" Those business interests which claimed to be progressive and enterprising, he said, were only entering "a plea for freebooting and filibustering."[57] The raid was an invasion of a friendly state by "gentlemen stock-jobbers"; Cecil Rhodes appeared to him as "a pirate in top hat and patent leather boots," Napoleonic "in his arrested moral development."[58] Grant instinctively sided with the God-fearing Boers, whom he had visited in 1888, against what he took to be economic imperialism masquerading as liberalization. "They were never understood in England," he said of the Boers; for sixty years British policy toward them had been one long "mistake." "They love freedom more than life," he declared, "they believe that the establishment of political conditions which will ensure the control of unscrupulous capitalists means white slavery."[59]

What dramatically changed Grant's mind about the tensions in South Africa, even though he never lost sympathy for the Boers, was President Kruger's telegram of October 1899 demanding the withdrawal of British troops from the borders of the Transvaal and challenging British

57 G. M. Grant, "Current Events," *Queen's Quarterly*, III (April 1896), 312.
58 *Ibid.*, IV (April 1897), 316.
59 *Ibid.*, VIII (July 1900), 77.

suzerainty. This, Grant argued, "substituted a new issue for the old ones" and he took some comfort from the facts that the "British ideal of civilization is the higher as well as in accordance with modern political principles," and "that the appeal from moral force to the God of battles was made not by us but by the government and people of the Transvaal."[60] That being the case, it befitted those Canadians who wanted their country to be a nation to understand that the survival of the Empire was at stake and not to raise hair-splitting constitutional points in opposition to full participation in the war. Such equivocations and qualifications as these were lost upon Colonel Denison, who thought pleasing preachers a difficult business, but though Grant came around to support the war and wholehearted Canadian action in it, he did so only hesitatingly and only after he had satisfied himself that the moral ambiguities had been resolved.

The most striking aspect of Grant's mind was his ability to see the unity of all experience and to preserve a careful balance between what was general and what was particular. He had as little regard for the mechanics of imperial federation or political parties as he did for the organizational differences which divided Christians. It was not these differences which distressed him, but rather the exaggeration of them until men forgot the common aim that they were meant to serve. He dealt with those who urged the submergence of Canada in an Anglo-Saxon confederacy, those who supported uniform, non-denominational, national schools, and those who wanted a single university in Ontario, in exactly the same fashion. Just as the united church for which he prayed would draw upon varied traditions and harness them to a single cause, similarly the different nations within the Empire would work harmoniously for the imperialism of mission.

III

When we study the lives of men, George Parkin wrote after reading Carlyle's biography of Cromwell, we glimpse the purposes of God in the governing of the world. "Their circumstances – their training – the influences under which they are thrown, the common acts of their everyday life are all means which He is using to prepare them to do the work He has for them to do."[61] It was characteristic of Parkin that he should see all history and his own life in this way, and that in his

60 *Ibid.*, VII (Jan. 1900) 252; Willison Papers, Grant to Willison, Nov. 22, 1899; G. M. Grant, "Introductory Chapter" to T. G. Marquis, *Canada's Sons on Kopje and Veldt: A Historical Account of the Canadian Contingents* (Toronto, 1900), 4–5.
61 Parkin Papers, vol. 74, notebook, 1871.

youth he should determinedly seek in scripture and in history his own avocation. His "mission" was education: he was a teacher long before he became an imperialist, "the prince of Imperialists and their first missionary," as the anti-imperialist John Ewart called him.[62] The desire to mould opinion and character, together with the religious fervour which suffused it, were the major strands of continuity in his life.

Parkin was the youngest of thirteen children born to a father who had emigrated from Yorkshire and a mother whose roots in New Brunswick ran back to the era of loyalist settlement. He knew at first hand what was meant by the hand to hand struggle with the forest and the land, and he understood from personal experience the educational handicaps that the children of pioneers faced. His early training was desultory and irregular; he attended the Normal School at St John in 1863, taught in a primary school, and entered the University of New Brunswick in 1864. His favourite teacher was Dr Loring Bailey, professor of chemistry and natural science, who had studied under Louis Agassiz at Harvard. So intrigued was Parkin with the study of nature, that he later wondered how it was that "the studies of those days did not turn me into the field of scientific research."[63] One of his student companions was George Foster who, like Parkin, was to teach in the grammar schools, lecture for the temperance cause, and become an imperialist. But while Foster was to leave his professorship in classics at Acadia University for politics, and in time serve in Conservative governments as minister of marine and fisheries, minister of finance, and minister of trade and commerce, Parkin remained with teaching. After graduating in 1867 he was appointed headmaster of the grammar school in the lumbering town of Bathurst and four years later came back to Fredericton as head of the collegiate school affiliated with the university. For enthusiasm and for winning the hearts of students, Parkin had few rivals. Bliss Carman said of him that he "was head-master, tutor, big brother, and hero to me all in one."[64]

During 1873–4 Parkin took a leave of absence and went to Oxford to study Latin, Greek, and history. For the young teacher who packed a jar of home-made jam in his suitcase, the journey to England was a veritable pilgrimage. Years afterward, he recalled the sensation that seized him upon his arrival at the university. It was an overwhelming experience "to grow up to manhood in the backwoods of Canada, filling one's mind with the details of English History, and having one's

62 John S. Ewart, *The Kingdom of Canada, Imperial Federation, The Colonial Conferences, The Alaska Boundary Dispute, and Other Essays* (Toronto, 1908), 53.
63 Parkin Papers, Parkin to Bailey, March 29, 1920.
64 *Ibid.*, vol. 107, Bliss Carman to Author [J. S. Willison], June 7, 1926.

imagination stirred by the writings of men famed throughout the English world," and then be transported to the very centre of British culture, to hear Ruskin lecture on art, to listen to Dean Stanley's sermons, to see Pusey and Max Muller, and the historians Stubbs, Freeman, and Froude in the flesh.[65] Parkin never lost this sense of veneration for Oxford and his year in England was the decisive experience in his life. He visited the public schools – Eton, Rugby, and Uppingham – and from Edward Thring, headmaster of Uppingham, he learned of the powerful role such institutions played in educating the future leaders of society. His friendship with Thring, whom he called "one of my founts of inspiration,"[66] redoubled his hopes for establishing a public school on the English model in New Brunswick and it also revealed to him a mind completely committed to the new imperialism. Parkin was secretary of the Oxford Union and there he came into contact with Alfred Milner who was to become one of the leaders of English imperialism. In a debate in 1874 Parkin spoke of the need for extending representation in imperial councils to the more important colonies and aroused Milner's interest in these "new" ideas.[67] This association was never severed. When Parkin returned to England in the spring of 1888 to gather material for a biography of Thring, he was introduced to the inner circle of the Imperial Federation League and was asked to undertake a lecture tour of Australia and New Zealand on its behalf. He leapt at the opportunity, resigned his position at Fredericton, and deferred writing the life of his teacher.

Parkin had joined the League in 1885 when its branches were established in the Maritimes and he had previously been invited by D'Alton McCarthy, president of the organization in Canada, and Sir Leonard Tilley, lieutenant-governor of New Brunswick, to undertake a tour of Ontario and Quebec. During 1888, G. M. Grant had delivered a few lectures on imperial federation in Australia, but Parkin threw himself into the work as though the whole imperial question depended upon his efforts alone. Between 1889 and 1895, when he came to Toronto as principal of Upper Canada College, he travelled thousands of miles throughout the Empire and published three books which constitute the most cogent case for union ever penned by a Canadian. His *Imperial Federation: The Problem of National Unity* (1892) was calculated to convey "a clear and continuous statement of Canadian

---

65 *Ibid.*, vol. 64, MS untitled, n.d.
66 Raleigh Parkin Collection, Parkin to Arthur Lee, Sept. 22, 1898 (copy).
67 *Ibid.*, file 3 contains a photocopy of the record of this debate. Milner's biographer credited Parkin with a great influence on his subject; see A. M. Collin, *Proconsul in Politics: A Study of Lord Milner in Opposition and Power* (London, 1964), 16–18.

ideas from a national point of view";[68] *Round the Empire* (1892), a descriptive account of the geography and resources of the Empire, was intended for use in schools and a year after its appearance fifty thousand copies had been sold;[69] and *The Great Dominion: Studies of Canada* (1895), a compilation of articles which originally appeared in the London *Times*, contained so appreciative an account of Canadian regions and prospects that the Dominion government subsidized its publication as immigration material.[70] These books and his speeches were really only amplifications of an article he had written for an American magazine in 1888. In capsule form it contained the fundamental premises of his imperial thought – the interest in geography, an understanding of the revolution in communications, the tendency to interpret geopolitics within the terms of social Darwinism, and the concern with demonstrating to the working classes that the preservation of the Empire was in their interest. And through it all there ran the burning sense of religious mission, the conviction that the British people had assumed "vast responsibilities in the government of weak and alien races," and the apprehension that if the Empire was not amalgamated Britain would within fifty years abdicate her foremost place to Russia and the United States.[71] Parkin had the gift of lucid exposition and his words ring with a certainty that came from religious conviction. Lord Rosebery said of Parkin that he was the only man to stump the Empire. A more accurate analogy, however, was the one Parkin chose: he called himself "a wandering Evangelist of Empire."[72]

Though these were Parkin's most productive and creative years, they were also the ones that carved the lines upon his face. He was oblivious to personal wealth and when he embarked upon his tour he abandoned comfort, a secure income, and a settled home life. (He had married a former student, Anne Fisher, "Nan," he called her, in 1878.) During the early 1890s the small income which he received from literary work and as correspondent of the *Times* was supplemented by the loans of generous friends like Sandford Fleming and an "endowment" of four hundred and fifty pounds a year from Milner.[73] Parkin refused a Scottish parliamentary seat and he turned down a lucrative post as publicity agent for the CPR. He was repelled, he told Nan, by "the fierce wrestle for success and wealth." "I fear," he added, that "you have

68 Fleming Papers, Parkin to Fleming, May 3, 1891.
69 *Week*, XI (Sept. 14, 1894), 999.
70 Parkin Papers, Diary, 1891–7, July 10, 1894.
71 G. R. Parkin, "The Reorganization of the British Empire," *Century Illustrated Monthly Magazine*, XXXVII (Dec. 1888), 187–92.
72 Parkin Papers, Parkin to Nan, Feb. 7, 1908 (copy).
73 *Ibid.*, Diary, 1891–7, May 27, 1893; vol. 107, memorandum, June 1, 1893.

a dreamer for a husband."[74] In spite of financial worries, frequent absences, and the death of two children, his marriage retained much of the delight and novelty of courtship. "I have been in love myself for the last twenty-one years," he told a bachelor friend. "Last Friday I stole away ... to our summer home to see my wife after ten days of separation, and it was all as fresh – and dreamlike – as if the twenty-one years had not intervened."[75]

All who met Parkin remarked upon his energy and religious fervour. He was six feet tall, loose-limbed, and spare, and his deep set eyes were grey-blue. In his dress he showed a penchant for well-cut suits of rough grey or heather mixture tweeds. Bliss Carman could only compare him with Theodore Roosevelt for driving power and compelling moral force. What sustained Parkin was a passionate religious feeling and a faith in the influence of Christianity in the world. This lay at the bottom of all his thought and unified his work as an educator and as an imperialist. Bishop Medley of Fredericton ("this great and good man whom I love so much")[76] had confirmed him in the Anglican faith, and at Oxford he had heard Wescott, regius professor of divinity, summon the Church of England to missionary work and ask it to rise to a realization of the obligation of imperial power. At the General Synod in Montreal in 1880, Parkin spoke of the obligation of the church "to grapple with the great task of supplying the wants of our great North West country" and to carry the gospel throughout the Empire.[77] Again and again he turned to scripture for inspiration and guidance: "I intend to get my books out and settle down for a good read in the Bible particularly," he told his wife. "I feel of late as if I wanted to have my mind soaked in it anew." After long voyages at sea he found it a "great happiness" to be able to go to church.[78]

Parkin's forte was his ability to seize upon an idea and communicate his own earnestness to others. He had been tongue-tied in his youth and had deliberately cultivated public speaking in YMCA gatherings and temperance meetings and had carefully studied the orations of Daniel Webster. He often judged others by the impact of their rhetoric; he was complimented when someone thought that he had modelled his own speeches on those of Richard Cobden. One who worked with him at Upper Canada College said that "He was the only man I have known who by the inspiration of an address, based on a real belief in human nature, could rouse boys to keep away from a neighbouring apple-

74 *Ibid.*, Parkin to Nan, June 12, 1894; July 14, 1895 (copies).
75 Raleigh Parkin Collection, Parkin to Arthur Lee, Sept. 29, 1899 (copy).
76 Parkin Papers, Parkin to Miss Erskine, May 1878.
77 *Ibid.*, Parkin to Miss Erskine, Sept. 22, 1880.
78 *Ibid.*, Parkin to Nan, Feb. 24, 1888; Oct. 30, 1892 (copies).

orchard."[79] What drove Parkin on and provided satisfaction to him was the assurance that he was "becoming a certain kind of power in Canada" and that people thought "I can give an impulse to forces of some kinds which few can. I myself have a belief that ... I could change the current of public thought on some questions in a very distinct way."[80]

He cared little for the economic argument for imperialism and was indifferent to the internal politics of its organizations. While conceding that an emphasis upon economics was necessary in order to appeal to certain groups, such as the working class, or in special situations, as in Canada in 1890 to counteract unrestricted reciprocity, he was suspicious of all attempts to make fiscal preferences the main item in the imperialist platform. Fearing that such an inversion of what he considered the priorities would make imperialism a "Protectionist dodge," he said that he never believed in the strategy of tariff reform though he had an unlimited faith in the ultimate goal.[81] Though he worked under the auspices of the Imperial Federation League he informed Denison that he had never taken an active part in its inner deliberations but "considered that my sphere was rather the actual working of the propaganda."[82] Just before the League collapsed from internal division in 1893, he said that it did not really matter to him and that its demise might even stimulate local and individual effort.[83] With a few others, including Sir John Seeley, regius professor of modern history at Cambridge and author of The Expansion of England (1884), he carried on the lecturing activities in England during 1894 as though the breakup of the League had been a minor occurrence.

While Parkin found in Upper Canada College an environment congenial to the application of his educational ideas, his seven years there were not altogether happy. Though he was brought into intimate association with Canadian imperialists like Colonel Denison who sat on the board of governors of the school, as did Frank Arnoldi, a vice-president of the British Empire League in Canada, and though Principal Grant and the University of Toronto historian, George M. Wrong, were invited to deliver the Sunday addresses to the boys, Parkin quickly learned that the college itself was not universally accepted as a Canadian Eton and that one who described education as the pouring of life into life, the transmission of the vital flame from mind to mind, was bound to encounter disappointments and frustrations. "The work is

79 *Ibid.*, vol. 107, W. L. Grant, "Private Memo for Sir John Willison [re] Sir George Parkin" [c. 1924–6].
80 *Ibid.*, Parkin to Nan, Dec. 11, 1892 (copy).
81 Fleming Papers, Parkin to Fleming, May 3, 1891; Feb. 23, 1906.
82 Denison Papers, Parkin to Denison, July 18, 1893.
83 Parkin Papers, Parkin to Nan, Nov. 23, 1893 (copy).

wearing and the vexations endless," he wrote in his diary: "I hope I am sincere when I say that I see no point in working, in pouring out one's life here – if it be not for the Christian ideal."[84] The source of his dejection was partly financial, for he was still repaying loans made to him six or seven years before; it was partly also due to his discovery that the masters did not look upon the work with the same sense of high seriousness as he did. His despondency was deepened as well by the obvious discrepancy between the reality of a public school in Toronto and the English ideal which he was then describing in his biography of Thring.

Parkin had all the failings of a rhetorician. He was an enthusiastic rather than a systematic teacher and he had little patience for humdrum administrative duties. Having seen so clearly himself the place of such a school in supplying leadership and cultivating character, he left much of the drudgery to the young instructors while he attended to public affairs. William Grant taught history and geography at Upper Canada between 1898 and 1902 and Stephen Leacock was a modern English master there from 1891 to 1899; both thought Parkin placed too much stress on good manners and accent and mentioned his English acquaintances too often. "Has he no friends below the rank of Viscount?" Grant asked Leacock. "Plenty," replied the humorist, " – back on the farm."[85]

Parkin had always been acutely conscious of his own upbringing in the backwoods and he had marvelled after his introduction to Lord Grey and Lord Rosebery at "how easy it is for one without money or position to get along and meet these people in a perfectly natural, independent and pleasant way." Remarking upon the life of one English peer, Parkin said that what struck him most was that while "I was still working on a farm, and wondering how I could get the means of educating myself he was at the top at Eton, and with the best homes of England open to him, which is itself an education."[86] Not a little of Parkin's ambition to create a school where youths would acquire finish and manners stemmed from his own experience. But not even those irritated by what they took to be an excessive emphasis upon conduct and comportment failed to recognize his real contribution in restoring the college to a station of acceptance and security and in inspiring his students. When Parkin was mentioned as a possible candidate for the presidency of the University of Toronto in 1906, Lord Grey described him as "no scholar; he is a little old, and his verbosity is

84 Ibid., Diary, 1891–7, Jan. 1 and 17, 1897.
85 Ibid., W. L. Grant, "Private Memo ..."
86 Ibid., Parkin to Nan, July 27, 1888 (copy); Parkin to his son, Raleigh, March 25, 1917.

like the scratch of a slate pencil to many; but, on the other hand, I do not know his equal for infusing enthusiasm into young men ... "[87] This was a much fairer judgment than that unkind cut, which William Grant heard, that Parkin was a good man for a one-night stand.

While Parkin regretted leaving Canada, he became organizing secretary of the Rhodes Scholarship Trust in 1902 with both a feeling of relief and a sense of a new challenge. Milner and Grey, who were responsible for his appointment, could scarcely have picked a more suitable exponent of Rhodes' idea for Parkin was, figuratively, one of the first Rhodes scholars. Like the sponsor of the scheme, he had attended Oxford rather late in life and entertained an almost mystical belief that what the university had awakened in him it would also kindle in others. He resumed his travels of the Dominions and also of the United States, laid the administrative basis of the plan, and everywhere explained how the education of young men at Oxford would further Anglo-American understanding and cement imperial unity. "You have simply created the Rhodes Scholarships as a great permanent institution, with an assured reputation ... ," Milner congratulated him in 1919 as Parkin was about to retire. "The system ... might have been a lifeless thing, if you had not breathed a soul into it."[88]

In the years between 1902 and his death in 1922, Parkin gradually lost contact with Canadian affairs. Though in 1917 he lectured in the Dominion in support of conscription and in the United States on Allied war aims, his visits were infrequent. His journeys under the auspices of the Rhodes Trust, however, put him in touch with imperially minded educators throughout the Empire, and his home at Goring, a village eighteen miles from Oxford, was close to the centre of things to enable him to call upon his friends like Kipling and Milner. William Grant, who held the Beit chair of colonial history at Oxford between 1906 and 1910, came to help him with his biography of John A. Macdonald. Parkin treated Macdonald as one of the first statesmen to see that national independence was not incompatible with continued co-operation within the Empire, a natural view, since the Canadian Prime Minister had told Parkin twenty years before that he agreed with his justification for imperial unity.[89] In 1911 William married Parkin's daughter, Maude; in 1917 he became principal of Upper Canada College, a post he held until his death in 1935. Parkin's other daughter, Alice, married young Vincent Massey.

87 Grey of Howick Papers, vol. 28, Grey to Byron Walker, Oct. 27, 1906 (copy).
88 Parkin Papers, Milner to Parkin, Dec. 10, 1919.
89 *Ibid.*, Macdonald to Parkin, Dec. 11, 1888. Macdonald was commenting on Parkin's article, "The Reorganization of the British Empire." Parkin's biography, *Sir John A. Macdonald* (Toronto, 1908), appeared in the Makers of Canada series.

Having never been fascinated by the legalistic aspects of imperialism, Parkin did not actively participate in the Round Table movement in which his two sons-in-law were involved. This movement was a loose association of small groups in England and the dominions which had come into existence in 1908 and 1909. Promoted by Milner and Lionel Curtis, they were devoted to an examination, through discussions and through the periodical, the *Round Table*, of imperial questions, and after the appearance of *The Problem of the Commonwealth* (1916) by Curtis, they concentrated particularly on constitutional problems. The group in Toronto included several of Parkin's friends, George Wrong, John Willison, and Arthur J. Glazebrook (who named his son, George Parkin de Twenebrokes Glazebrook, in honour of his godfather); a younger man, Edward Peacock, who had taught at Upper Canada under him; as well as Sir Edmund Walker, president of the Canadian Bank of Commerce, and Sir Joseph Flavelle, a leading industrialist and financier.[90]

Parkin's own interests, however, ran in another direction, to church affairs and social reform. He held memberships in many organizations whose names suggest their purposes – National Society for Promoting the Education of the Poor in the Principles of the Established Church, Society for the Study of Inebriety, British and Foreign Bible Society, Naval and Military Emigration League. During the war he continued to deliver lectures on his favourite theme, "Christian Responsibilities of Empire," and restated with renewed assurance that national policy and individual effort alike had to be based on the teachings of Christ for that alone would maintain the peace of the world. Peace, he said, was always threatened by the selfish passions in human nature which Christ had come to extirpate and had founded His Church to overthrow.

In the end, Parkin returned to the concerns which preoccupied him in youth. If there was any thought which he would like to leave for the benefit of those he loved, he wrote, any advice condensed from his experience, it would be this injunction from the Bible: "Keep innocency, and take heed unto the thing that is right, for that will bring you peace at the last."[91]

IV

Parkin, Grant, and Denison were the unchallenged leaders of the imperial movement in Canada in the late 1880s and the 1890s. Grant's

90 James Eayrs, "The Round Table Movement in Canada, 1909–1920," *Canadian Historical Review*, XXXVIII (March 1957), 1–20; Carroll Quigley, "The Round Table Groups in Canada, 1908–38," *ibid.*, XLIII (Sept. 1962), 204–24.
91 Parkin Papers, vol. 69, notes.

death in 1902 and Parkin's departure for England in the same year left behind Denison, whom another generation of imperialists, like Stephen Leacock, Andrew Macphail, and William Grant saw as a venerable figure from the past rather than as a source of guidance in the future. These younger men neither inherited the mantle of leadership of their predecessors, nor were they in agreement with every single particular of imperial unity as expressed by them. Those of Denison's generation had fought to preserve the British connection in a period of pessimism and to an incredible extent their thought was dominated by the fear of annexation to the United States and by the chief advocate of continentalism in Canada, Goldwin Smith.

Since his arrival in 1871, Smith had built a high reputation as a journalist of controversy, a deflator of Canadian self-esteem, and an intellectual to whom all problems could be submitted for confident comment and unambiguous judgment. Smith's intellect, his own secretary wrote, had "been developed at the expense of his heart."[92] His predilection for the apt epigram and his biting sarcasm and irony were his strengths as a writer, but they blocked his perception of the sentiments and emotions of the community in which he lived. Matthew Arnold traced Smith's acerbity to his isolation: he who had lived at the centre of British culture naturally found the new world lacking in many things.[93] A man who shared Smith's views and worked with him for many years concluded that apart from his wife he had "no deep affection for anyone ... He was interested in them insofar as what they did would promote his views."[94] Denison's encounters with the "traitor" were venomous and legendary; Grant was once moved to say that Smith suffered from "pure, unadulterated, unmanly spite, the quality in him that has poisoned his life work."[95] Parkin's *Imperial Federation* was in part written with the intention of offsetting the influence of Smith's *Canada and the Canadian Question* (1891), one of the most gloomy examinations of the Dominion ever written. There was scarcely an item of imperialist literature at this time which did not set forth a challenge, denial, or indignant dismissal of Smith's views, and in the heat of controversy the imperialists often forgot how many of his beliefs about society, education, and race they subscribed to themselves.

By 1900, however, the threat of annexation receded further every day and the contentions of Smith became as tiresome and irrelevant as the loyalism of Colonel Denison. The new generation of imperialists

92 Arnold Haultain, *Goldwin Smith: His Life and Opinions* (Toronto, n.d.), 69, 136.
93 Griffin Papers, Arnold to Griffin, April 19, 1885.
94 QUL, William D. Gregory Papers, MS Autobiography, 127.
95 Willison Papers, Grant to Willison, Jan. 15, 1898.

became preoccupied with the consequences of prosperity and industrialization, with the emergence in English and French Canada of a
nationalism which hoped for the breakup of the imperial system, and
with the problems of imperial defence. They did not so much change
the meaning of Canadian imperialism as they gave to it an altered
emphasis while retaining the substance of that belief.

Stephen Leacock is now remembered as Canada's most famous
humorist. In his long life he published so many books of funny stories
that one of his friends doubted whether any person had ever read them
all. But in the years between his arrival at McGill University in 1901
as a sessional lecturer in economics and 1910 when his rollicking
Literary Lapses appeared, the public recognized Leacock as the author
of some articles on government and politics, a widely used text, *Elements of Political Science* (1906), and a book on Canadian history,
and also as a spokesman of imperialism. Those who have tried to
establish Leacock's place in Canadian thought have generally concluded that he was a kindly humorist and that his imperialism was a
flirtation, or, in the words of Harold Innis, it "carried him from his
moorings" and threw him "off his stride."[96] There is, however, too
much of a coincidence between the underlying values in Leacock's
serious social commentary, his satire, and the ideas of Canadian imperialism in the prewar period to allow such judgments to remain unqualified. While the sheer joy of entertainment and the delight in making
money entered into his motives, many of his favourite notions originated in that phase of his career which has been lightly treated.

"I was born at Swanmoor, Hants, England, on December 30, 1869,"
Leacock wrote in the preface to *Sunshine Sketches of a Little Town*
(1912). "... My parents migrated to Canada in 1876, and I decided
to go with them." Brought up on a farm near Lake Simcoe, educated at
Upper Canada College and the University of Toronto, Leacock said
that he "took to school teaching as the only trade I could find that
needed neither experience nor intellect." He joined the staff of Upper
Canada as modern language master in 1891 and departed for the University of Chicago in 1899 to study economics and political science.
He received a PH.D in 1903 for a thesis on the doctrine of laissez-faire
and rose rapidly up the academic ladder at McGill until he became
head of the department of economics and political science, a position
he described as one which enabled him "to stop thinking altogether

96 H. A. Innis, "Stephen Butler Leacock (1869–1944)," *Canadian Journal of
Economics and Political Science*, X (May 1944), 219, 221. This interpretation
is accepted and supported by Ralph L. Curry, *Stephen Leacock: Humorist and
Humanist* (New York, 1959), a less perceptive account than Donald Cameron,
Faces of Leacock: An Appreciation (Toronto, 1967).

for months at a time."[97] Leacock wore carefully chosen, but deliberately oversized, expensive, tweed suits, and his tastes ran to ample entertainment, "preferably," wrote one who knew him well, "under an arrangement with Messrs. Chivas Brothers of Aberdeen."[98] In 1901 he married Beatrix Hamilton, a descendant of a United Empire Loyalist family and a relative of Sir Henry Pellatt, a Toronto magnate and builder of Casa Loma, whose enthusiasms were often more ridiculous than Leacock's satires on the wealthy could ever be.

Many allusions in his books, especially those references to his English ancestors, suggest that Leacock was acutely conscious of his social standing, and it is well known that he was extremely fond and careful of money. At his summer home at Orillia he behaved like a country squire. He saw himself as a cultured gentleman of late Victorian times who enjoyed an easy rapport with society, was accorded a relatively high estate by it, and moved easily among its leaders. But in the Canada of 1900–14 men of learning were pushed aside in the bustling search for profit and gain. Business was predominant and it set the tone of the entire community. The professor, Leacock discovered, "more than any ordinary person finds himself shut out from the general society of the business world," scorned because he "does not know how to make money."[99] The professor in turn lashed out at the sources of scorn. Those who have found in his satire a revulsion against "the unbridled acquisitiveness and arrogant commercialism of the early twentieth century" and a protest directed at "the corrupting influence of modern industrialism and the worship of material success,"[100] and those who saw him compelled to write to make money,[101] have isolated two reactions of the same, complicated mind. On the one hand, Leacock's toryism moved him to idealize the country life as the only basis for civilization and ridicule the men who were destroying it, and, on the other, he partially accepted the monetary standard of success which he attacked. He would show them, those who said professors could not make money, that he could make forty thousand a year selling funny stories. That would be the best joke of all.

Despite his impressive academic credentials, Leacock loathed that

97 Stephen Leacock, *Sunshine Sketches of a Little Town* (Toronto, 1947), v-vi, viii.
98 Andrew Macphail, "Stephen Leacock," *The Yearbook of Canadian Art 1913*, 7.
99 Stephen Leacock, "The Apology of a Professor," *University Magazine*, IX (April 1910), 178, 189.
100 Desmond Pacey, "Leacock as a Satirist," *Queen's Quarterly*, LVIII (Summer 1951), 212, 215.
101 Robertson Davies, "Stephen Leacock," in Claude T. Bissell, ed., *Our Living Tradition: Seven Canadians* (Toronto, 1957), 138–49.

specialized scholarship and research into minutia which had been inspired by science and imported to America from Germany. (Throughout his life, he thought Germany the homeland of all evils.) "Today," he wrote in 1910, "we are overridden in the specialities, each in his own department of learning, with his tags, and label, and his pigeon-hole category of proper names, precluding all discussion by ordinary people ... The broad field of human wisdom has been cut into a multitude of little professorial rabbit warrens." "History," he complained in 1909, "is dwindling into fact lore and is becoming the science of the almanac; economics is being buried alive in statistics and is degenerating into the science of the census; literature is stifled by philology, and is little better than the science of the lexicographers." This mechanical ordering of knowledge was replacing the kind of humanistic education which Leacock himself had received – the "older view of education," he called it, "thought about life, mankind, literature, art." And it was also "ultra-rational" and "hyper-sceptical" of traditional beliefs. In place of the authoritative code under which humanity had painfully acquired the moral habit, he said, was the "New Morality" of self-development and self-gratification. Modern scholarship, based on a misapplication of the doctrine of evolution from biology to human affairs, turned morals and ethics from fixed facts and imperatives into relative reflections of time and place. "All the old certainty has vanished," said Leacock. "There is no absolute sureness anywhere ..." The distinctive trait of modern learning was that it was able to refute everything and believe nothing. In the age of industrial capitalism, education was judged exclusively in terms of its practicality and its serviceability to business. "Education is synonymous with ability to understand the stock-exchange page of the morning paper, and culture means a silk hat and the habit of sleeping in pyjamas."[102] Leacock's defence of an integrated humanistic training, or rather his assault upon those attitudes replacing it, grew out of his temperamental toryism; so too did his nostalgic idealization of the farm. Seeing learning in this light, it is not surprising that his fame as a humorist exceeded his reputation as an economist.

The conservative values against which Leacock measured Canadian society and found it wanting would be of interest only to literary scholars were it not for the fact that these standards were the basis of his imperialism. There was an affinity between his satirical treatment of business and the general drift of the thought of his imperialistic

102 Stephen Leacock, "The Devil and the Deep Sea," *University Magazine*, IX (Dec. 1910), 616–26; "Literature and Education in America," *ibid.*, VIII (Feb. 1909), 3–17.

contemporaries. So well did he express the faith that Lord Grey described Leacock as one of those self-respecting citizens "who feel uncomfortable at the thought that he and other Canadians only contribute 50 cents to the Englishman's $7 to that Imperial Defence which secures the independence of Canada as well as that of England." Grey concocted a plan of "turning Dr Leacock loose on Australia and Canada, as an Imperial missionary. He has all of Parkin's enthusiasm for the Empire," said Grey, "and in style, matter and general effectiveness, is Parkin's superior."[103] During 1907–8 Leacock toured the Empire as a lecturer on imperial organization. His essay, "Greater Canada: An Appeal,"[104] published before he left, distilled the substance and conveyed the emotion of imperialism as few other writings did. Even his studies of responsible government in Canada ran in the grooves previously marked out by Parkin, Grant, and Denison.

Leacock's most intimate friend in Montreal was Andrew Macphail, professor of the history of medicine at McGill and editor of the *Canadian Medical Journal* and the *University Magazine*. They met at the Pen and Pencil Club, a gathering of artists and writers attended by the painters William Brymner, Maurice Cullen, and Robert Harris, and the poet John McCrae. Macphail was five years older than Leacock and a widower: his wife had died in 1902 leaving two children and a sizeable enough sum to allow him to discontinue his practice and devote more time to his literary and political interests. Though Leacock knew little about Macphail's early years in Prince Edward Island and his student days at Prince of Wales College in Charlottetown, McGill, and London, it was said that they grew to know each other's minds as few friends ever do. In contrast to the humorist, Macphail wore "an air of gloom and deliberation"; he was fond of fashioning mystifying epigrams so that it was sometimes impossible to tell what he really meant or thought. His mind, wrote Leacock, "was as a shadowed pond with shifting shades but no ripples"; he was possessed of "a stern set frame of beliefs and traditions from which he was unwilling to depart; he always hated idle scoffing, cheap rationalism, one might almost say, reason and logic itself, and he always loved the sterner ideas of conduct that went with the illumination of old beliefs. If there had been no Westminster Catechism, Andrew would have invented it for himself."[105]

103 Rhodes Trust Records, Ontario Scholarships, Grey to Parkin, Dec. 27, 1905; Grey of Howick Papers, vol. 28, Grey to Dr. Peterson, March 25, 1907 (copy).
104 Published in the *University Magazine*, VI (April 1907), 132–41, and reprinted in pamphlet form under the same title.
105 Stephen Leacock, "Andrew Macphail," *Queen's Quarterly*, XLV (Winter 1938), 446–7.

Macphail's home on Peel Street was a "man's house"; from the cellar to the second floor study, nothing was out of place. He had a passion for tidiness in his personal life, a quality made even more necessary after he lost the sight of one eye in an accident involving a heated bottle of soda water, and the doctors told him to prepare for the day when he would have to guide himself around the house in total and unending darkness.[106] Macphail was a brilliant conversationalist and preferred to entertain his friends at small dinner parties. Just as Leacock left for Orillia at the conclusion of each academic year, Macphail returned to the scenes of his boyhood on "the island." Disliking industrialism, he would assert that during his lifetime Canada had degenerated from a happy community of farmers, fishermen, and lumbermen into a country of wide extremes of wealth, unemployment, and a plutocratic domination. This was one of Macphail's sentiments which left Leacock doubtful about his seriousness.

There was a precision, an almost military orderliness, about Macphail. He had what one of his friends called "an ingrained preference for the soldier over the politician";[107] like Denison, he preferred the decisive and undebatable dictums of the military life to the squabblings of democratic politics. The historical subjects which later caught his interest were men of action and soldiers – T. E. Lawrence of Arabia, General Robert E. Lee, and Field Marshal von Hindenburg. He had, said Leacock, an exquisite exactness with words. "I have never met a man with a greater reverence for language," wrote Pelham Edgar, professor of English literature at Victoria College.[108]

In 1907 Macphail took the ailing college journal, the *McGill Magazine*, transformed it into the *University Magazine*, and helped make it one of the finest periodicals of political and literary comment to appear in English Canada between the expiry of the *Week* in 1896 and the appearance of the *Canadian Forum* in 1920. Though the magazine was ostensibly managed by an editorial committee representing three universities – McGill, Dalhousie, and Toronto – Macphail ran it practically alone, and paid the bills out of his own pocket without telling anyone. Writers of the imperial persuasion, Charles F. Hamilton and William Wood, G. M. Wrong and M. Hutton, Castell Hopkins and William Grant, all contributed to it, as did Leacock many times. That the leader of the agrarian protest movement, William Good, also wrote an appeal

106 Pelham Edgar, "Sir Andrew Macphail," *ibid.*, LIV (Spring 1947), 9–10.
107 J. A. Stevenson, "Sir Andrew Macphail," *Canadian Defence Quarterly*, XVI (Jan. 1939), 208.
108 Pelham Edgar, "Sir Andrew Macphail (1864–1938)," Royal Society of Canada, *Proceedings and Transactions*, third series, XXXIII, 148.

for free trade in a journal edited by a convinced imperialist who called himself the last conservative in Canada is not the least of the ironies of imperial thought in these years.

When the World War broke out Leacock was forty-five and Macphail fifty. Macphail served on the medical staff of the Canadian forces and was knighted in 1917. The *University Magazine* ceased publication in 1920 and his remaining eighteen years were taken up with writing essays and commenting on the Canadian scene in other periodicals. Until his death in 1944, Leacock continued to turn out his books of humour at a phenomenal pace, each one becoming kinder and more repetitious. Like Parkin and G. M. Grant, these two touched many facets of Canadian intellectual and cultural life, too many to be adequately dealt with in a study of their imperialism. But it is a testimony to the capaciousness of the movement for imperial unity that such different and strong personalities could find a home within it, and suggestive of the emotional power of the imperial ideal that bound them together.

2
Canada First

Canadian imperialism rested upon an intense awareness of Canadian nationality combined with an equally decided desire to unify and transform the British Empire so that this nationality could attain a position of equality within it. These two ideas have customarily been viewed as separate and mutually incompatible; for imperialists the sense of nationality and the ideal of imperial unity were interlocked and identical. The group of young men who founded the Canada First movement in the years after Confederation and attempted to arouse a stronger consciousness of uniqueness among Canadians and to impart meaning to the phrase, "new nationality," exemplified the way in which these two emotions fused into one. Though their main impact upon politics was made during the Red River insurrection of 1869–70, the original members of that group dramatically mirrored a way of thinking about Canada and the British connection which became the abiding and most distinctive feature of Canadian imperialist thought.

I

Canada First originated in the accidental meeting of five young men in Ottawa in the spring of 1868. Two years before, in April 1866, Denison had encountered a young journalist and civil servant who had himself only arrived in the capital of the Canadas with the transfer of government from Montreal in 1865. Henry Morgan had been in the civil service since the age of eleven and was then secretary to the Liberal politician, William McDougall. Though only twenty-four, Morgan had already published several books, chiefly editions and collections of the writings of others, including D'Arcy McGee's speeches on British North American union, descriptions of the 1860 tour of the Prince of Wales, and a series of biographical sketches of famous Canadians. A corresponding member of the New York Historical Society and a veritable Gradgrind in his respect for facts, Morgan later assiduously compiled and edited compendiums, directories, and bibliographies on a wide variety of subjects. While his work suggests a systematic rather than a creative intelligence, he entertained a rather exalted conception of the patriotic usefulness of biography. In a lecture delivered a few weeks before he met Denison, Morgan had contended that though "the narrative of our rise and advancement is full of noble and self-denying examples in the cause of Discovery, Civilization and Progress," no historian had appeared to record them. The great men of a nation, he said, were representative of the national character; they embodied and typified the spirit of the people which had produced them. Their personalities and achievements had to be rescued from oblivion for it was through understanding them that Canadians would come to know what Canada itself represented.[1]

It was through Morgan that Denison met the poet Charles Mair in the spring of 1868 when the Colonel once again descended upon the politicians to lobby for a position in the Militia Department. The short and slightly chubby Mair had gladly left his medical studies at Queen's College when asked by McDougall, then minister of public works, to undertake researches on the North-West in preparation for the Dominion's negotiations with the Hudson's Bay Company. Born in Lanark, Ontario – his father was a pioneer in the square lumber trade in the Ottawa valley – Mair had arrived in Ottawa with the manuscripts of sugary verses which, when published in the autumn as *Dreamland and Other Poems*, earned him the title of the Canadian Keats. Like Morgan, Mair believed that literature discharged a patriotic purpose. A native literature was both an infallible signal of the development of a national consciousness and the chief source of its nourishment.[2] To his new acquaintances in McDougall's office, Denison introduced a Toronto barrister, William Foster, a shy, gentle, and impressionable person who cared more for the intricacies of the law than did his impatient friend. Where the one was all impulsive activity, the other was a detached, dreamy litterateur more interested in turning a graceful phrase than an enemy's flank. Yet Foster was also concerned with economic policy. For some time he had been the chief editorial writer for the Toronto financial paper, the *Monetary Times*, which he had helped to establish, and he had published a cogent argument for the need to renew the recently cancelled Reciprocity Treaty.

Another, rather older, man shared Foster's interest in trade. Robert Grant Haliburton, the son of the crusty Nova Scotia loyalist who created Sam Slick, appeared in Ottawa as a spokesman of the Cape

---

1 *The Place British Americans Have Won in History: A Lecture delivered at Aylmer, L. C., on Thursday Evening, 22nd February, 1866 by Henry J. Morgan* (Ottawa, 1866).
2 Norman Shrive, *Charles Mair: Literary Nationalist* (Toronto, 1965).

Breton coal-mining interests which had suffered severely by the loss of the American market. Like the others, he was engaged in intellectual studies. Deeply interested in science, a member of the Danish Society of Antiquaries, and fascinated by the current revival of interest in the sagas of the Northmen and the myths of primitive people, Haliburton had already presented to the Nova Scotia Institute of Natural Science a paper comparing All Souls' Day, All Saints' Day, and their pagan antecedents, and another ambitious essay entitled "The Unity of Origin of the Human Race Proved by the Universality of Certain Superstitions Connected with Sneezing." Father Dawson, the Roman Catholic chaplain to the British troops stationed at Ottawa, was drawn to the group largely by his interests in literature, colonial questions, and the North-West. He wrote a favourable review of *Dreamland* for the Ottawa press and was to provide a warm letter of introduction to Bishop Taché of St Boniface on behalf of Charles Mair. Though he attended its early meetings, Father Dawson was soon forgotten as a founding member of the group.[3]

Though these men who gathered in Morgan's quarters in the Revere Hotel differed in character and interests, they shared much more than the oppressive atmosphere of the capital – "dull as ditch-water," Mair called it.[4] They had all been born in Canada and had all attended college; three were trained in the law. Except for Haliburton, who was thirty-seven, their average age was twenty-eight. Like the new Dominion itself they seemed on the threshold of promising careers. They were literary men who had either published or were on the verge of delivering some masterpiece to the public. And they were all to respond, in different ways, to the challenge that D'Arcy McGee had thrown down to the educated young men of the new nation. "I invite them," he had said, "not to shrink from confronting the great problems presented by America to the world, whether in morals or in government. I propose to them that they should hold their own, on their own soil, sacrificing nothing of their originality; but rejecting nothing, nor yet accepting anything, merely because it comes out of an older, or richer, or greater country."[5]

Like many others, they had been inspired by the anticipation of a

3 Henry J. Morgan, *In Memoriam: Recollections of Father Dawson* (Ottawa, 1895); *Proceedings at the Presentation of a Public Testimonial to the Very Rev. Æ. McD. Dawson, L.L.D., U.G., Etc., by Citizens of Ottawa. December, 1890* (Ottawa, 1891). At this presentation Father Dawson mentioned his membership in the Imperial Federation League.
4 TPL, G. T. Denison Papers, Mair to Denison, July 9, 1870.
5 D'Arcy McGee, *The Mental Outfit of the New Dominion*, offprint from the Montreal *Gazette*, Nov. 5, 1867.

broader and more purposeful national existence which Confederation made possible. Only a few days before they met McGee had been shot on an Ottawa street, and Denison was one of the eighty thousand that attended his funeral in Montreal.[6] McGee became their patron martyr and his speeches saluting the rising northern nation became their litany. They were conscious too that the stultifying relics of the past were quickly disappearing. Having come to maturity during the decade preceding Confederation, one of the most frustrating and bitterly partisan periods in Canadian political history, they all retained an abiding distaste for the mechanics of politics and prided themselves on their independence of party. They believed that the old colonial parties which had reduced the union to a sickening deadlock no longer had any reason to exist. With the death of old issues and the establishment of the political framework of the "new nationality," the Dominion would in the future become a great northern monarchical nation to rival the republic to the south. For these men who had known Canada only as a narrow strip of territory along the St Lawrence, the prospect of acquiring the North-West territory generated an indescribable sense of liberation from the past and faith in the future. Like Alexander Morris in the 1850s they surveyed British America's geographical extent, natural resources, and commercial advancement, and felt assured of dramatic progress in the future. "Who," Morris had asked, "considering our present and looking back upon the past, can doubt but that a great future is before these colonies? Nay, is it not manifest that the day must come when they will play no mean part in the world's history, and amid the ranks of nations?" Like him, they also came to believe that it was "our manifest destiny" to possess the west.[7]

Excited by the vision of McGee and Morris, and conscious that a new generation was coming to maturity in America, these young men were quick to resent any implications of inferiority with which the word "colonial" was loaded. When Denison's book on cavalry was published in the fall of 1868, the *London Review* wondered how a colonial dared instruct Her Majesty's horsemen on the need for reform. "We foresaw the difficulty," Denison told Mair, "... that I was a Colonist, a Colonial, a Provincial writer." Though the military journals were more favourable, "I hear the Army officers ... are shy about buying it ... They think -aw-that-aw dam'ned impertinences -aw- Volunteer aw – Colonist -aw – aw." Piqued by the snobbery he had encountered during his visit

6 G. T. Denison Papers, Diary, April 13, 1868.
7 Alexander Morris, *Nova Britannia: or, Our New Canadian Dominion Foreshadowed. Being a Series of Lectures, Speeches and Addresses* (Toronto, 1884), 38, 142.

to England during the summer and angered by the supercilious tone of the review, Denison protested that Canadians had to have more confidence in themselves and stop looking up to England as a superior country. The motherland should be held in reverence because of her history and because our ancestors lay in that hallowed ground, but Englishmen were only our brothers, our equals. He had, he said, "traversed their country, & I have come home feeling confident we have a finer country [,] a more intellectual chivalrous highspirited people, and one unspoiled by withering conventionalities."[8]

This sense of superiority and separateness, which Denison expressed in an intensely personal way, was subsequently amplified into a compelling doctrine by Robert Grant Haliburton. In his address, *The Men of the North and Their Place in History*, which was delivered in several centres in 1869, he fused the nebulous sentiment of his associates and his own knowledge of mythology to produce one of the most arresting themes in the emerging nationalist creed of Canada First. Lamenting the fact that British North American union had been accomplished in the prosaic manner more usual in the formation of joint-stock companies than in the founding of new nations, he advanced a view of the character of Canada which was designed to nourish an optimistic faith in its future. The distinctive character of the new Dominion, he proposed, "must ever be that it is a Northern country inhabited by the descendants of Northern races." Equating the adjective northern with toughness, strength, and hardihood, he argued that the diverse nationalities within Canada all shared a northern ancestry, and that the climate tended to instil and maintain the strenuous attributes of the Nordic races. Because of this racial heritage and their stern environment, Canadians were destined to assume in the new world the dominant role played by the northern people in Europe, and to preserve their vigour and cherish their institutions of liberty. Few of Haliburton's young friends could resist seizing upon his assurances that *"We are the Northmen of the New World."*[9]

Though these men shared a common aspiration and a delight in Canada's prospects, it would be an exaggeration to conclude, as Denison later claimed, that they either approached the subject of nationalism in a systematic fashion or that they met in solemn conclave and selflessly devoted themselves to the service of the state. Judging by their later allusions to their association in Ottawa in the spring of 1868, what

8 QUL, Charles Mair Papers, Denison to Mair, Dec. 30, 1868.
9 R. G. Haliburton, *The Men of the North and Their Place in History: A Lecture delivered before the Montreal Literary Club, March 31st, 1869* (Montreal, 1869).

stands out is their adolescent humour, horseplay, and bibulousness. The jocular and teasing letters that followed Mair's departure to the west in the autumn of that year began with Morgan's hope that he had arrived "without ... temptation in the shape of women and whiskey." Morgan wanted to know "the number of pretty girls on the Census role," and then added mischievously that "information has reached here of a little mishap on your part with a young feminine Nor'Wester."[10] In December 1868, Morgan and a friend came down to Toronto for the Christmas holidays and dined with Denison and Foster at the Queen's Hotel. "We four," the colonel reported, "drank one bottle of sherry [,] two bottles of Champagne, and two of claret," which seemed an excellent performance since Morgan had "taken the pledge," refused to imbibe, and "laid down on a sofa and went asleep ... We took advantage of the occasion and crowned him with all the formalities. As King Theodorus' crown was not convenient we were obliged to make use of an article of household furniture which is much more useful than ornamental and if it consisted of crockery it yet had a little gold about it as it belonged to a pattern which contained a good deal of gilding." With his sleeping majesty before them, and the sherry, champagne, and claret surging through their heads, it was little wonder that when Denison and Foster got around to discussing "points of public policy" they discovered that "for some reason our views were decidedly opposite to each other, but the conversation was pleasingly diversified by the old gentleman (Morgan's friend) interposing the remark at intervals that he understood us both and that he entirely disagreed with the views expressed on either side."[11] "Your ... references to a portion of the past," Foster warned Mair with mock solemnity, "were unfortunate if not immoral. Chamber maids ... orgies! Oh me! Morgan, Mair, Denison, Oh me!"[12]

Their disinterested dedication to the state, no less than their gravity and sobriety, has been overstated. It is curious for a group which arrogated to itself the slogan of Canada First and condemned the influence of political patronage, that Morgan and Mair were McDougall's protégés and that Haliburton and Denison had come to the capital to advance their own interests. Haliburton's pamphlet, *Intercolonial Trade: Our Only Safeguard Against Disunion* (1869), which has often been regarded as an anticipation of the National Policy,[13] exhibited an extra-

10 Mair Papers, Morgan to Mair, Oct. 25, 1868 and April 4, 1869.
11 *Ibid.*, Denison to Mair, Jan. 8, 1869.
12 *Ibid.*, Foster to Mair, June 10, 1875.
13 See, for example, W. S. Wallace, ed., *The MacMillan Dictionary of Canadian Biography* (Toronto, 1963), 262, or A. G. Bailey, "Literature and Nationalism after Confederation," *University of Toronto Quarterly*, xxv (July 1956), 419.

ordinary degree of special pleading. Haliburton's coal mine, said Denison, "ain't worth a damn while the reciprocity treaty is busted," and it was mainly concern over his own investment which brought the Maritimer to Ottawa in the spring of 1868 and again in 1869 when he was heard before the Privy Council "on behalf of the Nova Scotia coal interests."[14] In his pamphlet Haliburton pointed out that the only way to solidify the political connection between central Canada and the coast was through "common interests and commercial sympathy." Deploring the fact that Ontario and Quebec imported coal from Pennsylvania and Ohio while the fuel of the Maritimes was kept out of the American market by a high tariff, he proposed that a duty be imposed on American coal. Such protection would not only allay the general dissatisfaction with Confederation in the seaboard province and lessen Canada's dangerous dependence upon foreign fuel, but it would also provide a dynamic impulse to manufacturing and farming. The key to the growth of manufacturing in central Canada and to commercial expansion in the West Indies, he argued, was the reduction of the transport costs between Ontario and Nova Scotia. By favouring Nova Scotia coal in the markets of central Canada, an east-west economic flow would be created, transportation charges upon farm commodities as well as manufacturers would decrease, and commercial prosperity and political unity would be assured. Haliburton's argument for protection did not mention the transcontinental railroad nor the settlement of the prairies – policies which were just as central to Macdonald's National Policy as was the tariff. Nor perhaps was it even very original. It may well be that he owed more than he cared to admit to the influence of Henry Morgan who had been secretary to Isaac Buchanan, an Upper Canadian merchant and politician. In 1864 Morgan had edited the papers of Buchanan in which a strong case for the protection of Canadian industries had been made.[15] If Haliburton anticipated anything, it was not the National Policy but Dominion subsidies to the Nova Scotia coal industry.

In their early association, then, the original members of "the corner room set" were neither as single-minded, solemn, nor selfless as they have been portrayed. Though they shared much, they brought to their

14 Mair Papers, Denison to Mair, April 22, 1869.
15 Isaac Buchanan, *The Relations of the Industry of Canada with the Mother Country and the United States* (Montreal, 1864). In an earlier pamphlet, *The Coal Trade of the New Dominion* (Halifax, 1868), Haliburton referred to Buchanan's ideas. In the Montreal paper, the *New Era*, which he edited in the later 1850s, D'Arcy McGee outlined the whole concept of an east-west economy based upon the St Lawrence system, a facet of his thought described in R. Burns, "D'Arcy McGee and the New Nationality" (MA thesis, Carleton University, 1966).

discussions a wide variety of personal approaches. In the spring of
1868 these notions remained as incohesive as the group of individuals
that expressed them.

II

What catapulted the corner room set into history and provided an outlet
for their energies was the train of events that followed Charles Mair's
departure for the North-West. Appointed paymaster to the party which
was building a wagon trail between Port Arthur and Red River, Mair
soon fell in with John Christian Schultz, the leader of the Canadian
expansionists within the settlement. Schultz was welcomed into the
ranks of Canada First; he was, said Denison, a "damn good Kanuck."[16]
The personal connections between the young men who had worked in
McDougall's office, Schultz's followers in the colony, and Denison and
Foster in Toronto, were thus drawn tight. During the early months
of 1869, Mair published a series of letters in the *Globe* describing the
agricultural resources of the prairies in the language of manifest destiny.
Portage la Prairie, he proclaimed, was "the door, ... the narrow entrance
through which will flow the unspeakable blessings of free Government
and civilization ... [into] the larger and lovelier Canada – the path of
empire and the garden of the world."[17] "I am very glad to hear," Denison responded, "such good accounts of the resources and fertility of
the great North-West. When filled up with a loyal population and a
prosperous one, I have every confidence that in time it would prove a
great source of strength to the Dominion and together we men of the
North (as Haliburton says) will be able to teach the Yankees that we
will be as our ancestors always have been, the dominant race."[18] "We
must," he added, "send up Canadians to take possession of the country
but roads must be built at once."[19]

Never one to miss the opportunity of humouring his friend, Denison
explained at length why it would be impossible to send Mair a veloci-
pede, and, drawing upon Napoleonic precedents, he advised the poet on
how to withstand a siege. When assaulted, form a hollow square, "put
the whiskey and provisions inside, and tell them to come on ..."[20] The

16 Mair Papers, Denison to Mair, Aug. 11, 1869; G. T. Denison, "Sir John
   Schultz and the 'Canada First' Party," *Canadian Magazine*, VIII (Nov. 1896),
   16–23.
17 *Weekly Globe*, June 4, 1869.
18 Mair Papers, Denison to Mair, March 10, 1869.
19 *Ibid.*, Denison to Mair, April 22, 1869.
20 *Ibid.*, Denison to Mair, March 29, 1869.

imminence of martial exploits excited Denison's ambition: he had not only failed to secure the post of assistant adjutant general of cavalry, but he had been treated in so "insolent" and "overbearing" a manner by Sir George Etienne Cartier, the minister of militia, that he promptly resigned his commission. He never forgot or forgave this rebuff. When in the summer of 1869 Schultz informed private Denison of the sedentary militia that his name had been mentioned "in connection with a corps of Mounted Rifles which it was thought it might be necessary to organize for the protection of [the] Red River Territory," Denison inquired of Mair whether he should send a copy of his cavalry book to the *Nor'Wester*. Again his hopes had been stirred, again he was disappointed.[21]

But in the rapid staccato character of the events that followed – the growth of resistance in the Red River settlement, the exclusion of McDougall, the apparent paralysis of action at Ottawa, the shooting of the Orangeman, Thomas Scott, and the capture and subsequent escape of Schultz and Mair – Denison found a spacious field for his talent of bellicose propaganda. There were many who called for the head of Riel and revenge of the "loyalists," but none exceeded Denison in appeals for violence. With all the pungency of speech that made his Yorkshire ancestors synonymous with a brassy forcefulness, and out of the bitterness of frustrated ambition, Denison discharged his resentments upon the "traitors" – not the Hudson's Bay Company, or the politicians in general, but Cartier and the French Canadians. As the winter of 1870 turned into spring and as Foster was writing his inflammatory invocations in the Toronto press, Denison came to see the issue with crystal clarity. For him the martial gesture was invariably equated with national assertion and he urged that an armed force be sent both to subdue the rebellion and to maintain the honour of the nation. If this were not done, or if by some devious plot Wolseley's expedition was purposely delayed, compromised, or recalled, there must be a "scheme of armed emigration" of Ontario people to the west. Quick military solutions to puzzling problems came easily to Denison; so too did the model for his behaviour. In the series of crises that had preceded the American Civil War, a determined effort had been made by the free soilers in the north and the partisans of slavery in the south to promote armed immigration of their followers into the disputed territories of Kansas and Nebraska in order to fix the institutions of these areas before they assumed statehood. The issue at stake at Red River was no less monumental than the conflict of free soil versus slavery, for it also hinged on the question of what institutions were to be permanently stamped upon the garden in

21 *Ibid.*, Denison to Mair, Aug. 11, 1869.

the west. Because the fate of half a continent hung in the balance, there was no limit to the vigilante activities of Canada First. Schultz warned Denison that the French Canadians were trying to recall the Wolseley expedition: the tension and emotionalism had to be sustained. "I got ... the Rope which bound poor Scott's hands when he was shot," Schultz wrote. "I send it by express. Use it at Indignation meeting and then present [it] to the Master of [the] Orange Lodge."[22] When he learned that Cartier would pass through Toronto and be accorded an official guard of honour, Denison threatened that "we would take possession of the armoury that night ... and if anyone in Toronto wanted to fight it out, we were ready to fight it out on the streets."[23]

Behind Denison's menacing language lay a larger reason for his hostility to the aims of the French Canadians and the "half starved half breeds," a reason which Mair made explicit. Mair emphatically denied that the French should be accorded any special place in the west and in a letter to the editor of the Toronto *Telegraph*, he announced that

Ontario and the English-speaking people of Quebec have been milked long enough ... Thank God there is such a thing at last as a purely national feeling in Canada. There is a young and vigorous race coming to the front, entirely in earnest, and which is no longer English, Scotch or Irish, but thoroughly and distinctively Canadian ... It means strict justice to the French and nothing more – a fair field and no favour. It means moreover that this country [the North-West Territories] shall be British and not French and shall not be governed by the nominee of either priests or proletarians.[24]

A few years later Mair returned to this question and amplified the conception which had only been implied in Canada First's actions in 1869–70. The "mediaeval inertia and trammeled enterprize" of Lower Canada, he wrote, must not be transplanted to the west. Since the French Canadian lacked the dynamic impulse which made for material progress, his presence in the west would only stultify its development until "the swift extension of American settlement, and the intrusive fingers of American ambition" grasped it from Canada. ("In general," he wrote in another connection, "the Frenchman married the Indian and sank to the level of her tastes and inclinations. In general the Englishman married the Indian and raised her to the level of his own.") French-Canadian claims were not only incompatible with the rapid

22 TPL, Denison Papers, Schultz to Denison, July 20, 1870.
23. G. T. Denison, *The Struggle for Imperial Unity* (Toronto, 1909), 37.
24 TPL, Denison Papers, draft of Mair's letter to the editor of the Toronto *Telegraph*, enclosure in Mair to Denison, n.d., but probably 1870.

settlement of the west; they were also irreconcilable with the require-
ments of the Canadian national sentiment which the Canadian Firsters
espoused. It is the Celt and the Teuton who speak our language and the
"many-tongued" people of northern Europe, said Mair, who are destined to settle in the west. "How, then, if we wish ever to become a
homogeneous people, can we extend the parliamentary use of a
language which is limited of right to a certain Province? Either this
privilege must be confined to that Province, or we must be prepared
to sanction its extension to a host of incoming tongues ..." The "minor
nationalities" must sacrifice their individuality, he concluded, for the
sake of a homogeneous nationality and the onward movement. French-
Canadian rights, therefore, should be confined to the "prescribed
domain" of Quebec.[25]

The Red River insurrection profoundly affected both Denison in
particular and the Canada First group in general. His almost patholo-
gical insistence on plots and his over-dramatization of issues until they
could only be expressed in the language of loyalty versus treason had
worked in the atmosphere of crisis. They had, in fact, worked all too
well, and their success confirmed in Denison's mind the efficacy of his
style of politics. Twenty years later he was to employ the same tactics
and slogans against the annexationist movement. In addition, during
the rebellion the membership of Canada First increased to about thirty
and it acquired a more formal organization. The North-West Emigration Aid Society was created partly to provide a channel through which
propaganda was conveyed to the public and, as its name suggests, to
aid immigrants anxious to settle in the west. While the movement gained
in members, it lost the personal attachments of the corner room set.
Haliburton was living in Halifax, Morgan in Ottawa, and Mair in the
west; only Denison and Foster remained in Toronto. As a result,
Canada First became almost exclusively Toronto orientated and it
lost the heavy emphasis that the original members had placed upon
literary as opposed to political activities. The members who joined at
this time included Dr William Canniff, professor of surgery at Victoria
University and author of *The Settlement of Upper Canada* (1869),
George Kingsmill, editor of the Toronto *Telegraph*, Joseph McDougall,
son of the ill-fated governor of the North-West, J. D. Edgar, a Liberal
politician, and several of Foster's friends, like Hugh Scott, who worked
on the staff of the *Monetary Times*. No number of letters or affectionate
recollections could really bridge the geographical distances that sepa-

25 Charles Mair, "The New Canada: its natural features and climate," *Canadian
Monthly and National Review*, VIII (Aug. 1875), 156–64; [G. T. Denison],
Reminiscences of the Red River Rebellion of 1869 (n.p., 1873), 3.

rated the originators of the movement, nor could these obscure the fact that a very different association was taking shape.

III

In the aftermath of the Red River insurrection the Canada Firsters turned to consider the question of the future relationship of the new Dominion and Great Britain. Though observers at the time, as well as later historians, discovered perplexing obscurities and equivocations in their statements regarding Canadian political independence, the ambiguities in their thought arose not so much from a studied vagueness or confusion but rather from two contemporaneous tendencies which shaped their outlook. The first was the attitude toward colonies then prevalent in Britain. Since the abolition of the preferential trading system and the relaxation of formal political control in the 1840s, British public opinion and official policy moved in the direction of curtailing commitments and responsibilities in North America. Few Englishmen stated the basis of triumphant "Little Englandism" more persuasively than Goldwin Smith, disciple of Cobden and Bright, controversialist, and regius professor of history at Oxford. Colonies, he argued in *The Empire* (1863), were not only economic liabilities, but the whole spirit of exclusiveness militated against the realization of the mutual interdependence of nations and hence international peace. Canada especially seemed to epitomize all that was wrong with the Empire: it had taxed British imports, embittered Anglo-American relations, and refused in 1862 to vote the funds necessary for its own defence. Between 1865 and 1871 British statesmen pursued the aim of disengagement from North America partly in recognition of the supremacy of the United States on the continent, and partly to adjust to the changing balance of power in Europe. Whether British North Americans read Smith's book or the oracular pronouncements of the *Times*, or simply observed the drift of official policy, they could not doubt that the security and certainties of the past were finished.

The second tendency which bore heavily upon the deliberations of the Canada Firsters was the revival of American hostility to British North America during the Civil War. History had imprinted in their imaginations an image of an aggressive and voracious neighbour: their mentor, McGee, had said during the Confederation debates that "the acquisition of Canada was the first ambition of the American Confederacy, and never ceased to be so."[26] In the early years of the war it

26 P. B. Waite, ed., *The Confederation Debates in the Province of Canada 1865* (Toronto, 1963), 82.

had been possible to believe that the South's drive for independence might succeed and that a rough equilibrium of power would be created on the continent. Northern victory shattered that hope and, as William Foster noted in 1865, the thoughtful British North American had to recognize that if the union were restored an effort might be made "to apply to the whole of North America the modern and exaggerated reading of the Monroe doctrine." The unification of the United States meant the "overshadowing predominance of a single state" in North America and it consequently implied that for British America there could be no absolute independence. "She must lean somewhere for support," wrote Foster, "and her inclinations, if not her interests, lead her to prefer a species of dependence upon the mother country, which shall be something more, though perhaps not much more, than a national alliance."[27] Here then was the dilemma of Canada First. The new Dominion was weak and thinly populated, internally divided by sectional, racial, and cultural conflicts; it was confronted by an enormously powerful and hostile neighbour; and at the very moment that British support was most necessary, Canadians could no longer assume that it would be automatically given.

This sense of uncertainty underlay their speculation on the prospects of independence and accounted for much of their ambivalence and ambiguity. In the crisp language of his address, "The Duty of Canadians to Canada," Denison expressed the leading postulate of the Canada Firsters when he asserted that the development of Canadian national sentiment was the only way in which the drift to imperial disintegration could be checked. The major threat to Canada came from Britain because Englishmen not only considered colonial residents as inferiors but had acquired such a pounds, shillings, and pence basis for considering everything that they were unappreciative of colonial loyalty and oblivious to the benefits of the Empire. "If England stands by us," he told Mair, "we can always hold our own, and independence would be the worst thing for us now." If Canadians would only concentrate upon the material development of their country, take pride in their nationality, and discharge the responsibilities of a self-reliant people, then the exaggerated notions concerning "colonists" would soon disappear. With these illusions demolished, Englishmen would come to regard the Empire in a different light and they would be more willing to accord Canada the protection she required in order to develop. The Empire

27 W. A. Foster, "The Canadian Confederacy," *Canada First: A Memorial of the Late William A. Foster, Q.C., with introduction by Goldwin Smith, D. C. L.* (Toronto, 1890), 125–6. The article originally appeared in the *Westminster Review*, April 1865.

was the matrix in which the new nation would mature and Denison anticipated that in the future the Empire would be "united into one great power or confederation of great nations."[28]

In his celebrated address, "Canada First: or Our New Nationality,"[29] which was published in 1871, William Foster agreed with Denison's contention that the British connection would in time be transfigured into an "alliance of nations." He also understood that there could be no alliance of national entities unless there were national entities to combine in alliance, and he believed that if Canadians did not discard the habits of thought which identified them as colonials, the future imperial alliance would not be a combination of equals but simply an institutionalization of the colony-motherland relationship. Canadians could only come to think of themselves as the equals of the residents of Britain, and behave as though they did, if they were moved by a sense of nationality. Foster knew that "nations do not spring Minerva-like into existence"; the "foundations of our identity," he said, must be purposefully and conscientiously cultivated. Though the emergence of a Canadian consciousness had previously been inhibited by the fawning, butler-minded attitude of those whose loyalties were focused across the Atlantic, Foster predicted that "now that some of the traditions of the past are gradually losing their hold on the imagination of a new generation, that sentiment which so long found an outlet in declamation over the glories of the Mother Land, will draw a more natural nourishment from native sources."

Far more dangerous for national unity than this disappearing loyalism, however, were the diversity of peoples within Canada, the importation of old world quarrels, and the "asperities of race, creed, of interest" – all of which were aggravated rather than blunted by party politics. What Foster sought was "some common basis of agreement strong enough to counteract disintegrating tendencies," some article of faith which would nourish a sense of Canadian nationality. He found the sources of optimism in the record of material advancement, in the statistics of the growth of trade, territory, population, and railways. The rate of growth would be continued in the future; there was room enough in the Dominion for forty million people. He drew attention to the achievements of Canadians in war and pointed to their contributions to intellectual life. He praised the social fluidity of the new world and the political institutions which combined freedom with restraint and progress with stability. And he appealed to Haliburton's idea of the northern race: "The old Norse mythology, with its Thor hammers and Thor hammerings, appeals to us, – for we are a Northern people, – as

28 Denison, *Struggle*, 50–3; Mair Papers, Denison to Mair, June 8, 1869.
29 *Canada First: A Memorial*, 13–47.

the true out-crop of human nature, more manly, more real, than the weak marrow-bones superstition of an effeminate South." Above all, Foster understood that history was one of the most important vehicles for expressing and maintaining a sense of nationality.

Like other literary invocations to nationalism, Foster's manifesto exhibited a misty character because he was appealing for a sentiment and not preparing the platform of a political party. Nor was he advocating political independence from Britain. Had that been the case, it is doubtful whether that pillar of the British connection, George Brown, would have printed the address in the *Globe* even before it was actually delivered to any public meeting. The uncertainty concerning the future derived from the possibility that Britain might cut the connection. When Foster said that he no more advocated independence than the day of judgment he was not indulging in a meaningless metaphor: ultimate independence, like the day of judgment, was not in Canadian control.

Like his friends, Robert Haliburton considered the eventuality of independence, not because it emerged inexorably out of his nationalistic assumptions, but because it was forced upon his attention by British attitudes and diplomacy. The Washington Treaty of 1871, which made substantial concessions to the United States in the fisheries and the navigation of the St Lawrence but said nothing about compensation to Canadians for damages inflicted by the Fenian raids, had a traumatic impact upon the Canada Firsters. It confirmed the impression that Britain was more interested in pacifying the republic than in defending the interests of the Dominion and it moved Haliburton to write a harsh denunciation of Britain's dealings with North America. It would be incorrect to see in this condemnation, or in Haliburton's environmentalism, implications of independence. It is true that he believed that the American environment was moulding a profoundly different society and nationality than that which existed in the old country. "We are not Britons," he declared in 1870. "We are the descendants of Britons, but we are sons of the New World, cherishing fondly the traditions of the old world, but feeling that here 'old things have passed away, and all things have become new.' "[30] Haliburton's glorification of the social fluidity of Canada as compared with the rigid class structure of England, however, was only a more general statement of Denison's blast about "withering conventionalities" and Foster's boast that here "every man is the son of his own works" and that Canadians did not need any antique code or musty rules from a Herald's office to tell them what to respect.

Haliburton's review of British diplomacy, published in 1872, and

30 *Mr. Haliburton's Speech on The Young Men of the New Dominion*, reprint from the Ottawa *Citizen*, Jan. 27, 1870.

significantly subtitled "The Dream of the United Empire Loyalists of 1776," emerged out of a tradition of maritime imperialism which was at the heart of his family history. As early as 1851, his father, Judge Haliburton, had denounced British misrule in America and had contended that the invidious distinction between Britain and her colonies should be obliterated through imperial federation. The colonists, he wrote, "should be represented in Parliament, help to pass English laws, and show them what laws they want themselves ... It should be our navy, our army, our nation. That's a great word, but the English keep it to themselves, and colonists have no nationality."[31] This ideal of imperial unity, Robert Haliburton argued, had been planted in Canada by the United Empire Loyalists and nurtured by their sons, but their vision had turned out to be only an illusion, their sacrifice and exile were rewarded with contempt, and their hopes were betrayed by Englishmen who identified the Empire with the United Kingdom. The Treaty of Washington was but the latest instance of the ill-informed, misconceived, and fumbling British diplomacy which began with that extraordinary geographer Oswald and was invariably characterized by the sacrificing of Canadian interests for the sake of the Empire. The treaty proved that the British House of Commons could not legislate for the Empire as a whole. "Something formed on a wider basis will be needed to satisfy the aspirations and the wants of the widespread English race, and to stay the process of dismemberment."[32] What Robert Haliburton clearly sought was some kind of imperial association in which Canadians would secure control over foreign policy, or at least be able to correct the astigmatic character of British diplomacy, by representation in the councils that determined it. What he attacked was not the idea of imperial unity, but the blind insularity of Little Englandism. What he proposed was imperial federation, not autonomy. Those who have maintained otherwise have not explained why he later went to England, purchased the *St. James Magazine,* renamed it the *United Empire Review,* and turned it into an organ of the imperial revival, or why he himself described the pamphlet of 1872 as a "protest against imperial disintegration."[33]

What is confusing about Haliburton's lament, however, was the concluding warning that if Canadians had no alternative but to submit to such treatment, "we must tell the world that this is to be the last page in the history of British diplomacy in our affairs," and he went so far

31 Anon., *Haliburton: A Centenary Chaplet* (Toronto, 1899), 43.
32 R. G. Haliburton, *A Review of British Diplomacy and its Fruits: "The Dream of the United Empire Loyalists of 1776"* (London, 1872), vii.
33 *Haliburton: A Centenary Chaplet,* 9; Mair Papers, Haliburton to Mair, June 27, 1881.

as to propose a new departure in Canadian-American relations. If the aspirations of the loyalists could not be fulfilled because of Britain's anti-colonial policy, "we may hope, at some future day we may, by a reunion of the English race on this continent pave the way for a grander and wider union." The great unifying force of the day, he said, was race, and the power of blood operated in an inscrutable but irresistible fashion throughout the civilized world.[34] Haliburton's hope for racial reunion – by which he did not mean annexation – came naturally to one so steeped in the traditions of the Maritimes where the suspicion of the United States was never as strong as it was in Ontario, and his idea of the union of the Anglo-Saxons of the new and old worlds was to become a leading theme with the advocates of imperial unity in the following decades. Haliburton's call for a racial union on the continent, in short, was not incompatible with the aims of Canadian imperialism as those aims were later defined by imperialists.

And what of Charles Mair? In 1875 he admitted that independence was nothing compared to "the vastly nobler conception of the homologation of the whole Empire, the first great and permanent step towards a universal brotherhood of nations."[35] In the late 1880s he told Denison that he still adhered to these views, that he still hoped some "progress will be made in formulating a workable scheme for Imperial union." Such a union was only practicable, however, "if England could be brought to seriously consider the question." But the problem then, as in 1871, was in Britain. Were Canadians to stand still while the "greater question is held in abeyance at its fountain head? Why not go on, upon our old lines of Canada First, and carve out a nationality for ourselves in the meantime, ready at any subsequent period to become a component part of a Federation when time is ripe."[36] In his historical drama, *Tecumseh* (1886), Mair had General Brock utter the imperialist creed of Canada First:

For I believe, in Britain's Empire, and
In Canada, its true and loyal son,
Who yet shall rise to greatness, and shall stand
At England's shoulder helping her to guard
True liberty throughout a faithless world.[37]

Not for nothing did Mair later describe his verse as "one of the literary sources of Canadian Imperial sentiment."[38]

34 Haliburton, *A Review of British Diplomacy*, 9, 18–20.
35 Mair, "The New Canada," 161.
36 Denison Papers, Mair to Denison, Dec. 19, 1888 and April 20, 1889.
37 Charles Mair, *Tecumseh: A Drama* (Toronto, 1886), 101.
38 Denison Papers, Mair to G. N. Morang, March 14, 1901.

Denison, Foster, Mair, and Haliburton, the major founding members of Canada First, did not advocate a Canadian independence in isolation from the Empire. To a later generation it would seem so natural, indeed inevitable, that men who sought to instil a Canadian patriotism, and were so insistent upon the failures of British policy, could be satisfied only with a completely independent foreign policy. Their reaction was the opposite: they aimed at securing some voice in foreign affairs, but only within the imperial system. They did not represent the first stirrings of what was subsequently called autonomy; they were imperialists. Their response was the same as that of Joseph Howe who requested that a clear and distinct understanding be reached between Canada and Great Britain in order to prevent any more treaties of 1871;[39] the same as that which led G. M. Grant to conclude his book describing his trip across Canada in 1872 with the warning that neither the independence of four million faced with thirty-eight million Americans, nor cut and dried schemes for imperial federation, held the key to the Canadian future. Our only course, he said, was "to seek, in the consolidation of the Empire, a common Imperial citizenship, with common responsibilities, and a common inheritance."[40] The spirit of Canada First nationalism was perfectly expressed by Denison's friend, William Kirby, who told Tennyson that it is true that "we have but four millions of people in Canada ... but taking us individually we feel that we are the equals in *every respect* – and perhaps superior in loyal devotion to our Queen & flag to any four millions of our fellow subjects at home. – How dare they – and by what right *can they* suggest our severance from the Empire which is as much *ours* as *theirs*?"[41]

IV

In the agenda of the Canada Firsters the promotion of immigration assumed a central place. They were convinced that the North-West had to be speedily settled in order to make it British in racial character and institutions. In August 1870 they created the North-West Emigration Aid Society to publicize the territory and advise prospective settlers on the easiest means of transportation to it. By November Denison reported that although the society had hardly advertised its services many enquiries and applications had been received, and he estimated

39 J. A. Chisholm, ed., *The Speeches and Public Letters of Joseph Howe* (Halifax, 1909), II, 639–40.
40 G. M. Grant, *Ocean to Ocean: Sandford Fleming's Expedition through Canada in 1872* (Toronto, 1873), 366–7.
41 Cited in Lorne Pierce, *William Kirby: The Portrait of a Tory Loyalist* (Toronto, 1929), 228.

that between fifteen hundred and two thousand people would leave for the west in the spring.[42] Though this interest in settlement grew out of their concern with the North-West, it was also stimulated by the disappointing census of 1871 which showed that during the preceding decade the population of British North America had only increased from three to three and one-half million. If such a slow rate of growth was all that could be hoped for, said one observer, "many an aspiration for political independence must be checked, many a hopeful anticipation as to our national progress moderated."[43] How much indeed would it really matter that Canada had room for forty million if her population in fact was to remain a small fraction of that of Britain or the United States? Such considerations drove many into supporting the systematic promotion of British immigration into the new Dominion. In official quarters the Ontario government intensified its campaign to secure immigrants, and late in 1872 appointed Denison special commissioner of emigration and dispatched him to England.

Denison arrived in Britain at an auspicious moment. The industrial depression of the late 1860s had occasioned widespread distress and had stimulated agrarian discontent which received expression in the National Agricultural Labourer's Union and its paper, the *Labourer's Chronicle*. Under the leadership of Joseph Arch and dissenting lay preachers, the union demanded the abolition of the payment of tithes to the established church, an increase in farm wages, extension of the franchise to include farm workers, and an end to the "land monopoly." Especially instructed to co-operate with Arch and to ensure that at least three-quarters of the assisted immigrants were agriculturalists,[44] Denison lectured to farm labourers in Wiltshire and Dorset, to mechanics in London and Birmingham, and in Scotland and Wales; he quickly discovered plots of American immigration agents; and when landlords were alarmed at the prospect of their labourers departing, the Colonel attacked the "monied classes" in a letter to the *Times*. His lectures read like the literature of Canada, or rather, Ontario First. He praised the local control of local affairs; reminded his listeners that there were free schools and no established church; contrasted the demo-

---

42 TPL, Denison Papers, North-West Emigration Aid Society, circular #1; Mair Papers, Denison to Mair, Nov. 10, 1870.
43 Arthur Harvey, "The Canadian Census of 1871," *Canadian Monthly*, I (Feb. 1872), 102.
44 A sympathetic account of the movement is given by Arthur Claydon, *The Revolt of the Field: A Sketch of the Rise and Progress of the Movement Among Agricultural Labourers, known as the "National Agricultural Labourers' Union"* (London, 1874). Denison's mission may be followed in OA, "The Letter Book of G. T. Denison, Dec. 1872–Jan. 1874 while Special Commissioner from Ontario to England re immigration to Canada."

cratic character of the new nation to the rigid class lines in England; and emphasized that British people should remain within the Empire and not strengthen the United States. Until Denison persuaded him to visit Canada, Arch had conceived of emigration more as a threat to hold over British landlords than as an actual solution to agrarian unrest. But after a tour of Ontario in 1873 Arch was so impressed that he reported to the union that "Canada is a better land than England."[45] Over forty thousand copies of his address were reprinted by the Ontario government, and it was estimated that Denison's mission brought between eight and ten thousand agricultural labourers to Ontario.[46]

Denison's visit to Britain not only permanently shaped his views regarding immigration as a means of consolidating the Empire but it also brought him into contact with the personalities who were spearheading the imperialist revival in the motherland. The incipient imperial movement which led to the establishment of the Royal Colonial Institute in 1869 and to Disraeli's famous Crystal Palace address in 1872, was stimulated by the social crisis of the late 1860s and early 1870s and was associated with an agitation for state-aided emigration of the unemployed to the colonies. The leading figures of this movement, like Frederick Young and the Duke of Manchester, who was president of both the Royal Colonial Institute and the National Emigration League, were to exercise a decisive influence upon the nascent imperial impulse which led directly to the formation of the Imperial Federation League in the 1880s. Denison's contacts with these men were forged early and never severed; he had sent a copy of his book on cavalry to Manchester and as early as 1874 they were discussing Canadian representation in either an imperial parliament or a federal council.[47] Whenever the Duke visited Canada, as he did in 1873 and 1882, he stayed with Denison in Toronto. With the establishment of these personal connections, the imperialists of Canada First received encouraging news from their counterparts in Britain, for they now knew that Little Englandism did not march onward unopposed or unchecked. Despite this reassuring knowledge, however, Denison returned to Canada in 1874 to find Canada First in disarray.

V

From its origins the Canada First group had looked upon party struggles as an impediment to national unity. Partyism was incom-

---

45 Henry Simpson, *The Emigration Mission of Mr. Joseph Arch to Canada* (Liverpool, 1874), reprints his address.
46 *Week*, VII (March 21, 1890), 249.
47 Denison Papers, Manchester to Denison, July 5, 1874.

patible with nationalism because parties, or "factions," institutionalized and perpetuated the very sectional and racial differences which made a general Canadian sentiment impossible. With the frustrations of the early 1860s fresh in their minds, the Canada Firsters really believed that Confederation was the child of political deadlock. Was not union accepted, asked Foster, "because it offered a prospect of relief from that sickening political squabbling which party spirit carried to the greatest extreme and opened up a new arena in which statesmanship might win prizes worth contending for?"[48] Having been convinced by the proponents of Confederation that the broadening of the area of activity and interest would raise the calibre of politicians, these intellectuals looked forward to the end of pointless partisanship and they hoped to see in Canada the emergence of figures comparable to Gladstone in England and Bancroft in the United States, men who combined cultural interests with political service. Their attitude to politics was similar to some idealists' views of love: attracted to the noble ideal, they were repelled by the mechanics by which ideals can alone be realized.

While the idea of independence in politics was only one among many propositions with the corner room set, it became the major principle of a very different association in the early 1870s. Between 1871, when Goldwin Smith joined the movement, and 1873, when it formally entered politics as a third party, Canada First was totally changed in membership, and, to a degree, in intentions. In spite of his earlier attitude towards the Empire, it was possible for Smith to sympathize with these young nationalists because he shared their revulsion at partyism, the degeneracy of journalism, and political corruption. With Macdonald's compromise settlement of the rebellion, a course which Denison termed disloyal, the promulgation by a group of fervent ultramontanes in Quebec of a "Catholic Programme," which urged the formation of a Catholic group within the Conservative party, and the Pacific Scandal of 1873, few could reasonably maintain that the abominations of partyism were disappearing. When Denison unsuccessfully contested the constituency of Algoma for the Reform party in the election of 1872, Smith sent him fifty dollars as a token of support. "You and I differ ... in politics," he explained. "You are more for the Crown, I more for the people ... But I think I understand the issues of the late struggle; and, if I do, you have been fighting for purity of government and for the rights & honour of the nation."[49]

The adhesion of Goldwin Smith to Canada First coincided with the withdrawal of the original members. By 1873 Mair was running a store at Portage la Prairie, Haliburton was writing his imperialist articles in

48 *Canada First: A Memorial*, 89.
49 TPL, Denison Papers, Smith to Denison, Sept. 2, 1872.

England, and Morgan had been appointed keeper of the public records
by the Dominion government. With Denison absent from Canada for
lengthy intervals between 1872 and 1874 only the impressionable
Foster remained in Toronto and he was surrounded by new members
who had few personal connections with the founders. Many of the
individuals who joined the group at this time were young Toronto
lawyers like the Trout brothers, who had founded the *Monetary Times*,
and W. G. McWilliams, Foster's law partner, or close associates of
Smith, like G. Mercer Adam, editor of the *Canadian Monthly and
National Review*, a magazine established in 1872 in order to protest
against the party-dominated press and to decrease Canadian dependence upon American periodicals. Another was Thomas Moss, with
whom Foster had attended university and with whom he had worked
on Erastus Wiman's humour magazine, the *Grumbler*. In the autumn
of 1873 Moss was nominated as the Liberal candidate to represent West
Toronto in the House of Commons and Foster brought the Canada
First group to his support. A more formal organization grew out of this
successful intrusion into politics. The Canadian National Association
was founded in January 1874, and a National Club, modelled on the
English political clubs, was soon organized. William H. Howland, the
son of a former lieutenant-governor of Ontario, was nominated chairman of this association and a declaration of purposes was issued to
the public. The manifesto of the new party was a curious mixture of
the nationalistic aims of the old group and the interests of the newer
members in technical improvements in the electoral system. Though
both Smith and Denison believed that Foster drafted the platform, it is
quite possible that the declaration was the result of the contributions of
several individuals, with Foster emphasizing those points for which his
old friends had agitated.

The first plank – "British Connection, Consolidation of the Empire,
and in the meantime a voice in treaties affecting Canada" – is at once
the least mysterious and the most misleading. As we have seen, the
older members of Canada First preferred some kind of imperial association of national entities; they did not think in terms of an independent
foreign policy since, because of American dominance, Canada alone
could never have one. They hoped rather that by representation in
either an imperial council or in the imperial parliament Canadians could
influence foreign policy; at least they could dispel the misconceptions
about North American interests which had been the leading feature of
British diplomacy in the past. But given the apparent strength of Little
Englandism and the outright hostility to colonies then dominant in
British opinion, it must have seemed that such a possibility was very
far in the future indeed. This is why the call for the consolidation of the

Empire was so quickly followed by the phrase "in the meantime" – in other words, until some imperial consolidation could be achieved in which Canadians could influence policy in general, they wanted some interim voice to prevent the repetition of such disasters as the Treaty of Washington in particular. The call for imperial consolidation and a voice in treaties are therefore complementary.

Of the other ten proposals five stemmed directly from the concerns of the old group and were advanced as solutions to the problems that the new Dominion faced in the early 1870s. The call for a systematic encouragement of immigration grew out of the activities of the North-West Emigration Aid Society and the disappointing census of 1871. The proposal for an improved militia was designed to provide for the defence of Canada after the withdrawal of British troops and the injunction that such a force be under the command of Canadians comported well with the resentments against British officers. The skilfully balanced suggestion for a "tariff for revenue" and the "encouragement of native industry" ran back to the writings of Isaac Buchanan, Haliburton's appeal for protection to the Nova Scotian coal industry, and to the demands of Canadian manufacturers. As well, protection was presented as an alternative to the frequent failures to renew the reciprocal trade treaty with the United States. The idea of closer trade relations with the West Indies – "with a view to ultimate political connection" – had appeared earlier in Haliburton's pamphlets. The remaining five points of the platform advocated changes in the electoral system – an income franchise, the secret ballot, compulsory voting, a scheme for the representation of minorities, the elimination of property qualifications for members of the House of Commons, and reorganization of the Senate. Intended to secure a more faithful reflection of popular opinion and derived from American examples and mid-Victorian liberalism, these technical reforms were of the order to appeal to the young and ambitious lawyers who were joining the party.

In 1874 Canada First began publishing the *Nation*, a weekly journal which took its name from the major press organ of civil service reform in the republic. "Our main object," it declared, "is to look at all public questions not from the party but from the national point of view ... This was our meaning in calling our journal THE NATION, a name already borne by one which has done good service in the same way in the United States."[50] One of the dominant issues in American politics in the post-Civil War years was the attempt of liberal reformers to secure a more independent civil service and to reassert the role of the educated gentleman in political life. The chief spokesman for this movement was E. L. Godkin, a friend of Goldwin Smith and editor of the *Nation*.

50 *Nation*, Sept. 3, 1875.

Inspired by the Northcote-Trevelyan report of 1854 on the British civil service, animated by a disgust at the uncouth type of politicians who were assuming leadership of the democracy, and scandalized by the boodling which made the era of Grant synonymous with corruption, the reformers hammered away at the necessity for civil service reform in particular, and in 1872 supported a third party of Republican insurgency, nominated Horace Greeley for the presidency, but lost miserably.

While Canada First never emphasized civil service reform as heavily as its American counterpart, it none the less represented similar ideas, admitted the influence of the American parallel, and frequently cited with approval editorials of the liberal press in the United States. Almost every issue of the Canadian paper detailed contemporary incidents of political corruption to sustain its charges that the degeneration of political life was not peculiarly Canadian. "This is an age of grab," it announced in 1875; "An age ... [of] the Credit Mobilier, the Tammany Ring, the Canal Ring, the land grabbing Congresses, the fall of Jay Cooke and William C. Ralston, backpay, the salary grab, and other strange and debasing phenomena ..."[51] One of the most compelling parallels between the Godkin reformers and the Canada Firsters was that both groups were dismissed as "mere intellectuals." Though the Canadian movement contained no one of the stature of Henry Adams, their literary interests indelibly stamped them as men of ideas. They sought a press which was independent of political control, urged the infusion of "organic questions" into political discussion, and often expressed the feeling that as intellectuals, or custodians of culture, they deserved some more exalted place than the North American community was willing to accord them. Their alienation from political life was not a temporary aberration, but was to be a persistent theme of late nineteenth-century Canadian history.

While the *Nation* devoted primary attention to the degeneration of political life, the growing political influence of the Catholic Church was viewed with an equal degree of alarm. This concern formed one of the strongest links of continuity between the small group of the Riel resistance years and the vastly expanded movement of 1874–75. The resurgence of ultramontanism in Quebec during the early 1870s not only affronted the inherited Protestant prejudices of the Canada Firsters but conflicted with their belief that special interests should be submerged in a generous national outlook. In 1876 Denison told Mair that he had left Macdonald's party because "French Canadian Catholicism and Ultramontanism were rampant under the wing of toryism."[52] The claim of

51 *Ibid.*, Sept. 10, 1875.
52 Mair Papers, Denison to Mair, Feb. 20, 1876.

Bishop Bourget that the interests of the church must be the primary determining influence in voting seemed but a revival of the same old animosities which had brought the union to a complete deadlock, and it appeared too as but one reflection of a world-wide challenge. Aware of the conflicts between state and church over separate schools in the United States, the Canada Firsters were also reminded of Bismarck's *Kulturkampf*. After a visit to Germany in 1874, Robert Haliburton published a warning that the ultramontanes who were responsible for the rebellion at Red River and the decline of imperial power in Ireland, were also secretly at work in England. "In Germany civil and political liberty and the safety of the state have been endangered by the cry of 'the Pope and a divided kingdom!' The triumphant reply to this has been the watchword – 'The Emperor and our Fatherland!' In this country the same danger is awaiting us, and must be met by the same loyal response – 'the Queen and a United Empire!' "[53] One of the most watchful observers of ultramontanism was Charles Lindsey, biographer of William Lyon Mackenzie and author of *Rome in Canada: The Ultramontane Struggle for Supremacy over the Civil Authority* (1877), a lengthy history which set out to place the current conflicts into perspective. The *Nation* clearly revealed what Canada First meant by calling for the injection of organic questions into politics when it noted the growing power of the church and prophesied: "It is in this quarter that the great struggle is impending, and those who care for public liberty and civilization more than for place will speedily find themselves constrained to cast off unholy alliances, and take a stand in defence of their principles."[54]

The decision to form a party to combat factionalism, to organize a third party in order to combat the evils of party, left observers of Canada First confused and mystified. The adherents of the movement had a fairly definite conception of the role they sought to play and often declared that though they were opposed to existing Canadian parties there was nothing inherently wrong with a spontaneous combination to urge fundamental principles. Their newspaper contended that a movement to change opinion need not take the shape of a conventional party and that history was studded with examples, like the Anti-Corn Law League, the anti-slavery agitation, and the temperance crusade, of influential movements which attained their objectives without becoming political parties.[55] These illustrations explain both the reasons why they thought of Canada First in these terms and why they ultimately failed.

53 Denison Papers, vol. 18, R. G. Haliburton, "The Queen and the United Empire," reprint from the *St James Magazine and United Empire Review*, Jan. 1874.
54 *Nation*, Nov. 5, 1875.
55 *Ibid.*, Sept. 3 and Feb. 26, 1875.

Brought up with an unquestioning acceptance of progress and the belief that the minds of men were changed by incisive rational argument, they seemed unaware that inculcating a sense of nationality was far more complicated than launching an assault upon intemperance.

By 1875, with the *Nation* possessing a circulation larger in proportion to population than its American namesake, Canada First appeared healthy and virile. The National Club, Foster told Mair, had about four hundred members – "good furniture, excellent pub, nice company, best of liquor, unexampled cooking, great success."[56] But Foster was wrong, Canada First was dying. Its demise was implicit in its own short-lived effervescence. On October 1, 1874, Goldwin Smith delivered an address at the National Club in which he expressed the hope that the Empire in the future would become a "family of self-governing nations." Smith was by far the best-known figure to join Canada First and it was virtually inevitable that men like George Brown, who had been shocked by his trenchant views on Canada in the 1860s, should still equate his name with imperial disengagement and interpret his speech in the context of his earlier proposals.[57] But if Smith still adhered to these views it is strange that none of those members of Canada First who favoured some form of imperial co-operation perceived this. Denison maintained his friendship with Smith right down to the late 1880s and Charles Mair, writing in 1884, believed that though Smith's criticism of Canadian life was beneficial, his support of Canada First brought it much harm "before he was understood."[58] Smith had given Egerton Ryerson the impression in 1871 that he had been permanently cured of his "unqualified admiration" of the United States.[59] His biographer, moreover, by emphasizing that it was the failure of Canada First which permanently disillusioned him about the future of the Canadian nation, certainly implied that his position in the early 1870s was not what it had been in 1863 nor what it was to become in 1891.[60] But whatever his actual position in 1874, his reputation as the author of *The Empire* came back to haunt the party he joined. Because of this association and his criticism of the Toronto press, Brown's *Globe* launched an attack upon Canada First as a treasonous organization.

On October 3, two days after Smith's inaugural speech, Edward Blake delivered his celebrated Aurora address. With typical prolixity he alluded to the profound impression that the Treaty of Washington

56 Mair Papers, Foster to Mair, June 10, 1875.
57 J. M. S. Careless, *Brown of the Globe* (Toronto, 1963), ii, 328.
58 Denison Papers, Mair to Denison, Jan. 16 and April 16, 1884.
59 C. B. Sisson, ed., *My Dearest Sophie: Letters from Egerton Ryerson to his daughter* (Toronto, 1955), 210–11.
60 Elizabeth Wallace, *Goldwin Smith: Victorian Liberal* (Toronto, 1957), 263.

had produced in Canada and he recalled that he had suggested "that an effort should be made to reorganize the Empire on a Federal basis." Only if Canadians could secure some voice in foreign policy could their "national rights" be secured and their ambitions satisfied.[61] So effectively did Blake state the argument for electoral reform that the *Nation* reported that his "exposition of principles is identical on most points with the views which have found expression in these columns."[62] But the Canada Firsters were soon disabused of the notion that Blake would become their public spokesman and defender. The Liberal politicians could hardly remain indifferent to the new departure at Aurora, for Blake's speech, taken in conjunction with his previous erratic course in politics and his connection with Goldwin Smith, threatened a revolt against Brown and Mackenzie. Not only did the Aurora address serve to increase the vehemence with which the *Globe* denounced Canada First, but it failed to generate any substantial public interest in the question of imperial relations. "I was impressed," one observer noted, "by his statement that Canadians were four million people who were not free. I don't recall any person in our neighborhood [of South Norwich] who was particularly interested in this subject, nor do I remember anyone speaking to me about it."[63] "Blake's deliverances about the reconstruction of the Empire," Governor-General Dufferin confirmed, "seem to have fallen flat."[64] Even the original members of Canada First were dismayed at Blake's flippant remarks concerning the west, as when he said he was confident that a bushel of wheat would never go to England over a railway from the Saskatchewan to the seaboard. Whatever the intent of the Aurora address it certainly did not enhance the repute of Canada First. When Blake re-entered the cabinet in 1875, the expectation that he might give the movement the leadership it required was ended.

In 1876 the *Nation* stopped publication, and, though the National Club survived, the Canadian National Association, tainted with treason and leaderless, completely disintegrated. The founders of Canada First like Charles Mair, who had taken no part in transforming it into a political party, and Denison, who had opposed such a course, were tempted to blame those individuals who joined their ranks late and usurped their positions. "I have lived to see the germ of a national party strangled in the embraces of a Goldwin Smith," Mair grieved, "and ...

61 "*A National Sentiment": Speech of Hon. Edward Blake, M. P., At Aurora: with the comments of the Canadian Press Thereon* (Ottawa, 1874), 9.
62 *Ibid.*, 24.
63 QUL, William D. Gregory Papers, MS Autobiography, 48.
64 C. W. de Kiewiet and F. H. Underhill, eds., *Dufferin-Carnarvon Correspondence, 1874–1878* (Toronto, 1955), 81.

a policy of antagonism to the north west espoused by an Edward Blake."[65] Denison was less than acute when he attributed the collapse of the movement to one fifteen-minute speech by W. H. Howland in 1873 in which the president of the association declared that there was "too much toadyism to English aristocratic usages in this country" – "too much toadyism to titles."[66] While such a remark was found useful to those who sought to paint the group as disloyal, Denison did not explain how a speech delivered in 1873 killed a party that attained its largest following two years later. Nor did he seem to remember that his old friends had subscribed to exactly the same sentiments.

The strangest legacy of Canada First were the two contradictory accounts of its own existence. The only two published records of the movement – Goldwin Smith's introduction to a memorial volume to Foster, published in 1890, and Denison's autobiography which appeared in 1909 – were written by men who had not been in Canada during important phases of the movement's history. By 1890, moreover, Smith had become the chief propagandist of continental union, Denison had emerged as the major spokesman of imperial federation, and they were hopelessly separated by a venomous personal feud. In his brief treatment of Canada First, Smith nowhere mentioned Denison, though he did refer to Haliburton, Mair, Morgan, and Foster as precursors of the party, and he concluded that the Canada Firsters looked forward to Canadian independence. Denison, on the other hand, described the movement as a forerunner of the Imperial Federation League. In doing so, he did not so much misrepresent the thinking of the original members as he imparted to their chance meetings an exaggerated purposefulness and melodramatic zest for conspiratorial operations. While Smith blamed the party-dominated press for the movement's collapse, Denison believed the traitors who joined it compromised the party's loyalism.

In the face of such conflicting and retrospective evidence historians have been forced to speculate about the reasons for the party's collapse and more often than not they have done so in deterministic terms. Indeed, one of them believed that it was fortunate that Canada First failed because otherwise nationalism might have become a party question.[67] It has been implied also that the movement was fated to fail because it sought to define the indefinable, because its members were in such hopeless disagreement, and because the traditions to which they

65 Denison Papers, Mair to Denison, March 16, 1876.
66 Denison, *Struggle*, 60.
67 W. S. Wallace, *The Growth of Canadian National Feeling* (Toronto, 1927), 55.

appealed could not possibly find as much support in Quebec as in old Ontario. Regarded in the context of third party movements in North American politics, the disintegration of the movement scarcely appears surprising. It is true, of course, that the Canada Firsters were imprecise in defining goals, though no more so than the Young America or Young Ireland movements in that age of romantic nationalism, and that their attitude to politics was quixotic, though there were reasons for its being so. They were not the first or the last "Canadian nationalists" who were only spokesmen for Ontario, or Quebec, or the West, or the Maritimes. Not even originality can be placed against their shortcomings, for they were more adept at drawing together existing traditions than in stating dramatic and novel departures. Later imperialists recognized the Canada Firsters as their own ancestors, and rightly so, for they shared that group's chief assumption and were moved by the same anticipation.

Some of the original members of Canada First lost faith in this hope, some of those who joined the party in 1872–5 never had it, but Denison spoke for it right into the 1920s. After the breakup of the movement, Haliburton concerned himself with scientific researches and Foster with the law. Morgan remained in Ottawa, editing his cyclopedias, uninterested in politics. Exiled in the west which he came to love, Mair never forgot the loss of his manuscripts during the Red River troubles and in moments of despair and depression, as when the *Canadian Monthly and National Review* expired in 1882, he denounced Canadians as "literary eunuchs" and said he was "filled with shame & contempt & regret when I think that I am a Canadian." "As regards Canadian literature," he later added, "I have given more time and labor to it than it deserves ... I am done with the 'Canadian Public' which consists of mere cattle ... its true and only enjoyments (the heights of Canadian ambition in fact) are guzzling and drinking and rotten politics."[68] It was Henry Morgan who drew the perfect epitaph for Canada First. Those were the "happy days," he wrote, when we were all assembled, with the glasses full and the pipes aglow. "Those were the days when we made history & took our whiskey straight."[69]

68 Denison Papers, Mair to Denison, Aug. 20, 1882 and July 17, 1891.
69 Mair Papers, Morgan to Mair, Dec. 4, 1899.

3

The Loyalist Tradition

In the summer of 1884 the Imperial Federation League was founded in London and in Canada the descendants of the United Empire Loyalists celebrated the centennial of the migration of their ancestors. Though there was no apparent connection between these two events the loyalist tradition was to provide one of the most potent elixirs to Canadian imperial sentiment and the descendants of the loyalists were to constitute the major source of the League's support. This tradition expressed an indigenous British-Canadian national feeling and it flourished both because it provided a useful device by which the arguments of the advocates of Canadian independence could be counteracted, and because it bolstered the status of loyalist descendants by associating their ancestors with the foundations of national greatness. Of all the factors which served to awaken the tradition the nationalistic determination to recover the Canadian heritage and the conservative desire to preserve the guiding principles of that past were the most important. History in its broadest cultural sense was the medium in which the tradition was expressed and history was the final and ultimate argument for imperial unity.

I

The centennial of the arrival of the loyalists in Ontario coincided with the fiftieth anniversary of the incorporation of the City of Toronto and, during a week filled with various exhibitions, July 3 was set aside as "Loyalist Day." On the morning of that day the platform erected at the Horticultural Pavilion was crowded with civic and ecclesiastical dignitaries and on one wall hung the old flag presented in 1813 to the York Militia by the ladies of the county. Between stirring orations on the significance of the loyalist legacy, injunctions to remain faithful to their principles, and tirades against the ancient foe, patriotic anthems were sung and nationalist poetry recited. "Rule Britannia" and "If England To Herself Be True" were rendered "in splendid style" and "evoked great enthusiasm." "A Loyalist Song," "Loyalist Days," and "The Maple Leaf For Ever" were all "beautifully" sung. The Reverend Le Roy Hooker of Kingston read his poem, "The United Empire Loyalists" – "specially written for the occasion" – in which he talked of "the brave old Revolution days" and the "hero blood." In the afternoon a reception was held at Government House where William Kirby, Lieutenant-Governor John Beverley Robinson, and Lieutenant-Governor Aikins of Manitoba spoke movingly of the sacrifices of the past.[1]

The celebrations at Adolphustown and Niagara were similar to the one at Toronto both in general character and doctrinal content and all passed smoothly except for the objections of Goldwin Smith in the columns of the *Week* and the discordant note sounded by the Liberal politician, Sir Richard Cartwright. At Adolphustown, Cartwright declared that those who derived inspiration from the founders of Canada "can best do justice to the spirit of their forefathers by doing what they can to bring together in a union all English-speaking races in the world." Cartwright later reported that the idea that Canada might form a "link of union" between the United States and Great Britain was one of his deepest convictions and that his attempt to secure commercial reciprocity between Canada and the Republic, and thereby to create a community of economic interest between them, was but one external expression of it.[2] This was certainly not what most of the loyalist descendants took to be the burden of their heritage. Cartwright's hope for British-American friendship clashed head-on with their vituperative criticism of the United States and he scandalized the Denisons and the Kirbys. Apologizing to Kirby for not being able to attend the meeting at Niagara, John A. Macdonald wrote that "I have no doubt that the speeches at Niagara will be most effective answers to the late disloyal utterances of Sir Richard Cartwright and others. I am quite sure," he added, "that the country is sound to the core."[3]

If Macdonald's remark suggests the political utility of the loyalist centennial, then even more instructive for gauging the relevance of loyalism for subsequent imperialism are the personalities who sponsored the festivities, particularly in Toronto. The chairman of the committee of management and the moving force behind the whole idea of the celebration was William Canniff. Born near Hastings, Upper Canada, in 1830, Canniff had graduated from New York University

1 *The Centennial of the Settlement of Upper Canada by the United Empire Loyalists, 1774–1884: The Celebrations at Adolphustown, Toronto and Niagara* (Toronto, 1885).
2 *Ibid.*, 29; Sir Richard Cartwright, *Reminiscences* (Toronto, 1912), 283.
3 OA, William Kirby Papers, box #4, Macdonald to Kirby, June 30, 1884.

with a medical degree, had served in the Crimean War and as professor of surgery at Victoria University, and had been appointed medical health officer for Toronto in 1883. He was one of the leading amateur historians who did so much in the years following Confederation to recover significant aspects of the Canadian past. The chief impetus behind his historical work, he frankly admitted, was nationalistic. In a patriotic address delivered during the Civil War he declared that although Canadians "have not made a great mark in history, we have reason to be glad we have not such *marks* of sin as those which rest upon a slave-holding nation, marks which all the blood now being spilt cannot wash out. But we *have* a history – a history of not a few United Empire Loyalists who *did* choose to become pioneers into Canada rather than live under an alien flag. We have a history, not of a bloody revolution ... but of those gradual, and healthful changes" which constitute genuine progress, a history of internal improvement, rather than the "filibusterism" of "land pirates" and "Manifest Destiny." Those elements which lie at the core of British-Canadian nationality, he continued, were a "guided and controlled" liberty, popular education "tempered with Christianity," and the energies of the Anglo-Saxon race. Canniff appealed to the vision of the Anglo-Saxon empire which would ultimately "cover the whole earth" with the "English language, English laws and the English Protestant Bible."[4]

Dr Canniff was in several ways representative of the others involved in the fête of 1884. He had been an associate of the Canada First movement and, like his friend Denison, he belonged to the right wing of that group. He had made his denunciation of the party system and though he had declared in 1875 that Canadians "will be satisfied with nothing less than equality with the people of the United Kingdom," and seemed to dismiss the United States as a bogy rather than a real threat to Canada, he nevertheless believed that the strengthening of "Canadianism" would not only "tend to blend the French element with the Anglo-Saxon" but in no way compromise loyalty to Britain.[5] William Foster also sat on the committee that organized the centennial, but, burdened by the legal work which was even then sapping his strength and was to lead to his premature death, he made no declarations of principle and his presence appeared to be one of token support. And Charles Mair, though absent, was not totally removed in spirit, for at the same time that his Canada First friends were extolling the traditions

4 OA, William Canniff Papers, package #13, MS "Patriotic Address," n.d.
5 William Canniff, *Canadian Nationality: Its Growth and Development* (Toronto, 1875), 7, 14–15, 20.

of loyalism, Mair was writing his drama about Brock and Tecumseh which expressed in literary form the same propositions. In 1876 Colonel Denison had bewailed the disintegration of Canada First and had hopefully told Mair that if it were ever revived "it must be in a new dress, under a new name, and in some time of public excitement when some great rallying cry can form a pivot around which the young men can gather."[6] Denison perhaps may be excused for believing that the revival of loyalism in 1884 represented the reincarnation of Canada First.

The committee of management also included a number of historians who, like Canniff, produced books which embodied the loyalist cult. Egerton Ryerson, for example, whose two-volume study, *The Loyalists of America and Their Times* (1880), became one of the major literary sources of the tradition, was secretary-treasurer of the committee. Others who shared this interest in popularizing the loyalist past both in literature and in the commemorative celebration included Canniff Haight, David B. Read, Henry Scadding, William Withrow, and William Kirby. In yet another way, apart from the semblance of continuity with Canada First, the common interest in the past, and loyalist descent, Canniff seems representative of the sponsors of the centennial. By the late 1880s he became an enthusiastic advocate of imperial federation and equated faithfulness to the loyalist tradition as virtually synonymous with imperialism. With only a slight exaggeration it might be said that the list of those who sponsored the loyalist centennial in 1884 reads like the roster of the Imperial Federation League in Ontario in 1890. Aside from the ubiquitous Denisons, it included Principal Grant of Queen's University, D'Alton McCarthy, Sir Alexander Campbell, as well as many descendants of the old stock families like the Merritts and the Playters, whose contribution to the imperial ideology remains obscure but who in the end supplied the League with its most fervent adherents.

The loyalist centennial of 1884 was in itself a minuscule occurrence but in terms of the emergence of Canadian imperialism it was both symbolic and significant. In the enemies it made, no less than in the supporters it attracted, the celebration was a prelude or anticipation of the imperial federation movement of the later 1880s. And in the clash of ideas it occasioned it provided a foretaste of the wide-ranging debate over the Canadian future produced by the annexation threat. The literature of the centennial, moreover, contained the quintessence of the loyalist tradition and confirmed that an indigenous variety of

6 QUL, Charles Mair Papers, Denison to Mair, Feb. 20, 1876.

Canadian imperialism had appeared in certain quarters in Ontario by the early 1880s.

II

Traditions become the objects of justificatory invocations when they are under attack and not when their propositions are taken for granted and tacitly accepted. Despite the ringing certainty so characteristic of the loyalist proclamations of 1884, the praise of the loyalist past was generated in part as a response to the increasing criticisms of the British connection and the appearance of what the orthodox custodians of the loyalist tradition took to be an incipient independence movement of dangerous dimensions. The Denisons, Canniffs, and Kirbys vastly overestimated the strength of their adversaries but in a sense they also understood that the ancient foundations of Canadian loyalty to Britain could no longer be taken for granted. The institutional basis of tory loyalism had long before vanished with the dissolution of the state-church connection in Upper Canada and the abolition of the preferential tariff system. Though the makers of Confederation were unquestionably imbued with an allegiance to the Crown and an unbounded admiration of the British system of government, and though they thought of federal union of the North American colonies as in no way implying a weakening of the connection, the very achievement of Confederation stimulated a debate on the future of the new nationality which was to lead to what many regarded as strange and alien conclusions. Although this discussion was confined largely to publicists and intellectuals, it was none the less notable, hinging as it did on the question of whether the future of Canada would be total independence, annexation to the republic, or some kind of imperial association. This pamphlet and press debate was an expression of the fact that Confederation, to use Macdonald's phrase, was still gristle and not bone, and that the future was still an open question.

One of the commonplaces of the day was that independence was virtually identical with absorption into the republic. An appreciation of the powerlessness of the Dominion, the heritage of distrust of the United States, and frequent disputes over tariffs and fisheries combined to keep alive the suspicion and fear which underlay this view. The premier of Ontario, Sir Oliver Mowat, told an audience in 1892 that there were only two, not three, alternatives before Canada – annexation to the United States or connection with Britain. "If we are not for annexation," he said, "our clear policy as Canadians is for the present to cherish British connection whatever else any of us may be looking forward to in our political and national future."[7] Though the British connection was thought to be a necessary, even if only a temporary, condition for Canadian development, there were a few individuals like Goldwin Smith and William Norris who insisted that the sooner a forthright declaration of independence was made, the more quickly would Canadians develop a strong sense of patriotism and self-reliance.

Norris had joined the Canada First party during the waning period of its troubled history. In 1875 he published *The Canadian Question*, an incisive argument for independence, and during the early 1880s he penned a number of articles which presented some of the most trenchant critiques of the British connection. From the development of Canada in his own time Norris drew the conclusion that the movement towards a completely independent nationality was irreversible. The growth of internal self-government, the creation of independent Canadian churches, the withdrawal of the British garrisons, the establishment of the Canadian Supreme Court, and the enunciation of the National Policy of protection, all appeared to him as symptoms of the deeper drift of history. Norris was assured that separation from the Empire would not lead to annexation if Canadian independence were protected by treaty guarantees between Britain and the United States. The only thing that stood in the way of the realization of her destiny to become an asylum for the oppressed of Europe was the existence and lingering influence of an older generation of English colonists. Their "loyalty to a foreign power," he said, "is disloyalty to Canada." The height of their ambition "was reached when they received a smile from the Colonial Under-Secretary in Downing Street or an invitation to dinner from an English nobleman when they paid their periodical visit to Canossa." They still continue to "affect British citizenship and talk about 'our army' at the Cape, or about what 'our fellows' in Afghanistan have done."[8]

Until its demise in 1882 many pages of the *Canadian Monthly and National Review* were filled with arguments in support of Norris' contentions and spirited rejoinders. The Ottawa controversialist, William

7 *Centennial of the Province of Upper Canada, 1792–1892: Proceedings at the Gathering held at Niagara-on-the-Lake, July 16, 1892. And also the Proceedings at the Meeting in Front of the New Parliament Buildings, Toronto, September 17, 1892* (Toronto, 1893), 29.
8 William Norris, "Canadian Nationality," *Rose-Belford's Canadian Monthly and National Review*, IV (Feb. 1880), 113–18; "The Colonists Organ's Attack on Freedom of Discussion," *ibid.*, VII (Aug. 1881), 166–72; "Canadian Colonialism and Sir Francis Hincks," *ibid.*, VII (Nov. 1881), 501–6.

Le Sueur, who delighted in baiting the loyalists as much as he enjoyed confuting the reactionary clergy with the latest revelations of Huxley and Spencer, declared that loyalty was merely the deference and fidelity of an inferior to a superior and that its purpose was the preservation of the colonial status of Canada.[9] Though these exchanges were obviously only symptomatic of the unsettled state of the times and the desire of intellectuals to grapple with the problems of the country, the orthodox custodians of loyalism could not regard them with equanimity. Their response was epitomized by Colonel Denison's retort to Goldwin Smith at a meeting of the National Club in 1880 when the Colonel blurted out that argumentation for and against independence and annexation would have a "bad effect" and that he would debate the issue "on horseback with my sword."[10] "In 1884," Denison remembered, "the Independence agitation was probably more in evidence than at any period before or since."[11] During that year, William Norris and E. E. Sheppard, editor of the Toronto *Evening News*, continued the agitation for independence and they were supported by a few others. That the whole centennial celebration was an effort to counteract the "disloyal element" is implied in Denison's account of it; it was as much a reply to the "independence flurry" as it was a conscious attempt to arouse the pride and faith in the loyalist legacy. Insignificant as the debate might seem in retrospect, the fact that men could discuss the Canadian future as though the issue was a mere debating topic, affronted those loyalist descendants who felt as though the righteousness of their fathers had been questioned.

III

In large part the loyalist tradition was an attempt to associate the original loyalists, and, by implication, their living descendants, with the fount of national greatness. It was familial and ancestral pride which accounts for a good deal of the insistence that these founders of Canada had invariably been the very best people in the American colonies. The loyalist descendants who were so persistent in underlining their separateness from things American were, ironically, part of a social movement which was affecting their ancient foes. Canadians often

9 W. D. Le Sueur, "The True Idea of Canadian Loyalty," *ibid.*, VIII (Jan. 1882), 1–11.
10 G. T. Denison, *The Struggle for Imperial Unity* (Toronto, 1909), 63.
11 *Ibid.*, 64.

commented upon "the craze for heraldry and genealogies" which formed so curious a "social development of our neighbours" since the 1870s,[12] but they seldom plumbed the deep reasons for it. The concern evinced in the United States by "old stock," "Anglo-Saxon" families for tracing back their ancestry to the early days of the republic or to aristocratic associations in Europe arose partly from an attempt to recover social prestige and compensate for their impending or actual loss of political power in the years following the Civil War. The older families of the seaboard reacted to the chaotic social climbing of the gilded age and the appearance of the capitalists of "mere wealth" by asserting their role as custodians of culture and denigrating the parvenus for their lack of hereditary associations. These parvenus themselves often sought exactly such symbols of legitimacy, but it was largely the representatives of the older families who tried to bolster their prominence by proclaiming their superior patriotism. The heavy ethnological emphasis that they placed upon their Anglo-Saxon origins, moreover, suggests a reaction to the massive immigration of southern Europeans. The filiopietistic patriotic orders, like the Sons of the American Revolution (1889) and the Daughters of the American Revolution (1890), were open only to those who could trace lineal descent from the founding fathers. Of the one hundred and five of these orders in existence in the United States in 1900, seventy-five were founded after 1870. They became centres of a perfervid patrician patriotism in which a mark of notability was claimed by individuals simply because of their ancient associations with the origins of the republic.[13]

One need not read very far in the literature of British-Canadian loyalism to perceive a remarkably similar pattern in the assumptions of social superiority based on ancestry and patriotism. At no other time perhaps was the mark of honour, "u.e.," bestowed upon the refugees after the revolution, worn so proudly by its possessors. In biographical sketches of Canadian celebrities, loyalist ancestry was noted even before the date of birth, as though the very phrase "of u.e.l. descent" provided in itself an illuminating insight into character. Besides singing the extravagant praise of "our ancestors," the organizers of the centennial of 1884 also published a list of all those who had received crown lands as rewards for their allegiance, thereby providing

12 *Week*, xi (Nov. 9, 1894), 1190.
13 John Higham, *Strangers in the Land: Patterns of American Nativism, 1860–1925* (New York, 1963), 32; Wesley Frank Craven, *The Legend of the Founding Fathers* (Ithaca, 1965), chaps. iv–v.

a handy check-list of the founding families. And the local historical societies filled the pages of their published transactions with sketches of loyalist families, usually written by relatives, stressing past sacrifices for principle and tales of hardships in the forests of Ontario. The United Empire Loyalist Association was founded in 1896, devoted to "preserving historic records" and "keeping bright the spirit of loyalty in the inheritors of so noble an ancestry."

Though the Ontario membership remained small – 165 in 1898, 518 in 1905 – it was always pointed out that there were over seven hundred thousand descendants of the "Loyalist pilgrims," "the chosen ones," in Canada, and it was sometimes implied that because of their superior character they were still the guiding force of the whole Dominion. "The leading names among the sixty thousand of a hundred years ago," boasted Nathaniel Burwash, chancellor of Victoria University, "are still the leading names among the six millions of today."[14] John Bourinot reported that sixty members of various legislative assemblies in Canada in 1897 gave their descent as loyalist and he concluded that "the Loyalists still exert a direct influence in the legislation and government of this country" and that they "now number upwards of one-seventh of the total population of Canada."[15]

Despite the ease with which apologists like Bourinot could list descendants of the loyalists who were, like Foster, Tilly, and Tupper, influential in politics, or Sangster, Lampman, and Roberts, conspicuous in Canadian cultural life, their claims attest to an extraordinary degree of special pleading. Loyalist descent, as Richard Cartwright had shown, was no certain determinant of an individual's allegiance to the imperial cause, nor was it, as Roberts' life proved, an obstacle to furthering one's literary career in the United States. Moreover, many of those guardians of the loyalist tradition, who were foremost in associating their own place in society with an inflated interpretation of the achievements of their forebears, were not exactly pre-eminent in either political life or business. Denison was a police magistrate; Canniff, a medical health inspector; Bourinot, the clerk of the House of Commons; Parkin, a school teacher; and Kirby, trained in his youth as a leather tanner, earned his income as a customs collector.

14 Nathaniel Burwash, "The Moral Character of the U.E. Loyalists," *The United Empire Loyalist Association of Ontario, Annual Transactions For the years ending March, 1901, and March, 1902* (Toronto, 1903), 63.

15 J. G. Bourinot, "The Makers of the Dominion of Canada," *Canadian Magazine*, x (April 1898), 489; "The United Empire Loyalists of Canada," *Acta Victoriana*, xxiii (Dec. 1899), 142; "The Pre-Loyalists and U.E. Loyalists of the Maritime Provinces. (1760–1783)," *The United Empire Loyalist Association of Ontario, Annual Transactions, March 10th, 1898* (Toronto, 1898), 70–4.

To suggest in an unqualified and simplistic way that these men created the loyalist mystique and became imperialists in order to bolster their own social position or to compensate for their ineffectuality in political life would ignore their sincerity and distort the idealistic elements in their outlook. Their efforts to identify their families with the foundations of national greatness, however, could not but redound to their own personal prestige and social status. This psychological motive for loyalism does explain a good deal about its ideology. It accounts, at least in part, for the antipathy of Denison, Kirby, and Parkin, and many other imperialists towards men of business, as well as their attachment to an élitist view of political leadership. The great quarrel that Goldwin Smith and Denison waged over continental union was often worded in the language of social snobbery. Denison was just as scandalized that Smith, whom he referred to as a "tramp" and "Bohemian" of recent arrival, should be admitted to Toronto society as he was affronted by a public press debate on fundamental issues. And, as well, critical press commentary on the revival of the loyalist tradition rarely failed to associate it with an inordinate consciousness of social standing. "A U.E. Loyalist celebration," wrote an observer in the *Week*, "will never fail to awaken general sympathy. But we cannot afford to let a particular set of persons erect themselves into an aristocracy of Loyalty, to look down as a superior caste on the rest of the community, or to treat the country as their own creation and themselves as the appointed masters of its destinies. The descendants of martyrs," he thought it necessary to add, "are not the martyrs themselves."[16]

One of the advantages of being a Canadian imperialist came from associating with the aristocrats of England. The United Empire Loyalist descendants who fancied themselves as members of a native Canadian aristocracy were bathed in the reflected glory of their British counterparts who lent their illustrious names and titles to the Imperial Federation League and other agencies of imperialism. The memoirs of Canadian loyalists were filled with references to friendly discourses with their compeers or presentations at Court. Colonel Denison recalled one meeting at the Hotel Cecil in London in 1900:

Shortly after the Prince of Wales came in, and just afterwards Lord Salisbury, who spoke to the Duke of Devonshire and the Prince of Wales, and then looking about the room he saw me and crossed over at once and shook hands with me, and chatted for a minute in his usual friendly manner. As soon as he moved away several of my friends came to me and expressed surprise at the very cordial greeting

16 *Week*, III (Jan. 7, 1886), 84–5.

he had given me. I said, "Why should he not?" and then they told me that he hardly ever knew or remembered anyone, and was very exclusive.[17]

From another perspective, Castell Hopkins provided a penetrating insight into Canadian society at the end of the century when he remarked on the displacement of the old traditional families in British Canada by men of commerce and industry. In his history of Canada during the Victorian age, he noted that

> In English-speaking centres the old-time Loyalist clan with its official connections, hereditary sentiment and sympathetic touch with English social traditions, has largely passed away or else has experienced the loss of position which so often follows the loss of property or means. Successful merchants, well-to-do manufacturers and prosperous professional men have succeeded to its social place and traditions, and to these classes at the end of the century is due a society which has a curious commingling, in its customs and forms, of American freedom and British reserve.

Although Hopkins could recall only a few such families of hereditary associations in English Canada – the Denisons, Cartwrights. Robinsons, Tuppers – he believed that the hierarchical, ordered society of Quebec, with its instinct for rank and hostility to business, provided a far more congenial atmosphere for their survival than Ontario.[18] It was precisely this "loss of position" experienced by the old and once preeminent families that animated their desire, as in similar quarters in the United States, to establish and to publicize their connections with the fathers of the nation and to legitimize their social pretensions with the paraphernalia of heraldry. They took satisfaction in seeing their lineage documented in such records as Edward M. Chadwick's *Ontarian Families: Genealogies of United Empire Loyalist and other Pioneer Families of Upper Canada*, published in 1894 and quickly followed by a second volume devoted to delineating the social élite. They apparently remained undisturbed by those critics who pointed out that the original Upper Canadian loyalists were mainly illiterate backwoodsmen.

The evidence for this relationship between the loyalist cult and the social pretensions of the guardians of the tradition must necessarily be rather impressionistic. But though the association was probably unconscious in their own minds, its existence does account for some of the

17 Denison, *Struggle,* 273. For a similar description of a presentation to the Prince of Wales, written with the air of one revealing to country cousins the doings of the great, see G. S. Ryerson, *Looking Backward* (Toronto, 1924), 148–9.
18 J. Castell Hopkins, *Progress of Canada in the Nineteenth Century* (Toronto, 1900), 513.

peculiar features of the loyalist tradition and it is in keeping with the remark, which has often been made but never explored, that much of the attractive power of the British connection for Canadians was its function as a "status-symbol."[19]

IV

What distinguished the sentiment of loyalty to the British Crown and institutions in the later nineteenth century from its previous expressions was neither its identification with imperial unity nor the hostile view of the United States, but rather the emphasis upon historical antecedents. One reviewer without doubt overstated the case when he remarked that "the retrospective and historic spirit has eagerly seized upon the popular mind,"[20] but there was substantial evidence to sustain the impression that a growing consciousness of history and the past was marked in nearly every department of Canadian culture. In literary taste the decades after the mid-1880s witnessed an upsurge in the popularity of the historical romance,[21] and in painting, though there were of course counter-currents, the same retrospective spirit appeared. For example, Homer Watson, the painter of rural Ontario whom Oscar Wilde dubbed the Canadian Constable, conceived an epic series of pictures depicting the struggles and triumphs of the pioneers in Waterloo County.[22] It is therefore not surprising to find at the same time an intensification of interest in the Canadian past and the multiplication of books and articles describing it. The relationship between the recovery of the past and the emergence of an image of that past which expressed all the elements of the loyalist tradition was not completely fortuitous. Because it emphasized the hereditary forces in national development, the loyalist tradition was itself a potent stimulus to the growing interest in history. In turn, this tradition was influenced and inspired by the many efforts to create a cohesive historical heritage. Not all historical work during these years derived from the loyalist impulse, nor did all of it contribute to the loyalist cult. But history was the chief vehicle in which the loyalist tradition was expressed and that tradition depended for its credibility upon the assumption that the past contained principles to which the present must adhere if the continuity of national

19 F. H. Underhill, *The Image of Confederation* (Toronto, 1964), 31.
20 *Canadian Monthly*, vii (Aug. 1881), 213.
21 Gordon Roper, "New Forces: New Fiction 1880–1920," Carl F. Klinck *et al.*, eds., *Literary History of Canada: Canadian Literature in English* (Toronto, 1965), 281.
22 J. Russell Harper, "Homer Watson, a Painter of Rural Ontario," in National Gallery of Canada, *Homer Watson* (Ottawa, 1963), unpaginated.

life was to be preserved. The reasons for the growth of the retrospective cast of thought are therefore fundamental for understanding the emergence of the loyalist tradition.

Nationalistic history was just as much an instrument of survival for the British-Canadian loyalists as it was for the French Canadians. Like French-Canadian nationalist thought, indeed like any tradition, the loyalist tradition was romantic in outlook, backward-looking in orientation, and shot through with nostalgia. Both of these Canadian traditions centred on defeat and both sought to assuage the memory of conquest or disaster by invoking the images of some golden age in the past, by exalting the principles for which the ancestors had fought, and by glorifying the subsequent adherence to those principles and attitudes which were the foundations of nationalism. Defeat was traced to circumstances external to those principles. Defeat in no way affected their validity: indeed, it seemed but a purging, a preparation for their final triumph. Both traditions, moreover, placed a heavy emphasis upon hereditary associations and family history. The obsessive preoccupation of French-Canadian historians with genealogical researches was paralleled by similar efforts of local historical societies and patriotic orders in Ontario. The descendants of the United Empire Loyalists found in the revolution and the War of 1812 events of personal relevance which stemmed from familial experience. It is startling to realize how many English-Canadian historians in the late nineteenth century traced their roots back to the old loyalist families. Bourinot, Scadding, Canniff, Hannay, Read, Withrow, Ryerson, and Kirby were all sensitively conscious of their lineage. When in 1893 William Canniff told the Canadian Institute of Toronto that "to obtain a correct account of the inner life of a community, the historian must belong to that community and be imbued with the feeling, the longings and the aspirations of the people,"[23] he singled out the most important feature which shaped the writing of Canadian history.

While it was not until the late 1850s that the loyalist cult began to form and only in the mid-1880s that the loyalist tradition fully flowered, one of the major symbols of that tradition had appeared in the early years of the nineteenth century. The myth of the War of 1812 which focused upon the victory of the Upper Canadian militia under General Brock at Queenston Heights preceded by decades the literary formulation of loyalist hagiography. It was much easier for British Canadians to recall and celebrate the victory of 1812 than the defeat of 1783. This tradition of 1812, especially the exaggerated idea that the yeoman

23 Canniff Papers, package #12, MS "A Review of Historical Work in Upper Canada," read before the Canadian Institute, Toronto, Nov. 9, 1893.

militia and not the regular British forces provided the backbone of the defence of Upper Canada, originated with the Loyal and Patriotic Society of Upper Canada and it came directly from an exhortation of the Reverend John Strachan in which he declared that future historians would record that the militia "without the assistance of men or arms except a handful of regular troops" repelled the invasion.[24] This myth which the war itself had spawned was kept green and fresh long afterwards by the dominance of the Family Compact, the recurrence of the issues of loyalty versus republicanism, and the continuing fear of the United States.

In 1824 the government erected a monument to Sir Isaac Brock on the heights above Queenston and, when the remains of the general and his aide-de-camp were reinterred, a contemporary chronicler piously recorded that although "twelve years had elapsed since the interment, the body of the general had undergone little change, his features being nearly perfect and easily recognised, while that of Lieutenant Colonel McDonell was in a complete mass of decomposition."[25] When the monument was blown up in 1840 by a disaffected Irishman, a large crowd gathered at the site to consider building another, but two years later when Charles Dickens saw it, the column was still a "melancholy ruin." By 1856 another monument had been completed, much grander than the first one, taller, it was said, than any monument of either ancient or modern times, save Christopher Wren's memorial to the Great Fire of 1666. The aged worthies of the Compact, like Chief Justice J. B. Robinson, were again on hand to exalt the character of Brock and feed the militia legend.

For this generation the significance of Queenston Heights could only be rendered in the analogies of antiquity – Thermopylae, Marathon, Salamis. At the base of the peerless pillar were placed the busts of soldiers whose helmets, swords, and shields were emphatically classical. In patriotic orations, as in historical accounts of the war such as David Thompson's *History of the late war between Great Britain and the United States* (1832), Major John Richardson's *War of 1812* (1842), or Gilbert Auchinleck's *A History of the War between Great Britain and the United States* (1855), it was constantly emphasized that the

24 C. P. Stacey, "The War of 1812 in Canadian History," in M. Zaslow, ed., *The Defended Border* (Toronto, 1964), 333–4; G. F. G. Stanley, "The Contribution of the Canadian Militia During the War," in Philip R. Mason, ed., *After Tippecanoe: Some Aspects of the War of 1812* (Toronto, 1963), 28–48.

25 *The Battle of Queenston Heights: Being a Narrative of the Opening of the War of 1812, with Notices of the Life of Major General Sir Isaac Brock, K. B., and a description of the Monument Erected to His Memory*, edited by **John Symons, Esq.** (Toronto, 1859), 22–3.

British inhabitants of Upper Canada had taken up arms universally and that the chief significance of the conflict was that it demonstrated Canada's preference for the British connection and devotion to the British throne.

The remembrance of the War of 1812 and the celebration of the achievements of Brock and the militia were paralleled in the 1850s by the appearance of a body of literature extolling the United Empire Loyalists. Over seventy years by then had passed since the conclusion of the revolution had sent thousands of exiles into the northern forests. The last living links with the Simcoe era were expiring in the 1840s and it was the passage of this generation that first occasioned tributes to their character and political principles. While Egerton Ryerson believed that the United Empire Loyalists ceased to exist as a distinct class around 1815, it was the death of his father in 1854 which set him to thinking about recovering the memorabilia and documents to illustrate the life and times of those pioneers, "to vindicate their character as a body, to exhibit their principles and patriotism."[26] In a sermon preached at Trinity Church in St John, New Brunswick, in 1857, another divine took as his text "One generation passeth away, and another generation cometh" and sought to show that the central principle of the loyalists, their allegiance to the Crown, was firmly rooted in Biblical precepts and was still a vital principle which should shine as a beacon for the new generation.[27]

Though William Kirby's long poem, *The U.E.: A Tale of Upper Canada*, was completed thirteen years before its publication at Niagara in 1859, it was also, according to the preface, intended to "preserve traits of a generation of men, now alas! nearly passed away." Even more suggestive than this straightforward declaration is the actual plot of Kirby's epic. It does not deal primarily with the original loyalist migration at all, but centres on the arrival of Walwyn and his sons in the Niagara peninsula in the years after the Napoleonic wars. Walwyn, it is true, meets an old loyalist who communicates to the new arrivals the story of Indian warfare and scalping expeditions of the revolutionary days, but the main events of *The U.E.* involve the repulse of the American attack on Prescott Mill in the late 1830s. Kirby makes it clear that loyalty, and the host of virtues subsumed in that word, is not some peculiar attribute of the loyalists of 1784 or their descendants – indeed, he himself came to Canada only after the rebellions and re-

26 Egerton Ryerson, *The Loyalists of America and Their Times* (Toronto, 1880), II, 191.
27 Rev. J. W. D. Gray, *A Sermon preached at Trinity Church, in the Parish of St. John, N.B., on the 8th December, 1857, ... Designed to Recommend the Principles of the Loyalists of 1783* (St John, 1857).

ferred to himself as "the last of the loyalists" – but rather that loyalty stems from a particular social order and the agrarian life and that allegiance to an hierarchical order, the Church of England and the British form of government, are communicable, are, in fact, already a tradition. The virtual disappearance of the first-generation loyalists, he implies, does not affect the persistence of the ideology for which they fought. The purpose of *The U.E.* was to preserve the loyalist tradition as Kirby interpreted it and to hold it aloft as an inspiration and moving force to a generation which had no personal experience of "the heroic age."

In the 1850s, the celebration of the loyalist virtues and the victory of 1812 arose out of a conscious British-Canadian patriotism as well as from simple nostalgia and a didactic desire to inculcate conservative principles. What infused these symbols with such emotional force in the 1860s was the national spirit generated under the impact of the Civil War in the United States and the achievement of Confederation. In 1864 when another invasion from the south seemed imminent, one commentator revealed the emotional meaning evoked by the very symbol – 1812:

It carries with it the virtue of an incantation. Like the magic numerals of the Arabian sage, these words, in their utterance, quicken the pulse, and vibrate through the frame, summoning, from the pregnant past, memories of suffering and endurance and of honorable exertion. They are inscribed on the banner and stamped on the hearts of the Canadian people – a watchword, rather than a war-cry.[28]

The nationalistic desire to trace the life of the nation to its roots, to exalt its founders and defenders, not only gave an immense stimulus to historical work in general, but also nourished inherited traditions which otherwise might have withered away. D'Arcy McGee and the young men of Canada First fully realized that history was the most effective of all instruments for instilling a sense of national unity. "Patriotism," McGee once said, "will increase in Canada as its history is read."[29] In his Canada First address of 1871, William Foster summoned Canadians to realize the heroic elements in their history and assured them that the consciousness of a common past would provide a bond of union.

Though the quickening interest in the past originated in the nationalist impulse, it was sustained by other forces and examples. At the very

28 William F. Coffin, *1812: The War and Its Moral: A Canadian Chronicle* (Montreal, 1864), 18.
29 Thomas D'Arcy McGee, *Speeches and Addresses chiefly on the Subject of British-American Union* (London, 1865), 94.

time that Canadians were calling for a national historical literature, the volumes of Francis Parkman were flowing from the press. His description of life under the French regime was regarded not only as one of the finest efforts of the historical imagination but also as an outstanding example of what could be accomplished with the materials and themes of Canadian history. While a later generation of historians would both question Parkman's reputation for exactitude and repudiate the assumptions which guided his work and frequently obtruded throughout his narrative, his influence upon Canadian historiography was greater than that of any other individual during the nineteenth century. Canadian historians copied his books extensively; they imitated his prose style, usually with little success; they incorporated his judgments of the French Canadians and the old regime because they obviously shared them; and reviewers invariably compared Canadian books to his. While one critic said of Parkman that he had "invaded"[30] the field of Canadian history, a more typical judgment was that of William Withrow, editor of the *Methodist Magazine*, who wrote that the American's work "is not exceeded in extent nor, we think, in fidelity to truth, in careful research, in ability and interest by the great works of Gibbon, Grote, Hume, Macaulay." Withrow urged every Canadian to "study the fascinating story of the founding of Canada by the brave pioneers of empire whom the genius of Parkman has made to live and move and act again."[31] By demonstrating to nationalists who were so conscious of the uses of the past that there were large issues like the struggle between liberty and absolutism, as well as heroic figures and romantic incidents in Canadian history, Parkman came to enjoy a popularity among Canadians which could not be approached by Motley, Prescott, Green, or Macaulay, all of whom dealt with themes external to Canada and whose writings, though popular, did not have the same immediacy.

Scarcely less influential than Parkman in strengthening the conception of romantic history and in inspiring the retrospective spirit was the example of Sir Walter Scott. The Bard of Abbotsford had long before rejected the universalist doctrines of the enlightenment and the age of cold reason and had retreated into the attractive lore of the borderland. The historical novels in which he sought to recapture the delicate and fragile strands of medieval traditions, to savour the texture of locale, and to focus on organic relationships were extremely popular in mid-nineteenth-century English Canada, and they gave a strong stimulus to the development of the historical romance and the attempt

30 T. G. Marquis, "English-Canadian Literature," in A. Shortt and A. G. Doughty, eds., *Canada and Its Provinces* (Toronto, 1914), xii, 496.

31 *Methodist Magazine*, xxxii (July 1890), 87.

to recapture the traditions and legends of Canadian regions. While Charles Mair read a good deal of Scott during his boyhood, the most enthusiastic devotees of the bard's works were William Kirby and his friend, Sir James LeMoine of Quebec. LeMoine published many essays describing the natural beauty and local history of the St Lawrence and one of these sketches became the basis for Kirby's *The Golden Dog* (1877), an historical novel set in the last days of New France. Kirby found in Scott's borderland tales the perfect technique with which to describe the loyalist tradition in the Niagara region as well as the chivalric and hierarchical social order of the French society on the St Lawrence. And even more than LeMoine, Kirby also accepted the anti-industrial philosophy which underpinned Scott's toryism. What Scott had done for the borderland and LeMoine for the St Lawrence, Kirby set out to do for the loyalists of Niagara. If Mark Twain exaggerated when he held Scott responsible for the American Civil War, because his novels of chivalry and romance helped to sustain the Southerners' mystique of the conservative plantation life, then it would be no more of an exaggeration to say that, at least as far as Kirby was concerned, Scott also helped to inspire the Canadian loyalist tradition. Romanticized versions of incidents in Canadian history, especially the War of 1812, abounded in the late nineteenth century and were presented in dramas like Charles Mair's *Tecumseh* (1886) and Sarah Anne Curzon's *Laura Secord* (1887), in poetical collections like William Kirby's *Canadian Idylls* (1888), and in children's novels like Agnes Maule Machar's *For King and Country* (1874).

During the 1880s a novel and discordant note of pessimism crept into the pleas for a national history and the invocations to remain true to the past. While the exuberant and optimistic nationalism represented by the Canada Firsters stimulated the desire to popularize Canadian history, even more influential in promoting the appeal to tradition were the economic depression and political upheavals of the 1880s. It is in times of trial that the sense of nostalgia for a heroic history is heightened and in the midst of turbulence and change that traditions are most useful for maintaining the assurance of security. The mood of doubt, disillusionment, and uncertainty which culminated in the late 1880s provoked many of the appeals to the certainties of the past. "We should study the history of the past for our guidance in the present," wrote G. M. Grant in a review of yet another volume from the industrious and unimaginative Kingsford. "History is indeed that revelation which, as Carlyle says, no one in or out of Bedlam can question. Most of all should the lover of his country, anxious that the good ship should steer a steady course, know all that can be known of the views of those who built and freighted her." Changing metaphors, and revealing his deep conservative respect for the organic continuity of the generations, Grant emphasized that a nation is an "organization," or organism, "and every break in the continuity of its life is injurious. In vain have been the thoughts, the wisdom and the sacrifices of our fathers, as far as we are concerned, unless we take the trouble to understand the principles on which they acted. Especially when clouds overhang our future," he emphasized "is there the greater need to look to the past for light. If we do so [,] we shall find that, notwithstanding differences in circumstances, the identity of principles may easily be discerned."[32] That there were "principles" embedded in Canadian history and that allegiance to these principles was a sacred obligation of their own generation, was an attitude implicitly shared by many Canadian imperialists and certainly by the majority of those who believed themselves faithful to loyalist principles. It was largely this conservative frame of mind which made the loyalist tradition so meaningful and which made history itself appear so central to nationalism, so necessary in time of crisis.

Despite the fervent appeals for a national history, the bulk of Canadian historical literature written in the late nineteenth century was narrowly local, even parochial, in character. The period was truly the golden age of local history and the local historical society became the chief instrument for popularizing the past. Between 1882 and 1896 no less than fifteen local historical organizations appeared in Ontario alone and, though some of these actually represented the enthusiasm of only a few devoted individuals, their appearance none the less did mark a substantial growth of an interest in history. The proliferation of these societies in Ontario and the other provinces was one aspect of a wider North American concern with local history. In the decade after 1880 over eighty similar societies were established in the United States[33] and Canadians explained their own purposes and worded their appeals for government funds in terms of the American example. The founders and members of the historical societies were not primarily concerned with disinterested and detached antiquarianism. These societies were dedicated to "establish and strengthen the spirit of patriotism among all classes of people in Canada, by circulating patriotic literature, by public lectures and readings," by celebrating "notable anniversaries," conducting military reinterments, and erecting monuments.[34]

The chief purpose of the Pioneer and Historical Association of

32 *Week*, IX (Aug. 12, 1892), 586.
33 David Van Tassel, *Recording America's Past: An Interpretation of the Development of Historical Studies in America, 1607–1884* (Chicago, 1960), 186–90.
34 *Seventh Annual Report of The Lundy's Lane Historical Society, July 25, 1894.*

Ontario, its president announced, "is to foster the spirit of British Canadian nationality, which shall remain strong and steadfast for generations to come."[35] In keeping with this avowed purpose their publications were almost exclusively devoted to the hardships of the United Empire Loyalists and the incidents of the War of 1812. One of their more macabre activities was the reinterment of the bones of soldiers who had been killed during the war and whose remains had either been buried with little care at the time or remained outside consecrated soil. The buckles and buttons recovered were treated like religious relics; one reinterment ceremony at Lundy's Lane was referred to as a "Holy Task."[36] The association also led the agitation for the building of monuments commemorating engagements of the War of 1812 and by the later 1890s had secured government financial support for the erection of memorials to keep fresh the memory of the victories at Lundy's Lane, Crysler's Farm, and Chateauguay. There is much to be said for regarding these historical societies as branches of the Imperial Federation League.

The rhetoric of the imperialists like Denison, as well as of defenders of the national protectionist policy like Macdonald in 1891, was pervaded by the retrospective spirit. In his last election address in 1891, Macdonald pointed to the many "material objections" against unrestricted reciprocity and said that these were not "the most vital." He appealed to the descendants of those French pioneers who had brought civilization to the wilderness and he invoked the memory of that loyal band of British subjects who had given up everything that men prize most and began life anew in hardship in order to maintain their allegiance to their sovereign. Of the descendants he asked, "what have you to gain by surrendering that which your fathers held most dear?"[37] An officer of the Imperial Federation League recalled that presenting the argument as one between unrestricted reciprocity and continentalism against the British connection "enabled us to appeal to the old dream of the United Empire Loyalists ... It gave the opportunity of appealing to our history, to the sacrifices of our fathers ... and the victories of the war of 1812."[38] In the months preceding the election, Denison and his friends arranged demonstrations in the public schools to celebrate "Canada's glorious Thermopylae," the Battle of Queenston Heights, and the *Empire* offered a flag for the finest essay on the

35 Address of Canon Bull, Pioneer and Historical Association of the Province of Ontario, *Proceedings and Annual Report, 1895–96* (n.p., n.d.), 9.
36 *Dominion Illustrated: A Canadian Pictorial Weekly*, VII (Nov. 21, 1891), 487.
37 Sir Joseph Pope, *Memoirs of the Right Honorable Sir John Alexander Macdonald* (Toronto, n.d.), 776.
38 Denison, *Struggle*, 85.

subject of the patriotic influence of raising the flag over the school houses.[39] When Goldwin Smith asked whether it was really "loyal to turn our Public Schools into seedplots of international enmity by implanting hatred of the Americans in the breasts of our children?" and when he lamented that two generations had not effaced "the evil memories of 1812,"[40] Denison's retort was to say that all virile people had a national sentiment and that only the inculcation of Canadian patriotism would defeat the annexationist policy.

Few imperialists were in a more strategic position for employing history to arouse national sentiment than Denison's friend, Sir George Ross, minister of education of Ontario between 1883 and 1899 and subsequently premier of that province. Ross supported efforts to teach more Canadian history in the schools and his *Patriotic Recitations and Arbor Day Exercises* (1893), a book of instructions and readings designed to help teachers celebrate Canadian and imperial holidays, bore on its fly-leaf Bismarck's dictum: "We owe to our schools the thankful task of strengthening the feeling that we are all Germans." Ross gave firm personal backing to the suggestion made by a member of the Wentworth Historical Society that a day be set aside in all schools for patriotic exercises. The result was Canada's original contribution to the calendar of imperial festivities – Empire Day, first celebrated in May 1899. That celebration, one Canadian magazine proclaimed, should be

> a gathering up of the patriotic fragments of the school year for a right loyal feast – a day when our history, past and present, might be enrolled with becoming dignity and ceremonial; a day when our national hymns and patriotic songs might be heard and our hearts set a-glow with the recital of the heroism of the United Empire Loyalists, and our sons live over in their boy-life the Homeric age of Canada.[41]

According to its authors this occasion was not intended to be a holiday; it was calculated to provide an opportunity in which the reality of the Empire and Canada's place within it were to be impressed on the minds of the young.

There was no better way to arouse popular interest in the past than in commemorative exhibitions. In 1876 at Philadelphia the United States had celebrated the centennial of the Declaration of Independence with

39 *Empire*, Oct. 9 and 14, 1890.
40 Goldwin Smith, *Loyalty, Aristocracy and Jingoism: Three Lectures Delivered Before the Young Men's Liberal Club* (Toronto, 1891), 24; *Canada and the Canadian Question* (Toronto, 1891), 108.
41 *Canadian Magazine*, xxi (May 1903), 78–9. For the history of Empire Day see Castell Hopkins, *The Origins and History of Empire Day* (n.p., 1910).

massive display, and the spread-eagle oratory was directed at strengthening national unity, especially in reuniting the North and the South, and at extolling the material progress of the nation as evidence of the soundness of republican institutions. Canadians of the loyalist persuasion saw in the American centennial attempts to vilify their ancestors in particular and demonstrations of hostility to British America in general. They responded with the loyalist centennial celebration in 1884 and renewed their ancestors' pledges of fidelity to the British Crown and the unity of the Empire. Canadian nationalists allowed few other anniversaries to slip by unnoticed and uncelebrated. The one-hundredth anniversary of the Constitutional Act of 1791, the four-hundredth anniversary of the voyage of the Cabots, and the three-hundredth anniversary of the founding of Quebec were made focal points for reminding Canadians of their heritage.

The cultural milieu in which the loyalist tradition flourished was one in which men had discovered the utility of history for inculcating national sentiment. The tradition was conceived in response to the deeply felt need to create a cohesive national heritage and it represented an attempt to impart an historical dimension to conceptions of British-Canadian nationality. Had it originated only as a negative reaction to the "independence flurry" or as a cult to exalt the patriotic status of particular individuals, the tradition would not have exerted such a powerful impetus to imperialism.

V

The loyalist tradition began, as did all myths of national origins, with the assertion that the founders of British Canada were God's chosen people. Partly because so many exponents of the tradition were themselves descendants of the loyalists and partly because of the necessities of nationalist hagiography, the original United Empire Loyalists were portrayed as a superior, cultured, and elevated class of men. They were, it was maintained, "the very cream of the population of the Thirteen Colonies. They represented ... the learning, the piety, the gentle birth, the wealth and good citizenship of the British race in America."[42] William Kirby said that the loyalists included "judges, lawyers, legislators, clergymen, soldiers, merchants, yeomen and handicraftmen" and that they were of "the purest blood" of the old colonies.[43] And

42 James H. Coyne, "Memorial to the United Empire Loyalists," Niagara Historical Society, no. 4 (Niagara-on-the-Lake, 1898), 8.
43 *Centennial of the Settlement of Upper Canada*, 109–10.

J. G. Bourinot testified that "No country in the world ever received a higher class of immigrants."[44] Just as the Puritan divine had once boasted that England had been winnowed of her choicest people for the migration to New England, the loyalist descendants declared that the population of America itself was sifted and "its very choicest men selected by Providence for the peopling of this Dominion!" The United States was thus drained of "their noblest elements" and "suffered a moral loss which they have never made up for to this day." The migration of the United Empire Loyalists, declared the Chancellor of Victoria University in the modern language of evolution, "was the 'natural selection,' to borrow Darwin's phrase, which sifted these sixty thousand out from the three million of the Colonists."[45] Like the mythical account of the origins of the American people which was popularized by Southern patriots in the pre–Civil War period, this conception of the loyalist origins of British Canada had much more relevance as a symbol of nationalism than as an objective explanation of the past. The Southern myth, which maintained that the founders of the slave states were the aristocratic cavaliers of the English Civil War and the Yankees descendants of the plebian Roundheads, obscured the real social origins of the first settlers in the American South; similarly, the loyalist cult inaccurately portrayed the founders of British Canada. For whatever might be said about the genteel social backgrounds of the Maritime loyalists, the majority of these refugees who came to the upper St Lawrence and the Niagara region were farmers and frontiersmen and assuredly not what Kirby meant by the very best blood of the old colonies.

According to the tradition, the most important characteristic of the loyalists, apart from their social prominence, was their attachment to principle. The chief evidence of this steadfast adherence to moral values was their behaviour during the American Revolution. Writing during the late 1860s, "a period of great irritation to Canadians," William Canniff argued that the central cause of the colonial revolt was that the rebels were "actuated mainly by mercenary motives, unbounded selfishness and bigotry." The Declaration of Independence was concocted by smugglers, office seekers, and slave-owners, and it was only a last resort taken "when the king's forces required taxes; when they could not dispossess the tories of the power and emoluments of office."[46] The "boasted struggle for liberty," Denison concurred, "was closely mixed up with a desire on the part of the masses to rob and despoil those who

44 Bourinot, "The United Empire Loyalists of Canada," 131.
45 Burwash, "The Moral Character of the U.E. Loyalists," 59.
46 William Canniff, *History of the Settlement of Upper Canada (Ontario) with special reference to the Bay Quinté* (Toronto, 1869), vi–vii, 45–6.

had acquired property." The "lawless elements" were led by impe-
cunious lawyers and unsuccessful merchants, by shipowners who lived
by smuggling, and by men on the verge of bankruptcy."[47] To under-
score the selfish and pecuniary motives of the rebels not only provided
a way of contrasting the loyalists' sacrifice for "principles" but tended
as well to identify republicanism with disobedience, lawlessness, and
vulgar materialism. While the rebels were "unprincipled," moved only
by the prospects of gain, the loyalists were motivated by religious precepts. The loyalists, said Canniff, "were honest, devoted, loyal, truthful,
lawabiding and actuated by the higher motives which spring from
religion."[48] They obeyed the sacred precept of scripture – "Fear God
and honour the king." Kirby thought it a fact of immense significance
"that the U.E. Loyalists, leaving all other possessions behind them,
brought with them the ten commandments, the Bible, and the sacred
vessels of the communion, as the most precious relics of their old
homes." Just as the United States lost its "best blood" by the loyalist
exodus, so too a huge blank was left by the removal of the religious
influence upon society, a loss which "American history is now daily
recording."[49]

In the loyalist lore the records of individual suffering were lovingly
culled and retold, usually with much emotion and embellishment. The
sacrifices of property, position, and comfort which the loyalists made
were central to the literature of the tradition. "In some instances," ran
one account of these privations, "the cattle that were browsed upon
felled trees in the forest were from time to time bled, that the blood
might be had for food, so fierce and close was the struggle for life."
Less horrendous but equally touching was the spectacle of "ladies
brought up in luxury and comfort [who] might be seen in the early
spring woods gathering in their aprons and baskets the swelling buds
of the basswood for food for themselves and for their children."[50]
Whether expressed in poetical form, as in William Kirby's "The Hungry
Year," or in Canniff's densely detailed description of the early settlement of Upper Canada, the record of hunger, the tales of old bones
passed from household to household to provide sustenance in times of
famine, offered irrefutable proof and confirmation of the loyalists'

47 G. T. Denison, "The United Empire Loyalists and their Influence Upon the
   History of this Continent," Royal Society of Canada, *Proceedings and Transactions*, second series, part I, 1905, XXXI. This address is virtually the same as
   his article, "The United Empire Loyalists," in J. Castell Hopkins, ed., *Canada:
   An Encyclopaedia of the Country* (Toronto, 1898), I, 104–19.
48 Canniff, *History of the Settlement of Upper Canada*, 625.
49 *Centennial of the Settlement of Upper Canada*, 110–11.
50 *A Centenary Study, Upper Canada. A Paper Read Before the Lundy's Lane
   Historical Society*, by the Rev. E. J. Fessenden, B.A., Rector of Chippawa,
   Ont. (n.p., n.d.), 21–2.

allegiance to principle and indicated testimony of God's stewardship. Not for nothing was the loyalist exodus most often compared to the Israeli's flight from Egypt.

It was reiterated that the loyalists did not come to Canada to better their condition, to secure land, or to flee persecution. They went forth, said Chancellor Burwash, "to face discomfort and poverty and suffering and want for the sake of their principles."[51] Though the definition of these principles differed slightly in various formulations of the tradition, the two central ideas at the heart of the loyalist legacy were taken to be the "British constitution" and the ideal of imperial unity. It was these two principles that the United Empire Loyalists had defended, preserved, and transmitted to all Canadians. And it was obligatory, a "sacred trust," that these two principles be in turn passed on intact and unimpaired to the future.

Because the United Empire Loyalists made a deliberate choice at the time of the revolution for monarchical institutions over republicanism and because they established British North America upon this secure basis, it was to them that Canadians owed the fact that they lived in the freest country on the face of the globe, that they enjoyed the highest type of political freedom, and that they inherited by birthright all the principles of British constitutional liberty. In the loyalist tradition the "British constitution" was identified with a deeply conservative instinct as well as with a particular body of representative institutions, procedures, and customs. It was praised not only because it was "British" but because it was conservative. All explanations of the loyalist legacy and all attempts to suggest what the principle of loyalty itself encompassed, evoked the leading postulates of traditional Burkean conservatism. The analogies which were employed to explain it were those of natural and organic life; the words which appear most often in the loyalist rhetoric were order, stability, allegiance, service, law-abiding, authority, tradition, inheritance, continuity. In a sermon preached in St John, New Brunswick, in 1857, Reverend J. W. D. Gray set forth the central conviction of the old loyalists and urged his parishioners to diligently cultivate "that spirit of *submission to lawful authority* which lies at the foundation of loyalty to your earthly Sovereign."[52]

All appeals for loyalty harked back to this spirit. A text-book history of Canada, published in 1876, explained that the adherents of the royal cause in the revolution "felt that loyalty to the sovereign was

51 Burwash, "The Moral Character of the U.E. Loyalists," 59; for a similar statement of their motives see Alexander Fraser, ed., *Brock Centenary, 1812–1912: Account of the Celebrations at Queenston Heights, Ontario, on the 12th October, 1912* (Toronto, 1913), 45.
52 Gray, *A Sermon Preached at Trinity Church*, 14. Italics in original.

their first and highest duty," an obligation enjoined upon them by instinct, tradition, and the religious precepts to fear God, honour the king, and "be subject unto the higher powers; for there is no power but of God."[53] Loyalty, said Egerton Ryerson, was not merely a sentiment or emotional affection for the representative or person of the sovereign; "it is a reverence for, and attachment to, the laws, order, institutions and freedom of the country."[54] Loyalty in its simplest and most recurrent formulation was a reverence for law and order and a desire to be peaceably and quietly governed. This respect for order and authority was, according to Colonel Denison, the "great doctrine," the "foremost article" of the United Empire Loyalist creed,[55] and it was also the central principle of the British constitution.

What the loyalists brought to Canada in 1783 was not the actual institutional apparatus of the British constitution, but, more important, its inner spirit. Behind this insistence upon authority rested a train of assumptions dear to the tory mind – the respect for history, the primacy of the community over individual selfishness, society conceived as an organism of functionally related parts and structured to reflect different human aptitudes, religion as the mortar of the social order, and the distrust of materialism. Rarely were these convictions made explicit, partly because those who believed them had inherited them and accepted them without much thought, partly because the conservative mind in general engages reluctantly in political speculation and displays an aversion to spinning out theories. It was when the Canadian tory viewed the social turbulence and violent disruptions in the United States during the late nineteenth century that he became, as will be seen, more explicit about his preferences and even more convinced of the wisdom of the forefathers.

The second principle for which the loyalists had made their sacrifice was the ideal of imperial unity. The "arduous and glorious task to which Providence had assigned them," wrote one historian, was "to transplant in this new soil British laws and British institutions, and to guard and transmit to their successors the germ of a great idea – the solidarity of the British race and empire."[56] The moving principle of duty in the hearts of our forefathers, said Kirby, was "To keep the empire one in unity."[57] Even Liberals like George Ross, who could not accept the authoritarianism which the loyalists had espoused, nevertheless hailed

53 Lovell's History of the Dominion of Canada and other parts of British America (Montreal, 1876), 122.
54 Ryerson, Loyalists of America, II, 449.
55 Denison, "The United Empire Loyalists and their Influence ... ," xxxi.
56 Coyne, "Memorial to the United Empire Loyalists," 5.
57 Centenial of the Settlement of Upper Canada, 124.

them as "Imperial Federationists All" and contended that "the first impulse towards that imperialism which so marks the colonial feelings of to-day, came from that little band of exiles."[58] Colonel Denison informed the Royal Society of Canada that the whole issue of imperial federation was "really the question of endorsing and approving and endeavouring to carry into effect the principles for which the United Empire Loyalists struggled and fought."[59] This identification of the loyalist legacy with Canadian imperialism did not depend primarily upon the fact that the loyalists had ostensibly fought to prevent the disruption of the Empire and it certainly did not stem from the knowledge that at the time of the revolution they had advanced plans to give colonials representation in the imperial parliament. In the loyalist tradition the ideal of imperial unity was presented as a Canadian, not a British, idea. "Imperial Federation [is] of Colonial – not of English – origin," wrote George Parkin.[60] Had the loyalists not made their stand for imperial unity in 1776, it was often implied, there would have been no Empire in 1880. The motherland had betrayed the ideal of imperial unity in her free-trade aberration, when her public men accepted Turgot's view that colonies must inevitably fall away like ripe apples from the tree of empire. It was the United Empire Loyalists who remained faithful to the "national idea," as Parkin termed it, and nurtured it in Canada. The imperial revival in Britain in the late 1860s and early 1870s seemed but a return to the ideals of the Canadian loyalists.

Not only had the United Empire Loyalists practically originated this idea of imperialism, they had also defended it virtually alone. Within the framework of this tradition, which took the central theme of Canadian history to be adherence and allegiance to the principles of the British constitution and imperial unity, the most meaningful episode was the defence of Canada in the War of 1812 by the loyalists and their descendants. In the year 1812, declared a minister in 1888,

> when our peaceful Canadian settlements were invaded by hordes from the neighbouring Republic ... Loyalist heroes, now advanced in years, with their sons at their side, fought under General Brock and other noble soldiers. Invasion followed invasion, but at the end of the struggle not a single inch of Canadian territory had been

58 G. W. Ross, "Some Characteristics of United Empire Loyalists, and their Influence on Canadian History," *The United Empire Loyalist Association of Ontario, Annual Transactions, March 9, 1899* (Toronto, 1899), 39.
59 Denison, "The United Empire Loyalists and their Influence ... ," xxxix.
60 G. R. Parkin, "Imperial Federation," *McGill University Magazine*, I (April, 1902), 185; see also, Sir George R. Parkin Papers, vol. 66, MS "The Historical Relation of Canada To The Idea of A United Empire," n.d.

wrested from the British Crown. Thus we owe it mainly to the U.E. Patriots that one half the Continent of North America remains to-day under British rule.[61]

The loyalist tradition fused the militia legend which had originated early in the nineteenth century with the cult of the loyalists. In the invocations to loyalism it was repeatedly stressed that the burden of defending Canada in the War of 1812 fell upon Canadians. Great Britain, wrote one historian, was exhausted by nearly twenty years of conflict and still engaged in a strenuous struggle against Napoleon. Until near the close of the war she could furnish only scanty military aid.[62] With little outside support and outnumbered by the Americans, the patriotic yeomanry of Upper Canada "forsook ploughshare and broadaxe, seized sword and musket, and rallied to the standard of Brock ... Every clearing became a drill-hall, every log cabin an armoury."[63] It was even implied that had not inept British generals like Provost interfered the militia might have overthrown the republic.

The militia legend was the very heart of the loyalist tradition for two reasons. Firstly, to emphasize the role of the regular British soldiers would have tended to subtract from the fame of the loyalist settlers and deprive the war of its national meaning. In the nationalist myth, it was the *Canadian* people who repelled invasion, and for the keepers of the tradition the Canadian people included the French Canadians. "We do not exclude the French of Lower Canada," said Canniff, "... for we remember how they stood firmly by the side of our fathers in the fight for Old England in 1776 and 1812."[64] "There is no French or English when our country's rights are in question," another enthusiast told the Lundy's Lane Historical Society, "we are all Canadians."[65] The second reason why the role of the militia was inflated in the tradition was because they had defended and preserved imperial unity. The war, wrote James Hannay in the preface to his history of the conflict entitled *How Canada Was Held for the Empire* (1905), "ought to be regarded as Canada's first and greatest contribution to the work of empire building." When critics of the imperial connection like Goldwin

61 Rev. R. S. Forneri, *The United Empire Loyalists and the Memorial Church, Adolphustown, Ontario* (Belleville, Ont., 1888), 6–7.
62 Rev W. H. Withrow, *A Popular History of Canada* (Toronto, 1885), 340.
63 W. R. Nursey, *The Story of Isaac Brock: hero, defender and saviour of Upper Canada, 1812* (Toronto, 1908), 82.
64 *Centennial of the Settlement of Upper Canada*, 22–3.
65 *Canada in Memoriam. 1812–14. Her Duty in the Erection of Monuments in Memory of her Distinguished Sons and Daughters. A Paper read July 25, 1890, by Mrs. Curzon, of Toronto, at the Annual Commemoration of the Battle of Lundy's Lane, of 1814, before the Lundy's Lane Historical Society* (Welland, 1891), 5.

Smith argued that loyalty was nothing but dependence upon British protection, or that Canadians never had and never would make a genuine contribution to the defence of the Empire in which they took such a verbose pride, the response of the loyalist was to point to the War of 1812 as evidence that the burden of imperial defence had not been borne by Britain alone.

Scarcely less eminent in the loyalist tradition was the figure of General Brock. Praise of him stretched the resources of the language as well as the historical record. Biographical accounts customarily noted that he was born in 1769, "the same year which gave birth to Napoleon and Wellington."[66] Denison called Brock "the greatest national hero of Canada"[67] and Charles Mair asserted that "the Canadian people ... look upon him as the Americans look upon Washington."[68] Books of children's stories referred to the British soldier as "our own."[69] From the poet Charles Sangster came the ultimate apotheosis:

> Some souls are the Hesperides
> Heaven sends to guard the golden age,
> Illuming the historic page
> With records of their pilgrimage;
> True Martyr, Hero, Poet, Sage:
> And he was one of these.[70]

Brock came to hold such an exalted place in the loyalist tradition because his death at Queenston Heights was associated with the victory of the militia. That battle occurred during the opening phases of the war when Canada was almost denuded of British troops and the defence had to rely upon the yeomanry more than at any other time during the conflict. Since it was under the leadership of Brock that the people rose up to preserve Canada for the Empire, the hero-worship of Brock and the militia legend were indissolubly fused.

The United Empire Loyalists, then, were described as the makers, founders, and defenders of Canada because it was they who laid the basis of those institutions and habits of thought which their admirers regarded as the cornerstones of Canadian nationality. The tradition

66 Coffin, *1812: The War and Its Moral*, 36.
67 G. T. Denison, *Soldiering in Canada* (Toronto, 1900), 17.
68 Charles Mair, *Tecumseh: A Drama* (Toronto, 1886), "Notes," 198.
69 Agnes Maul Machar and T. G. Marquis, *Heroes of Canada* (Toronto, 1893), 85; Katherine A. Young, *Stories of the Maple Land: Tales of the Early Days of Canada for Children* (Toronto, 1898), 111.
70 Charles Sangster, "Brock," in W. D. Lighthall, ed., *Songs of the Great Dominion* (London, 1889), 254–5.

credited them with implanting in Canada the British constitution and the impulse towards imperial unity. To preserve the one and work toward the realization of the other were treated as a sacred duty because the entire tradition was predicated upon the belief that the past, or history, exercised obligations upon the present. Society was an organism with roots stretching back into history; to disturb those subtle and delicate strands of continuity, or what Egerton Ryerson once called "the mysterious links of connection between grandfather and grandson,"[71] was itself an unholy thing leading to disastrous consequences. The loyalist tradition symbolized the preservation of continuity of British national life in the new world and it enjoined all Canadians to maintain that connection. For the loyalists had brought to Canada not only the particular principles of the British constitution and imperial unity, but the entire corpus of cultural and political accomplishment of the British people. The consciousness and realization of the fact that Canadians enjoyed this heritage because of the sacrifices of their own ancestors imparted a peculiar psychology to Canadian imperialism.

The descendants of the United Empire Loyalists did not claim that Canadians possessed the most desirable form of government solely because of the beneficence of Englishmen, nor did they call for admittance to the governance of the Empire in a tone of servility. When critics like Norris denounced their obsequious colonialism, he misinterpreted the very decided and independent attitude of men like Denison. It is quite true, of course, that one of the refrains most often invoked by them was the boast that Canadians, because they were British subjects, could legitimately take pride in belonging to a great and powerful Empire. Beneath this boast may be discerned a feeling that Canada was insufficient and restricting. Many appeals for imperial unity dwelt upon what one proponent called the "sense of exclusion, the want of weight" which bore heavily upon Canadian minds.[72] "At present," another imperialist added in 1897, "the issues Canadian statesmen have to deal with are too restricted ... How petty our interests, how small most of our public questions, how narrow our sympathies."[73] Canada, in short, was confining, powerless, new, and raw; the allegiance to the Empire offered compensation. But this sense of belonging was frequently transformed into a desire for participation. Echoing Kirby's remark to Tennyson, an imperialist saluted "Our Empire" and said that "It is just as much ours as it is the empire of the British people living in any part

71 Ryerson, *Loyalists of America*, II, 449.
72 *Canada and the Empire: A Speech by Gilbert Malcolm Sproat, Agent-General for British Columbia* (London, 1873), 8.
73 Francis Blake Crofton, *For Closer Union: Some Slight Offerings to a Great Cause* (Halifax, 1897), 7.

of it."[74] In insisting that the Empire was theirs, these Canadians were resting their claims upon their status as Britons and their right to possession upon the fact that it was their forefathers who had made the sacrifices for the Empire in North America. Canadian imperialism centred on the hope that Canadians would eventually attain full citizenship within the Empire and acquire a huge influence – some would say a controlling influence – over its affairs. The loyalist tradition coloured this imperialism; it was the vehicle for a curious variety of Canadian nationalism.

Because of this, those imperialists who did not share any family connections with the original loyalists none the less regarded the United Empire Loyalists as a symbol of imperialism. Charles Mair, for example, told Denison that there was something distinctive and definite about the phrase in 1812 but in 1884 he believed "it applicable all round to those who think that the destinies of our people in all parts of the world are to be wrought out through a close attachment of the whole imperial system." In that sense, "I feel that I am as much a U.E. Loyalist as you or anybody."[75] Again and again the advocates of imperial unity returned to identify their cause with the founders of Canada and claimed that they were working within the tradition for identical ends. For those Canadians the very word "imperialism" conjured up the image of the loyalists, their sacrifices and ideals. The loyalist tradition gave to Canadian imperialism a domestic and native tone, a feeling that the movement grew out of Canada's own past and was part and parcel of Canadian history. It also imparted to imperialism an almost indescribable sense of mission and destiny. Though the tradition began with a defeat, its custodians did not think of themselves as a vanquished people. Their psychology was exactly the opposite of defeatism. Out of disaster in 1783, the United Empire Loyalists had seized victory in 1812 and had established in Canada a form of government which was superior to republicanism. They had also implanted the ideal of imperial unity to which the motherland was returning. The British Empire belonged to Canadians, the power it represented was rightly theirs to share, because of the sacrifices of the loyalists. Animated by this vision, the loyalist descendants and those who regarded the United Empire Loyalists as the founders of the nation looked forward to the steady extension of Canadian authority until it overshadowed the power of the republic from which their ancestors had fled. In the loyalist tradition imperialism was a form of redemption.

74 *Imperial Federation League in Canada: Speech Delivered at Paris, Ont., on January 19th, 1888, by Alex. McNeill, M.P., Vice-President* (n.p., n.d.), 6.
75 G. T. Denison Papers, Mair to Denison, Nov. 29, 1884.

4

Progress and Liberty

Canadian imperialism was dominated by appeals to the past primarily because its exponents regarded history as the repository of enduring and valuable principles and not because they sought to escape into some secure and idealized Heroic Age. Convinced that Canadian development must proceed in harmony with these principles, the imperialists felt they had to define and defend them. This is why so large a portion of the literature that was ostensibly calculated to promote imperial unity dwelt instead upon Canadian history and especially upon the achievements of the United Empire Loyalists. In addition to exalting the loyalist tradition, imperialists contended that the history of the Dominion was essentially the story of material progress and the steady advance of liberty and self-government. For them, all Canadian history was ceaselessly moving toward one irrefragable conclusion – the acquisition of full national rights and freedom within an imperial federation.

I

This conception of history was rooted in the belief in progress, in the conviction that history was the record of steady improvement in material conditions and in intellectual and moral life. The idea of progress was the major certitude of Victorian culture and the extent of progress was invariably measured in material terms because it was assumed that the physical surroundings exercised a powerful role in shaping the human mind. The implications of the idea of progress were obviously incompatible with conservatism but even conservatives could hardly deny the external indications of material improvement however much they doubted the possibility of perfecting human nature. The faith in progress ran far back into the intellectual history of western Europe and in the mid-nineteenth century improvement was regarded as self-evident. Confirmed by the technological innovations of the industrial revolution, identified with the ineluctable processes of evolutionary science, it was startlingly obvious in the colonial environment. Who in

Upper Canada in the 1850s could deny the progressive tendency of history when, to use the language of that day, cities stood where only two generations before the redman and his wigwam prevailed?

The chief value of history was that it affirmed and detailed the relentless march of improvement by contrasting the state of things in some remote time with the high level of society in a later age. With varying degrees of emphasis and qualification the theme of progress was the burden and the integrating principle of nearly every historical account of Canada in the nineteenth century. In John McMullen's *History of Canada from Its First Discovery to the Present Time* (1855), Alexander Munro's *History, Geography, and Statistics of British North America* (1864), William Withrow's *A History of Canada for the Use of Schools* (1876), Castell Hopkins' *The Progress of Canada in the Nineteenth Century* (1900), and John G. Bourinot's studies of political and intellectual development, progress was the standard employed to appraise the past and improvement was the chief lesson confirmed by it. "What a contrast does history recall!" exclaimed Munro in 1864. With an abundant use of statistics which was typical of all such accounts, he compared the colonies in his time with the state of affairs a hundred years before. A century ago, he wrote, the total population of British America did not exceed one hundred thousand, now the people of Canada West alone number nearly one and a half millions. Then only sixty-seven vessels, measuring five thousand six hundred tons, entered the harbour of Quebec; now two thousand two hundred vessels, measuring nine hundred and twenty thousand tons, annually ascend the St Lawrence. In the past the total number of children attending schools did not exceed those now in the classrooms of Prince Edward Island; in 1864, over eleven hundred educational institutions were disseminating the blessings of education to six hundred and fifty thousand pupils. On and on ran the statistical record, gauging the increased railway mileage, the acreage cleared, the commodities exported, and the books and newspapers published, all testifying to the onward course of improvement.[1] Few aspects of progress attracted so much attention as speed; it seemed that history itself moved more swiftly and dramatically than at any other time. "In the present age," McMullen wrote in the mid-1850s, "when our rivers and lakes are covered with floating palaces, which traverse their waters at the rate of twenty miles an hour; when railroads annihilate space, and the electric telegraph speaks with the rapidity of the lightening's [*sic*] flash it is difficult to form an ac-

1 Alexander Munro, *History, Geography, and Statistics of British North America* (Montreal, 1864), 58, 66.

curate idea of the condition of matters in Canada sixty years ago, or what a 'slow people' our Canadian ancestors were."[2]

The nineteenth century, said Parkin in 1868, was characterized by "an amount of change, improvement, and general advancement, which far exceeds in nature and extent, the accumulated progress of many preceding centuries," and, because "the minds of men are moulded by their surroundings," improvements in the material sphere resulted in the intellectual and moral elevation of the people. The "national intelligence and material wealth," it followed, "ever go hand in hand."[3] Invariably measurements of physical improvements were followed by descriptions of a burgeoning cultural and intellectual life. Bourinot, who agreed with Macaulay's opinion that every improvement in the means of locomotion benefitted mankind morally and mentally, described the intellectual development of the Canadian people as though the life of the mind was but a reflection and effect of social and political causes. "In point of time," wrote another observer in 1872, "the material progress of every country necessarily precedes the intellectual; indeed, they stand to one another some-what in the relation of cause and effect." Whether the settler values or is indifferent to culture, ran the explanation, his own work was an unconscious instrument of its advancement. "Every acre of wild land cleared by the axe of the woodman, every bushel of grain taken to the rude mill on the creek, every little hoard saved from the fruits of toil, will contribute to the intellectual progress of the generations to come."[4] The chroniclers of improvement not only tended to regard the appearance of intellectual activity as an indication of the extent of progress, but they also ascertained its dimensions in the same fashion as they measured the growth of railways. "At the recent Indian and Colonial Exhibition, in London," wrote one litterateur in 1887, "no fewer than 3,000 volumes, all by native authors, were shown in the library of the Canadian section, and this exhibit, as you know, by no means exhausts the list of books actually written by Canadians, during a century of time."[5] An editor commented in 1901 that Canadian literary progress was verified by the "increased yearly output of Canadian books." In 1868 the number of copyrights issued

2 John McMullen, *The History of Canada from Its First Discovery to the Present Time* (Brockville, 1855), 213.
3 Sir George R. Parkin Papers, vol. 107, MS "Railways in their Financial, Moral and Social Aspects," and MS "Education," 1868.
4 *Canadian Monthly and National Review*, I (Jan. 1872), 93.
5 George Stewart, Jr., "Literature in Canada," in *Canadian Leaves: History, Art, Science, Literature, Commerce. A Series of New Papers read before the Canadian Club of New York* (New York, 1887), 131.

numbered thirty-four, in 1898, seven hundred and two. "No country on the face of the globe," he submitted, "has produced, proportionately, so many volumes of verse as Canada."[6] Progress was not only conceived in material and tangible terms, but even in intellectual matters it was treated as quantifiable.

The principle of progress supplied a ready scheme by which the various phases of Canadian history were judged. All periods were not equal in their contributions to development; indeed, it was maintained that Canadian history began in a complete state of stagnation and only by slow evolution attained the speed and breadth of improvement characteristic of the middle nineteenth century. For McMullen the Indian races were destitute of the arts, industry, and the desire to ameliorate earthly conditions, and hence there was no reason to regret that Canada had been transferred to other people. The old regime fared no better: it was, he said, characterized by mental sluggishness and a torpid repose. The French "desired no innovations – no improvement of any kind"; they were "fond of pleasure," "unreflecting," "indolent," "superstitious"; they "knew nothing of that sober steady love of constitutional liberty that animates every true Briton."[7] Bourinot in 1900, like McMullen in 1855, concluded that a survey of the history of New France "will not give any evidence of political, economic, or intellectual development."[8] It was interesting only because it provided a base of comparison with what was to follow. Progress and advancement dated from the British conquest. Typifying the universal judgment of English Canadians in the late nineteenth century, the Methodist clergyman and historian William Withrow wrote that

> The conquest of Canada by the British was the most fortunate event in its history. It supplanted the institutions of the middle ages by those of modern civilization. It gave local self-government for abject submission to a foreign power and a corrupt court. It gave the protection of Habeas Corpus and trial by jury instead of the tribunals of feudalism. For ignorance and repression it gave free schools and a free press. It removed the arbitrary shackles from trade, and abolished its unjust monopolies. It enfranchised the serfs of the soil ... It gave an immeasurably ampler liberty to the people, and a loftier impulse to progress, than was ever before known.[9]

6 John A. Cooper, *Canada Under Victoria* (Toronto, 1901), 64–5.
7 McMullen, *History of Canada*, 385–6, 389.
8 J. G. Bourinot, *Canada Under British Rule, 1760–1900* (Cambridge, 1900), 3.
9 W. Withrow, *A History of Canada for the Use of Schools* (Toronto, 1876), 102.

From 1759, or 1763, the tempo of history increased. In the histories of the Dominion published in the later nineteenth century, as well as in sermons and patriotic orations, the unmistakable impression conveyed was that since the coming of the British the Canadian past was substantially the chronicle of phenomenal material growth. In a sermon at St John commemorating the arrival of the loyalists in New Brunswick, one clergyman perfectly communicated the enthusiasm for progress:

From a waste and a wilderness, where no sound was heard but the voice of the forest bird, or the roll of the waves upon the beach, the rush of waters over the falls, or the regular beat of the Indian's paddle, while the only dwellings were an occasional encampment of the wild children of the forest, we have now our present city with its thousands of inhabitants, its thirty or forty churches, its public buildings, its free schools, its courts of justice, its growing and increasing commerce; its lines of railway connecting us with the whole American continent, its steam communication with Europe; its telegraphic connection with every part of the world, and its every facility for making it wealthy and successful, prosperous and happy.[10]

This delight in material improvement was quite obviously rooted in objective reality; it was when men so easily assumed that the spectacular rate of growth would continue almost indefinitely into the future that their accounts betrayed the excessive optimism characteristic of the faith in progress.

On few subjects did such descriptions verge more upon the fanciful than in the predictions concerning the future size of the Canadian population. Nearly all discussions of the "new nationality" followed a similar pattern: spokesmen began by calling attention to past improvement; they measured the magnitude of the Dominion's natural resources and territory, and usually implied or openly stated that ultimately the number of people in Canada must correspond to her huge area. D'Arcy McGee, Alexander Morris, and the Canada Firsters clearly anticipated that the population would increase dramatically and enormously. Charles Mair believed that in terms of "mere numbers and material advantages" Canada may "eclipse even England" and Denison invariably spoke of his country as potentially the most populous nation in the Empire. In 1905 he called upon Canadians to look forward to the day when "we will have one hundred or one hundred and fifty million

10 *The Landing of the Loyalists. A Sermon by the Rev. James J. Hill, M.A., Rector of the Parish of St. John. Preached at Trinity Church on May 18th, 1873* (St John, 1873), 5–6.

people."[11] In 1875 Alexander Mackenzie, the epitome of sober judgment and cautious accounting, told a Scottish audience that "a larger population will inhabit the British portions of North America than now inhabit the British isles";[12] thirteen years later Wilfrid Laurier gave it as his opinion that Canada "will some day number a larger population than Great Britain."[13] In the atmosphere of optimism nurtured by the wheat boom, Sir George Foster, minister of trade and commerce, predicted that "in fifty years the population of Canada should be close on 50,000,000 people";[14] another imperialist thought that within a century the figure would be "at least a hundred millions";[15] still another ascertained that with the settlement of the west, the limit of the Canadian population would probably be "one hundred millions."[16] But few exceeded the lyrical language of Stephen Leacock when he summoned Canadians to recognize the inevitable greatness of their country. To those who argued that the smallness of her population prevented Canada from assuming an imperial role, he replied: "A little people, few in numbers, say you? ... Aye, such a little people, but growing, growing, growing, with a march that should make us ten millions tomorrow, twenty-millions in our children's time and a hundred millions ere the century runs out."[17] Such heady estimations appeared reasonable to those nationalists who had surveyed the extraordinary advances

11 G. T. Denison Papers, Mair to Denison, Nov. 24, 1884; *Empire Club Speeches: Being Addresses Delivered Before the Empire Club of Canada During its Session of 1904–05* (Toronto, 1906), 122.

12 *Speeches of Hon. Alexander Mackenzie during his recent Visit to Scotland with his Principle Speeches in Canada since the session of 1875* (Toronto, 1876), 21.

13 O. D. Skelton, *Life and Letters of Sir Wilfrid Laurier* (Carleton Library Edition, Toronto, 1965), I, 110.

14 *The Call of Canada: An Address by the Hon. George E. Foster ... at the City luncheon organized by the Royal Colonial Institute, June 12th, 1912* (n.p., n.d.), unpaginated.

15 W. D. Lighthall, *The Governance of Empire: Being Suggestions for the Adaptation of the British Constitution to the Conditions of Union among the Overseas States* (Montreal, 1910), 5.

16 W. H. Montague, "Thoughts About Canada and Australia," *Empire Club Speeches ... 1903–04* (Toronto, 1904), 47.

17 Stephen Leacock, "Empire and Education," *Empire Club Speeches ... 1906–07* (Toronto, 1907), 284. In *My Discovery of the West* (London, 1937), 278, he estimated Canada's potential population as 250 million. The most extravagant predictions were those of the writer Edmund Collins who said in 1887 that "the valley of the Saskatchewan, according to scientific computation, is capable of sustaining 800,000,000 souls," and the painter John A. Fraser who contended "that the valley and delta of the Fraser River are alone capable of supporting a population as large as that of Great Britain." See Collins, "The Future of the Dominion of Canada," in *Canadian Leaves*, 16, and Fraser, "An Artist's Experience in the Canadian Rockies," *ibid.*, 235.

of the past and who accepted Laurier's sanguine proclamation that the twentieth century would belong to Canada just as the nineteenth had belonged to the United States.

The other dimension of progress was the rise of liberty. The chronicles of its advance also began with the conquest and proceeded to trace its ever upward course from the Quebec Act of 1774 and the Constitutional Act of 1791 to the struggle for responsible government and Confederation. Looking back from the vantage point of 1889 Bourinot saw in this process the finger of Providence. There has been, he wrote,

> a steady development ever since England, the birth-place of free institutions, took the place of France, so long the home of an absolute, irresponsible autocracy. It took a century to bring about the changes that placed Canada in the semi-independent position she now occupies, but as we review the past we can see there was ever an undercurrent steadily moving in the direction of political freedom. Politicians might wrangle and commit the most grievous mistakes; governments in England and Canada might misunderstand public sentiment in the colony, and endeavor to stem the stream of political progress, but the movement was ever onward and the destiny that watches over people as well as individuals was shaping our political ends, and, happily, for our good.[18]

These twin themes of material growth and the expansion of liberty constituted the burden of Canadian history as the imperialists understood it. They did not believe that this was irreconcilable with the praise of the loyalists' principles because they conceived of progress as merely multiplying and strengthening desirable things. They pointed out, for instance, that the fact that Canada had gradually and peacefully come to enjoy a degree of self-government was in itself a major justification for the loyalists' refusal to dismember the Empire in 1776. Beneath the glorification of progress there sometimes lurked a desire for compensation or security, especially during the later 1880s when economic stagnation and loss of population were so obvious. There would come a time, too, when some imperialists would grow more emphatic in their denunciation of what modern progress implied – particularly industrialism and the decline of the agricultural avocation. But in general their uncritical acceptance of progress did much to instil a sense of confidence and certainty that underlay their faith in the greatness of Canada.

18 J. G. Bourinot, *Federal Government in Canada* (Baltimore, 1889), 27.

II

Whenever imperialists spoke of progress, or the impulses behind this phenomenon, they associated it with the British constitution and racial capacity. Bourinot assumed a direct causal relationship between liberal political institutions and advancement in all spheres of life. The "auto-cratic, illiberal system of government" in New France, he wrote, resulted in "complete social and political stagnation."[19] In another context, he asserted that "as the political privileges of the people have been enlarged and they have enjoyed the fullest measure of self-govern-ment ... all branches of industry have attained larger proportions and the territory and wealth of the country have expanded."[20] In this study of the intellectual development of the Canadian people, he reiterated that "the extension of political rights had a remarkable effect in stimu-lating the public intelligence and especially in improving the mental outfit of the people."[21] For him, the extension of liberty released energies, instilled self-reliance, and broadened the outlook.

Since the British constitution was regarded as the most perfect embodiment of liberty, it was also the most effective instrument of progress. Seldom was the praise of progress so extravagantly attri-buted to that constitution as during Queen Victoria's Jubilees in 1887 and 1897. To read one Jubilee speech is to know the whole genre, and entirely representative of the Canadian variety was the report of the Toronto celebration of 1887 compiled by a local customs official, Conyngham Taylor. All the sermons, addresses, and orations occa-sioned by the anniversary, said Taylor, "expatiated on the theme of the Victorian age."[22] In summing up the leading feature of the period from 1837 to 1887 as well as distilling the substance of the praises of it,

19 J. G. Bourinot, "Local Government in Canada: A Historical Study," in H. B. Adams, ed., *Johns Hopkins Studies in Historical and Political Science*, fifth series, V–VI (Baltimore, 1887), 19.
20 J. G. Bourinot, "Canada: its National Development and Destiny," *Quarterly Review*, CLXIX (July 1889), 3–4.
21 J. G. Bourinot, *The Intellectual Development of the Canadian People* (To-ronto, 1881), 22–3.
22 Conyngham C. Taylor, *The Queen's Jubilee and Toronto Called Back from 1887 to 1847* (Toronto, 1887), 389. For other outpourings of the Jubilee spirit see *Souvenir of the Queen's Jubilee: An Account of the Celebration at the City of Saint John, New Brunswick, in honor of the Jubilee Year of the Reign of Her Most Gracious Majesty, Queen Victoria* (Saint John, 1887); Rev W. T. Herridge, *A Sermon Preached in St Andrew's Church on the Occasion of the Queen's Diamond Jubilee* [Ottawa, 1897]; N. F. Davin, *The British Empire: A Speech Delivered at the Banquet in Boston celebrating Her Majesty's Dia-mond Jubilee* (Winnipeg, 1897).

Taylor wrote that "No equal period in the history of the world has witnessed such advances in science and speed, such rapid development in the useful arts, such an increase of comfort, liberty and enlightenment." Then followed the inevitable array of facts and statistics attesting to the growth of population, territorial acquisitions, the increase in commerce and wealth, and the multiplication of shipping tonnage. "These are marvellous facts and figures of material progress within one reign," the liturgy continued, "but what is quite as important is the fact that the enlightenment, enfranchisement and bettered condition of the masses, the growth of civil liberty, of art and culture, have kept pace with the vast strides in population, trade and wealth. Newspapers, schools, churches and benevolent societies have grown as never before ... Laws have improved, humanity advanced, wages increased, and the prime necessities of life cheapened ..." Having divulged the spirit of that age, this typical statement then proceeded to extol the character of the Queen. She exemplified the womanly virtues; her "natural self-reliance" and the "patient heroism of widowhood" were commended.[23] The apostrophes to progress and the praise of the personal qualities of the Queen were always coupled because these spokesmen found the root cause of progress to be in the institutional system which she symbolized. Like Bourinot, they idealized the constitution as the protector of liberty which was the source of progress.

While the cause of progress was in this manner traced back to the British constitution and to freedom, the capacity for liberty was even more often regarded as a particular characteristic of certain races. That the Anglo-Saxon race displayed a special genius for self-government and political organization seemed as undeniable to many English Canadians as did the idea that history was the record of progress. Racial explanations were conventional as well as respectable within the cultural milieu of the later nineteenth century and imperialists had no monopoly over them. The familiar language of racism, however, frequently concealed confusion: it is not clear, for instance, whether they generally believed racial character to be permanently fixed and unchangeable or whether they really thought that habits and aptitudes could be learned and acquired. Sometimes the phrase "Anglo-Saxon race" was simply a synonym for a total culture which was itself understood to be the product of history and not only racial instincts; sometimes, race was quite explicitly associated with the biological analogies of Darwinian science. However vague and confused it might be, race was none the less frequently identified with aptitudes for liberty

23 Taylor, *The Queen's Jubilee*, 375–6, 389.

and self-government. Imperialist literature is replete with allusions to the fitness of the Anglo-Saxon race in this respect. Parkin asserted in 1892 that "A special capacity for political organization may, without race vanity, be fairly claimed for the Anglo-Saxon people."[24] Over twenty years before, Robert Haliburton had traced the origins of representative institutions back to the tribes of northern Europe.

The most comprehensive exposition of this interpretation of the racial basis of liberty was submitted by J. G. Bourinot in his numerous historical and constitutional studies. While these books may appear at first sight rather remote from the preoccupations of imperialists, they in fact offer an amplification of the assumptions behind the opinions about race and they afford a more penetrating glimpse into a way of thinking that was common to many imperialists. Bourinot was receptive to the ideas and conceptions which were transforming the study of history and political science in the second half of the century and in the works of Edward A. Freeman, regius professor of history at Oxford, and his American disciples, John Burgess of Columbia University and Herbert Baxter Adams of Johns Hopkins, he encountered a thesis concerning the evolution of political institutions which he found especially relevant to Canadian history. The fundamental principles which these scholars endeavoured to apply to the study of the past were that the substance of history was past politics; that historical change, like change in nature, was slow and evolutionary; and that the factor of race provided the thread of continuity in the development of political institutions. In his *Comparative Politics* (1873), Freeman argued that the business of the political scientist was to classify political constitutions and he proposed that the similarities in the institutions of the ancient Teutons, Greeks, and Romans which could not be explained by direct transmissions, or identical responses to similar problems, could be accounted for by postulating the existence of a single race which had developed elementary forms of representative government. This Aryan race, as he called it, had been broken up into three separate "nations," Romans, Greeks, and Teutons; each of these possessed the "seeds" of liberty as a racial inheritance; and, as a consequence, wherever they went they carried with them the impulses to liberty. It was, in short, a common racial possession which accounted for the existence of parallel governmental forms in different places and at different times. The Teutonic races, including Saxons and Normans, had brought the seed of liberty to Britain; in time it was carried across the Atlantic to America. There thus existed, these scholars claimed, a direct evolutionary relationship between the primi-

24 G. R. Parkin, *Imperial Federation: The Problem of National Unity* (London, 1892), 1.

tive assemblies of the Teutonic tribes of northern Europe, the folkmoots of Saxon England, and the New England town-meetings.[25] Like his mentors, Bourinot accepted race as determinant in the development of political institutions; he dutifully noted that the origins of Parliament "must be sought in the early assemblies of our English ancestors ... who came from the seacoast of northern Germany and of Denmark";[26] and he placed the familiar story of the evolution of self-government in Canada into the framework of this Teutonic origins thesis.[27] Seen from this perspective, the steady development of liberty in Canada since the conquest was not so much the result of incident and circumstance, but the consequence of ineluctable racial instinct. Translated into the context of 1890 what this meant was that Canadians – and Bourinot included the French Canadians because they were of Norman descent – would not remain content with a partial freedom. Extravagant as his contentions may appear, their net effect was to sustain the nebulous impression that the moving force behind liberty and progress was something irresistible. The zest for freedom was "in the blood."

III

So much for the past. This view of Canadian history as progress was found relevant not in and for itself, not even because it bore in an objective sense a resemblance to the past. It was meaningful because it expressed the imperialists' conclusion that history moved in a desirable direction and it brought additional support to their hopes for the future. As nationalists, they found themselves in 1889 or 1908 in a rather ambiguous position. Canada had evolved from a complete state of colonial tutelage, through responsible government and Confederation, to a position which appeared to them temporary and transitional. Canada, said George Ross in 1908, was still a "dependency"; she was virtually independent in the control of internal affairs but possessed no influence in foreign relations, no voice at all on the issues of peace and war.[28] No imperialist accepted this as a permanent state of things and

25 E. A. Freeman, *Comparative Politics* (London, 1873), 1–36.
26 J. G. Bourinot, *How Canada is Governed* (Toronto, 1895), 57.
27 J. G. Bourinot, *Canadian Studies in Comparative Politics* (Montreal, 1890). This aspect of his historical thought is investigated in C. Berger, "Race and Liberty: The Historical Ideas of Sir John George Bourinot," Canadian Historical Association, *Annual Report*, 1965, 87–104.
28 *Shall Canada Be Always A Dependency of the Empire? Extension of the address by the Hon. Geo. W. Ross at the banquet tendered to Viscount Milner by the National Club, Oct. 28th, 1908. Col. Geo. T. Denison in the Chair* (n.p., n.d.).

none believed that it could exist for very long. All of them fervently maintained that Canadians would not rest content with political rights which were less than those exercised by citizens of Britain and thought that complete citizenship could only be secured within an imperial association. To them it appeared clear and axiomatic that imperial federation was the logical culmination of the drive toward full freedom which was implicit in Canadian history.

Because he was one of the first British North Americans to regard the achievement of responsible government as a precondition for imperial federation, Joseph Howe was accorded a prominent place in the imperialist tradition. To Howe, "responsible government had conferred upon colonials only the partial rights of British citizens. As a natural extension, the Empire ought to be reorganized without delay to confer these rights in all their fullness."[29] The Nova Scotian had enunciated this idea at an inhospitable time, but by the 1890s he and his contemporary, Judge Haliburton, who had held to the same notion, were regarded by the advocates of imperial unity as the fathers of the movement. Howe's biographer, G. M. Grant, admitted that "We are, all of us, pupils of Haliburton and Howe."[30] George Parkin explained that responsible government "was the fundamental idea upon which the whole political system, not only of Canada, but of all the self-governing colonies of England, rests." Anyone who followed through the principle of responsible and representative government could come to no other conclusion than that of Howe.[31] Stephen Leacock arrived at the identical estimate of the other father of Canadian self-government – Robert Baldwin. Baldwin's principle was a colonial invention, Leacock emphasized, and it neither signified our exclusion from the rest of the world nor was it the "negation of imperialism." It was rather "the only true and rightful basis upon which an actual theory of imperial relations could be established." It was, in fact, "the first step towards ... a more complete consolidation of the British Empire."[32]

Whether or not they acknowledged the intellectual paternity of Howe or Baldwin, all imperialists identified imperialism with an extension of Canadian freedom and her rise to nationhood. Castell Hopkins saw the entire movement for imperial unity arising from the determination of

29 J. M. Beck, "Joseph Howe: Opportunist or Empire-builder?" *Canadian Historical Review*, XLI (Sept. 1960), 202.

30 Cited in anon., *Haliburton: A Centenary Chaplet* (Toronto, 1899), 44.

31 G. R. Parkin, "Imperial Federation," *McGill University Magazine*, I (April 1902), 186–7.

32 Stephen Leacock, "The Political Achievement of Robert Baldwin," *Addresses Delivered Before the Canadian Club of Ottawa, 1903–1909* (Ottawa, 1910), 162–2. See also his "Responsible Government in the British Colonial System," *American Political Science Review*, I (May 1907), 355–92.

the colonies to become great nations. "They desire," he wrote in 1889, "to have a controlling interest in the managing of foreign affairs" and they could "only have it by some system of Imperial Federation."[33] "Imperial Federation, from a Canadian point of view," G. M. Grant elaborated, "means simply the next act in a process of political and historical development that began in 1763." It meant "the full development of self-government" and its accomplishment would mark "the placing of the copestone on that structure of Canadian nationality which we have been working at so long." He defined imperial federation "as a union between the Mother Country and Canada that would give to Canada not only the present full management of its own affairs, but a fair share in the management and responsibilities of common affairs," and he emphasized that imperialists believed that Canadians "are determined to be the peers and not the dependents of their fellow-citizens in the British Isles."[34]

These imperialists believed that there was as much inevitability in the movement from colony to nation through the imperial alliance as the advocates of complete Canadian independence, like John Norris or John Ewart, found in the evolution to autonomous nationhood. They agreed with Ewart that Canadian political history was simply "the relation of our rise from complete subordination to almost complete independence."[35] Like him, they believed that Canada's development had reached, or would very soon reach, a point when the final instalment of liberty, the exercise of power in relation to other states, would come. Some of them would even have accepted the analogies Ewart drew between individual and national maturity when he wrote that "Independence means responsibility; responsibility, self-reliance; and self-reliance, the sentiment of nationality."[36] Where they differed from him was not in the belief that the parent-child relationship must end but rather in the manner in which it was to be ended.

33 *Imperial Federation: The Journal of the Imperial Federation League*, IV (May 1, 1889), 107.
34 G. M. Grant, *"Imperial Federation": A Lecture Delivered in Victoria Hall, Winnipeg, on September 13th, 1889* (Winnipeg, 1890), 1–2, 4–5, 8. For additional statements linking imperial federation with the extension of Canadian self-government and the acquisition of full political rights, see J. G. Bourinot, "The National Development of Canada," *Canadian Monthly*, IV (March 1880), 337; John A. Cooper, "Self-Government and Imperialism," *Queen's Quarterly*, XI (Jan. 1904), 245; Sir John S. Willison, "Some Political Leaders in the Canadian Confederation," *The Federation of Canada 1867–1917* (Toronto, 1917), 74.
35 John S. Ewart, *The Future of Canada, A Perplexed Imperialist, The Canadian Flag, Etc.* (n.p., [1907]), 30.
36 *Report of the Canadian Club of Winnipeg together with the Inaugural Address of the First President, Mr. J. S. Ewart, K.C., 1904–1906* (Winnipeg, n.d.), 17.

How closely the imperialist case for extended Canadian control over her affairs paralleled that of the anti-imperialist view may be illustrated in detail by reference to the sacrifice theory of diplomacy which came to occupy a major place in these two outlooks. One of the strongest arguments marshalled by imperialists to underline the claim for a greater Canadian influence upon foreign affairs was the claim that they could no longer afford to allow Britain to sacrifice imperial interests in North America. The early expressions of this contention, in the responses of Joseph Howe and Robert Haliburton to the Washington Treaty for instance, critically assumed that Englishmen had been woefully deficient in their knowledge of North America; that they had negotiated away "Canadian" territory either out of ignorance of geography or a misguided sense of benevolence towards the United States; and that the only way a repetition of such settlements could be avoided was by bringing the Canadian point of view and influence to bear upon diplomacy affecting the Dominion. One of the most effective statements of this position was written by none other than Colonel Denison in 1895,[37] and the conclusion which he drew from his review of British diplomacy in America was the same as that enunciated by Haliburton back in 1872. "We want the Mother Country to consult with us," said Denison, "... not as a matter of favour, but under imperial federation as a matter of right."[38]

Paradoxically, this sacrifice thesis which was thus employed to buttress the case for imperialism, also cut the other way and was invoked to strengthen the anti-imperialist argument for an independent Canadian foreign policy. "We take the record of diplomacy of Great Britain in so far as Canada is concerned," said Laurier in 1907, "and we find it is a repetition of sacrifices of Canadian interests." We have "suffered" particularly on boundary matters, and "we have come at last to the conclusion that upon this point ... we would do better by attending to the business ourselves rather than having it trusted to the best men that can be found in Great Britain."[39] The unpopular Alaska Boundary decision of 1903 not only provoked such sentiments as this one, but also triggered a far-ranging debate on the significance of the British connection in general. On the one side were ranged those who agreed with the general drift of John Ewart's argument in his *Kingdom of Canada* (1908) and *The Kingdom Papers* (1912). With a profusion of citations and the style (so imperialists complained) of a prosecuting lawyer,

37 G. T. Denison, *Canada and Her Relations to the Empire* (Toronto, 1895).
38 *Imperial Federation: Report of Speech Delivered by Col. Geo. T. Denison at Guelph, Ont., on Friday, March 29, 1890* (n.p., n.d.), 3.
39 Cited in Andrew Macphail, *Essays in Politics* (London, 1909), 251–2.

he argued that the British connection had been, and continued to be, a baneful influence in Canada; that whatever benefits Canadians derived from it were incidental and accidental; and that the record of British diplomacy in North America was something no Englishman could dwell upon without humiliation and shame. A forthright declaration of independence, he urged, was justifiable and urgent. Separation from Britain would not cut Canada away from a "mother"; it would free her from an "owner."

Ranged against Ewart were the younger imperialists like W. L. Grant and Andrew Macphail as well as the Toronto lawyer, R. S. Neville, KC, who was, reported Governor-General Grey, "eager to knife that knave Ewart up to the hilt."[40] Realizing the dangers implicit in Denison's one-sided criticism of British diplomacy, they produced historical articles on boundary negotiations to destroy the myth of sacrifice and to demonstrate that the most outstanding feature of North American history was not what Canada had lost, but that in the face of American expansion across the continent the northern half of America remained in the Empire at all. During 1907 and 1908 Macphail's *University Magazine* carried a series of essays on the Ashburton Treaty of 1842, the Oregon settlement of 1846, and the Alaska award in an effort to offset the view projected by Ewart, and, more particularly, the implications that were drawn from it. What Macphail and his imperialist associates objected to was not the desirability of extending Canadian power. What they found distasteful was that the claim to the treaty-making power was based upon a myth instead of the frank acknowledgment that the very growth of the Dominion inexorably led to a larger role in international relations.

Both imperialism and the kind of anti-imperialism that Ewart represented were pervaded by a similar sense of dissatisfaction with Canadian dependence and both looked forward to a broadening of Canadian influence. In substance the disagreement between Ewart and these imperialists was not a struggle between autonomy on the one hand and a reactionary urge to maintain the colonial status quo on the other. The disagreement arose over the means by which "liberty" would be extended.

If the critics of imperialism denied that it represented a nationalistic urge to end the colonial status they were even more insistent that its advocates failed to state precisely how the Empire was to be changed

40 Grey of Howick Papers, vol. 28, Grey to A. Glazebrook, Feb. 15, 1909 (copy). For critical treatments of Ewart's case, see W. L. Grant, "Mr. J. S. Ewart's View of Canadian History," *Queen's Quarterly*, XXI (April, May, June 1914), 473–85; R. S. Neville, "British Diplomacy," *Empire Club Speeches ... 1908–1909* (Toronto, 1910), 40–7.

to accommodate the large Canadian influence. It was repeatedly pointed out that imperialists offered no practical plan of union which would not infringe upon the measure of self-government that Canada already possessed. Despite the appearance of such tracts as Archibald McGoun's *A Federal Parliament of the British People* (1890) and Granville Cunningham's *A Scheme for Imperial Federation* (1895) or the fact that Parkin devoted a chapter of his comprehensive *Imperial Federation* (1892) to such proposals, imperialists expended very little time thinking about technical constitutions which would give Canadians representation in an imperial parliament or council. This was due, moreover, to deliberate intention and preference rather than to a failure of constructive effort. From their reading of history, their conservative predisposition, and their understanding of the British constitution, they were not merely suspicious of paper constitutions but decidedly hostile to such theoretical speculations. Bourinot, for example, whose knowledge of constitutional history could easily have been put to use in drafting a scheme of federal union, expressed disdain for such activity. In 1866 he had dismissed Joseph Howe's plan for the reorganization of the British Empire as "wild and chimerical" and "quack medicine" mainly because it had been advanced as an alternative to British North American union.[41] Bourinot supported Confederation and along with many others saw it as a step towards a vaster imperial federation. Certainly he shared the opinion of another that Confederation "has been one step in the direction of a general imperial consolidation."[42] The union of 1867 not only provided the model for local unions elsewhere in the Empire, but for Canadian imperialists it represented a historical example of how the Empire itself would someday be formally unified. Confederation, wrote Bourinot, "at times afforded a fruitful theme of discussion in the press, and even in Parliament, but it never assumed a practical shape until the political difficulties of Canada forced her public men into the consideration of a national idea. So it may be with this question of Federation of Great Britain and her Dependencies."[43]

For men whose understanding of political evolution was acquired from British writers like Walter Bagehot and Sir Henry Maine, who

41 J. G. Bourinot, *Confederation of the Provinces of British North America: "Re-published from the 'Halifax Evening Reporter' of the 10th, 13th, and 17th November, 1866"* (Halifax, 1866), 3–4.

42 H. Scadding, as reported in the *Empire*, July 10, 1890.

43 J. G. Bourinot, *The National Development of Canada, A Paper Read at the Royal Colonial Institute, January 20, 1880* (London, 1880), 20. He reiterated this point in "Canada: its National Development and Destiny," 22.

spoke of the cohesive role of custom and of imperceptible organic growth, there was something unnatural about mechanical and revolutionary alterations. In 1872 G. M. Grant dismissed with disdain constitution-making in the style of Abbé Sieyes; in 1900 he reaffirmed that "I do not look for any startling Constitutional change or any paper scheme for re-organizing the Empire. That is not the way of the British."[44] "The British Constitution," Denison reminded the historian Goldwin Smith, "is unwritten; it has 'broadened down from precedent to precedent,' always elastic, always adapting to changing conditions. So should the idea of British unity be carried out."[45] The very phrase "imperial federation" was itself misleading in the sense that it suggested something concrete, technical, and constitutional, whereas the imperialists read into it a bewildering variety of meanings. One even objected to the word federation because it conjured up "visions of federal councils, new constitutions, expensive legislatures and selfish office-holders."[46] Others made it quite plain that they did not agree on any specific and ultimate scheme of union. Denison equated imperial federation with an "alliance among a number of self-governing nations" co-operating through periodic conferences;[47] George Foster foresaw "a deliberative, directive body," but only in the distant future.[48] William Canniff asserted that the aim of imperial federation was to transform the colonial status into one in which "Canada will no longer be regarded as a dependency, but as an auxiliary power, possessing equal rights with Britain in parliamentary representation, and sharing with her the responsibilities pertaining to the welfare of the Empire."[49] But while these men were at variance in their interpretation of the final form of co-operation or association, most of them distrusted sudden and abrupt changes. The prevailing Darwinian cast of thought made it appear more natural that institutional alterations be slow and evolutionary. Parkin perhaps best summed up the Canadian imperialists' conclusions on this

44 G. M. Grant, *Ocean to Ocean: Sandford Fleming's Expedition through Canada in 1872* (Toronto, 1873), 366; "Introductory Chapter," T. G. Marquis, *Canada's Sons on Kopje and Veldt: A Historical Account of the Canadian Contingents* (Toronto, 1900), 6.
45 G. T. Denison, *The Struggle for Imperial Unity* (Toronto, 1909), 215.
46 Thomas MacFarlane, *A United Empire: Paper Delivered Before the Montreal Branch of the Imperial Federation League in Canada, Monday, 21st December, 1885* (n.p., n.d.), 3.
47 Denison, "Imperial Federation ... ," 3; Denison Papers, Denison to Grey, June 24, 1905 (copy).
48 George E. Foster, "Some Problems of Empire," *United Empire: Royal Colonial Institute Journal*, new series, III (Dec. 1912), 960.
49 OA, William Canniff Papers, package #13, MS "Conditions in Canada," April 6, 1888.

subject when he said in 1887 that "we should still keep as far as possible from any great political reconstruction, but watch for every point where common interests can be strengthened or new ties formed."[50]

Their hostility to drafting constitutional schemes was also powerfully reinforced by their sense of Canadian nationalism. To have institutionalized the Empire through some federal arrangement in the later nineteenth century would have frustrated the chief end Canadian imperialism sought to realize. The disparity in the size of populations and power between Canada and Great Britain was so great that a federalization at that time would simply have frozen and made permanent the colonial status. The imperialists wanted to advance the absolute political equality of Canadians by extending their influence within the imperial system, but they were certainly not unmindful of the fact that in the 1880s or 1890s Canada required time in which to develop and establish internal consolidation. They had an enormous faith in Canada's future. Contemplating her vast territory and the swiftness of her progress in the past, they hoped that a country which was more than thirty times the size of Great Britain, endowed with abundant natural resources, and destined to contain a population exceeding that of the old country, would truly become the centre of the Empire. To debate plans in face of such a hope as this appeared to be a diversion of energy; the business of the imperialists was to forward the growth of the Dominion in order to hasten a destiny which seemed as fixed and certain as the rising of the sun. Yet even if one took the most literal rendering of imperial federation to mean Canadian representation in the imperial Parliament who could seriously argue that Canadians would be perpetually outvoted by the representatives from the more populous places? Stephen Leacock was deadly serious when in 1906 he suggested that to the 670 members of the British Parliament should be added 166 from the colonies. This was fair, he estimated, because the population of Britain was forty-two million, while the colonies possessed only some ten millions. "Objectors will," he confessed, "... put forth the statement that the colonial few would become swamped"; it is true that we "cannot realize all we wish now, but we will develop with our growth." A Canadian population of a hundred million was within the possibilities of the twentieth century while the limits of the British population had already been established.[51] With such growth would come power and equality, perhaps even dominance.

The imperialists, then, were assured that Canadian history exhibited

50 Sir Sandford Fleming Papers, Parkin to Fleming, Jan. 27, 1887.
51 Stephen Leacock, "The Imperial Crisis," *Addresses Delivered Before the Canadian Club of Toronto Season 1905–06* (Toronto, n.d.), 117.

an extraordinarily rapid material growth and the slow and gradual acquisition by colonials of the political rights of British subjects. They were anxious to secure the substance of these rights, to secure for Canadians the same voice upon imperial matters that citizens of Great Britain already possessed. This, they were certain, could be accomplished only within some form of imperial association, and, equally, it could only come when Canadians were not only ready to assume responsibilities but also when their material development enabled them to do so. This drive toward full national rights was taken by imperialists to mean the culmination, not the subversion, of the principle of responsible government.

5

The Canadian Character

Like nationalists everywhere, the Canadian imperialists assumed that the people whose ideals they expressed possessed a distinctive national character which was the product of racial inheritance and social training, environment and historical experience. Running through their critique of republican society and their interpretation of the Canadian past was the belief that Canadians were pre-eminently a loyal and law-abiding people not given over to the erratic and hectic behaviour of their neighbours. Scarcely less dominant in their image of the national character was the impression that the northern climate imparted to it a high degree of energy, vigour, and strenuousness. Urged on by the desire, natural to all nationalists, to conceive of a single people sharing common characteristics, some imperialists managed to accommodate the French Canadians into their composite image of the Canadian character far more easily than they were able to accept the strange immigrants from central, eastern, and southern Europe.

I

Certain that the Canadian population must increase until its magnitude bore a close relationship to the physical size of the country, imperialists also supposed that the geographical situation of the nation must profoundly affect the character and outlook of her people. Few contentions ran through nationalist thought so persistently as the idea that the northern location of Canada gave its inhabitants peculiar qualities. There were those, of course, who reacted with indignation to foreign commentaries upon the weather, especially the winter. In 1855 one writer reassuringly noted that the harshness of the Canadian winter would be moderated as the forests were cleared and the lands brought under cultivation, an opinion reiterated fifty years later by an official publication of the Department of Agriculture.[1] In the decades after the publication of R. G. Haliburton's lecture on the men of the north,

1 J. Sheridan Hogan, *Canada: An Essay: to which was awarded the first prize by the Paris Exhibition Committee of Canada* (Montreal, 1855), 53; Canada,

however, Canadian nationalists of all persuasions stopped apologizing for their climate and extolled the influence of the snow and cold upon their character. Isolating the most distinctive feature of the weather – the Canadian winter – they often buttressed the very mistaken impression concerning that season which their ancestors had sought to dispel. The adjective "northern" came to symbolize energy, strength, self-reliance, health, and purity, and its opposite, "southern," was equated with decay and effeminacy, even libertinism and disease. A lengthy catalogue of desirable national attributes resulting from the climate was compiled. No other weather was so conducive to maintaining health and stimulating robustness. "A constitution nursed upon the oxygen of our bright winter atmosphere," exclaimed Governor-General Dufferin, "makes its owner feel as though he could toss about the pine trees in his glee."[2] After studying the statistics of diseases collected by surgeons at British and American army stations, one medical authority concluded that the salubrity of the climate increased, and that mortality arising from digestive, respiratory, and nervous disorders decreased, as one moved northwards. The climate, this doctor contended, was most "favorable to the highest development of a hardy, long-lived, intelligent people"; the future occupants of the soil – and he was emphatic on the point that they would be a "*Canadian* people" – "will be a taller, straighter, leaner people – hair darker and drier and coarser; muscles more tendinous and prominent and less cushioned."[3] Another doctor believed that it was all to our advantage that "we have a rigorous winter and that the climate is a bit hard at times" for from struggle would come strength and from strength, superiority. In the future, he predicted, "the most virile nation on this continent will be to the north of the great lakes."[4] To the testimony of scientists was added the impressions of poets. Writing of the climate of western Canada, Charles Mair praised its lightness, sparkle, and dryness. "The atmosphere," he added, "is highly purified, joyous and clear, and charged with ozone – that element which is mysteriously associated with soundness of mind and body."[5]

Department of Agriculture, *Canada: Its History, Productions and Natural Resources* (Ottawa, 1905), 11.

2 William Leggo, *History of the Administration of the Earl of Dufferin in Canada* (Toronto, 1878), 599.

3 W. H. Hingston, *The Climate of Canada and its relations to Life and Health* (Montreal, 1884), 94, 265–6.

4 Dr William Osler, "Anglo-Canadian and American Relations," *Addresses Delivered Before the Canadian Club of Toronto Season 1904–05* (Toronto, n.d.), 65.

5 N. F. Davin, ed., *Homes for the Millions. The Great Canadian North-West* (Ottawa, 1891), 11.

On the moral and intellectual level, no less than in the purely physical, the climate was held to be the promoter of straight-thinking and moral purity. The clear and frosty air seemed incompatible with lax morality; the voluptuous living characteristic of southern climes was impossible in the northern zone. The climate, George Parkin claimed, imparted "a Puritan turn of mind."[6] The long winters forced men to cultivate thrift and forethought and it enabled them to pursue intellectual studies, a fact which allegedly explained why northern peoples were invariably better educated than the Latin races.[7] Compared even to the "warm, moisture-laden atmosphere of the British Isles" the sharp and clear air of northern America was calculated to make perception more accurate and more penetrating. "The Canadian is supereminently quick-witted," wrote one observer, because the very air of his country has "tonic properties."[8]

Of all the characteristics of a northern people the desire and capacity for liberty was the one most often singled out for comment and eulogy. "Wherever snow falls," Emerson had written, "there is usually civil freedom." The northern latitudes not only nourished exactly those traits like self-reliance and rugged independence most necessary to the functioning of self-government, but it was also claimed, as we have seen, that the institutions of liberty had originated among the tribes of northern Europe. Certified by the respectable political science of the time, this conception treated the capacity for liberty as a "seed," indwelling in the blood, especially in the northern blood, and its proponents traced the migration of freedom from the ancient Scandinavian and German communities to Britain, the United States, and Canada. In the Dominion, in a climate so similar to the environment in which it was born, liberty was destined to thrive and flourish, permanently immunized from those malignant forces which sapped its strength in warmer climes. Residents of southern zones, wallowing in a surfeit of plenty, were deficient in hardihood and the spirit of liberty. Hence, progress, or the forward motion of society, was most marked in northern countries while southern nations remained stagnant, unprogressive, notable only for frequent political upheavals.

Not the least fortunate aspect of the Canadian climate was that it kept the Dominion uncontaminated by these weaker races. Parkin called the climate "one of our greatest blessings," "the most valuable asset that the country has," not only because it nurtured and maintained certain

6 G. R. Parkin, *The Great Dominion: Studies of Canada* (London, 1895), 215.
7 Rev. F. A. Wightman, *Our Canadian Heritage: Its Resources and Possibilities* (Toronto, 1905), 46.
8 Arnold Haultain, "A Winter's Walk in Canada," *Nineteenth Century and After*, L (Sept. 1901), 558.

characteristics but also because it functioned, in Darwinian terms, as "a persistent process of natural selection" by discouraging the immigration and successful settlement of tramps and lower races. That labour problems were unknown in Canada was due both to the abundance of land and to the fact that the "Canadian winter exercises upon the tramp a silent but well-nigh irresistible persuasion to shift to a warmer latitude." The United States thus served as a "safety-valve" for Canadian social problems. The stern climate, moreover, ensured that the Dominion would have no Negro problem "which weighs like a troublesome nightmare upon the civilization of the United States." Nature itself decreed that she would have no cities like New York, Cincinnati, or New Orleans which attracted "even the vagrant population of Italy and other countries of Southern Europe." "Canada," he emphasized, "will belong to the sturdy races of the North-Saxon and Celt, Scandinavian, Dane and Northern German, fighting their way under conditions sometimes rather more severe than those to which they have been accustomed in their old homes." Stable and ordered development were hence assured: the climate was "a fundamental political and social advantage which the Dominion enjoys over the United States."[9]

Descriptions of Canadians as a northern people were particularly insistent upon including the French Canadians, for they had both demonstrated their capacity to settle and multiply in the inhospitable environment and they were also continually influenced by the same refreshing winds as their English-speaking fellow citizens. The similarity of climate throughout Canada, declared the vice-president of the National Club of Toronto, was "creating ... a homogeneous Race," sturdy in frame and stable in character.[10] The French and English were not merely being "welded together" by the common climate: it was frequently pointed out that in their racial backgrounds there were no vital differences between them. Genealogists had demonstrated that the majority of the original French settlers had come from Brittany and Normandy; since the Normans themselves were descendants of the Scandinavian invaders of the ninth and tenth centuries who had gone on to conquer Britain, it could be claimed that both British and French contained elements of the northern strain. The historians William Wood

9 Parkin, *Great Dominion*, 213–5; *Imperial Federation: The Problem of National Unity* (London, 1892), 205; "The Relations of Canada and the United States," *Empire Club Speeches: Being Addresses Delivered Before the Empire Club of Canada During its Session of 1907–1908* (Toronto, 1910), 160–1.
10 F. B. Cumberland, "Introduction," *Maple Leaves: Being the Papers Read Before the National Club of Toronto at the "National Evenings," During the Winter of 1890–91* (Toronto, 1891), vii–viii.

and George Wrong both thought it a fact full of meaning that the two peoples were identical in racial origins and that they shared such good stock.[11] The poet Wilfred Campbell saluted this consanguinity in verse:

> They, too, our brothers,
> Loyal Canadians,
> Valorous, chivalrous,
> Sons of Montcalm; –
>   . . .
> They are not alien,
> Helot, out-cast,
> But blood of the old blood,
> Norman of William,
> Victors at Hastings,
> Builders of England,
> Heirs of your wonderful
> Glorious past.[12]

Sharing heroic northern antecedents and subjected to the same exertions by the climate, French- and English-speaking Canadians seemed divided only by superficialities.

Allusions to the beneficial action of winter obtruded in serious history as well as whimsical song, nationalist invocations as well as painting. Advantages large and small were traced back to its influence. The snow, it was said, covered and protected fall crops, and the frost broke up the soil as thoroughly as a plough, thereby saving farmers much toil.[13] Ice and snow protected the three thousand miles of northern frontier, thus "greatly relieving national expenditure and contributing much to our sense of security."[14] Joseph Howe challenged the view that the northern climate would prevent a great increase in population by observing that in the south "a man may do without a wife; but in the long cold nights of our winters he cannot sleep alone. Large, vigorous, healthy families spring from feather beds in which Jack Frost compels people to lie close."[15] So recurrent was the northern

11 W. Wood, ed., *The Storied Province of Quebec. Past and Present* (Toronto, 1931), I, 3; G. M. Wrong, *The Two Races in Canada, A Lecture delivered before the Canadian Historical Association, Montreal, May 21st, 1925* (n.p., n.d.), 4–5.
12 Wilfred Campbell, "Show the Way, England," *The Collected Poems of Wilfred Campbell* (Toronto, 1905), 306.
13 J. G. Bourinot, *Canada as a Home* (London, 1882), 13.
14 Wightman, *Our Canadian Heritage*, 280.
15 J. A. Chisholm, ed., *Speeches and Letters of Joseph Howe* (Halifax, 1909), II, 277.

theme in the imaginative literature published in Canada during the early twentieth century that one critic was moved to complain that the "whole of Canada has come to be identified with her northernmost reaches" and that in "modern folk-geography Canada means the North."[16] The image of Canada projected by some of the paintings by members of the Group of Seven was that of "a long, thin strip of civilization on the southern fringe of a vast expanse of immensely varied, virgin land reaching into the remote north." "Our whole country," one of these artists wrote, "is cleansed by the pristine and replenishing air which sweeps out of that great hinterland." The north – with its clear and sharp outlines which could never be apprehended with the techniques of old world art – was more than an interesting locale to paint: it was a mirror of the national character. To Lawren Harris at least this clean psychic atmosphere and its cleansing power was a distinctive Canadian advantage over the congestion of the more southerly parts of North America.[17] In yet another sphere of expression the lines from "O Canada," which celebrate the nation's strength and freedom, harked to the northern theme. Not even in a brochure intended to attract visitors to the Muskoka lakes could Canadians refrain from informing prospective American tourists that they would enter a land in which hardy Northmen resided, men who in the future would exercise "the same potential influence upon their neighbours lying to the south that the northern nations have in the older continent of Europe."[18]

It was with little effect that Goldwin Smith reminded Canadians that the heat of their stoves was no less enervating than that of the sun, for nationalists contemplated, reformulated, and refined the northern theme again and again. With all its ramifications, the concept became a vehicle for expressing their faith in themselves and the distinctiveness of their character. Canadians, ran the conclusion, were a strong and serious race, enjoying advantages over Britain as well as the United States. Canada, alone of all the Dominions, lay above the forty-fifth parallel, and because of the energy inherent in the personality of her people she was surely predestined to assume an important position in the world.

16 Lionel Stevenson, *Appraisals of Canadian Literature* (Toronto, 1926), 245, 253.
17 Lawren Harris, "The Group of Seven in Canadian History," Canadian Historical Association, *Annual Report*, 1948, 30; National Gallery of Canada, *Lawren Harris: Retrospective Exhibition 1963* (Ottawa, 1963), 33.
18 *"Picturesque Canada": The Northern Lakes of Canada, Their Summer Resorts and Sporting Districts* (Toronto, 1876), 5.

II

Whatever comfort they may have received from claiming that French and English Canadians shared the northern environment and ancestry, the presence of Quebec defied the imperialists' desire for a sense of Canadian nationality rooted in the same language, identical traditions, and similar racial characteristics. With its announced objective of consolidating the Anglo-Saxon race and its appeal to the English-Canadian heritage, it is hardly surprising that imperialism appeared alien and threatening to French Canadians. Canadian imperialism, moreover, was nourished in the atmosphere of cultural conflict which was provoked by the hanging of Riel and the attack upon separate schools, and all too often the actions of its spokesmen in politics, no less than the general tenor of their ideology, confirmed their hostility to French-Canadian aspirations. "Shall a French nationality or an English nationality govern this Dominion?" asked one excited author in 1884.[19] Imperialists not only accepted the legitimacy of this question but ultimately gave only one answer to it. The president of the Imperial Federation League in the late 1880s was D'Alton McCarthy, the head of the Equal Rights Association which was formed to combat papal interference in Dominion affairs. The majority of the thirteen members of the House of Commons who voted for disallowance of the Jesuit Estates Act, which had been passed by the legislature of Quebec to extend financial compensation to the order for the lands it had once held and had appealed to the Papacy to adjudicate the settlement, were ardent imperialists. When disallowance failed, McCarthy sought to abolish the official status of the French language in the North-West and his Equal Rights campaign led directly to the end of the separate schools in Manitoba. The Orange Order in Ontario provided some of the most vociferous advocates of imperial unity, and it often appeared that to the motto of one race, one flag, one throne, they wanted to add, one religion. On the individual level, George Sterling Ryerson, who became president of the United Empire Loyalist Association, also supported the anti-Catholic crusade of the Protestant Protective Association, and James L. Hughes, a Toronto school inspector and devoted imperialist, was one of the first to suggest the formation of a Protestant party to combat the interference of the Pope in Canadian affairs which had been provoked by the Jesuit Estates Act.

Despite such associations as these, however, there was nothing inevitable and unalterable about the partnership of imperialism and

19 *Week*, I (July 17, 1884), 519.

Orangeism. McCarthy, G. M. Grant, Denison, and Parkin were never members of the Orange Order and even McCarthy – whose agitation received the support of Clarke Wallace, grand master of the Orange Association of British North America – personally believed that "it is not religion which is at the bottom of the matter but that it is race feeling."[20] Convinced that the French sought to extend their language, laws, and institutions from Quebec into Ontario, Manitoba, and the North-West Territories in order "to subdue this country to Frenchmen, or to make it a French nationality,"[21] McCarthy was determined to settle the question once and for all in his generation before it had to be decided by bullets in the next. In presenting his resolution calling for the elimination of official recognition of the French language in the North-West, he told the House of Commons that it was expedient in the interest of national unity of the Dominion that there should be a community of language among the people of Canada.[22] Though the brunt of his attack fell upon the language rights which had grown, he said, to such "monstrous proportions," he went far beyond these in claiming that if the French Canadian were ever to be a Briton in thought and feeling, "he must learn to cherish, not merely our institutions, but our glorious past, and to look forward with us to a still more glorious future."[23] Wallace also agreed that the only choice Canada had was to become an independent nation within the Empire with one law, one language, and no privileged race or religion. The alternative, he warned, was disintegration amid sectarian warfare.[24]

Neither Wallace nor McCarthy spoke for all imperialists. In 1888 the Imperial Federation League claimed that sixty members of Parliament were enrolled in its ranks,[25] and while some of these obviously joined primarily because of opposition to unrestricted reciprocity, or for other political reasons, the fact that only thirteen voted for disallowance of the Jesuit Estates Act indicates that League membership was

20 Fred Landon, "D'Alton McCarthy and the Politics of the Later 'Eighties,' " Canadian Historical Association, *Annual Report*, 1932, 46.
21 *Equal Rights Association of Ontario: D'Alton McCarthy's Great Speech Delivered at Ottawa, December 12th, 1889* (Toronto, n.d.), 26.
22 *Speech of Dalton McCarthy, M.P., on the French Language in the North-West, Tuesday, 18th February, 1890* (Ottawa, 1890), 3.
23 *Equal Rights Association*, 11.
24 John P. Buell, "The Political Career of Clarke Wallace" (MA thesis, University of Toronto, 1961), 59.
25 *Imperial Federation League in Canada. Speech Delivered at Paris, Ont., on January 19th, 1888, by Alex. McNeill, M.P., Vice-President* (n.p., n.d.), 2. In 1890 it was reported that one quarter of the members of the House of Commons were members of the League: *Imperial Federation: The Journal of the Imperial Federation League*, v (June 1890), 31.

not an infallible measure of support for Equal Rights, still less for Protestant supremacy. It was, moreover, precisely because of his connection with the Equal Rights movement that McCarthy was removed from the presidency of the League in 1891. "You see," G. M. Grant explained, "we wish to keep the League non-partizan, till we can persuade Canadians generally that it is in the common interest."[26] McCarthy's activities, Denison frankly added, "were so unsatisfactory to the French Canadians that the prospect of the League obtaining their support would be hopeless while he remained President."[27] The initiative for replacing McCarthy came largely from Grant and Sandford Fleming: other figures in the League like Thomas Macfarlane of Ottawa and Archibald McGoun of Montreal wanted him to retain the position. The League, in short, was split on the issue of Equal Rights, just as it was divided over the whole French-Canadian question.

Deeply held convictions, as well as considerations of political strategy, governed Grant's response to the cultural crisis. He regretted the incorporation of the Jesuits for the same reason that he condemned Protestant sectarianism: both varieties of religious extremism endangered the prospects of Christian unity in Canada. Grant took no part in McCarthy's movement because he believed in provincial rights, which meant "a frank recognition that there are different types of sentiment and thought among us, and that it is right to give room for the free development of these."[28] Nor did he agree with those who maintained that a uniformity of language or race was an urgent requirement for national unity. Such a supposition, he scornfully wrote, was "an abstract conception scarcely worth refuting ... The highest form of national life does not depend on identity, but rather on differences that are transcended by common political interests and sentiments." While recognizing the existence of dissimilar nationalities within Canada, but carefully noting that the population was "mainly composed of the two great historic races that have taken root in the land," he anticipated that the day would come when the French Canadian would teach his children English so that they would not be handicapped for life in America and that "the British-Canadian, finding that the man who is master of two languages is often preferred to him, resolves that if he cannot speak French his children shall."[29] Rejecting simplistic formulas for uniformity in language, Grant was also suspicious of the idea that a non-denominational or national school system was desirable. For him

26 OA, Sir Alexander Campbell Papers, Grant to Campbell, Jan. 21, 1891.
27 G. T. Denison, *The Struggle for Imperial Unity* (Toronto, 1909), 194.
28 G. M. Grant, "Our National Objects and Aims," *Maple Leaves*, 14–5.
29 G. M. Grant, "Canada and the Empire. A Rejoinder to Dr. Goldwin Smith," *Canadian Magazine*, VIII (Nov. 1896), 77.

education was incomplete and socially useless unless it was grounded in "moral training," and such training, he was certain, could not be inculcated without the sanction of religion. "The state," he argued, "has the right to insist on moral training as indispensable to national well-being; and as the only religious sanctions effectual with children are those acknowledged by their parents, every encouragement should be given for the application of these, consistent with the rights of others and with the maintenance in every community of well-equipped schools."[30] Because he was so insistent upon the development of a moral and law-abiding people and less concerned with whether the schools in which they were educated were Catholic or Protestant, Grant contended that the Manitoba government should not have summarily abolished the dual system of education but simply reformed it. He expected, indeed, that separate schools would increase in number and he specified that constitutional guarantees for minority rights in education be extended throughout the entire Dominion.

Though Grant was no more representative of all imperialists than was McCarthy, he was not an isolated and atypical figure. Colonel Denison, rather surprisingly perhaps, was unstinting in his praise for Laurier's settlement of the Manitoba schools question; he pointed to the various languages and religions in Switzerland to prove that such difference did not make national unity impossible; and he informed Charles Mair that "We cannot be a great country unless we understand that we must give and take, and that our constitution must give all classes freedom and fair play."[31] Denison and Grant were nationalists who believed that the Canadian peoples were united by profoundly important traditions and aspirations and that Canada was a legitimate and viable nation. One of the reasons why they sought to discourage the kind of rhetoric and suspicions spawned by the Equal Rights Association was that they felt it merely played into the hands of the continental unionists. It was Goldwin Smith, as well as McCarthy, who was most emphatic in maintaining that the racial tension was intractable and irrepressible. "To make a nation," Smith wrote in 1889, "there must be a common life, common sentiments, common aims, and common hopes. Of these, in the case of Ontario and Quebec, there are none." Quebec, in fact, looked forward "to being a nation of herself ... not only cancelling Wolfe's victory but realizing the visions of Louis XIV."[32] The more convincingly Smith showed that Confederation had failed to bring

30 G. M. Grant Papers, vol. 25, clipping from the *Interior*, Aug. 15, 1895.
31 G. T. Denison Papers, Scrapbook, 1897–1915, clipping from the *Globe*, Oct. 19, 1899; QUL, Charles Mair Papers, Denison to Mair, July 31, 1895.
32 *The Bystander: A Monthly Review of Current Events, Canada and General*, new series (Dec. 1889), 78.

together French and English, the stronger would be his case against the survival of Canada, and, consequently, the more powerful his argument for continental unity. This was why Mair deplored the "fashion of certain annexation newspapers to rail at what they chose to call 'French aggression,' "[33] and why some imperialists deliberately minimized the extent of the cultural conflict. They were able to do this largely because they had succeeded in adjusting the French Canadians into their conception of the national character. Some of the characteristics which they attributed to the French were inherited notions, some were products of observation and based upon fact, others were gathered indirectly from literature and history. It was not so much intellectual consistency that held this image together but rather the nationalistic determination to think of Canadians as "one people."

In the foreground of the imperialists' image of the French Canadians was the idea that history offered irrefutable proof of their devotion to British institutions and allegiance to the British Crown. Their loyalty had been tested in the American Revolution and the War of 1812; they had helped to preserve Canada for the Empire and had justified the hopes of those who had extended freedom to them. The French Canadians, Denison declared in a Dominion Day address in 1889, "are our own people" and we should never forget

> that our fellow-Canadians in the Lower Province, in 1775, saved the country for us. I hope they will never forget that in 1812, when this country was in danger and our national life came within one ace of being destroyed, our fellow-Canadians of French blood stood side by side with our own people. At Chateauguay they knelt down and prayed to God to prosper their arms and defend their country. They prayed under the rites of the Roman Catholic religion, and God blessed them as he blessed us when we prayed the same prayer under the rites of the Protestant religion. ... Let us remember, for goodness sake, first of all that we are Canadians ... Let us remember that we have a people on our border whom our Premier, Mr. Mowat, has described as a hostile people.[34]

French-Canadian loyalty was usually ascribed to the beneficence of the British Empire because it was the only world state in which minorities could retain local traditions. Compared to it, the United States stood for uniformity and homogeneity. The imperialists did not need to look

33 Denison Papers, " 'The Land We Live in!' Mr. Chas. Mair's Speech at the Banquet Given to Col. Irvine in Prince Albert, N.W.T., from the Prince Albert Times," enclosure in Mair to Denison, Feb. 12, 1889.
34 *Ibid.*, Scrapbook, 1888–97, unidentified press clipping.

very far to find confirmation of their view of French-Canadian loyalism. The often-quoted remark of Sir Etienne Taché that the last shot fired in defence of the British Empire in North America would be fired by a French Canadian seemed to them a more accurate reflection of the opinion of Quebec than the discordant separatist doctrines of the Quebec Premier, Honoré Mercier. Writers like Benjamin Sulte and James LeMoine, who were accepted by some as authentic spokesmen of the French-Canadian outlook, repeatedly proclaimed that the most important theme in the history of Quebec was its attachment to the Empire. "Should the day ever unhappily come that there remains but one faithful Colony," Sulte wrote in 1905, "Quebec will be that Colony."[35] From one of Laurier's French-Canadian colleagues came the assurance that loyalty to the Empire was "one of the most undeniable characteristics of the French-Canadian nationality";[36] another averred that the conquest, by bestowing upon the French-Canadian Roman Catholics guarantees for their laws, language, customs, and religion, was ordered by Providence.[37] Even Armand Lavergne, *nationaliste* and colleague of Bourassa, informed a select Toronto audience that the nationalists of Quebec "are willing and ready to give their last drop of blood for the defence of the British flag and British institutions in this country."[38]

The imperialists recognized that the loyalty of the French Canadian had a peculiar quality in that it sprang from the calculation that their rights would be more secure within the Empire than in any other system. Because their attitude to the Empire did not result from racial associations or culminate in a desire to participate in the government of it, it seemed to imperialists restricted and negative. But though it differed from the loyalist tradition of Ontario and the Maritimes, French-Canadian loyalism played no small part in the imperialists' assessment of the prospects of their cause. "Our position here," Denison told Joseph Chamberlain in 1902, "is very difficult on account of the two million French Canadians who cannot have the sentiment of Imperialism as we of English descent naturally have." Because he assumed the French to be loyal and sound, and because he believed that political leadership was a matter of leading the "inert masses," Denison tended to dismiss active anti-imperialism in Quebec as the product of demagogues who

35 Benjamin Sulte, "The French-Canadians and the Empire," in C. S. Goldman, ed., *The Empire and the Century* (London, 1905), 423.
36 L. P. Brodeur, "The Loyalty of the French-Canadians to the Empire," *Empire Club Speeches ... 1903–04* (Toronto, 1904), 95.
37 Rodolphe Lemieux, cited in M. A. Banks, "Toronto Opinion of French Canada during the Laurier Regime, 1896–1911" (MA thesis, University of Toronto, 1950), 133.
38 Armand Lavergne, "National Defence as Viewed by French-Canadians," Canadian Military Institute, *Selected Papers* (Welland, Ontario, 1910), 98.

imagined differences which did not really exist. Imperialists should therefore do nothing which would only provoke extremists and supply them with an issue. A cash contribution for imperial defence, for example, was out of the question, because "the French will raise the cry of 'Tribute' and demagogues will make trouble."[39] Denison understood that French-Canadian loyalism did not lead to positive imperialism, but he was also certain that the majority would not engage in promoting imperial disintegration. If intemperate attacks upon the French were stopped and if an imperial tariff arrangement could be presented so as to appeal to their economic self-interest, then they would in time be brought into line.

The conservative social order of Quebec received almost as much praise from imperialists as did the tradition of steadfast loyalty. Throughout the nineteenth century English-speaking Canadians had regarded the French as lacking in the spirit of progress. In their histories they painted the French regime as a period of "torpid repose," exhibiting neither political advancement nor material development. It was, they agreed, noteworthy only for its "picturesque" features. In his description of the conflicts of the 1830s, McMullen conveyed a widely held impression when he wrote that the British

> were foremost in all great public measures of utility, in the building of steamboats, in commerce, in agricultural improvement, in liberal educational measures, in the social elevation of the industrial classes, and thus kept full pace with the progressive spirit of the age. The French population, on the other hand, clung to ancient prejudices, ancient customs, and ancient laws, with the unreasoning tenacity of an uneducated and unprogressive people. They remained an old and stationary society, in the midst of a new and progressive world.[40]

Frequently invoked during the tensions of the late nineteenth century, this conception of the French as an unprogressive people lingered long and became one of the commonplace fixtures of the English-Canadian mind. There were some imperialists, however, who were attracted to Quebec exactly because of its "backwardness." They discovered in the province conservative principles, traditional values, and a hostility to capitalism which they themselves admired and shared. It is true, of course, that they sang the eulogies of progress and welcomed material growth, but a deep undercurrent of suspicion pervaded their attitude toward industrialization and urbanization. They had been repelled by

39 Denison Papers, Denison to Chamberlain, Feb. 22, 1902 (copy).
40 John McMullen, *The History of Canada from Its Discovery to the Present Time* (Brockville, 1855), 389.

the social atomization in the United States and were fretful and apprehensive lest the same fate overtake the Dominion. They consequently sympathized with what were commonly understood to be the guiding ideals of French Canada.

Like William Kirby, who idealized the chivalrous and feudal values of the French regime in his historical novel, *The Golden Dog* (1877), imperialists as different as Castell Hopkins and G. M. Grant viewed French-Canadian society in the late nineteenth and early twentieth centuries through a romantic veil. It seemed to Hopkins that the educational system of Quebec, with its emphasis upon religious observances, duties, morals, and manners, as opposed to business affairs and material interests, had very much to commend it. "Is the final test of life," he asked, "happiness and contentment, or is it ambition, restless change, and money?" Hopkins left no doubt of his own preference: he glorified the society in which "families still frequently maintain a position of hereditary distinction"; where the social principle of mutual obligation survived; and where the suffragettes, those "advanced women" whom he abhorred, were not to be found.[41] In an article in which he weighed the quality of Canadian life in 1909 with what had prevailed in the past, one of the few encouraging signs he found was that Quebec remained a "special religious influence and conservative force."[42] Grant also admired the social role of a church which was not his own and he described French-Canadian society as an altogether beautiful Christian civilization. For over a hundred miles along the St Lawrence, he wrote, everything was "clean, orderly, idyllic. It is Arcadia in the nineteenth century, Arcadia with steam-boats, steam sawmills, the electric light and little native ponies drawing little, rude primitive carts." It troubled neither of these imperialists that Jean Baptiste did not worry his soul about "progress."[43]

Grant called the French Canadians "children of the soil" and many imperialists continued to think of them primarily as agriculturalists even after significant numbers of them were beginning to move into the urban centres. Throughout the nineteenth century many of the intellectual exponents of French-Canadian nationalism had recommended the agricultural vocation as the most secure economic basis for *la survivance*. They tended to identify industrialism with foreign ownership and an alien mentality and they feared that it would destroy the tightly knit

41 J. Castell Hopkins, *Progress of Canada in the Nineteenth Century* (Toronto, 1900), 505–6, 513–4; *French Canada and the St Lawrence* (Philadelphia, 1913), 382–3.
42 J. Castell Hopkins, "Canadian Life and Character," *University Magazine*, VIII (April 1909), 304.
43 Grant, "Our National Objects ... ," 11–12.

parish society. For different reasons, which will be suggested later, Kirby, Denison, and many other imperialists frequently expressed a deep rooted preference for agrarian values and also identified industrialism with a hateful materialization of life. For them, the archetype of the French Canadian was the *habitant* who was conventionally noted for his frugality, courtesy, hospitality, and his attachment to the land. English-Canadian writers turned from the clash and clamour of business life to the stable and traditional rural society of Quebec with both a sense of relief and a thankfulness that there was still a corner of America where the capitalist ethic had not completely triumphed. In a passage which typified this reaction, the essayist Byron Nicholson wrote in 1902:

> In the keen competition, and maddening hurry, and heartless strife of the present day, the peaceful and contented French-Canadian of this generation, especially if he belongs to the humbler classes, may not be well adapted to play a leading part. His natural inclination not to be grasping, his quiet life, his domestic disposition, his conservative tendency, all predispose him against wildly struggling in that mad rush for worldly pelf which is so distinctive of this plutocratic age ... And is it altogether a disadvantage to us, restless and dissatisfied Anglo-Saxons as we are, to have for our neighbours a race of people, who, by their comparative indifference to Mammon, are constantly reminding us that this life, with its many false ambitions, evanescent honours, and ephemeral glories, is not everything?[44]

In a similar spirit the historian G. M. Wrong turned from "the turmoil of the city streets in Toronto" and from the clank of factories in Quebec City, to the little village of St Augustin, an idyll of the simple village life. It was in the countryside, he said, that France was to be found, in the sober, prudent, and industrious farmers who were indifferent to progress and suspicious of change.[45] Here at least was stability and quiet.

This conception of French-Canadian character was certainly not confined to imperialists, nor was it merely the consequence of a well-meaning desire to turn what had so often been denounced as backwardness into a spiritual advantage. It arose partly from a literary and

44 Byron Nicholson, *The French-Canadian: A Sketch of His More Prominent Characteristics* (Toronto, 1902), 113–14. Nicholson also praised French-Canadian "business qualities" and predicted that in time a large number of them would figure among "Canada's merchant princes."
45 G. M. Wrong, "St. Augustin," *University Magazine*, XII (Feb. 1913), 65–76.

artistic quest for quaintness in the late nineteenth century when painters especially eagerly seized upon the picturesque features of French-Canadian life, the habits and morals of the country people, and inadvertently helped to shape an exaggerated image of the entire province.[46] The poetry of William Drummond, of whom it was said that "he discerned ... the true nature of the Habitant, and interpreted the soul of one-third of our people to the other two-thirds,"[47] concentrated upon peasant life and the strange speech of Little Bateese and Johnny Courteau and also sustained the same general impression. And, in a slightly different fashion, so too did the essays collected by G. M. Grant in *French Canadian Life and Character* (1899) and William Wood's *In the Heart of Old Quebec* (1913). While it grew out of the romantic temptation to seek out and exalt the peculiar and the quaint, this image was not entirely the product of patronizing English Canadians. In 1909 the premier of Quebec, Sir Lomer Gouin, told the Canadian Club of Toronto that the habitant was the "original type" of Quebec just as the United Empire Loyalist was the original type in Ontario. "Happy in his home and contented with his lot," Gouin reported, "the Habitant's light-heartedness and freedom from worry displays itself in a variety of picturesque and innocent amusements."[48]

An invariable accompaniment of this appreciation of the conservative social forms of Quebec and her loyal background, was an idealized picture of the heroic character and grandeur of French-Canadian history. Though this portrait was derived primarily from Francis Parkman's popular works, it was additionally strengthened by Canadians like Kirby who shared the Bostonian's romantic view of history. Fixing upon great figures and dramatic historic moments rather than anonymous social forces, Parkman's books were peopled by explorers, missionaries, and soldiers who strode across the continent larger than life, and, exemplified by LaSalle, his heroes were the personifications of energy and will, mastery and vigour. The scale of their exploits and the heroic quality of their efforts did much to counterbalance the equally tenacious opinion that the old regime was bereft of freedom and material progress. The impression conveyed by this romantic history proved congenial to those of the imperialist persuasion for they

46 Russell Harper, *Painting in Canada: A History* (Toronto, 1966), 244.
47 S. E. Dawson, "A Plea for Literature," Royal Society of Canada, *Proceedings and Transactions*, third series, 1908, appendix A, LXVI.
48 Sir Lomer Gouin, "The Habitant of Quebec," *Addresses Delivered Before the Canadian Club of Toronto Season 1909–10* (Toronto, 1910), 43–51. Nearly two generations later the *Preliminary Report of the Royal Commission on Bilingualism and Biculturalism* (Ottawa, 1965), 79, noted that "in almost all the English-speaking provinces a large proportion of people still think of Quebec as an archaic, rural society."

tended to see the martial spirit as an indispensable ingredient of a healthy nationalism, and, like Parkman, they admired strenuous masculinity. It was claimed that the French Canadians were not only descended from the best and most honourable blood of France, but that the primary feature of their settlement had been the preponderance of the military element. "The two races which mainly contribute to the making of the Canadian people," said one imperialist, "possess a birthright of military spirit derived from long lines of warlike ancestry."[49] In a book of children's stories entitled *Heroes of Canada* (1893), seventeen of the nineteen valiant figures described were French Canadians of the old regime. A reading of this book, said G. M. Grant, would encourage British-Canadian youth to "think all the more of their French-Canadian fellow citizens."[50] This view of the heroic character of the French reached its apogee in the celebration of the tercentennial of the founding of Quebec in 1908. The re-enactment of the military achievements of French-Canadian arms, said William Wood, demonstrated that the "Anglo-Saxon is not the only adventurous race of modern history."[51]

Heroic and loyal, contented and conservative – these were the characteristics of the French as the imperialists understood them. Even the idea of race was employed to underline similarities and reconcile differences. Implicit in a good deal of the literature describing the position of the French in Canada was the notion that their collective qualities formed a necessary counterpoise to Saxon character and that the interaction of the two races would provide distinctiveness to the Canadian nationality. This notion was ultimately grounded upon racial stereotypes: the grace and cheerfulness of the French would combine, it was said, with the drive and will of the Anglo-Saxon. The citizens of Quebec, said Sir Alexander Galt in 1881, as descendants of the Latin race, were distinguished for "industry and thrift," "courtesy and bonhommie." Though not the peer of the Anglo-Saxon in enterprise, the French Canadian "is certainly more than his equal in those amenities which beautify life and cast a charm over even the hardships of the backwoods."[52] "The greater impulsiveness and vivacity of the French Canadian," wrote Bourinot, "can brighten up, so to say, the stolidity and ruggedness of the Saxon. The strong common-sense and energy of the

49 Lt. Col. W. E. B. O'Brien, MP, "The Growth of a Military Spirit in Canada," Canadian Military Institute, *Selected Papers* (Toronto, 1891–2), 37.
50 Sir Sandford Fleming Papers, Grant to Fleming, Jan. 27 [1893]. The book was written by A. M. Machar and T. G. Marquis and published in Toronto.
51 William Wood, *In the Heart of Old Canada* (Toronto, 1913), 90.
52 *The Future of Canada: A paper read by Sir A. T. Galt G.C.M.G. before the Royal Colonial Institute ... January 25, 1881* (n.p., n.d.), 3.

Englishman can combine advantageously with the nervous, impetuous activity of the Gaul."[53] In the imagination, even if nowhere else, the two races, embodying definite aptitudes, flowed together, intermingled, and made the Canadian character unique.

In their attempt to harmonize the French Canadians with their conception of the national character the imperialists showed some sincerity, ingenuity, and not a little blindness. By thinking in such terms they often concealed from themselves the degree to which imperialism was repugnant to French Canadians. And, beneath their rosy allusions to the past, racial characteristics, and aspirations held in common, there lurked a different order of considerations. Even the most conciliatory among them remained assured that the French Canadians were destined to become an ever smaller minority within the Dominion. G. M. Grant reminded Goldwin Smith that while in the eighteenth century all Canada was French, in 1891 six of the seven provinces were English-speaking. "In half a century," he predicted, "the number of Provinces will probably be doubled and Quebec alone will be French." Very soon "most of the emigration from the northern countries of Europe will be obliged to flow into our North-West, and then into the vacant spaces of the Maritime Provinces ... The whole of that immigration will be English-speaking after the first generation. Is not this future as certain as the rising of to-morrow's sun?"[54]

George Parkin's entire assessment of the French-Canadian question and its bearing upon the prospects of imperialism hinged upon the same confidence in population growth. "The relative influence and numbers of the French element in Canada," he wrote in 1892, "will never be greater than they are at present." The French element would steadily decrease in importance, he believed, because of the migration to New England, the fact that Quebec received no immigration from France, and because their high birth rate was offset by an equally high mortality rate. They would remain, of course, attached to their language and religion and they should receive toleration from English Canadians. But the conclusion was inevitable that the French Canadians "can never dominate Canadian development, or permanently block the general movement of the Dominion in any given direction."[55] The French themselves once believed that they could attain numerical superiority in the west and thereby dominate the Dominion. This dream, announced an imperialist in 1911, had proved to be an illusion. They could no longer

53 J. G. Bourinot, *The Intellectual Development of the Canadian People* (Toronto, 1881), 16.
54 *Week*, VIII (May 15, 1891), 382.
55 G. R. Parkin, *Imperial Federation*, 153–62; *Great Dominion*, 127–47.

prevail by force of numbers; soon, ran the implication, they would cease to be even a troublesome minority.[56]

The very forces of growth and development which were pushing Canada toward nationhood within the Empire were at the same time removing the major obstacle to that realization. The imperialists expected that the party system would faithfully reflect this changing reality of power and that parties would cease to be so concerned with bowing to the opinions of Quebec. The imperial impulse in English Canada was unmistakable and potent, and, after all, English Canadians were the majority; the business of political leadership, as Parkin phrased it in criticizing Laurier's temporizing, was "to boldly lead the country along the path that the British Majority is ready to take – with an assurance that Quebec would sufficiently follow him."[57] There were those who cautioned against such bluntness and maintained that such remarks only delayed the ends they were meant to achieve. The solution, after all, was simplicity itself. The influence of the French was inexorably decreasing; they had to support imperial consolidation if the majority wanted it; given their strong attachment to British institutions and their suspicion of the United States there was simply no other course. The more sympathetically they were treated the sooner would they realize that they had nothing to fear from the dictates of destiny.

Yet even the counsellors of moderation, and Denison was one of these, revealed their real intentions in times of crisis, as in 1917, when rhetoric could no longer obscure the gulf that separated French and English Canadians. The formation of Union government to enforce conscription against the opposition of Quebec, was regarded as the final triumph of Canada First. After fifty years, Denison exulted, "my party had got into power." It took a long time for our principle to prevail, he told Mair, but prevail it had: the best elements of the two parties had combined to place the interests of Canada and the Empire first. The victory of the Union government signified "that Canada does not intend to be ruled any more by the French."[58] All the British provinces were united against Quebec and the game the French had played since Confederation of balancing one party against the other could be played no more.

This conclusion does not mean that the views of Denison and his associates on the French Canadians were necessarily fraudulent and in-

56 James Cappon, "Canada's Relation to the Empire," *Queen's Quarterly*, xix (Oct., Nov., Dec. 1911), 90–1. For a similar statement see Theodore H. Boggs, "Canada and the French-Canadian," *University Magazine*, x (Feb. 1911), 51.
57 Lord Minto Papers, Parkin to Minto, March 24, 1902 (copy).
58 QUL, Charles Mair Papers, Denison to Mair, Oct. 24 and Dec. 29, 1917, and March 18, 1918.

sincere rationalizations. It was quite possible to believe that the French had many desirable qualities and that they were destined to play a small and rather docile role in the future of Canada. In fact, the more one was convinced of their numerical unimportance, the more one could glorify their character.

III

While the imperialists did not doubt that the Canadian population would increase to an enormous size and that the majority would be English-speaking, they grew more and more apprehensive at the massive growth of immigration after the mid-1890s and particularly in the years immediately preceding the First World War. In the past the Dominion had received only a few immigrants from southern, east-central, and southeastern Europe and Canadian critics of the United States had maintained, with varying degrees of self-satisfaction, that it was a blessing that their country did not have an immigrant problem on the American scale. They believed that the non-northern European immigrants were largely responsible for political corruption and social turmoil in the United States and that they posed a fundamental threat to the Anglo-Saxon leadership of the republic. "The United States," declared one magazine in 1891, "are welcome to the Hungarians, Poles, Italians and others of that class; they are, as a rule, wretchedly poor, make very poor settlers, and bring with them many of the vices and socialistic tendencies which have caused such trouble to their hosts already. Renewed efforts should ... be made by our government to induce more of the hardy German and Norwegian races to remain here."[59]

Having had little previous experience of eastern Europeans and holding these negative and critical opinions of immigrants in the United States, it was only natural that some Canadians should become concerned and worried over the ever growing number of "foreigners" brought into the Dominion by Clifford Sifton's aggressive immigration service and publicity campaigns. Misgivings about these people was no singular preoccupation of imperialists. Rev. J. S. Woodsworth, whose determination to arouse Canadian Methodism to an awareness of its social mission arose partly from his personal acquaintance with immigrant communities, drew attention to the existence of different "race stocks" in the country and, referring to the experiments of Luther Burbank in grafting plants, warned that what the scientist had done "in a small way with fruits and vegetables we are doing on a gigantic scale with the human species." The flow of immigration should be subject to regulation, compulsory education introduced, and the franchise should

59 *Dominion Illustrated: A Canadian Pictorial Weekly*, VI (April 11, 1891), 338.

not be given automatically to Galicians who looked upon the vote as something to be sold.[60] J. A. Macdonald, editor of the *Globe*, shared Woodsworth's alarm over what would happen to Canadian citizenship and political standards if the "large masses of alien and undemocratic immigration," particularly of orientals "who are by nature and instinct undemocratic," remained unchecked.[61] And because the immigration policy of the Laurier government was endangering the racial dualism upon which the Canadian nationality rested, Henri Bourassa also condemned it for heedlessly sacrificing long-term goals for short-term business advantages.[62]

Estimates by imperialists of the ultimate impact of the strangers upon the Canadian national character were invariably confused and compounded by previous knowledge of the example of the United States. In 1899 the editor of the *Canadian Magazine* rebuked the government for bringing in outlandish foreigners while failing to subsidize the migration of English-speaking Canadians from Ontario to the west. "Is Canada to become," he queried, "as rude, as uncultured, as fickle, as heterogeneous, as careless of law and order and good citizenship as the United States?"[63] Charles A. Magrath, member of Parliament for Medicine Hat who once said his imperialism was a kind of religion, published a comprehensive survey of the immigrant problem in the west and analysed its dangers in terms of American precedents. Drawing heavily upon the literature of American commentators, usually restrictionists, he advised that determined programmes had to be undertaken to instil into the new arrivals an understanding and appreciation of the ideals of the British people. "We believe," he wrote, "that there are many sections in southern and eastern Europe very many years behind in the march of civilization, occupied by people ground down by centuries of oppression, many of whom cannot understand the meaning of liberty, which to them is licence, and who evidently have an intense hatred for the majesty of the law." What happened to the neighbouring republic should serve as an example, he said: "It is our privilege to take advantage of their experience."[64] As George Foster calculated in 1912, Canada faced a comparatively more difficult task than the United States

60 J. S. Woodsworth, "Canadians of To-Morrow," *Canadian Club of Toronto, Season 1909–1910* (Toronto, 1910), 139, 148.
61 J. A. Macdonald, "Canadian Clubs and Canadian Problems," *Canadian Club of Toronto, Season 1907–1908* (Toronto, 1908), 256–7.
62 Henri Bourassa, "The Nationalist Movement in Quebec," *Canadian Club of Toronto, Season 1906–07* (Toronto, 1907), 61.
63 *Canadian Magazine*, XIII (May 1899), 89.
64 Charles A. Magrath, *Canada's Growth and Some Problems Affecting It* (Ottawa, 1910), 54; "Stray Thoughts About Canada and the Empire," *Canadian Club of Toronto, Season 1911–12* (Toronto, 1912), 70.

because while the Americans had ninety million people to assimilate one million newcomers annually, the Dominion with eight million had to absorb five hundred thousand each year. In other words, while the United States had ninety-two people to absorb each immigrant, Canada had only sixteen.[65]

Though the question of the possible effect non-British immigration would have upon Canada's imperial future was constantly raised, imperialists were not driven into advocating total exclusion of certain groups, although they certainly retained their suspiciousness and watchfulness. The imperialists could appreciate the force of such remarks as that of a British observer who drew attention to the indiscriminate settlement of "Russian and Galician Jews, Greeks, Germans, Dutch, Poles, Hungarians, Italians, and even Syrians and Turks" and inquired whether there was anything to prevent "Canada from becoming entirely 'Americanized' and severing its connexion with the British Empire?"[66] They could also understand the sentiments of R. B. Bennett of Calgary who asked the members of the Canadian Club of Toronto whether they would permit the destiny of Canada to be determined "by men who have no love for our traditions, who know not of them, and have none of our reflected aspirations?"[67] But in general they were satisfied that it was possible to make these heterogeneous nationalities into British subjects. They were assured, moreover, that because these people settled on the land their disruptive impact on urban centres would be slight, or alternatively, that the most troublesome types would be prevented from coming, discouraged by the severity of the climate. "By the vigour of the North-west winter," wrote the political economist Adam Shortt in 1895, "the country is preserved from the overflow of Southern Europe."[68]

That repository of so many nativist trepidations, Colonel Denison, showed little fear over the presence of even Americans on the prairies. He was certain that once an imperial tariff was arranged and Canadian agricultural commodities accorded preferential treatment in the British market, they would support imperial unity on economic grounds alone. In addition, it was felt that the cultural patterns already fully imprinted upon western Canada would limit the extent to which immigrants could

65 George E. Foster, "Some Problems of Empire," *United Empire: Royal Colonial Institute Journal*, new series, III (Dec. 1912), 957.
66 Basil Stewart, *"No English Need Apply" or, Canada as a Field for the Emigrant* (London, 1909), vi, 47.
67 R. B. Bennett, "The Northwest Provinces and their Relation to Confederation," *Canadian Club of Toronto, Season 1911–12* (Toronto, 1912), 198.
68 A. Shortt, "Some Observations on the Great North-West," *Queen's Quarterly*, III (July 1895), 14.

alter Canadian values and standards. It augured well for national unity, Principal Falconer of the University of Toronto maintained, that the fundamental character of the west had been established by migration from the east before the large influx of foreigners took place. "Older Canada," he wrote, "sent out her sons to possess the new lands, and these first settlers belonging to the stronger races from which the older portions of Canada were colonized established the type of new life. Older political, social and religious ideals are so essentially inherent in the character, that, like hardy seeds wafted by ocean currents to distant shores, they reproduce in the new environment fruit similar in quality to that which was found in their former home."[69] "Manitoba," a westerner added, "is a duplicate of Ontario."[70] The educationists, missionaries, and settlers from the east had indelibly stamped upon the west the Canadian character, that is, the character of the Maritimes and Ontario, and consequently immigrants and their children had standards to which they could accommodate themselves and values and institutions which would present them with "Canadianism."

In spite of such hopeful signs and assurances as these, imperialists none the less positively preferred to see Canada settled by agriculturalists from the British Isles, a preference which had been shared by the Canada Firsters as well as John A. Macdonald. Imperialists looked with dismay and disappointment upon the migration of British people to countries outside the Empire, notably to the United States, and they often wished that the British government would help in channelling its surplus population to the Dominions. "I am told," George Ross informed a meeting of the British Empire League in 1901, "that the annual emigration from your shores numbers about 100,000, and we get only about 10,000 of them ... If you want to put us in a position in which we can be of more assistance to the Empire, give us your surplus population."[71] Canada required farmers, said Ross, people who would settle the west, produce food for Britain, and thereby strengthen the imperial union. "One of the primal and most enduring bonds is blood and race," added George Foster and, in order to preserve Canadian allegiance to the ideal of Empire, it was necessary "to keep the British stock dominant."[72] The encouragement of immigration from Britain, he was convinced, would also relieve social pressures within England and cure

69 Sir Robert A. Falconer, "The Unification of Canada," *University Magazine,* VII (Feb. 1908), 4.
70 J. A. M. Aikins, "Manitoba and its Relation to Confederation," *Canadian Club of Toronto, Season 1911–12* (Toronto, 1912), 132.
71 *Addresses Delivered by Hon. G. W. Ross During His Recent Visit to England and at the Meeting on His Return* (n.p., [1910]), 15–16.
72 Foster, "Some Problems of Empire," 953, 957; see also *Address Delivered in the Drill Hall, Victoria, B.C., by Hon. George Eulas Foster ... on 'Canada Within the Empire,'* Tuesday, February 18th, 1913 (n.p., n.d.), 3.

unemployment. Parkin thought that one city-bred Englishman, if properly selected and trained, would be worth more to western Canada than all the Doukhobors put together,[73] and W. L. Grant, alluding to all the foregoing advantages, proposed a systematic and state-directed programme of British immigration which he called the "imperialism of peace."[74]

While wishing to see fewer foreigners and more Britishers, yet accepting the continental Europeans as necessary for the economic development of the country and hopeful of the possibility of making them into British subjects, the imperialists all remained hostile to the idea that these arrivals would alter the Canadian character as they understood it. It was this fear that frequently motivated the warning that a careless concentration upon economic expansion was betraying and undermining the Canadian nationality. Stephen Leacock, whose contempt for "the Galicians," as all the east-central Europeans were indiscriminately labelled, was a life-long habit, dismissed the fusion theory of Canadian nationality with sarcastic scorn. "Poles, Hungarians, Bukowinians and any others ... will come in to share the heritage which our fathers have won," he wrote: "Out of all these we are to make a kind of mixed race in which is to be the political wisdom of the British, the chivalry of the French, the gall of the Galician, the hungriness of the Hungarian and the dirtiness of the Doukobor [sic]."[75]

The undercurrent of misgivings and disquietude, sometimes derision and dread, which obtruded in the rhetoric of imperialism and in other quarters as well before the World War, culminated in 1917 when those who had been born in the lands of the central powers and who had been naturalized since 1902 were disfranchised. The racial, sectional, and class antagonism intensified by the war, combined with the distrust of foreigners which wartime propaganda magnified, impelled some Canadians into a renewed questioning of the unselective immigration policy and led others into a black pessimism concerning racial degeneracy. In a bitter assessment in 1920, Andrew Macphail reminded Canadians of the law that whenever races are mixed the lower always prevailed. "The melting pot," he said, "... means that instead of the pure race from which we have come, we shall have a mongrel race, and this mongrel race is making itself known in Canada as a result of the immigration we have had."[76]

73 *United Empire*, new series, III (March 1912), 216.
74 W. L. Grant, "The Imperialism of Peace," *Arbor*, I (Nov. 1910), 7–10.
75 Stephen Leacock, "The Political Achievement of Robert Baldwin," *Addresses Delivered Before the Canadian Club of Ottawa, 1903–1909* (Ottawa, 1910), 164.
76 Andrew Macphail, "The Immigrant," *Canadian Club Year Book, 1919–1920* (Ottawa, 1920), 171.

Canadian imperialism, then, had in common with all nationalist ideologies a definite conception of what the national character encompassed and what its destiny would be. According to this view, Canadians were British in their historical associations, political ideals, their preference for law and order, and their capacity for self-government. They were, French and English alike, a tough and masterful people, inured to the stern climate of a northern nation whose population would in time exceed that of Britain. While the French Canadians were recognized as having exhibited an unchanging loyalty to the Empire and added distinctive charm to the Canadian character, they were also understood to be least enthusiastic for imperial unity. Their opposition to imperialism, however, was of small consequence and could only be significant temporarily because the rapid growth of the English-speaking section of the population, including the "foreigners" who would be assimilated to the prevailing ideals, would in the end exert a total dominance over the Canadian nationality.

6

Critique of the Republic

At every turn Canadian imperialists were forced to consider Canada's relationship to the United States. On this subject as on many others, they differed among themselves, but for various reasons, real or imagined, they were all convinced that the republic represented an undesirable social order. Their view of the United States was neither uniformly hostile nor was it completely uninformed; certainly it was not totally fabricated out of bitterness and traditional animosity. It gained much of its force from what was happening within that country itself during the late nineteenth century as well as from inherited predispositions and nationalist sentiment.

I

One of the curious features of Canadian views of the United States was that, while geographical proximity afforded countless opportunities to examine the nature of American society, Canadians have never produced significant interpretations of American life that could rank with the travelogues of Charles Dickens or Mrs Trollope, let alone the monumental study of Alexis de Tocqueville. It may well be that in the later nineteenth century their capacity for understanding was blunted by prejudice, but even the liberal nationalists of the 1920s and 1930s who thought of Canada as an interpreter in the Anglo-American relationship accomplished little in the way of explaining American society to foreigners. Lacking such a body of native literature Canadians have traditionallly employed critical accounts of the United States written by Europeans, usually Englishmen, or by Americans who portrayed shortcomings within their own country. In the 1880s, for example, such books as Woodrow Wilson's *Congressional Government* (1887) and *The State* (1889), which praised the British cabinet system and pointed out the weaknesses of the division of powers in the American constitution, or James Bryce's *The American Commonwealth* (1888), which judged that the corruption of municipal government constituted the major failing of American democracy, confirmed much that was inarticulately felt by Canadians. Undoubtedly John A. Macdonald's secretary, Sir Joseph Pope, read Matthew Arnold's appraisal of American life as fundamentally too uniform and uninteresting with as much interest as an anonymous reviewer in the *Week* perused Josiah Strong's *Our Country* (1885), a catalogue of the various perils facing the republic – immigration, Romanism, Mormonism, intemperance, socialism, the growth of irresponsible wealth, urbanization, and the imminent exhaustion of cheap lands in the west.[1] While it has been argued that in the early nineteenth century Canadian views of the United States were lacking in both understanding and information,[2] this was certainly not the case in the decades after 1880. Indeed, one of the reasons why the imperialists were able to isolate particular events and developments as objects of reprehension and censure was the ready availability within Canada of American books, periodicals, newspapers, and magazines. So accessible were American publications, in fact, that in the years after 1900 the imperialists themselves began denouncing these instruments of "Americanization" and proposing counter-measures such as the reduction in postal rates on British magazines and the formation of an imperial intelligence union.

The most extreme and caustic portrayal of American life emanated from the descendants of the United Empire Loyalists and their chief spokesman, Colonel Denison. Their centennial celebrations in Toronto provided an excellent occasion for voicing extravagant and fantastic denunciations of the moral character of Americans, but not even the descendants of the loyalists were of one mind on this matter. At the centennial ceremonies in New Brunswick in 1887 a completely different outlook prevailed. At St John the Union Jack and Stars and Stripes were displayed together, the Lieutenant-Governor, W. D. Wilmot, set the tone of the speech-making when he declared "that no feeling of hostility now exists between ourselves and our American cousins"; and the mayor of the city averred that "we are now as one nation."[3] This regional difference in views of the United States was generally characteristic of imperialists: Parkin and Grant never matched, and were even offended by, some of Denison's more hysterical prognostications. Upper Canada had borne the brunt of attack in 1812–14 and, as

1 Matthew Arnold, *Civilization in America from the Nineteenth Century for April, 1888*. Pope's copy is in the pamphlet collection, Public Archives of Canada. The review of Strong's book is in the *Week*, IV (Dec. 16, 1888), 37.
2 S. F. Wise, "Through the Lace Curtain: Canadian Views of American Democracy in the Pre-Civil War Period," Canadian Association for American Studies, *Bulletin*, II (Winter 1967), 46–68.
3 New Brunswick Historical Society, *Loyalists' Centennial Souvenir* (St John, 1887), 11, 16, 33.

Denison once pointed out, every generation of Toronto citizens had seen the dead bodies of her defenders carried along the streets. The Maritimes, in contrast, had profited from that war and there was no Maritime tradition of 1812. Fear of the power of the United States was heightened in the inland province which was far removed from the protective arm of British sea power, and, as well, in so far as "anti-Americanism" functioned as a defence of the national protectionist policy, Ontario had a more substantial economic interest in it than did the seaboard provinces. But to whatever origins this difference may be traced the more temperate attitude towards the United States was one of the leading features of Maritime imperialism.

II

The major component of the Canadian image of the United States was the idea that the British constitution was superior to republicanism. When that Yankee pedlar, Sam Slick, observed that "our constitutions don't differ no great odds," he uttered a judgment which few Canadians in the 1880s would endorse. "We have the freest institutions and most direct self-government in the world ... ," the *Canadian Methodist Magazine* boasted in 1880. "We are free from many of the social cancers which are empoisoning the national life of our neighbours. We have no polygamous Mormondom; no Ku-Klux terrorism; no Oneida communism; no Illinois divorce system; no cruel Indian massacres."[4] As this remark suggests, when Canadians praised the British form of government, they were speaking not so much about the external, legalistic husks of a constitutional system, nor were they lauding a specific representative or administrative apparatus. They praised the British constitution because it was both a sounder system in which desirable character was developed and a more effective instrument for promoting the maximum of social progress without social instability. Their remarks implied an interpretation not so much of government but of society and the motives for social behaviour.

The conviction that the democratic republicanism to the south was unstable and chaotic was deeply embedded in the Canadian mind. The men who forged Confederation were imbued with an abiding suspicion not only of the division of powers in the American federal system but of the erratic and unpredictable course of democracy in general. D'Arcy McGee, whose Catholic conservatism was reinforced by the principles of Edmund Burke, criticized the process of excessive democratization which the United States experienced in the early years of the nineteenth

4 *Canadian Methodist Magazine*, XI (Feb. 1880), 188.

century. While the basis of the monarchical form of government, he said, "is humility, self-denial, obedience, and holy fear," pure democracy "is very like pride – it is the 'good-as-you' feeling carried into politics. Pure democracy asserts an unreal equality between youth and age, subject and magistrate, the weak and the strong, the vicious and the virtuous. But the same virtues which feed and nourish filial affection and conjugal peace in private life, are essential to uphold civil authority; and they are the virtues on which the monarchical form of government alone can be maintained." The scheme of Confederation, he once argued, "will enable us ... to resist the spread of this universal democracy doctrine."[5] What McGee condemned, and what de Tocqueville had earlier isolated as the most striking feature of the United States, was the social atomization, the erosion of recognized standards of authority, and the rejection of precedent which affected every facet of American life.

One of the most lucid expositions of the contrast between British and American social principles was offered by an Irishman, Nicholas Flood Davin, in a speech delivered in Toronto in 1873 under the auspices of the local St George's Society.[6] Though Davin had only recently arrived in the country and had never visited the United States, he submitted a cogent condemnation of republicanism which was published as the second pamphlet in the nationalist series, the first being William Foster's *Canada First*. Like Macaulay and Lord Durham before him, Davin asserted that it was the frontier, not the republican form of government, that kept America free from despotism. "If despotism, an impossibility in Great Britain, is out of the question for the present in the United States," he said, "it is not because of the nature of the government, or of the civilization, but because of the immense waste of unoccupied territory lying westward. Subduing this under the influence of sanguine hopes of wealth ... absorb[ed] all the restless and adventurous elements of Society." American society was neither sufficiently organized nor compact, and the day would come when the social conditions in America would resemble those in the old world, and then the liberty of the people would need to be protected by something more substantial than an ephemeral frontier. Despotism would become pos-

5 Thomas D'Arcy McGee, *Speeches and Addresses chiefly on the Subject of British-American Union* (London, 1865), 131, 300.
6 N. F. Davin, *British versus American Civilization, A lecture delivered in Shaftesbury Hall, Toronto, 19th April 1873* (Toronto, 1873). See his "Remarks Suggested by President Garfield's Death," *Rose-Belford's Canadian Monthly and National Review*, VII (Dec. 1881), 621, particularly for his observations on the role of "the vast unoccupied country to the west" in preventing internal social strains.

sible in the United States, he predicted, because Americans rejected the cardinal social principle which had maintained and nourished liberty in Britain – the respect for rank and hierarchical order. Because they had repudiated the inevitability of the gradations of social rank as expressing in outward form human differences and inequalities, there could be but one motive for behaviour. "In the United States – as in every purely democratic community – where there is nothing to differentiate one man from another, but wealth, nothing therefore to aim at but wealth, character becomes materialized, and love of personal well being usurps a disproportionate and unhealthy place in the mind."

Against this uniformity and materialism, Davin contrasted the British ideal of hierarchical order and multiplicity of motives for social action. Assuming as a "general truth that the more numerous the forces contending in a community, the more shall we find individuality, originality –rich, moral and intellectual life," he attributed British freedom to the fact that for a thousand years the monarchical, aristocratic, ecclesiastical, and democratic principles have been contending for domination in the nation, "none ever obtaining complete mastery." In such a variegated society there existed many motives for conduct, while in America the principle one was money-making. "The notion of society in a democracy is a uniform one, and the system of life provides no image of a high development of graceful and accomplished humanity." Davin presented the fundamental choice to Canadians, reminding them that their decision would put the stamp on thousands of generations:

> Which is preferable – a society in which mammon is supreme; wealth the only test of merit; without ... love for long enduring toil tending toward glorious objects ... a society restless, undignified, unshapely, unlovely; or that fair order in which degrees of rank provide various motives and enrich the standard of merit: in which the love of fame is sure to be active; in which greatness is out of reach of none and difficult of access for all; which, broad based on the will of a great and proud people, rises up by bright gradations until it culminates in the calm and by-faction-unsullied figure of the Sovereign[?]

Though many commended the British system with equal zeal, few revealed so vividly as did Davin the common assumptions behind the conviction that Americans were a materialistic people.

Canadians were no less convinced that the looseness and licence of American society were due to the absence of the cohesive power of religion. Writing in 1881 the constitutional historian, Alpheus Todd, pointed out that Canadian loyalty was not some transient emotion but an enduring principle, "powerful enough to enable us to withstand many vicissitudes before consenting to exchange our free institutions ... for any other form of government upon earth." The chief advantage which Canada received from the British connection, Todd wrote, was "the inestimable advantage of stable Christian government, which affords to individuals the utmost possible freedom consistent with wholesome restraints upon the excesses of democratic opinion or the license of profanity." By Christian government he did not mean a state church, but rather "the distinct responsibility of a Christian government to respect the revealed laws of God, to enforce the decorous observance of the Christian Sabbath, and generally to protect and uphold the institutions of Christianity." The Christian religion, Todd believed, was part and parcel of the British constitution: "the entire framework of our polity is pervaded with ennobling influences and restraints of religion." The Americans, on the other hand, deliberately left out of their constitution any acknowledgment of a Supreme Being, declared "the people" the source of all power, and expressed no national preferences for Christianity over Judaism, Mohammedanism, or infidelity. Though the American people, he wrote, may be remarkable as a God-fearing people, they have repudiated any "necessary connection between religion and politics." In the United States "there is a grievous lack of the restraining influences of government to repress the abuses of free thought, in social and religious matters. Witness the liberty allowed in that country to the growth ... of Mormonism in the western territories, and the reckless blasphemies of Ingersoll – both of them awful growths and developments of free thought ... Such abominable and injurious outcomes of the right of private judgment could not assuredly have originated or have been permitted to take root in England, or in any of her colonies."[7]

Other Canadian scholars commented at length upon the instability of American political institutions. During the late 1880s books and popular articles offering comparative treatments of the British, American, and Canadian constitutions appeared in increasing numbers and not a few were written with the intention of strengthening an attachment to British institutions. J. G. Bourinot, who was one of the first Canadian political scientists to detail the exact differences between the Canadian and American forms of government, was certain that the Canadian determination to oppose annexation arose largely from the belief that American republicanism was an inferior and troubled form of govern-

---

7 Alpheus Todd, "Is Canadian Loyalty a Sentiment or a Principle?" *Canadian Monthly*, VII (Nov. 1881), 523–30. Ingersoll was an American politician and lawyer who held unorthodox religious views.

CRITIQUE OF THE REPUBLIC

ment.[8] A lawyer told the Toronto branch of the Imperial Federation League that if "on a comparison of the two systems we find good reason to consider that the British system ... is far preferable to that of our neighbours, a valuable weapon for Canadian use is added to the armoury of the Federation League."[9] Disclaiming originality, he added that one need only consult the expert judgments of British and American writers like Bryce, Wilson, Bagehot, Maine, and von Holst. The Canadian desire to remain British, ran a typical article in the *Week*,

> is the outcome of [the] conviction that Republican institutions are too loose and vague in their influence on the human mind to ensure the highest form of national stability and prosperity; and that a constitutional monarchy, wisely limited, is invested with characteristics of steadiness and permanence such as do not belong to any development of republicanism the world has ever seen. The immense patronage in the hands of an executive having only a brief term of power; its irresponsibility to the people while in office; the quadrennial upheaval of the whole nation to elect its chief magistrate; the elective judiciary; the power of the mobocracy; the constant under-working of secret political leagues ... have created a deeply-seated preference for British institutions [in Canada] ... Without claim to prophetic mantle ... one may safely predict that Canada will never be annexed to the United States.[10]

When the premier of Ontario itemized the reasons for opposing absorption into the republic, he was voicing the common wisdom in emphasizing "CANADIAN CONSTITUTIONAL SYSTEM SUPERIOR TO THAT OF THE UNITED STATES."[11]

However much Canadian critics might have been moved by traditional antagonism their beliefs regarding the failures of American government were in no small part a product of what was happening within the United States during the later nineteenth century. It is a commonplace of American political history that in the 1870s and 1880s the moral and intellectual tone of political life was low and that political conflicts were predominantly concerned with patronage rather than principle. In the early 1870s, Boss Tweed's theft of $100 million from

8 J. G. Bourinot, "Why Canadians do not favor Annexation," *Forum*, XIX (May 1895), 276–88.
9 A. H. F. Lefroy, *The British versus The American System of National Government, being a paper read before the Toronto branch of the Imperial Federation League on Thursday, December 18th, 1890* (Toronto, 1891), 7.
10 *Week*, VIII (Dec. 5, 1890), 5.
11 *The Reform Party and Canada's Future. An Open Letter From the Hon. Oliver Mowat, Premier of Ontario, to the Hon. Alexander Mackenzie, M.P. for East York, and formerly Premier of Canada* (Toronto, 1891), 27.

the city of New York, the well-publicized peculations and depravities of the carpetbag regimes in the former Confederate states, the Credit Mobilier and "whiskey ring" scandals, all served to confirm the ancient Canadian idea that American government encouraged and made possible corruption and irresponsibility. To such sophisticated critiques of American government as Bryce's *American Commonwealth* were added the assertions of the farmers who contended that they were being victimized by a conspiracy of economic interests and their political power negated by corrupt electoral arrangements. The Populist Party which emerged in the early 1890s denounced the essentially undemocratic character of American politics and its platform of 1892 called for the Australian ballot, the direct election of senators, and the initiative and referendum. Social disruption as well as political impurity seemed proven by events. The most conspicuous characteristic of American society was instability and the loosening of social ties under the impact of industrialization, urbanization, and immigration. In the 1880s the evils resulting from these developments became subjects of anxious debate and Americans became especially concerned about the survival of democracy in the face of business domination. It was in this decade too that the original impetus was imparted by such men as Henry George, Edward Bellamy, and Josiah Strong to the many-sided, moralistic, progressive movement. The violence which Canadians always associated with American society seemed confirmed by the great strike of 1877, the Haymarket massacre of 1886, the labour conflicts at Homestead in 1892 and the Pullman plant in Chicago in 1894, as well as by the march of Coxey's army of the unemployed upon Washington during the winter of 1893–94. So massive were the problems of social violence, business domination, and political corruption that some historians were to wonder subsequently how the United States escaped a bloody revolution in these years, and so substantial were the perils to the republic – described and denounced by Americans themselves – that those Canadians who sought to underline the dangers of annexation had a rich and abundant range of facts to draw upon.

Canadians found American contempt for law, order, and control manifested in nearly every sphere of social life. The statistics of divorce and crime were regular features of accounts of the United States. The dean of the faculty of law of McGill University claimed that "divorce is in the United States, proportionately to the population, more than 320 times as common as in Canada." In the forty years after 1867, while "the various states of the union have dissolved 1,274,341 marriages, Canada has been slowly compiling the beggarly total of 431 divorces." Since the family was regarded as the very cornerstone of a stable, conservative society, its dissolution was treated as a relapse into barbarism.

Of all the causes tending to increase the rate of divorce in the United States, and these included the nervous irritability of leading a life at high pressure and the economic independence of women, the one most often mentioned was the rejection of restraint. "The same spirit which, carried to the extreme length, is manifested in lynchings and murders finds a milder expression in the intolerance of control in the family."[12] Because his position as chief magistrate in Toronto gave him access to comparative criminal statistics, Denison became a specialist in American criminal history. Lawlessness and violence, he said, had been rampant in the republic for a hundred years, and "life is now more unsafe in the United States than in any civilized or semi-civilized country in the world." "There were 1,500 convictions for murder across the line in 1883, and only 93 hangings, while 118 people were lynched. The chances of a murderer escaping after he is convicted in the United States are sixteen to one. The number of murders in England amount to 237 per annum in each ten millions; in the United States they are 820, or three times as many." "The frontier settlements in Canada," he declared on another occasion, "were orderly, while the revolver, the bowie-knife, and 'Judge Lynch' ruled along the borders of civilization in the United States."[13] If Denison's criminal statistics lent an aura of objectivity to the contention that Americans were lawless, observation of contemporary American life reinforced the same point: in 1891 eleven Italians were lynched in New Orleans; in the late 1880s the number of Negroes lynched increased spectacularly. Within a single generation Canadians had seen three presidents of the United States assassinated: Lincoln in 1865, Garfield in 1881, and McKinley in 1901.

The diversity of maladies afflicting American society did not discourage efforts to attribute them to a single source. It was not in economic change that Canadian critics located the cause of these problems but rather in the fundamental principle announced by the revolutionaries of 1776. One need not be surprised at the Homestead riots, the Chicago strike, resorts to violence and murders, declared the president of the United Empire Loyalist Association in 1896, for "did not the Revolution teach Americans that if your neighbour does not agree with you, you may shoot him, confiscate his property, and injure him to the utmost of your ability?"[14] "The United States began with an act of

12 F. P. Walton, "Divorce in Canada and the United States: A Contrast," *University Magazine*, IX (Dec. 1910), 579–96.
13 *The Centennial of the Settlement of Upper Canada by the United Empire Loyalists, 1784–1884. The Celebrations at Adolphustown, Toronto and Niagara* (Toronto, 1885), 68, 96; *Imperial Federation: The Journal of the Imperial Federation League*, IV (Feb. 1, 1889), 32.
14 George S. Ryerson, *The After-Math of a Revolution: Being the Inaugural Address as President of the United Empire Loyalist Association, Delivered November 12, 1896* (Toronto, 1896), 11.

lawlessness," wrote the editor of the *University Magazine*, "and their conduct ever since has been marked by that spirit." They could have no social organization because they espoused an unworkable theory of society. Rejecting the binding force of convention and the legacies of the past, possessing no secure anchor in human nature, lacking a sense of obligation and bereft of all principles except money-making, American society stood as a living proof of the essential truth of Walter Bagehot's epigram that men cannot adopt a constitution any more than they can adopt a father.[15]

III

In their descriptions of the United States Canadians seldom failed to mention the existence of perilous racial problems. In the years before the Civil War they had looked upon the institution of slavery as both a social cancer with which they did not want to be contaminated and a proof of the fraudulence of American professions of democracy. In the late nineteenth century the presence of millions of Negroes within the United States was regarded as a possible source of turmoil and social tension. The American people, said an imperialist in 1889, "have all the elements at work for a civil strife in over 7,000,000 of negroes, whose cruel treatment at this hour in Southern cities may any day lead to a social convulsion."[16] "We may even venture," wrote another Canadian in a self-congratulatory vein, "... to compare ourselves favorably in some respects with the United States ... We have no 'nigger question' ... no lynch law."[17] The systematic disfranchisement of Negroes in the period following Reconstruction and the growth in the number of lynchings provided Parkin with substance for a sermon on the insincerity of American political democracy. "Should the Dominion be annexed to the United States," he wrote in 1892, "all the voting weight of Canada within the union would for a generation to come scarcely balance this single negro element of America's population, supposing that, in accordance with Canadian ideas of political justice, the negroes should be allowed (as they are not now) to exercise their legal right."[18] While

15 Andrew Macphail, "New Lamps for Old." *University Magazine*, VIII (Feb. 1909), 18–35.
16 John Hague, *Canada for Canadians: A Royalist "Roland" for the Annexationist "Oliver," A Paper Read Before the Toronto Branch of the Imperial Federation League, in Association Hall, Toronto, the 23rd January, 1889* (Toronto, n.d.), 7.
17 James Duff, "Alexander McLachlan," *Queen's Quarterly*, VIII (Oct. 1900), 133.
18 G. R. Parkin, *Imperial Federation: The Problem of National Unity* (London, 1892), 136. For other instances of how the "negro question" figured in Canadian pictures of the turbulent republic, see Rev. George Bryce, *A New Nation,*

insisting that under British conceptions of liberty the Negro would have the vote, Parkin none the less contended that Canadians should be thankful for not bearing the heavy burden of integrating the weaker races into their society.

The treatment of the North American Indian also provided an opportunity for censoriousness. In the two decades after the Civil War, Indian warfare was a constant theme in western history and it is no accident that two of the major literary sources which present critical pictures of the United States – William Kirby's *Canadian Idylls* (1888) and Charles Mair's *Tecumseh* (1886) – examine this topic at length. Though both are set in the period of the War of 1812 the impression is unmistakable that Kirby and Mair were not unmindful of the implications of the fact that the Indians had supported Brock and the British connection. In Kirby's "Pontiac," the old chief, White Ermine, tells the young Clifford:

> In this Dominion only – God be praised!
> Old English law and justice, and the rights
> Of every man are sacredly maintained.
> Here conscience lives, and the bright covenant chains
> Were never broken with the Indian tribes.
> We grow and prosper, and unenvied rise,
> And in the social race win many a prize,
> Our wigwams change to houses, wood and stone;
> Our forests turn to fields, our gardens grow
> With fruits and flowers – our barns are full of corn:
>
> . . .
>
> Now casting off the skins and mantles rude
> Of our old life, we don the seemly garb
> Of Christian men and women, worship God,
> And make the laws that govern us, and stand
> Not wards, but freemen, of this glorious land.[19]

While Mair's lament over the disintegration of Indian culture was not the major theme of his drama, his condemnation of American brutality in their relations with the noble savage nevertheless strengthened the impression which Kirby conveyed.

The enormous increase in the numbers of immigrants from southern and eastern Europe entering the United States attracted almost as much

or "*The First Quarter-Century of the Dominion*". *Being the president's inaugural Lecture to the Manitoba College Literary Society* (n.p., 1893), 5; G. T. Denison Papers, Scrapbook, 1897–1915, clipping from *St John Sun*, Jan. 20, 1898.

19 William Kirby, *Canadian Idylls* (Welland, Ontario, second edition, 1894), 66.

attention in Canadian discussions as did the record of social conflict. The slow shift in the sources of immigration from north and north-western to south and southeastern Europe during the 1880s coincided with the growing turbulence and violence in American society. The census of 1890 revealed that Italians and other southern European nationalities had greatly increased in numbers. This was regarded in some quarters as undesirable and dangerous because it was widely believed that southern races were incapable of self-government and that they were debasing the standards of American democracy. The immigrant became a scapegoat for the urban reformer who charged that he was responsible for the degeneration and corruption of city government; the conservative who believed the outlandish arrivals were bringing the alien ideology of socialism to the republic; the Protestant who feared the growth of Catholic power; and, in a qualified way, the spokesman of labour who feared the competition of cheap, immigrant workers. While the resurgence of American nativism and anti-foreignism was generated more by the general insecurity attendant upon industrialization and economic dislocations than by the objective character of the immigration itself, the idea became fixed in the minds of many that the immigrants were chiefly responsible for the incidents of violence in American society and the corruption of republican institutions.

Canadians tended to accept this American view of the "new immigration" and when the annexationists contended that the consanguinity of British Canadians and Americans provided a basis for continental unity they were met with the reply that the United States was no longer an Anglo-Saxon country. "Once it was," said Denison, "but since the revolution it has been the dumping ground of Europe, and they are forming a community there entirely different in its characteristics from ours."[20] A reviewer in the *Week* in 1888 saw the growth of undesirable immigration as one of the main threats to America, "especially as the element of the population in which the republican tradition of self-government resides is completely stationary, if it is not actually decreasing; while elements, untrained to self-government and in many cases revolutionary, are pouring in."[21] What have Canadians to gain by joining the republic? asked John A. Macdonald in 1890. "It is a great country, but it will have its vicissitudes and revolutions. Look at the mass of foreign ignorance and vice which has flooded that country with socialism, atheism and all other isms."[22] The amazing inundation of immigration which "is steadily diluting the Anglo-Saxon element and diminishing

20 *Centennial of the Settlement of Upper Canada,* 102.
21 *Week,* iv (Dec. 16, 1888), 37.
22 *Empire,* Oct. 2, 1890.

the relative influence of the native American," added Parkin, was one of the many practical reasons why Canadians should not commit the fortunes of their country to an alliance with those of the great republic.[23] In the apocalyptic language of American restrictionists, another Canadian equated this immigration with contamination and "degeneracy in the physical pedigree" and opined that "the moral and intellectual standards of Americans are bound to fall by reason of the immoral, illiterate, restless and degraded human importations from the eastern world."[24]

Before the turn of the century Canadians could hold such views because the Dominion itself had relatively few immigrants from southern and eastern Europe and because it could be claimed that the stern climate would prevent them from ever entering the country. But to whatever sources Canadians attributed the fortunate absence of Negro and immigrant problems in their own country, their knowledge of their existence in the republic strengthened a determination to remain apart. It might well be, John A. Macdonald admitted, that the good sense and patriotism of the American people would triumph over the internal troubles, but "it is better for us to keep aloof from the possibility of being partners to these struggles."[25]

IV

Had the Americans not adopted the eagle as their national symbol, Canadians would probably have still associated their neighbour with that predatory bird. Scarcely less prominent in their image of the republic than the feeling that republican institutions were unstable, was the conviction that the Americans had always been, and generally remained, hostile to the realization of a Canadian nationality. "Most Canadians," Castell Hopkins reported in 1893, "believe today that the United States has shown a steady, deliberate dislike of their country and has pursued a policy more or less injurious to their interests." Seldom at a loss for illustrative detail, Hopkins elaborated:

The Oregon boundary dispute; the Maine boundary troubles, settled, it was thought, most unjustly by the Ashburton Treaty; the San Juan question; the abrogation of the fishery clauses of the Washington Treaty; the Atlantic Coast fisheries dispute; the refusal to allow

23 Parkin, *Imperial Federation*, 134–5.
24 F. Clement Brown, "Canadians Abroad," *Canadian Magazine*, VIII (Jan. 1897), 257.
25 Watson Griffin Papers, Macdonald to Griffin, Feb. 2, 1891.

Canadian volunteers to cross American territory during the North-West Rebellion and prcviously to the completion of the Canadian Pacific Railway, although dozens of American regiments had passed through Canadian territory during the Civil War; the annexation of Alaska in order, as Secretary Seward once pointed out, to prevent British-Canadian extension on the Pacific Coast and to strengthen American influence in British Columbia; the Behring Sea fisheries dispute and the unfriendly manner in which Canadian sealers have been treated; the McKinley bill and its injurious agricultural schedule; the Alien Labor law, and its aggressive enforcement against Canadians; the constant threats regarding the Canadian Pacific Railroad; and refusals to entertain any proposition for fair reciprocity – all these things have combined to make Canadians as a rule consider the inhabitants of the Republic what the Liberal Premier of Ontario once termed them, "a hostile people."[26]

In the late 1880s the chronicle of American plots, invasions, and aggressions against Canada, especially the tradition of 1812, awakened from its slumbers in the folios of Ryerson and Canniff and entered the roster of arguments against commercial union. "The war of 1812 can never be recalled too often," announced the *Empire* on October 13, 1890, the anniversary of the Battle of Queenston Heights, "if we are a people wise enough to learn from the experience of the past." "I have always preached it to our people," Denison candidly admitted, "that the Yankees are our greatest if not only enemies and that we should never trust them."[27] He claimed that history showed the republic to be an aggressive, grasping, and hostile neighbour, and, in what was virtually a paraphrase of D'Arcy McGee's speech supporting Confederation, Denison said that the Americans "wanted Florida, and they took it; Louisiana and Alaska they annexed; California and Mexico they conquered; and Texas they stole." They "swindled" Canada out of half the State of Maine, left no stone unturned to conquer British America, and cancelled the reciprocity treaty of 1854 "in the hope that it would produce annexation."[28] The commercial union movement was a conspiracy and its sponsors like Goldwin Smith and Erastus Wiman were of the same treasonous breed as the Montreal merchants in 1849, Mallory and Wilcocks in 1812, and Thomas Paine in 1776.

26 J. Castell Hopkins, "Canadian Hostility to Annexation," *Forum,* xvi (Nov. 1893), 326.
27 oa, William Kirby Papers, Denison to Kirby, Jan. 14, 1888.
28 G. T. Denison, *The Struggle for Imperial Unity* (Toronto, 1909), 93; McGee's speech is reprinted in P. B. Waite, ed., *The Confederation Debates in the Province of Canada 1865* (Toronto, 1963), 81–2.

Denison's intuitive impressions were sometimes corroborated by the statements of Americans who were as flamboyant in their faith in manifest destiny as he was in his loyalism. In 1888 he discovered one of the classic formulations of American continentalism, W. H. H. Murray's address on Continental Unity. Boldly declaring that he voiced "the prophecy of Geography, of common blood and language, kindred institutions, like laws, commercial necessities and political institutions that are identical," Murray drew attention to the rivers running north and south and the great plains shared by both countries as evidence of "God's design and Nature's unity." The continent was evidently designed for free trade, he said, and commercial intercourse meant the brotherhood of men. But Murray specified that the benefits of American trade should not be extended to Canada as long as she remained a colony. To grant reciprocity without political incorporation would only delay the dictates of manifest destiny. "So long as Canada remains as she has been and is to-day," he concluded, "comparatively weak in population, in developed resources, and in military power, she is not a subject of serious concern to us." But if her population grew to twenty and then forty millions, he added, and these words were heavily underlined in the Colonel's copy of the address, "we of the Republic shall never stand idly by and see a great power build up, either on the southern or northern side of us ..."[29]

A nationalist from the tip of his spurs to the plume on his helmet, Denison adduced from this warning and his reading of history that the United States would never permit Canada to become the most powerful nation in the Empire. Less justifiably, perhaps, he accepted such declarations as Murray's as representative of the views of the entire American people and tended to brush aside reminders that Americans scarcely ever thought of Canada because he never measured the potential success of a policy by the number of people who supported it. It was an axiom with him that a few resolute individuals could change the course of history as, indeed, he and his Canada First friends had in 1869–70. Denison's conclusion had all the stark simplicity of a syllogism: Canada would in time become one of the greatest states within the Empire; history and the announced intentions of the proponents of manifest destiny made it clear that the United States would never willingly share the continent with another major state; Canadians should therefore never put themselves into a position where they depended upon the republic. "We should be as friendly as possible with the United

29 G. T. Denison Papers, vol. 19, *Continental Unity. An address by W. H. H. Murray delivered in Music Hall, Boston ... December 31, 1888* (Boston, 1888), 1, 6–7, 28.

States," he reiterated, "but never depend upon them, never do anything to put ourselves in their power."[30]

How foolish, thought Goldwin Smith, that this eccentric patriot should continue to believe that the principle motivating force of American policy was hostility to Canada and landgrabbing, manifest destiny. Americans, Smith wrote in 1891, had "absolutely no thought" of conquest, "no craving for more territory"; the southern violence and western lawlessness which had forced them into the War of 1812 were things of the past.[31] Such reassurances, coming from the chief continentalist in Canada, were suspect at the best of times and manifestly denied by the Behring Sea dispute and the crisis over tariff policy. The image that history had fixed in Canadian minds of a bellicose republic persisted into the late 1890s not only by the inertia of tradition but also because of the resurgence of American expansionism, which began with the war against Spain in 1898, the annexation of the Pacific islands and Puerto Rico, the subjection of the Philippine rebellion, and culminated with the big stick diplomacy of Theodore Roosevelt in the Caribbean. In these years the warnings of D'Arcy McGee appeared more relevant than the confident assurances of Goldwin Smith.

Apprehensive nationalists like Denison constantly remarked upon this revival of manifest destiny and tended to explain America's belligerence abroad by reference to her internal problems. They knew, either from personal experience or history, that a domestic crisis within the United States might mean another Fenian-type raid or even a war with Britain. They remembered that Secretary of State Seward had urged Lincoln in 1861 to declare war on some European power in order to avoid a catastrophic war between north and south. It was for this reason that some Canadians regarded the social violence within the republic as a possible source of danger to the Dominion. "The Yankee finances are in a deplorable condition," Denison told Kirby in 1895, "and financial distress and ruin is hovering over them. This even may force them into war." Later he added that economic depression was aggravated by "a great amount of poverty among a population accustomed in every walk of life to comparative luxury and among this mass of poverty an enormously wealthy class of millionaires living in the most ostentatious and wasteful extravagance ... If McKinley & the Gold bugs get control for four years, I dread that they will bring on a foreign war to save control of the Govt, and if so they can make no war that would be so popular as one against England."[32]

30 Ibid., Denison to Lord Grey, June 24, 1905 (copy).
31 Goldwin Smith, Canada and the Canadian Question (Toronto, 1891), 276.
32 Kirby Papers, Denison to Kirby, Dec. 26, 1895; Aug. 18, 1896.

Even for those who did not anticipate that the capriciousness of republican politics would end in war or revolution, American expansionism and the fact of her overwhelming dominance upon the continent reinforced the connection which Canadians had always maintained between British support and Canadian survival. This was one of the most worn and tattered themes in loyalist rhetoric and the major certitude of political life. "As to independence," John A. Macdonald queried in 1890, "how long could we stand as an independent republic? ... What could Canada do in the Behring sea controversy without England at our back?"[33] The imperialists claimed to understand the realities of power and they continually reminded those who advocated Canadian independence outside the Empire what the Dominion's fate would be. "Were Canada to declare for independence," one of them warned, "she would only enjoy such rights as her stronger neighbour permitted. Such an independence would be an expensive sham and a disastrous unreality." "A careful study of the history of Columbia and Panama, of Mexico, Texas and California," he added, "must dampen the ardour of those who advocate Canadian independence, unless, indeed, they advocate it as a step towards the incorporation of the Canadian provinces and territories into the United States."[34]

Cautioning those whose desire for independence was invigorated by the unpopular Alaska boundary decision and alluding to the fate of the Philippines, Panama, the Spanish West Indian Islands, and Hawaii, George Foster asserted in 1903 that independence for Canada would mean living under "the shadow of an overmastering power in whose heart of hearts is embodied the idea that it is her destiny to possess the whole North American continent."[35] The ultimate result of the Little Canada policy, William L. Grant elaborated, would make genuine freedom of action impossible. If Canada chose to defend herself, defence costs would drain her resources and hinder social progress. If she relied upon the protection of the United States, her fate would be even worse. "If they protect us, they will exact in return the full measure of dependence; the country which they will protect is not a country which makes its policy at Ottawa, but a country which has its policy dictated from Washington ... Our position under the protection of the United States would be precisely similar [to that of a kept woman]. I wish no such harlot's independence for my country."[36]

33 *Empire*, Oct. 2, 1890.
34 J. M. Clark in *Imperial Federation*, V (May 1, 1890), 121; *The Future of Canada: Address delivered by J. M. Clark, K.C. before the Mulock Club, Toronto* [on 23, November, 1903] (n.p., n.d.), 2.
35 George E. Foster, *Canadian Addresses* (Toronto, 1914), 117–18.
36 W. L. Grant Papers, vol. 15, MS Address, 1910 or 1911, 16.

With that satirical invective of which he was a master, Stephen Leacock rejected the contentions of those who claimed that Canada had no need to make contributions to the defence of the imperial system because she was shielded by the Monroe doctrine. Such an assumption, he said, only operated as a soporific on the minds of those who did not know whether Monroe's principle connoted a "Spiritual belief or a resolution of the Sons of Scotland," and it had no relevance to America's actual position at the beginning of the twentieth century. "Monroe's creed of America for the Americans has been altered to mean America for the Americans and as much else of the world's surface as can be obtained at a profitable figure." Surely, he said, it was a dangerous illusion to expect that the United States would suspend the simple calculus of national self-interest whenever she dealt with Canada.[37] What was uppermost in the minds of Leacock and W. L. Grant was the hope that Canada would achieve national stature and an influence in world affairs through the acceptance of responsibility within the Empire. To insist, as did advocates of independence like Ewart or defenders of the status quo like Laurier, that Canada would be protected by the United States, offended their conception of national self-reliance and ran against the whole drift of their nationalism. They believed that because of the peculiar genius of the Empire it was possible for Canada to retain full self-government and attain influence which would not be possible in a North America dominated by the United States. Wilfred Campbell spoke for all imperialists when he said that Canada's only choice was "between two different imperialisms, that of Britain and that of the Imperial Commonwealth to the south." If Canada was ever to be a nation, "we must in self-defence stay within the British Imperial system; whereas to enter that of the American means sheer annihilation of all our personality as a people." In the end the choice was reduced to "Imperialism or Imperialism."[38]

V

Despite the enduring themes of suspicion and apprehension in this image of the United States, the hypercritical and captious propositions which pervaded the Denisonian rhetoric were checked by several counter-currents from the mid-1890s onwards. The critical view of the republic, of course, did not vanish from the literature of imperialism,

37 Stephen Leacock, "Canada and the Monroe Doctrine," *University Magazine*, VIII (Oct. 1909), 351–74.
38 Wilfred Campbell, "Imperialism in Canada," *Empire Club Speeches: Being Addresses Delivered Before the Empire Club of Canada During its Session of 1904–05* (Toronto, 1906), 38, 40.

nor did Canadian intellectuals find American internal problems any less fascinating. But the defensive and negative tone characteristic of the predictions of the loyalists' descendants diminished in vigour and decreased in frequency. There could be no greater contrast in attitudes toward the United States than those of Denison and G. M. Grant, whose intense sense of nationalism never ended in the denigration of the United States. Believing that every nation had a divine mission to contribute something to the good of humanity, Grant maintained that all Canadian experience pointed to the role she must perform in world history. That "divine mission" was to create a British North American nationality which would become a "living link," a permanent bond of union, between Britain and the United States. As a "British-American" state Canada seemed peculiarly fashioned to heal the schism which had divided the Anglo-Saxon people since 1776. Canada, Grant declared in a sermon in 1887, "was American because the atmosphere, climate and other physical conditions under which people grew up, determined to a great extent their character and place in history. But it was also British, because we have inherited from Britain not merely that which the United States has inherited, language, literature, laws and blood, and the fundamental principles of civil and religious life, but also continuity of national life." History and environment had combined to produce a nation evidently designed to function as a "mediator" and Grant looked forward to "a moral reunion of the English-speaking race, commercial union based on free trade, a common tribunal and a common citizenship, if not more."[39]

There was another quarter from which similar sentiments were heard. In his *Canada and the Canadian Question* (1891) Goldwin Smith argued that, apart from the obvious economic benefits, commercial union between Canada and the United States was desirable because it would facilitate the moral federation of the Anglo-Saxon race. To this objective, said Grant, we "heartily subscribe"; it was, indeed, the ultimate aim of imperialism. But no Canadian could agree that this noble hope was to be realized by a second disruption and the elimination of Canada. Canadians had been sceptical of the ideal of racial reunion because in the past it had been so often accompanied by the suggestion that the most certain way of creating Anglo-Saxon amity was through disengaging British power from the continent, perhaps even allowing Canada to drift into the American orbit. Grant accepted the end but

39 G. M. Grant Papers, vol. 25, clipping from the Toronto *Mail*, Feb. 14, 1887; G. M. Grant, "Our National Objects and Aims," in *Maple Leaves: Being the Papers Read Before the National Club of Toronto at the "National Evenings," During the Winter 1890-91* (Toronto, 1891), 1-34; *Week*, xII (Nov. 8, 1895), 1189.

rejected the means. The best way of gaining the friendship of the United States, he said, "– and we all wish to gain it – is by preserving our own self-respect and maintaining our own rights." It was because Grant so fully shared Smith's hope that he reviewed the bystander's book more in a spirit of sorrow and regret than vengeance and outrage.[40]

During the late 1890s and the first decade of the twentieth century several factors served to make the ideas expressed by Grant a major theme in imperialist circles. The peculiar conditions of the late 1880s and early 1890s which had underlain the vituperative and negative picture of the United States gave way to an ebullient optimism concerning the Canadian future. The faith in Canadian progress was restored by the swift momentum of economic development and settlement and it received an enormous stimulus by Canada's participation in the Boer War, an experience which for imperialists signified one more step towards maturity and nationhood. The novelist, Sir Gilbert Parker, discovered a very different spirit in Canada in 1905 from that of twenty years before. Then "the question was, *Whither now?* That question is no longer asked. The country, its people, know where they are going; there is no longer national uncertainty; the Canadian stands no longer at the cross-roads – he is on the straight path of his destiny; national expansion under the British flag, complete control of his own affairs, but sharing in the general responsibilities of the Empire to which he belongs ..."[41] This return of confidence did much to dispel the uncertainty and insecurity which had earlier been discharged through the censorious and fearful allusions to the republic.

The optimism of the Laurier boom coincided with the development of the rapprochement between Great Britain and the United States. Britain's abandonment of splendid isolation and America's rise to the status of a world power stimulated a feeling in certain quarters in both countries that the two nations required each other's sympathy and support in international affairs. The rediscovery of common traditions and purposes was largely the product of power politics but it was enormously strengthened by a sense of racial consanguinity and common mission. During his visit to the United States and Canada in 1887, Joseph Chamberlain, the apostle of Anglo-Saxon unity, was profoundly affected by the vision of racial co-operation. "As I passed through England and the United States, and again when I crossed the boundary

40 *Week*, VIII (May 1 and 15, 1891), 348–50, 380–2. For a similar statement that imperialism sought union of the English-speaking peoples, see Thomas MacFarlane, *Within the Empire: an Essay on Imperial Federation* (Ottawa, 1891), 81.
41 Sir Gilbert Parker, "Canada, After Twenty Years," *Canadian Magazine*, XXVI (Dec. 1905), 107.

of the Dominion," he told a Toronto audience, "there was one idea impressing itself upon my mind at every step, indelibly written upon the face of the two vast countries, and that was the greatness and importance of the distinction reserved for the Anglo-Saxon race – (cheers) – that proud, persistent, self-asserting and resolute stock which no change of climate or condition can alter, and which is infallibly bound to be the predominant force in the future history and civilisation of the world."[42] Though there were exceptions, Canadian imperialists became the most effusive exponents of Anglo-Saxon co-operation. During his work for the Rhodes Scholarship Trust, George Parkin explained that the training of prospective American leaders at Oxford would pave the way to understanding and he especially emphasized that both branches of the race were confronted with the task of uplifting the backward races throughout the world.[43] The liberal imperialist, J. S. Willison, summed up the approach when he told the Canadian Club of Boston in 1905 that Canada possessed "a potent influence in preserving the good understanding that has so happily developed in recent years": "we shall stand together," he affirmed, "for the spread of Anglo-Saxon civilization."[44]

In the realm of diplomacy, the rapprochement led to the settlement of many minor disputes which had embittered Canadian-American relations in the past. Writing in 1911, Andrew Macphail drew attention to the series of treaties which had settled the fisheries and boundary problems and concluded that fear and hatred of the United States had completely vanished. There is not, he said, "any cause of public disagreement ... there is now between ourselves and our neighbours an absolutely clean slate."[45] This judgment that the treaties had removed the irritants upon which hostility to the United States had fed was slightly premature for the reciprocity election of 1911 was to reinvigorate a good deal of the ancient rhetoric. Denison's rigidity defied all changes in circumstance and he was to warn that reciprocity in 1911 was engineered by the same old conspiratorial clique of 1891.

Yet the younger generation of imperialists like Macphail, W. L.

42 Sir Willoughby Maycock, *With Mr. Chamberlain in the United States and Canada, 1887–88* (Toronto, 1914), 104. For a comprehensive examination of this theme, see Israel T. Naamani, "The 'Anglo-Saxon Idea' and British Public Opinion," *Canadian Historical Review*, xxxvii (March 1951), 43–60.
43 G. R. Parkin, "The Relations of Canada and the United States," *Empire Club Speeches ... 1907–1908* (Toronto, 1910), 157–68.
44 J. S. Willison, *Anglo-Saxon Amity* (Toronto, 1906), 3, 14. See also his *United States and Canada*, a pamphlet published by the American Branch Association For International Conciliation, Oct. 1908.
45 Andrew Macphail, "The Cleaning of the Slate," *University Magazine*, x (April 1911), 186.

Grant, and Leacock, whose experiences did not run back to the crises of the Civil War years and whose minds were unaffected by the bitter wine of the loyalist legacy, found it increasingly irrelevant, irresponsible, and impossible to repeat the slogans of the 1880s. Macphail was a most interested and sympathetic observer of the American progressive movement, and he was concerned with the social problems of the republic not primarily because they afforded opportunities for making invidious comparisons but because he saw at work in the United States the same forces which were transforming Canada into an industrial state. He had no patience with those who contrasted American society with some idealized social order in the north. "For a generation," he once wrote, "we have been the thank-Gods of America. We were not like those republicans and sinners ... who lived to the southward, with whom it was dangerous for simple-minded people like ourselves to have any truck or trade."[46] The American people, wrote another imperialist, "are something like twenty years ahead of us in public morality, in civic righteousness, in political virtue; our Pharisaic complacency is one of the things I wish to upset."[47] The United States had traditionally presented Canada with both a standard of democracy and a model of corruption, but who could say that the "politico-business alliance" in Canadian politics was really different from its American counterpart, or that the municipal corruption in Montreal was less demoralizing than that of Philadelphia. The United States was still an example, still a bad example; but it stood as a warning of what Canada might become if men of conscience did not denounce the irresponsibility of business and correct the short-range views of politicians. Imperialists like Macphail and Leacock did not need anyone to remind them that Canada was in America, for when they attacked the subordination of learning to technical training, or condemned the preoccupation with materialism, or voiced sympathy with those classes which were not participating in the flush times, they did not think of Canada as isolated from the problems of the United States. Their knowledge of these problems in the republic and the realization that industrialization had reproduced many of them within Canada, turned them, as we shall see, into Canadian social critics, not anti-Americans.

VI

The Canadian image of the United States was composed of a cluster of conceptions and assumptions suffused by a traditional emotion. Though

46 Macphail, "Patriotism and Politics," *ibid.*, xiii (Feb. 1914), 2.
47 C. F. Hamilton, "Ultimate Politics," *Queen's Quarterly*, xvii (July 1909), 77.

its main propositions were largely inherited they were invigorated in the later nineteenth century by the sense of insecurity within Canada, developments in the United States, and a Canadian nationalism which asserted and underlined what it took to be the essential differences between the two North American countries. The term "anti-Americanism," invented in another age, is too loaded with unsavoury connotations and too ill-defined to faithfully encompass outlooks which ranged from Denison's conspiratorial fantasies to G. M. Grant's hopes for Anglo-American understanding. It is suggestive of an unwarranted sense of superiority, an inordinate preoccupation with describing the failures of a good neighbour, and a tendency to attribute to Americans expansionist motives which they did not harbour. Though imperialists were unacquainted with the term anti-Americanism, they frequently disclaimed any hatred of the United States which it implies. One of them explained that comparisons of the Canadian and American constitutions were undertaken "not with any desire to disparage the people of the United States or their Constitution, but merely to bring out by way of contrast more strikingly the superior excellence of our own from the point of view of political freedom."[48] Another denied that Canadian writers were necessarily motivated by malice and misled by prejudice just because they did not offer insincere adulation: the reign of lawlessness in the republic, he said, was a matter of record not of opinion.[49] And, it should be added, that the greater obedience to the law by Canadians compared to Americans was not some imaginative invention but a feature which nearly everyone who has contrasted the two countries has remarked upon.[50]

What lay behind this Canadian critique of the United States was not malevolence but nationalism. These imperialists in fact offer testimony to the truth of the old saw that a nation is a society united by a common error as to its origins and a common aversion to its neighbours. As Canadian nationalists, completely convinced that Canada possessed certain attributes, especially a stable form of government and a law-abiding character, which differentiated her as a nation, they found they could most easily explain these things, and build up an attachment to them, by comparing them to the institutions of their neighbours which

48 A. H. F. Lefroy, "Canadian Forms of Freedom," The United Empire Loyalist Association of Ontario, *Annual Transactions for the Year Ending March 9th 1899* (Toronto, 1899), 114.
49 Macphail, "Canadian Writers and American Politics," *University Magazine,* IX (Feb. 1910), 3–17.
50 A recent example is Seymour Martin Lipset, *Revolution and Counter-Revolution – The United States and Canada,* Institute of International Studies, University of California, reprint no. 193 (Berkeley, n.d.), 29.

they felt were not only different but obviously inferior. This was hardly a unique by-product of nationalism. In a discussion of the European image of the United States, an English scholar thought it "useful to remind Americans of their own venerable tradition of xenophobia. Almost from the beginning the New World has explicitly repudiated the Old, defining its own virtues as the precise antithesis of the supposed vices of Europe."[51] To which an American historian recently added that "British and European society has served as a model of what the United States should *not* be, bringing America's concept of itself into focus and providing a foil against which American achievements may be measured."[52] Canadians also could most effectively describe those possessions which they felt made them a distinctive people by contrasting them with what existed in another country, especially since that country was founded upon principles diametrically opposed to everything they held dear. In this sense, the critique of the republic was not primarily a fretful, sterile, and rootless phenomenon, although admittedly it sometimes appeared to be just that in the hands of the loyalists; it was rather, and it is this that makes it significant for a history of nationalist thought, the other side of the conception of Canada as a British country, stable, ordered, and destined to become a great imperial power.

51 Marcus Cunliffe, "European Images of America," A. M. Schlesinger, Jr., and Morton White, eds., *Paths of American Thought* (Boston, 1963), 510.
52 Russel B. Nye, *This Almost Chosen People: Essays in the History of American Ideas* (Toronto, 1966), 48. Italics in original.

7

Social Criticism and Reform

In Britain, the United States, and Canada the relationship between imperialism and social reform was intimate and direct. Imperialists in all three countries were at one in their search for values, both personal and political, which would check the spirit of commercialism and the social atomization of their time. The American Theodore Roosevelt and the English imperialist, Alfred Milner, found such standards in a masterful policy abroad and social reform at home. Imperial power, after all, depended upon a strong and stable internal society.[1] For many reasons this social reformist strand of imperialist thought appeared in Canada only in an attenuated form. Because the Dominion lagged so far behind Britain and the republic in the state of her industrialization and its attendant social problems, Canadian imperialists before 1900 most often assessed the connection between the proper, balanced society and imperialism in terms of the British experience. But in the decade before the World War they presented one of the most sweeping indictments of Canadian society to appear before the agrarian revolt of the 1920s and the radicalism of the 1930s.

I

One of the fundamental features of Canadian imperialist social thought was an idealized conception of agriculture and a tendency to regard it as the most healthy foundation of national life. Nothing revealed Denison's romanticism more graphically than his deep-seated distaste for industrialism, his abomination of the business credo, and his belief that Canada was, and would always remain, predominantly an agrarian country. By social outlook and family tradition he was predisposed to feel that life on the land was more natural and durable than the shifting and rootless existence of urban masses, and like the other members of

1 Bernard Semmel, *Imperialism and Social Reform: English Social-Imperial Thought, 1895–1914* (London, 1960); W. E. Leuchtenburg, "Progressivism and Imperialism: The Progressive Movement and American Foreign Policy, 1898–1916," *Mississippi Valley Historical Review,* xxxix (Dec. 1952), 483–504.

Canada First, his sense of nationality had been inspired by the anticipation that the prairies would be settled by millions of farmers. Along with many European military thinkers, the Colonel believed that the agriculturalists were the mainstay of national defence for they not only had a fixed stake in the country but they also possessed, according to him, "physique and intelligence ... a good seat on a horse and a general knowledge of the use of the rifle." "A small amount of drill and a little practical training and reconnoitring duty," he wrote, "would make these men a most valuable force for defensive war."[2] Whenever he spoke of the people of Canada, Denison invariably accorded priority to the farmers. "The people of this country," he said in 1884, "are the farmers ... who have cleared the fields, who till them, and who produce the food that feeds us." The population, he added, also included factory workers, those engaged in trade and commerce, and "citizens who build her cities and work in them."[3] In 1884, of course, this description had some relationship to social reality, but Denison was not so much analysing class structure as he was expressing a value judgment in favour of the agrarian way of life.

The romantic poet, William Kirby, shared his friend's admiration for the old and stable order. Denison had no ear for the cadences of poetry and his only interest in literature was confined to the soundness of the ideas it propounded. When Kirby sent him a copy of his collected poems in 1894, the Colonel characteristically responded by saying that he wanted to "spread the good doctrines they contain."[4] All through Kirby's work there ran a note of dissatisfaction and revolt and the conventional romantic theme of the primacy of emotion and imagination over cold, rationalistic logic. In his drama, *The U.E.: A Tale of Upper Canada*, published in 1859 but written in 1846, the year which marked the triumph of laissez-faire in Britain, Kirby glorified nature and contended that conservative social principles were inseparable from the agricultural matrix. Loyalty, order, and religion, he believed, had been nurtured in the agrarian setting in Britain and were being destroyed by industrialization. The hero of his drama, Walwyn, resolved to migrate to British America in the years after Waterloo and he expected to find in the new world an Arcadia where ordered freedom and stability could be maintained. May Canada, Kirby interjected, ever keep "Thy British Freedom and thy rural reign." The west to him was not a place where

---

2 G. T. Denison, "The Cavalry Charge at Sedan – The Autumn Manoeuvers – The Moral they Convey," *Canadian Monthly and National Review*, I (Jan. 1872), 52.
3 G. T. Denison, *The Struggle for Imperial Unity* (Toronto, 1909), 67–8.
4 OA, William Kirby Papers, Denison to Kirby, Oct. 27, 1894.

men sought refuge from the evils of feudalism, monarchy, and class privilege of the old world, nor was it an environment where people were transformed. It was rather an agrarian paradise to which the essence of British freedom was transferred and where it would flourish in isolation from those sinister forces that were destroying it in Britain. Though Kirby praised the hum of trade in the cities of Toronto and Montreal, his heart was really with the old loyalist settlers who "had lived an honest country-life, / Apart from towns and politics and strife." Their simple loyalty, he made clear, received its ultimate sanction from religion. A life close to nature was profoundly religious because it was so exposed to "God's loving anger."[5]

For Kirby, the enemy of tradition, of the deferential social order, and of the mystical association of loyalty and religion was the rationalism of the eighteenth century, and in one powerful symbol he stated his rejection of its end product. As Walwyn passed up the St Lawrence he saw the grass and trees reflected in the calm river – the image of nature. The steamboat, however, disturbed the water, broke up the pattern, and distorted the order of creation:

> Gigantic power of Steam! fit emblem thou
> Of iron days and mighty toil below,
> When man to earth inverts his searching eyes
> And worships Vulcan in a modern guise.
> When his imaginings no longer brook
> God's comment traced in nature's mystic book,
> But as the subtle serpent, seeks to be
> Wise through the fruit of the forbidden tree.[6]

This rejection of individualism and industrialism pervaded everything that Kirby wrote. It provided the link of continuity between his drama of 1859 and his novel, *The Golden Dog* (1877), in which he commended the feudal and chivalrous social principles of New France, and it was never far from the surface in the disquisitions of those philosophical Indians who populated his poems. It seemed to Kirby that the distrust of sentiment, the economic calculus, the exaltation of machinery over nature, and the destruction of agriculture, were all inextricably bound together in the ideology of laissez-faire liberalism. Disquieted by these manifestations of modernity, he retreated into an idealized pastoral life in which alone the true social order was represented.

5 William Kirby, *The U. E.: A Tale of Upper Canada* (Niagara, 1859), 56, 89–90, 93.
6 *Ibid.*, 44.

It may appear at first sight a very long distance between Kirby's poetry and imperial trade policy, between the rich imagery of the romantic imagination and the curt, business-like language of those who advocated an imperial preferential tariff. But the social ideas to which Denison and his friend adhered profoundly affected their conception of trade policy and their understanding of Canada's place within the Empire. Not the least menacing aspect of the movement for closer commercial relations with the United States was that it appealed to exactly that class which they took to be the real strength of the nation. The challenge of unrestricted reciprocity imparted a powerful impetus to the growth of imperialist sentiment in Canada and it forced the loyalists to propose an alternative imperial trade arrangement. Romantic though he was, Kirby warned his friend that imperialists should learn a lesson from the annexationists and present imperial federation as a material question. Long after the threat of reciprocity lifted, preferential trade continued to be the keystone of Denison's practical imperialism. When the branches of the Imperial Federation League were reconstituted in 1896 as the British Empire League in Canada, Denison became president of the new organization and remained its chief spokesman on trade affairs for over fifteen years. He specified that Britain and the colonies should impose a duty ranging between five and ten per cent on every article of foreign manufacture and that the revenue collected in this fashion should be placed in an imperial defence fund controlled by a council of representatives of Britain and the colonies. He was, in addition, especially emphatic upon securing preferential treatment for Canadian agricultural products in the British market. While these concise resolutions seem self-explanatory devices for securing imperial unity, they were grounded upon a general conception of national interest in which the agrarian character of Canada was assumed, and, at least for Denison, they were intended to realize objectives which were essentially non-economic in character.

Denison scornfully repudiated the notion that the whole national future of Canada would be decided by pecuniary standards. He once said that no nation had ever contributed to its own obliteration for the sake of making a few cents on its eggs or a few cents a bushel on its grain. "I am not interested in manufacturers at all," he candidly and truthfully avowed; "I am not interested in trade or business in any way, so have no personal interest in one or the other."[7] He did not reject unrestricted reciprocity with the United States because it was unprofitable, but because he did not want to place the Dominion in a position

7 G. T. Denison Papers, Denison to Chamberlain, Feb. 16, 1901; Denison to Senator Pulsford, Feb. 24, 1912 (copies).

of depending upon a nation which had shown little sympathy to it in the past and because he did not want any connections to stand in the way of the future commercial union of the Empire. He believed an imperial trade system desirable and necessary, moreover, in order to arrest the ruinous effects of laissez-faire. Free trade had deliberately sacrificed British agriculture in order to secure world-wide industrial supremacy: in the long run it had failed to achieve this ambition and had produced disastrous social consequences within England. After a visit to Britain in 1897, Denison penned a pessimistic warning of the degeneracy which had followed the decline in farming and the concentration upon industry. A "majority of the children of England," he wrote, "instead of being reared in the open country, under the dome of heaven, are being huddled in crowded towns, under a pall of factory smoke, among the soot-begrimed walls of narrow courts and alleys paved with cinders, without a blade of grass or a green leaf to be seen."[8] Such conditions, he felt certain, had undermined the physique of the race to the point that in a great national emergency England's defence would rest with undersized, weakly looking boys. This physical deterioration was paralleled by a decline of traditional ideals and values. He shared Kipling's gloomy feeling that the blind and narrow materialism, the aimless getting and spending, and the loss of the spirit of strenuous adventure, would reduce England to the fate of Nineveh and Tyre. Denison sensed this fate in the scrawny children of the slums, in the aestheticism and homosexuality of Oscar Wilde, and in the average Englishman's disinclination to peer behind the imposing Jubilee façade and see what a generation of "free traitors" had really done to British power. "I can see," Denison told a friend in 1899, "that the day is fast approaching when the selfishness, luxury, and worship of gold above everything else in England is going to destroy the British race unless the new blood in the Colonies, will leaven the mass."[9]

Like some English imperialists, Denison thought that it was possible to reproduce in the outer-empire, especially in Canada, a simpler state of society, free from the hectic social pressures and overcrowding of the motherland. A tariff preference on Canadian produce in the British market would provide an economic incentive to the expansion of agriculture and the settlement of the prairie west, and create there a healthy and athletic people who would compensate England for her town-dwelling population. In military terms, moreover, such a tariff would

8 G. T. Denison, "The Present Situation of England, A Canadian Impression," *Nineteenth Century*, XLII (Dec. 1897), 1011.
9 Sir Sandford Fleming Papers, Denison to Fleming, May 6, 1899; Sir George R. Parkin Papers, Denison to Parkin, April 19, 1895.

decrease Britain's dependence upon potentially hostile nations for her foodstuffs, and it would build up in Canada a reserve of soldiers. "We want trade advantages," he asserted, "not because they will make us rich but because they will fill our empty plains & make us strong & thereby a source of power to the Empire by being able to provide food to feed the English people and men to defend the fields in which it grows." There was little point in talking of military and naval defence until the heart of the Empire was made secure in terms of food supply for "if England goes under it would be very uphill work for Australia & Canada to hold their own and a great Empire would be gone for want of forethought."[10] Pursuing this logic to its conclusion, Denison proposed that Britain restore her own agriculture even if this involved tariff discrimination against the colonies, though he assumed that additional food would still come from those sources. "What should be done," he said, "is to provide a tariff that will protect and build up agriculture again, and put the people back on the farms. They are the best people a country has."[11]

The whole bias of Denison's military and social thought suggests that he visualized a Canada in which industrial establishments were only subsidiary to an agrarian economy. Because his conception of national interest was rooted in an admiration for the agricultural life, he was quite willing to reduce tariff protection on Canadian industry in return for a British preference on Canadian foodstuffs. On this point, Denison could readily appreciate Goldwin Smith's sentiments when that apologist for commercial union with the United States wondered why there should be such "a passion for propagating factory life on a large scale" in Canada when the result in England had been "degeneracy" and the growth of a potentially revolutionary class.[12] It is clear, too, that Denison's social criticism was addressed primarily to Britain. The Empire in which Canada was to grow and gradually reach a position of power was weakest at its heart. As time went on, Denison gradually found himself a stranger in the Canada of the Laurier boom. A true representative of the old established families, he regarded the *nouveau riche* with an aristocratic disdain. Toronto had changed for the worse, he told Mair in 1911; "Parvenus are as plentiful as blackberries and the vulgar ostentation of the common rich is not a pleasant sight."[13] Repetitiously voicing his praise of agriculture and his aversion toward businessmen,

10 Denison Papers, Denison to G. D'Esterre Taylor, Jan. 26, 1901 (copy).
11 *Ibid.*, Scrapbook, 1909–25, clippings from *Sidney Post*, Aug. 12, 1909, and *Ottawa Free Press*, Aug. 5, 1909.
12 *Handbook of Commercial Union: A Collection of Papers Read Before the Commercial Union Club, Toronto* (Toronto, 1888), 197.
13 QUL, Charles Mair Papers, Denison to Mair, Dec. 31, 1911.

dismissing socialism as a fallacy which appealed to "shallow minds," he showed little understanding of the forces which were transforming Canadian life. His response to the problem of industrial conflict and labour unrest was in keeping with his character: he was quite willing to lead a charge of light cavalry against the strikers on the Toronto street railways.

II

Though G. M. Grant was mindful of the national advantages of a large number of farmers who tilled their own land, his social thought was very different from that of his impulsive associate. Denison's outlook was circumscribed by military considerations: the children of the slums offended his sense of military efficiency, not his humanitarianism. Grant's attitude, on the other hand, was determined by the conviction that Christianity must be made socially meaningful. He was one of the major religious leaders in late nineteenth-century Canada who sought to shift the church away from an exclusive concentration upon individual salvation and turn it to the path of social service. He was a precursor of that social gospel which culminated with J. S. Woodsworth and Salem Bland.

In the 1880s the dominant voice of Canadian Protestantism was still that of the Toronto churches during the printers' strike of 1872 when the clergy expressed concern for the workingmen as individuals but disapproved of class organizations and resorts to force. At a time when the editor of the influential *Canadian Methodist Magazine* was still explaining strikes with quotations from Samuel Smiles concerning the lack of thrift and sobriety among the working orders, and when an Anglican clergyman blamed the alienation of workmen from the church partly on the failure of ministers to take an interest in economic problems,[14] Grant was already studying the mysteries of the wages question. While his preoccupation with this major social issue was a natural outgrowth of previous training and a desire to obliterate the fictitious demarcation between secular and spiritual affairs, it was immediately provoked by a reading of Henry George's *Progress and Poverty* (1877) and inspired by the social gospel movement in the United States. When Grant first read George's book, which had roused the reformist impulse in so many North Americans, he was captivated and "carried away" with the argument that the only solution to the growth of poverty amid plenty was for the state to charge a single tax on the unearned increment

14 *Canadian Methodist Magazine*, XXIII (March 1886), 208; Letter to the editor of the *Canadian Churchman*, Nov. 5, 1891.

of land. Though he was thoroughly ignorant of economics and sociology at the time, Grant later admitted that George had "set me thinking; forced me to read more widely & inquire more diligently."[15] Inquire he did, and in time Grant attained a reputation as one of the foremost Canadian sympathizers with the revival of the Christian conscience across the border. He was attracted to Josiah Strong's Evangelical Alliance which typified the early social gospel in its determination to make the churches see and accomplish their "social mission." A branch of the alliance was founded in Montreal and at its meeting in 1888 Strong and Washington Gladden, another pioneer of the social gospel, delivered addresses on co-operation in Christian work and on the vital question of capital and labour. Grant was asked to become a vice-president of the Montreal branch of the Evangelical Alliance, but hesitated because the assembly seemed more interested in combatting the perils of alcohol and Romanism than in social justice.[16]

In intellectual content Grant's version of the social gospel did not depart substantially from that of his American counterparts.[17] He feared that if Christianity assumed no constructive role in the conflict between capital and labour, religion itself would become irrelevant and the social structure would be deprived of its moral basis. Like Strong and Gladden, he sought a middle course between the unjust and inadequate capitalist wages system and the socialist demand for the elimination of private property. Grant believed that both the Marxian socialists and the Single-Taxers were wrong in assuming that the poor were getting poorer and the rich richer. Statistics, he said, "prove that the working-classes are steadily getting a better share than they once had of the good things in life." Convinced that individualism was too ingrained in the character of the English-speaking peoples for land nationalization to be anything more than an academic proposition, he also felt that neither co-operative enterprises nor the organization of labour into unions were final solutions to industrial warfare. Co-operatives could succeed in areas where only small resources of capital were required and consequently they were no substitute for the private ownership of the means of production. The unionization of labour invariably called

15 G. M. Grant Papers, vol. 15, MS "Progress & Poverty – A Criticism," n.d.
16 *Vital Questions. The Discussions of the General Christian Conference held in Montreal, Que., Canada, October 22nd to 25th, 1888, under the auspices and direction of the Montreal Branch of the Evangelical Alliance* (Montreal, 1889), 212–3.
17 The following four paragraphs are based on: G. M. Grant, "The Wages Question," *Alliance of the Reformed Churches Holding the Presbyterian System: Proceedings of the Fifth General Council, Toronto, 1892* (Toronto, 1892), 351–62; Grant Papers, vol. 25, clipping from the *Weekly Witness*, Oct. 5, 1892; and vol. 16, MS "Practical Preaching," n.d.

forth "the organization of capital, and a mutually destructive war between the two has been the result."

Grant rejected the extreme variety of laissez-faire preached by Herbert Spencer and William Graham Sumner. "We are face to face with pressing questions," he said, "and Mr. Spencer offers no solutions." The state was more than an aggregation of individuals: it was "an organic unity that has to discharge different duties at different times." Society as a whole had rights which were as sacred as those of the individual. Grant none the less retained the belief that the economic laws as enunciated by the "authorities in orthodox political economy" must be recognized by those who wished to cure society's ills. Inequality in human capacity and inequality in remuneration could not be questioned; nor indeed could Malthus's law of population. There was nothing meritorious, said Grant, in getting married before one could support a family. Far from being unworthy of God, the principle to which Malthus had called attention, "is one that should induce men to develop their intelligence & practice self-restraint."

The conclusion to which Grant was driven did not involve wholesale institutional innovation nor any serious tampering with the capitalist system. Though it appeared natural to him that the state should in time levy a graduated income tax and an inheritance tax in order to pay for social betterment, his faith was placed in altering the convictions and behaviour of individuals. "The solution is to be found," he said, "in recognition and assertion of the Trusteeship of Capital and the moralization of Labour." The anchor of his social gospel was the principle that "superiority in capacity must prove itself by superiority in service"; the practical implement of trusteeship was profit sharing.

If Grant's contentions appear rather naïve to a different age which equates preaching with ineffectuality and is suspicious of the kind of reform which is addressed to the reformation of character as opposed to the redistribution of property, it should be kept in mind that the degree to which he believed in the possibility of instilling a sense of responsibility was the measure of his faith in the transforming power of Christianity. And it should be remembered too that in Canada in the early 1890s the idea that the church should deal with the capital-labour conflict at all was a revolutionary departure. It is of some significance that a report of his address on the wages question delivered before the Presbyterian Synod in 1892 noted that he failed to get a sympathetic hearing partly because some thought the subject not germane to the purposes of the synod. An American clergyman perhaps spoke for the majority of Canadian ministers when he said that he felt no enthusiasm for such discussions and that the best service of the church lay not in debating with Henry George but in inculcating a proper sentiment in favour of those "into whose hands God has put money, and on the part of those who are earning their living by their labour."

III

For Parkin, as for Grant, there was a direct connection between the social gospel and imperialism. The Christianization of the social order meant more than simply attaining industrial peace, more even than reasserting the relevance of religion. The social gospel was a necessary ingredient of imperialism; or, put another way, it was an expression on a different but interconnected level of the sense of mission. The ends of both were identical and the realization of the civilizing mission abroad was dependent upon the existence of a sound society in the imperial state. Without a purified and healthy social order within, the imperializing nation would not only lack the strength for the exercise of power but it would also project its own evils into those lands over which it held sway. For men who believed that God had placed upon the progressive peoples a duty and an obligation to uplift and civilize the "backward races" of the earth, social reform appeared as a test of Christianity itself.

Largely because he was in closer contact with English imperialists and British society, Parkin drew out these implications much more explicitly than did Grant. In his writings of the early 1890s this concern with the health of society was not as pronounced as it was to become in the decade before the World War, though Parkin, like Joseph Chamberlain, had frequently dwelt upon the need to preserve the Empire because the welfare of the working class depended upon it, and he was certainly aware of the social advantages of immigration within the imperial system. His friend, Alfred Milner, grew progressively more troubled lest the two essential components of imperialism – "national strength and imperial consolidation on the one hand and ... domestic reform and social progress on the other" – became separated. Imperial power depended ultimately upon the "welfare and contentedness of the mass of the people."[18] With his personal connections among the leading imperialists in England and his wide reading in the literature of the movement, Parkin could hardly remain uninfluenced by this major theme in British imperial thought, nor could such a sensitive conscience as his be unaffected by the slums and poverty he saw everywhere in Britain. With genuine pain he told his wife of the "swarms of pale look-

18 Viscount Milner, *Speeches Delivered in Canada in the Autumn of 1908* (Toronto, 1909), 75–6.

ing operatives going home at meal time" from the Dundee jute factories
– mere children, scarcely larger than his own.[19]

It was Benjamin Kidd's *Social Evolution* (1894) which provided
Parkin with an answer to the question of how a convinced social Darwinist could support social reform. "Kidd's book," he wrote, "capti-
vates me more and more."[20] The heart of Kidd's treatise was the contention that though the dynamic of social progress was competition,
rivalry and strife, the struggle for existence between individuals within
society, was being transcended by the struggle between societies or
states. Rejecting both the collectivism of the Marxians and the individualism of the Spencerians, Kidd argued that at any given time each individual, pursuing his own selfish ends, was acting in opposition to the
society to which he belonged. What tended to check and blunt this individualism, however, was the force of religion which provided an "ir-
rational" motive for altruism and selfless effort. Within any social system, Kidd wrote,

> there is maintained ... a conflict of two opposing forces; the disinte-
> grating principle represented by the rational self-assertiveness of the
> individual units; the integrating principle represented by a religious
> belief providing a sanction for social conduct which is always of ne-
> cessity ultra-rational and the function of which is to secure in the
> stress of evolution the continual subordination of the interests of the
> individual units to the larger interests of the longer-lived social or-
> ganism to which they belong.[21]

Kidd did not believe that competition within the state would be totally
suspended. Evolution would only change its character; crude laissez-
faire would be transformed into a "higher," "more efficient" competition based on equal opportunity for all. This development, he assured
his readers, was in the interest of the state which must prepare for gigantic struggles in the future. What Kidd implied was that the Christian
religion was at the very centre of social development and this is why
Parkin thought the book so valuable in an age of doubt. Equally important, Kidd strengthened the belief that social reform was entirely
compatible with, indeed it was dictated by, the changing character of
social evolution.

Parkin grew increasingly preoccupied with social questions and his
appeals were invariably phrased in biological analogies of Darwinian

19 Parkin Papers, Parkin to Nan, Jan. 23, 1892 (copy).
20 *Ibid.*, Parkin to Nan, March 21, 1894 (copy).
21 Benjamin Kidd, *Social Evolution* (London, 1894), 102.

science. One of his favourite devices was to compare the people emigrating from Britain to seeds. "Every emigrant ship that leaves our shores," he explained, "carries the seed of nations. Seedsmen say that all their seeds are tested before they are sent out. How much more need that this should be true of the seed of nations."[22] In emphasizing the necessity for maintaining the stamina of the imperial race, he arraigned the "evils that flow from the competitive processes by which wealth is accumulated" and pointed to the millions "living in congested centres under conditions so bad that the vigour of the race is being sapped and its character and physique lowered, entailing enormous waste of the human material that gives strength to the body politic." The responsibility for degeneracy, he said, lay in the rich West End of London, not in the slums. It lay with the idle rich "who place pleasure before public service" and "who are content to enjoy the advantages of wealth without its responsibilities." If those "parasites" who inhabit the West Ends of our cities, he wrote, "would devote the same amount of intense personal interest, the same free application of capital, and the same amount of scientific skill to dealing with the East End slums that they use in providing themselves with motors and other modern appliances of civilization, we should not have to wait an unlimited number of years to improve East End conditions."[23] For Parkin, the failure to grapple with social distress signified the defeat of the imperial ideal which hinged on Christian responsibility. The degree to which a man felt the sense of obligation to others, he believed, was the most penetrating test that could be applied to the sincerity of his Christianity. If men were insensitive to the poverty and degradation of the English working classes, then they did not have in them that spirit which alone gave imperial power any moral meaning. A nation which exercised far-reaching rule over subject peoples simply "cannot neglect in its own homes the vital questions of Duty and Discipline." Every year, he pointed out, thousands of administrators are sent out to the Empire. Every one of them, "from the viceroy down to the civilian clerk and common soldier is weighed in the balance and judged by ... subject populations as the products and examples of our own Christian Civilization." The church, state, and school had the duty to "keep pure and wholesome the fountain of national life which flows out on other lands," and these institutions must throw themselves with concerted energy upon the "social problems which place such a terrible strain on life and character, especially in our

22 Parkin Papers, vol. 66, MS "The better preparation of English Youth for service in the Outer Empire," n.d., 5.
23 G. R. Parkin, "True Imperialism," *United Empire: The Royal Colonial Institute Journal*, new series, II (Dec. 1911), 846; Parkin, Speech at the annual dinner of the institute, *ibid.*, III (June 1912), 497.

cities."[24] Like Grant, Parkin was less concerned with institutional reform than in applying Christian principles to society.

IV

Before 1900 Canadian imperialist social criticism was mainly aimed at the old country. Grant's social gospel was more prophetic of things to come, more an outgrowth of his world-view, than a direct response to Canadian conditions. Though the report of the Royal Commission on the Relation of Labour and Capital of 1889 had located widespread instances of factory evils, it was not without some justification that Grant noted in 1894 that the grave social problems depicted in American reformist literature were apparent in the Dominion only in their "first beginnings."[25] Even when Grant died in 1902, the forces which were to transform Canada from an agricultural to an industrialized nation were just gathering momentum. In the decade before the World War, however, the phenomenal pace of economic development and its mounting social costs, drew an ever-growing volume of criticism from various segments of the community. While the complaints of the farmers about the high tariff were the most obvious and have traditionally received the largest amount of attention, the general spirit of restlessness was swelled by members of the professional classes – particularly professors and clergymen – who had to live on relatively fixed salaries while prices rose sixty-four per cent between 1897 and 1906,[26] by city-dwellers who deplored the corruption discovered in the municipal government of Montreal in 1909, and by some intellectuals who regarded the age of Canada's great barbecue as a disgraceful debauch.

In such an environment it was no longer possible to believe that class tensions and strikes were peculiarities of older countries or the results of defective republican principles. Before the war, the mood of discontent did not attain either an amplitude or a political embodiment comparable to the progressive movement across the border. Socialism, most observers agreed, was a negligible factor in Canadian life.[27] In

24 Parkin Papers, vol. 66, MS "May 24th 1915: The Call of Empire to the Nation"; vol. 69, MS "The Church in the Empire," n.d., and MS "Chapter House, Oxford," n.d.
25 G. M. Grant, "The Religious Condition of Canada," *Queen's Quarterly*, I (April 1894), 318.
26 Andrew Macphail, "Protection and Politics," *University Magazine*, VII (April 1908), 239.
27 O. D. Skelton, *Socialism: A Critical Analysis* (New York, 1911), 309–10; E. J. Kylie, "The Menace of Socialism," *Empire Club Speeches: Being Addresses Delivered Before the Empire Club of Canada During its Session of 1908–1909* (Toronto, 1910), 120.

1909 O. D. Skelton, then a professor of political economy at Queen's, could write that the question of regulating industrial combines "has scarcely as yet been an issue in our politics." "We have," he added, "long considered ourselves immune from the evils of trust domination which afflicted our cousins to the South. Muckraking and trust-busting have never been acclimatized among our popular sports." In spite of such qualifications, Skelton sensed that a "vague but determined demand for governmental action is arising."[28] The explosion of social unrest which followed the World War had its origins in the social changes of the Laurier era, and it was these conditions within Canada which gave imperialist social criticism both an intensity and an immediacy which it did not have before.

The flowering of the American progressive movement during the presidential administration of Theodore Roosevelt exercised a profound effect upon imperialist thought. Though its beginnings ran back to the social gospel, agrarian protest, and resentment against the domination of business in the late nineteenth century, this reform movement had its deepest impact upon American politics in the years after 1900. The literature it produced, whether sophisticated academic treatises or the excited exposés of the muckrakers, was monumental in quantity and bewildering in the range of social disorders examined. Political observers in Canada could hardly escape the influence of this movement if for no other reason than that the influx of American books and magazines which they frequently deplored carried the ideas of progressivism into the Dominion. Information which was not derived directly from such periodicals as *McClure's* could be obtained easily from the summaries provided by Canadian publications. In *Queen's Quarterly*, for example, James Cappon, dean of arts at Queen's University, regularly called attention to the "literature of exposure" – to Ida Tarbell's examination of the Standard Oil Company and Lincoln Steffens' investigations of corruption in city governments. "The magazines," Cappon reported, "have been teeming with articles on the grafters of St. Louis and Philadelphia, the meat packers of Chicago, the insurance officials of New York, the magnates of Wall Street and their performances, the injustice of railway rate preferences, the adulteration of patent medicines ..."[29] Many of the leading American spokesmen of progressive reform, moreover, appeared before Canadian audiences to state the burden of their cause. A member of the Canadian Club of Toronto who regularly attended its meetings in the decade after its founding in 1902 would have been exposed to nearly every facet of this many-sided movement. He would have heard, to name but a few, Jacob

28 O. D. Skelton, "Current Events," *Queen's Quarterly*, XVI (Jan. 1909), 294.
29 James Cappon, "Current Events," *ibid.*, XIII (April 1906), 368.

Riis on city improvement; Charles van Hise, president of the University of Wisconsin and an authority on the regulation of trusts; Rev. Lyman Abbott, confidant of Theodore Roosevelt and an exponent of the "new nationalism"; the economist Richard T. Ely; Washington Gladden; Gifford Pinchot, a champion of conservation; and William Taylor, whose name became a synonym for scientific management. Even William Jennings Bryan appeared before the first meeting of the Empire Club of Toronto.

In a different age Canadians might have been tempted to congratulate themselves on being free from the malignancies which these progressives sought to cure, but after 1900 those like James Cappon, Andrew Macphail, and Stephen Leacock could not remain oblivious to the fact that what had previously seemed to be American problems were now Canadian ones as well and that the politico-business alliance which Roosevelt sought to sever in the United States did not differ, except in size, from the one emerging within the Dominion. Their pleas for social and political reform were customarily prefaced by appreciative allusions to the American movement and some went so far as to invert the traditional response of Canadians to social malaise in the United States. They grew painfully aware that compared to what Cappon called the "revival of conscience" across the border and the determined efforts of the progressives to restore order and organization to society, the Canadian public remained lamentably indifferent to similar evils within their own country.

Despite these outside influences and social changes within Canada, imperialist social criticism retained a remarkable continuity. The essential difference between the social views of Denison and those of Macphail is one of degree and sophistication, not of kind and content. Few developments generated more apprehension than the relative decline in the rural population, few themes were as dominant as the vague feeling that Canadian development was unbalanced and unhealthy. The preference for agriculture and the expectation that it would continue to be a dominant factor in Canada, was reinforced and strengthened at the very time when agriculture was rapidly losing its primacy. "From the very nature of the case," said George Foster in 1901, "Canada's rural population must always be preponderant – though she has many cities of magnitude and will have many more. This means a well distributed population – comparative absence of poverty, and that robustness of morals and simplicity of life which are essential elements in any people."[30]

For those who identified the preponderance of rural life with such

30 Sir George E. Foster Papers, vol. 78, MS "Canada, at the Opening Century," 1901, 7.

virtues, the growth of cities at the expense of the countryside appeared less a sociological problem and more an assault upon the very fibre of national life. A committee of the Canadian Senate was appointed in 1912 to consider the "Unsatisfactory Character of the Movement of Population" by which was meant the drift to the city, not the arrival of unassimilable immigrants. The Board of Social Service and Evangelism of the Presbyterian Church in Canada commissioned a study of rural depopulation in order to discover what the church might do to arrest the exodus from the Ontario countryside.[31] Such studies usually found the causes of this undesirable phenomenon in the loneliness and isolation of farm life compared to the misleading glamour of cities, the decreasing profitability of agriculture, and even in the widespread impression of the farmer as a backward specimen of humanity or a "hayseed." Imperialists praised the efforts of the tobacco magnate and philanthropist, Sir William Macdonald, who gave liberally in the cause of agricultural education and sponsored the school garden movement. Just as agricultural education was designed to make farming more profitable and hence deter abandonment of it, so too the purpose of attaching garden plots to schools was quite frankly intended, among other things, "to encourage the cultivation of the soil as an ideal life-work" and to "train the rural population to remain in the country."[32] Governor-General Grey, an admirer of Macdonald, announced with his customary zeal that the "most pressing problem of the time ... is how to reestablish the people in a profitable and beautiful life upon the land."[33] "An agricultural population," wrote one McGill professor, "is a nation's greatest strength. Canada must try to avoid the weakening from which Great Britain has suffered, through the drain of her agricultural population to the cities, by making the life of Canadians who live on the land more attractive ..."[34] Wilfred Campbell, the unofficial poet laureate of Canadian imperialism, had one of his fictional characters voice a desire which was close to the hearts of many imperialists, when that character said that he preferred the old ways and conditions to the

31 John MacDougall, *Rural Life in Canada: Its Trend and Tasks* (Toronto, 1913).
32 R. H. Cowley, "The Macdonald School Gardens," *Queen's Quarterly*, XII (April 1905), 399, 418. Macdonald's purposes were lucidly explained by one of his supporters in James W. Robertson, *The Macdonald College Movement: An Address Before the National Education Association of the United States at Denver, Colorado, July 7, 1909, Reprinted from the Proceedings of the Association, 1909* (n.p., n.d.).
33 Grey of Howick Papers, vol. 28, Grey to Sir William Macdonald, Dec. 31, 1909 (copy).
34 John L. Todd, "The Site of a University," *University Magazine*, IX (April 1910), 208.

clashing of capital and labour and hoped that men would some day "have the common sense to go back to the country and till the soil."[35]

It was not nostalgia alone that led Andrew Macphail to regard the decline of agriculture as a symbol of everything that was going wrong with the new Canada. We cannot live by cities alone, he wrote in 1911; "if the country districts decay, the whole of Canada is bound to decay as well." So completely did this urban intellectual accept the agrarian myth that he dismissed the traditional image of the farmer as a be-whiskered individual wielding a pitchfork as a jest, but said that the impression of a city-dweller as a fat man sitting in an easy chair, smoking a cigar, and reading a newspaper, "is a serious matter." Like Southey and Wordsworth he found no peace in industrial cities, and like Ruskin and Morris he found no aesthetic satisfaction in the products of the machine. "The machine myth," he believed, "was at an end." Men long ago realized that the factory was a curse socially and politically; now they were beginning to understand that it was a failure even in economic terms. Everywhere they were turning away from "the rottenness and barbarity of the products of the factory" to articles made by hand craftsmanship.[36] The factory system seemed to Macphail a gigantic instrument of human enslavement. It was no longer possible to see the steam engine as the herald of an age in which men would work less, when "a new earth would arrive with leisure and comfort for all." The Lancashire cotton spinners who tried to destroy the first jenny were profoundly right: through a sure instinct they knew that their children would be imprisoned in factories.[37] Macphail knew better than to counsel a wholesale return to the land, to an idealized society of a mythical past or to the blissfully rural Prince Edward Island of his youth. But he still felt that human nature could no longer stand the clank of machinery and a fraudulent existence cut off from the soil. Will we ever see the green earth again, he asked with Matthew Arnold, shall we ever drink the feeling of quiet any more?

Torn between the fear that industrialism was destroying something ineffably good and the hope that life in Canada would always be rural, Macphail turned upon the entire drift of Canadian development in his time with a denunciatory intensity reminiscent of Carlyle. For thirty years, he wrote in 1908, "we have resolutely turned our faces from an agricultural and pastoral life, from the simple joys that go with these

35 Cited in Carl F. Klinck, *Wilfred Campbell: A Study in Late Provincial Victorianism* (Toronto, 1942), 203.
36 Andrew Macphail, "Prince Edward Island," *Addresses Delivered Before the Canadian Club of Toronto, Season of 1911–12* (Toronto, 1912), 48–59; Macphail, "The Cost of Living," *University Magazine*, XI (Dec. 1912), 536.
37 Macphail, "The Cost of Living," 540.

occupations," to the machine, the factory, and the slum.[38] The protective tariff had been instituted without regard for social consequences and without much thought for the kind of society it would produce. Protection, he argued, had nearly always been adopted for political reasons, seldom for economic ones. The economic growth of the United States was due to an abundance of natural resources, that of Germany to the education, energy, and self-reliance of her people. In neither case was the tariff the major factor in development. In all countries, the end results of protection were the creation of a shoddy aristocracy of money, an aggravation of sectional and class jealousies, and the establishment of a pernicious alliance between politicians and businessmen which conspired against the national interest and bred corruption. All our troubles, ran Macphail's diagnosis, began when "public politics and private finance were allowed to intermingle" and "when we adopted the principle that one part of the community should be compelled to support another part, when certain favoured persons were protected at the expense of less favoured persons." The politico-business alliance was at the root of the corruption of political life as well as the degradation of society and until it was severed, until the motives of business ceased to be the guiding values of statecraft, there could be no justice and no peace.[39]

What Macphail particularly objected to was the notion that business, by which he meant a specific interest group as well as capitalistic standards in general, constituted the best measurement for national action. By its very nature business sought pecuniary profit without thought for the social context in which it operated. Admitting no goals apart from profits, it was indifferent to nationalism, religion, and education. It judged all these only insofar as they were related to its dominant concern. Because business interests and the economic calculus were paramount, Canadian growth had been unhealthy and unbalanced. The declining position of agriculture was but one symptom of this; the large number of unselected immigrants brought into the country without any thought for the future national character was another. Warning that the nation's interest was not identical with the good of its capitalists, Macphail would have been satisfied with nothing less than a group of disinterested leaders who stood above the contending classes and clash of special interests and legislated for the good of the whole nation. Completely consistent in his rejection of "business," Macphail sym-

---

38 Macphail, "The Dominion and the Spirit," *University Magazine*, VII (Feb. 1908), 14.
39 Macphail, "Consequences and Penalties," *ibid.*, XIII (April 1914), 172, 174; "Protection and Politics," 243–51.

pathized with the farmers' attack upon protection and their advocacy of a lower tariff. For too many years, he said, they had "been milking the hind teat."[40] And he heaped scorn on Joseph Chamberlain's conception of the Empire as a commercial proposition. A sense of despair and futility pervaded Macphail's social commentary. Beyond advocating a decrease in the tariff, he anticipated no concrete solutions to the contemporary malady. He discarded the proposals of organized labour, the attempt of the churches to uplift the masses, and even adult education because these appeared to him as but slightly different manifestations of the fundamental evil – the definition of the social good in terms of cash and comfort.

The belief that business values were inadequate and insufficient, demoralizing and corrupting, ran deep in imperialist thought. Article after article in Macphail's *University Magazine* dwelt upon this theme at length, no others quite achieving the combination of moral indignation and severity as those by Stephen Leacock. Like Macphail, Leacock located the main misfortune of his day in the penetration of the business spirit into the church, the university, and politics. Remarking upon the "literary sterility of America," and making clear that "Canada is in America," he attributed it in part to the fact that "business, and the business code, and business principles [have] become everything."[41] In his most biting satirical work, *Arcadian Adventures with the Idle Rich* (1914), Leacock paid his respects to the hustling ministers who no longer cared for religion, the university folk who no longer cared about learning and scholarship, the deceitful political reformers, the mindless wizards of high finance, and the inane social habits and mores of the rich in general. It would not be unprofitable to compare Leacock's satire on the wealthy with the mordant wit of the American economist Thorstein Veblen under whom he studied at the University of Chicago and from whom he learned that "human industry is not carried on to satisfy human wants but in order to make money."[42] Where Veblen couched his assault upon predatory businessmen, conspicuous consumption, and the sabotage of industrial efficiency and productivity by financiers in the indirect and involuted language of his peculiar social science, Leacock conveyed the same message in what were often mistaken for innocuous humour stories. Given his caustic assessment of the business civilization in the period before the First World War, it was not surprising that Leacock should turn to the problem of social justice in

40 Macphail, "The Dominion and the Provinces," *ibid.*, XII (Dec. 1913), 555.
41 Stephen Leacock, "Literature and Education in America," *ibid.*, VIII (Feb. 1909), 16.
42 Leacock, *My Discovery of the West* (London, 1937), 171.

1920, and, while rejecting socialism, endorse a forward-looking policy of state-directed reform to ensure equality of opportunity.[43] Nor was it out of harmony with these early predispositions that in 1935 he wrote the introduction to Prime Minister Bennett's first radio address explaining a Canadian New Deal in which Leacock recapitulated his denunciation of the extremes of laissez-faire and socialism and spelled out the aim of tory reformism – "the regulated state, preserving the stimulus of individual reward, but with a fairer set of rules to apply it."[44]

The indictments of Macphail and the satire of Leacock did not compose the limits of the reactions of imperialists to the primacy of commercialism. Castell Hopkins, who stigmatized "the greed of gain as the dominant aspiration of the day," could only counsel a return to the ideals of the past which had been "inadvertently or wilfully abandoned."[45] Another, William D. Lighthall, one-time mayor of Westmount, helped organize the Union of Canadian Municipalities in order to check business oppression on one front. The age of competition, he recognized, was over: "Public ownership, in fact – national and municipal – is the only refuge to which we can look from the evils of monopoly."[46] The policy for the future, he wrote in 1904, lay in public ownership of utilities and closer national control of lands and forests. The abuses of irresponsible wealth, not wealth itself, bore the brunt of his attack. The historian W. L. Grant, who combined the family tradition of Grant and Parkin, gave the clearest and most explicit formulation to the reformist side of imperialist thought. In my mind, he wrote, "Imperialism has two sides, a resolute attempt to solve our problems of [imperial] organisation and of social reform." Imperialism to him was a "system of life" and those who identified it exclusively with a high tariff and a big navy left unanswered the central question of what kind of society these instruments were intended to institutionalize and defend. For Grant, the two "inseparable" aspects of imperialism were social service and strength – an attitude of social responsibility and a desire to make Canadian society a place in which every man, woman, and child had the chance to develop the best that is in them, and strength which would protect that society in a world of imperfection, anger, and unreason. The history of Great Britain, no less than that of the republic, he said, was proof that a great country was not made by setting an

43 Leacock, *The Unsolved Riddle of Social Justice* (Toronto, 1920).
44 Leacock, "Foreward," *The Premier Speaks to the People: The Prime Minister's January Radio Broadcasts issued in book form. The First Address* (Ottawa, [1935]), 5–7.
45 J. Castell Hopkins, "Canadian Life and Character," *University Magazine*, VIII (April 1909), 296, 304.
46 W. D. Lighthall, "The People as Municipalities," *Addresses Delivered Before the Canadian Club of Toronto, Season 1904–05* (Toronto, n.d.), 35. For an extended statement see his *Canada, A Modern Nation* (Montreal, 1904).

energetic people to exploit natural resources. To expect that out of an individualistic scramble for wealth would automatically emerge a great people, he wrote, was the strangest fiction ever to enter the head of an economist. Individualism had broken down and the only means of reconciling the interests of civilization with industrialism was to extend the "organizing and supervising power of the state, and in some cases state ownership." Only in this way could a less mechanical and more humane society be preserved in Canada.[47]

Though it did not coalesce around a single proposal for reform, imperialist social thought possessed a high degree of unity and coherence in its arraignment of business standards. It must have often seemed simply unconstructive negativism, harping as it did upon the desirability of agricultural life, the misgivings about an urban, industrial civilization, and the insistence upon checking the decline and deterioration of the older certitudes. Even Leacock's satire may be seen in this light, for satire is in a sense a tacit acceptance of the thing satirized, a recognition that it is permanent. Yet the undercurrent of escapism and hopelessness was only a single facet of a very complex outlook. On a more positive level, these imperialists adhered, sometimes in an inarticulate way, to the traditional conservative conceptions which envisaged society as composed of functionally and organically related parts knit together by the impalpable filaments of mutual obligation and history. In this idea lay the source of affinity between their toryism and the impulse to reform. It is neither incongruous nor paradoxical that some of the strongest attacks upon business domination should come from tory imperialists for conservatives in Canada have frequently led the way in using state power to enforce a conception of the national interest which was more than the sum of special interests and assuredly not the result of the pressure of a single interest. Whether this arose from plain pragmatism, opportunism, or ideological commitment is open to debate, but the story of the creation of the Ontario Hydro, the Manitoba Telephone System, the Canadian National Railways, the Canadian Broadcasting Corporation and Bennett's abortive reform programme, has convinced some observers that the kinship between Canadian conservatism and socialism is evident in the historical record as well as in ideology.[48] When in 1911 Sir Robert Borden affirmed the Burkean principle that a nation is a continuous partnership between the

47 W. L. Grant Papers, vol. 15, MS "Canadian Ideals and the Canadian Navy," 1911; untitled MS, 1910 or 1911; W. L. Grant, '*A Nation of Prophets, of Sages, and of Worthies': A Speech Delivered on 18th December 1917 ... On His Installation as Headmaster of Upper Canada College* (n.p., n.d.), 10–11.
48 G. Horowitz, "Conservatism, Liberalism, and Socialism in Canada: An Interpretation," *Canadian Journal of Economics and Political Science*, XXXII (May 1966), 143–71.

dead, the living, and generations unborn, and warned that wealth which was irresponsible and acquired by unjust means "is and will be a menace to the political structure of this country,"[49] he voiced ideas which were deeply embedded in the imperialist mentality. There were imperialists, of course, who remained indifferent to this warning; some who completely believed it, but, like Denison, were unable to distinguish the antics of individuals from profoundly impersonal social changes; others, like Macphail, who never quite got beyond the preliminary stages of chastising evils to the point of suggesting remedies; and, still others, who, like W. L. Grant and his father, did both. But wherever one locates these imperialists in the tradition of Canadian social criticism, the significant thing is that they were critics and that their conception of imperialism was completely bound up with that fact.

49 R. L. Borden, "Some Problems of the Canadian People," *Addresses Delivered Before the Canadian Club of Toronto, Season 1910–11* (Toronto, 1911), 137.

8

Democracy and Leadership

In their attitude to party government the imperialists remained faithful to the Canada First tradition. Though the collapse of that movement demonstrated that the hoped for dissolution of the colonial parties and the end to bitter partisanship was premature, it did nothing to shake the hostility to "partyism" among the original members of that group and among Canadian intellectuals generally. The conventional condemnation of the sordidness and corruption of party politics, the questioning of whether party was an altogether indispensable instrument of government, and even an exasperation with democracy itself, increased in frequency and grew more and more specific in the later years of the nineteenth century. Though the imperialists' dispraise of both politicians and the behaviour of political parties was at times quixotic, it was also fed by certain objective realities and was usually prefatory to proposals for reform which involved education and the training of a leadership élite rather than institutional or mechanical alterations.

I

The revolt against party government in Canada expressed the disgust of an intellectual class and not simply the discontent of a particular group of imperialists. "It is rather an ominous fact," wrote one clergyman in 1882, "that, both in this country, and in the United States, there are a great many respectable and intelligent people who refuse to have aught to do with politics."[1] Those guardians of culture in the United States like Henry Adams and James Russell Lowell, as well as liberal editors like E. L. Godkin, felt estranged from the political life of their times partly because democracy appeared incapable of producing a group of devoted and disinterested leaders who stood above the clash and

---

1 Rev. Hugh Pedley, "The Study of Canadian Politics," *Rose-Belford's Canadian Monthly and National Review*, VIII (April 1882), 361. The American parallel is discussed in Richard Hofstadter, *Anti-Intellectualism in American Life* (New York, 1964), 172–96.

clamour of special interests. American democracy, it seemed to them, had fallen into the hands of men untutored in social responsibility and without any conception of leadership except pandering to the whimsical mob. These American critics had their counterparts in Canada among men of all shades of opinion. The distaste for the chicanery of politicians and the undignified and pointless wars between parties united such various figures as the continental unionist Goldwin Smith and the loyalist Colonel Denison, the French-Canadian nationalist Henri Bourassa and the imperialist Stephen Leacock, the engineer Sandford Fleming and the controversialist William Le Sueur. The historian John G. Bourinot doubted whether the tendency of democracy and the presence of highly educated individuals in politics were at all compatible, and the poet Archibald Lampman, who, like Bourinot, observed the statesmen at close range in Ottawa, greeted the coming of "The Modern Politician" as a successor to the kings of old,

> Blinding the multitude with specious words.
> To them faith, kinship, truth and verity,
> Man's sacred rights and very holiest thing,
> Are but the counters at a desperate play,
> Flippant and reckless what the end may be,
> So that they glitter, each his little day,
> The little mimic of a vanished king.[2]

This sense of alienation from politics and disdain for its practitioners which runs so persistently through the literature of these years can only be partly explained in terms of individual frustration or jealousy.

The anti-political language of Canada First, for example, could soothe the disappointment that Denison felt at failing to achieve a military command or a seat in the House of Commons. "If I had to go to Ottawa," he told Mair in pathetic sentences of self-justification, "I would have to associate with about the most contemptible and wretched society on this continent. Politicians ... Contractors, jobbers, wirepullers & frauds outside of the Civil service & in it ... toadies & timeservers, men without opinions or ideas, and without the courage to express them if they had any[,] needy embarrassed deadbeats most of them, living beyond their means and defrauding all who trust them. You can imagine the aversion I should have to place my family as they are growing up in such an atmosphere."[3] But this scion of the Toronto loyalists none the less refused a CMG in 1903 because he realized, as Goldwin Smith had said, that such honours had become "merely one of the taps in the

2 Malcolm Ross, ed., *Poets of the Confederation* (Toronto, 1967), 82.
3 QUL, Charles Mair Papers, Denison to Mair, Dec. 31, 1882.

party bar,"[4] and he feared that accepting one on the recommendation of the Laurier government would compromise his reputation for political independence.[5] Neither Parkin nor Grant ever sought an elective office and both rejected safe constituencies when offered them. While always insisting that imperial unity was not a question of party politics, they supported whichever party they thought was most progressive in carrying imperialist measures. They could preen themselves on their own adherence to principle, of course, largely because they did not bear the responsibilities of those whom they derided, and they could continue to deluge politicians with hortatory letters, letters always filled with free advice and predicated upon the assumption that those who wrote them represented detached and objective opinion, without being bothered by any sense of their own effrontery. It is significant that imperialists in politics, like George Ross or George Foster, who shared so many articles of the faith, were far less censorious of the foibles of party and less impatient with partisanship than their associates who had little intimate contact with the mechanics of government.

When personal bitterness and estrangement are taken into account, however, there remain several compelling reasons why these imperialists adopted a critical view of party government. The suspension of partisanship which had made Confederation possible proved to be only temporary and after a brief confusing interlude parties were consolidated and extended. While imperialists generally favoured John A. Macdonald's aims of integration and territorial consolidation, they grew more and more appalled by his technique of attaching special interests to the national government through favours or simply through government appropriations. They found it increasingly difficult to distinguish between the degree to which these policies were designed to foster national unity and the extent to which they only served the purposes of a party. The huge expenditures that this kind of nation-building entailed, moreover, appeared wasteful and unjustifiable to men like Grant who had a Gladstonian regard for money as a sacred trust and who stood for fiscal retrenchment in government.

Party control of patronage was hardly altered by the meagre instalment of civil service reform in the 1880s. In 1895 one civil servant observed that while Britain had a public service "absolutely free from all taint of political interference" and while the Americans were "dealing blow after blow at the spoils system," Canadians were satisfied "with a

4 *The Bystander: A Monthly Review of Current Events, Canada and General,* new series (May 1890), 225.
5 G. T. Denison Papers, Lord Minto to Denison, Oct. 23, 1903; Denison to Minto, Oct. 24, 1903 (copy).

Civil Service law which simply prescribes a very elementary qualifying examination, as a condition of eligibility, and then hands over all appointments to the politicians and their committees."[6] The Macdonald system of preserving unity through the distribution of government concessions, especially to large business enterprises, was accepted by the Laurier administration after 1896, and in the prosperous period before the World War it appeared to many that this technique and the vested interests created by it had become so firmly established as to be virtually ineradicable. "We bribe whole provinces by special subsidies or railroad extensions"; wrote O. D. Skelton in 1913, "we give cold justice to the districts ill-advised enough to differ in politics from Ottawa, and warm favours to the discreet. We bribe constituencies with public works, needed or not ... We bribe individuals by giving them contracts for which the country pays, or, if less important, by jobs in the country's service."[7]

Five years before he published *Sunshine Sketches of a Little Town* (1912), in which he lampooned the parochial and pecuniary concerns evident in "The Great Election in Missanaba County," and seven years before he exposed the deceitfulness of the fighters for clean municipal government in *Arcadian Adventures with the Idle Rich* (1914), Stephen Leacock mocked the "mud-bespattered politicians of the trade, the party men and party managers." "Harsh is the cackle of the little turkey-cocks of Ottawa," he wrote, "fighting as they feather their mean nests of sticks and mud, high on their river bluff."[8] The World War made Leacock doubt many things, but it only reinforced his previous contention that materialism and the business credo were at the root of the degeneration of political life. Those who looked around and saw the "rise of the great trusts, the obvious and glaring fact of the money power, the shameless luxury of the rich, the crude, uncultivated and boorish mob of vulgar men and over-dressed women that masqueraded as high society," may be excused, he said, from feeling that democracy could not cure its own debilities. "We have," Leacock added, "tolerated with a smile the bribery of voters, the corrupting of constituencies, the swollen profits of favoured contractors, the fortunes made in and from political life, the honours heaped upon men with no other recommendation to their credit than their bank accounts."[9] Canadians must realize

6 W. D. Le Sueur, "Problems of Government in Canada," *Queen's Quarterly*, II (Jan. 1895), 206.
7 O. D. Skelton, "The Referendum," *University Magazine*, XII (April 1913), 213; O. D. Skelton Papers, MS "Bettering our Politics," n.d.
8 Stephen Leacock, "Greater Canada: An Appeal," *University Magazine*, VI (April 1907), 136.
9 Stephen Leacock, "Democracy and Social Progress," in J. O. Miller, ed., *The New Era in Canada* (Toronto, 1917), 17, 32.

that the debasement of politics was only a consequence of the definition of individual merit and national progress in terms of dollars and cents and the identification of government with the broker state mediating between interests, mainly economic interests.

Leacock and his imperialist associates were not alone in tracing back the opportunism of Canadian politics to the total dominance of material issues. James Bryce, who had earlier pleased not a few Canadians by his critical assessment of certain aspects of American democracy, also studied Canadian democracy and came to much the same conclusion as Leacock, saying that "a game played over material interests between ministers, constituencies and their representatives, railway companies and private speculators is not only demoralizing to all concerned, but interferes with the consideration of the great issues of policy ..."[10] Though Bryce's critique of Canadian political life appeared in 1921 it rested upon impressions and evidence ranging back half a century.

Repelled by the perpetual preoccupation with material matters and critical of the alleged inability of party politics to transcend endless concentration upon the immediately practical, imperialists were in addition worried over the future of democracy itself. For those born in the middle years of the nineteenth century democracy was a new and untried thing, well known among Canadians for its undignified and turbulent effects upon the United States. Canadians had traditionally expressed a preference for the authority, order, and deference inherent in the monarchical principle as opposed to the American experience with the sovereignty of the people and universal manhood suffrage. The fathers of Confederation often linked the creation of the new nationality with the maintenance of a political system which was profoundly different from American democracy. "The difference between our neighbours and ourselves," said George Etienne Cartier, "is essential. The preservation of the monarchical principle will be the great feature of our confederation, whilst on the other side of the line the dominant power is the will of the masses, of the populace." Americans themselves admit, he added, that their "government became powerless owing to the introduction of universal suffrage, in other words, that mob rule supplanted a more legitimate authority."[11] "The great question to be asked in deciding whether or not a man shall exercise the franchise," declared Macdonald in 1870, "was whether or not he has a sufficient interest or stake in the country to be entrusted with a share in its government."[12]

10 James Bryce, *Modern Democracies* (New York, 1921), ii, 504.
11 John Boyd, *Sir George Etienne Cartier, Bart.: His Life and Times* (Toronto, 1914), 222.
12 Cited in W. L. Morton, "The Extension of the Franchise in Canada: A Study in Democratic Nationalism," Canadian Historical Association, *Annual Report*, 1943, 77n.

So gradually was the franchise broadened in Canada that no memorable series of enactments marked its course. The Dominion Franchise Act of 1885 established low but complicated property qualifications which were to be uniform in Dominion elections, and, though provincial franchises were broader, it was not until the Dominion Election Act of 1918 that universal suffrage became the basis for federal elections. Because they shared the sentiments of Cartier and Macdonald, because their conservatism was so inextricably bound up with their understanding of Canadian nationality, and because they were aware of the fears occasioned in conservatively minded circles in Britain by the second and third reform bills, some imperialists were alarmed at the expansion of the electorate. When Lord Salisbury told Denison in 1886 that the new electors enfranchised by the third reform bill "have no understanding of the issues before them – and several parliaments must pass before they take any but the most purely pecuniary interest in politics,"[13] he was using language which this descendant of the colonial patricians could well understand and appreciate.

It is extremely doubtful if Denison ever accepted the legitimacy of democracy for very often his immoderate criticism of party politics challenged the very substance of popular sovereignty. In his eccentric political science, "the people" were always described as loyal and sound; they were always the "silent masses" who had no way of making their true sentiments known. The duty of men like himself was to act as a mouthpiece of the "inert" populace. Of his leadership of the anti-reciprocity movement, he wrote: "I was only one of a band of men who voiced the feelings of the silent masses of the Canadian people."[14] Because the people were docile and lacking in initiative they had to be led. The trouble, however, was that the politicians either whipped up artificial agitations and appealed to the base and selfish interests of the voters, or they were so overcome with timidity and fear of consequences, that they did nothing at all. "I am afraid," the Colonel told a friend in 1898, that "the present system of government by politicians, depending upon the popular vote, places our destinies often in the hands of men afraid of their own shadows."[15] Political vacillation and timorousness, he said, were the results of the "extended franchise and the new idea of turning things upside down and looking for the brains in the feet." After a visit to England in 1894, he announced that the British House of Commons had deteriorated since he first saw it. "The landed gentlemen of England ruled England in the past and were the

13 Denison Papers, Salisbury to Denison, April 16, 1886.
14 oa, William Kirby Papers, Jan. 11, 1894.
15 Sir Sandford Fleming Papers, Denison to Fleming, Dec. 3, 1898.

men who built the Empire." With the broadened franchise, "it will not take long for the mob to destroy what great & able men have built up."[16] Predictably, he regarded the attack upon the powers of the House of Lords, taxation of the aristocracy, and "other revolutionary movements" as efforts of Lloyd George "to rob the land owners in order to bribe the mob to keep him in office."[17]

No other imperialist shared Denison's antediluvian toryism but many did agree that the unwieldy and ill-informed electorate had something to do with the lack of decisiveness and the absence of clarity in Canadian politics. While ostensibly accepting democracy, they none the less remained suspicious of the doctrine that one man was as good as another and sceptical of the contention that all citizens were equally well qualified for the work of government. In a lecture at the University of Toronto in 1901, William Le Sueur drove to the heart of the problem which bothered these intellectuals when he asked, "Why do practical politicians shrink so much from dealing with large questions?" "On the one hand," he explained, "government is committed to the people; and it is so far assumed that they are capable of performing the political duties thus devolved on them. On the other hand it is a matter of certainty that the majority of the voters are not very good judges either of the larger questions of politics, or of the details of administration." Between the politicians who had a "morbid sensitiveness to what they call public opinion" as well as a healthy fear of what an unscrupulous opposition would do with any positive and constructive proposal, and the voters who could so easily be excited by slogans and words, the large and fundamental issues were lost.[18] People cannot afford to go on accepting democracy in the same unthinking and unconcerned way as they did electric lights and the municipal water supply, wrote Andrew Macphail in 1912, nor could they continue priding themselves on their liberty while at the same time transferring powers upon non-elected commissions and boards designed to cure the very disorders which democracy had produced. Democracy, he said, clearly lacked an initiating drive;[19] it was so unmanageable, so lacking in cohesiveness. The imperialists did not require foreign commentators like André Siegfried and James Bryce to inform them that Canadian parties had no

16 Denison Papers, Denison to A. H. Loring, July 31, 1893 (copy); Kirby Papers, Denison to Kirby, Oct. 4, 1894.
17 Denison Papers, Denison to A. Milner, Oct. 14, 1913 (copy).
18 W. D. Le Sueur, *The Problem of Popular Government: A Lecture delivered in the Chemical Building, University of Toronto, February 23rd, 1901* (n.p., n.d.), 9, 13.
19 Andrew Macphail, "The Tariff Commission," *University Magazine*, xi (Feb. 1912), 34.

ideological consistency and that they lived on long after their principles had lost relevance, or that while it was obvious that politicians were concerned with attaining power, power was most often used to perpetuate itself. "Democracy," said Leacock, "cannot work of itself."[20]

Beyond censoring the materialization of politics and lamenting the deficiency of purposeful leadership, there was one further feature of this critique of party government which dwelt upon the role of parties in pandering to a minority group. Disquisitions on the evils of party were often little more than indirect assaults upon "French domination." Scandals in which French Canadians were involved were frequently interpreted as proof of their defective sense of political responsibility. Commenting upon the announcement of a French-Canadian politician that he would not contest the constituency which he formerly represented because he could not afford it, the Week in 1892 revealed that these men "have never been taught to look upon the franchise in its true light, as a sacred trust to be used conscientiously for the good of their country and their fellow-men."[21] To such a point of revulsion and moral indignation did the Langevin-McGreevy scandals drive G. M. Grant that he privately admitted that he hoped a French Canadian would never again be given control of a money-spending department, a proposal which was, of course, tantamount to excluding them from the cabinet altogether.[22] In 1887, with the divisive consequences of the execution of Riel fresh in mind, the Week advanced an additional condemnation, saying this time that British and Protestant civilization in Canada would be safe if only the British and Protestant element were not constantly torn into factions "whose reckless rivalry betrays it into the hands of a weak but united force."[23] In not dissimilar circumstances in 1917 Parkin complained that in face of a great national emergency the parties went on talking their "jargon" while "our English people ... divide and play for the French vote."[24] Denison regarded the influence of Quebec as a distortion of the wishes of the majority of Canadians and, as we have seen, he looked upon the formation of union government as the culmination of the anti-party tradition of Canada First and a certification that his party had finally attained power. These imperialists saw the French Canadians as simply another "faction," one which was becoming less and less significant. Any compromise with this fac-

20 Stephen Leacock, "Empire and Education," Empire Club Speeches: Being Addresses Delivered Before the Empire Club of Canada During its Session of 1906–07 (Toronto, 1907), 295.
21 Week, IX (March 25, 1892), 259.
22 Fleming Papers, Grant to Fleming, Aug. 20, [1891].
23 Week, IV (Jan. 13. 1887), 104.
24 W. L. and Maude Grant Papers, Parkin to Maude, Aug. 12, 1917.

tion which jeopardized imperialism was therefore looked upon as a betrayal of the national future by spineless politicians.

II

The political thought of Canadian imperialism was grounded upon an élitist conception of leadership. Imperialists did not believe that democracy by itself would automatically produce a group of enlightened and educated leaders who would hold in check the extravagances and excesses of popular rule and give the state some direction; indeed, they held the crudities of democracy responsible for the withdrawal of the "best people" from political life and their replacement by vulgar, machine politicians. If such leadership could not be expected to come from the party system as it then existed, where then was it to come from? This problem occupied a major place in the imperial thought of G. M. Grant and Parkin mainly because they realized that the fate of imperialism was dependent upon the degree to which such leadership was forthcoming.

From the 1880s onward, Grant looked everywhere for indications that the rigidities of party were subsiding. Like Goldwin Smith, he believed that the party system was only an incident, a stage "through which nations pass in endeavouring to attain self-government," and he saw no reason why institutionalized parties, which were unnecessary for the administration of the churches, banks, and joint stock companies, should be thought so necessary for the government of the state.[25] He did not deny the possibility of disagreements between men over principles; his main criticism of the parties in fact was that by enforcing discipline through the caucus they compelled individuals to compromise their most fundamental beliefs. This unanimity, he said, twisted the conscience, lowered high ideals, and destroyed self-respect. Emphasizing the way partyism corrupted individuals, it was natural that he looked to political mavericks and insurgent movements as heralds of the end of the sacrifice of political individualism to party dictates. Grant admired Edward Blake's decision after the election of 1891 in issuing the West Durham letter in which he stated his criticism of the Liberal party's commercial policy, and he regarded the Patrons of Industry as a progressive force partly because they sought to break up the two-party system in Ontario. He told D'Alton McCarthy that he was "in sympathy with the fundamental principles on which the Equal Rights movement is based" for similar reasons.[26] Though he refused to give

25 G. M. Grant Papers, vol. 15, MS "Our Political Duties," n.d.
26 D'Alton McCarthy Papers, Grant to McCarthy [1889].

his support to McCarthy's campaign against French-Canadian language rights in western Canada because he recognized that it could only discredit imperialism, Grant nevertheless sympathized with a man who was determined enough to break with his own party and sacrifice his prospects of advancement within it for the sake of the principle of equal rights for all, special privileges for none. His application of that principle may have been perverse and wrongheaded and the strategy of the movement faulty, but at least McCarthy had the courage of his convictions. There is little reason to doubt that had he lived Grant would have similarly welcomed Joseph Chamberlain's break with his party in 1903 over the issue of imperial preferential trade.

The curse of party, however, could not be ended by such exceptional actions as these. Grant believed that the disgraceful features of party government would not disappear until public education had attained a certain level. There had traditionally been, he said, two forces which had checked partyism in England: one was a wealthy, leisured, and cultivated class whose highest ambition had been to serve the state; the other was the relatively large class of independent and educated men who controlled the organs of public opinion. In Canada neither of these buttresses of independence was powerful enough. The press, said Grant, was not only based upon business principles and unconcerned with educating the people, but it was also almost completely dominated by party interests.[27] "The democracy rules now," he noted in 1889, "... and it must be educated before any great political change can be effected with safety."[28] The role of the imperialists, he told Denison, was not to influence governments directly, but "to Educate public opinion."[29] By themselves, politicians would not lead any forward movement on the imperial question, or for that matter, on any question, and it therefore fell to intellectuals both to educate the people so that when the time for decision came it would be made intelligently and to generate popular pressure for specific measures. Parkin made the same point when he reported that Laurier had told him in 1902 that "as a politician he was not willing to look far ahead, and could only touch national questions as they became practical." The politicians, said Parkin, have given up leadership; somebody else must take it. Our business was "to work to create the public opinion which makes politicians act."[30]

Grant's own work as principal of Queen's was guided by the aim of producing educated and informed leaders who would devote themselves to the service of the state. It is not accidental that public servants like

27 Grant Papers, vol. 16, MS "The Defects of Journalism in Canada and how to Cure them," n.d.
28 Sir George R. Parkin Papers, MS by Grant on imperial federation [c. 1889].
29 Denison Papers, Grant to Denison, April 9, 1898.
30 Parkin Papers, Parkin to Nan, Jan. 23, 1902 (copy).

O. D. Skelton and Adam Shortt created a strong connection between that university and the Canadian civil service, nor was it fortuitous that one of the first proposals for a school of journalism in the Dominion came out of Queen's in 1903. Even the dominant school of political economy at that institution was applied and practical. *Queen's Quarterly* was created partly with the intention of providing a non-partisan organ for the consideration of public questions, as had the *Week* and the *Canadian Monthly and National Review* before it. Though Grant looked forward to a cabinet made up of the best men from all parties, and even hinted that he favoured the abolition of the Senate, he placed his faith in men who would refuse to be bound by party. There was no other way to improve political life, he concluded, than "by appealing to the nobler elements in all men; by utilizing the forces inherent in the church, the press, the school and the college, and bringing these to bear effectually on the people generally." If strong, independent, non-party men could not be found, "then the country is not fit to be free. If Canada cannot supply them, it is useless to struggle for national existence."[31]

Grant's faith in the capacity of educators and publicists to exert a profound effect upon the popular mind and hence upon the course of politics was shared by other imperialists, especially by Leacock and Macphail who were university figures, and by Parkin, Ross, and Foster who had themselves been teachers. We must face the fact, said Leacock, "that in the modern world a university is not a cloister, that a university must be prepared to be an acting part of the driving machinery of civilization."[32] These men had almost as much contempt for withdrawn intellectuals as they had for the generality of politicians. The failures of Canadian politics, said Macphail, must be attributed to "those who are content to stand afar off proclaiming their own holiness, disdaining the labour and sweat of those who carry on the government of the country."[33]

Whatever else might be said about the political philosophy of Parkin and Leacock who travelled widely through the Empire carrying the message of imperialism, or G. M. Grant who worked as tirelessly for that cause as he did in building Queen's, or Denison, always ready, figuratively speaking, to challenge traitors on horseback, they can hardly be called inactive armchair imperialists. When they spoke of decided leadership they were thinking of men exactly like themselves.

There were, of course, others who looked to more technical means

31 G. M. Grant, "Current Events," *Queen's Quarterly*, II (Jan. 1895), 266; *ibid.*, v (April 1898), 332.
32 Leacock, "Empire and Education," 292.
33 Andrew Macphail, "Theory and Practice," *University Magazine*, XII (Oct. 1913), 395.

to set the state of politics in order. Most imperialists favoured civil service reform. W. L. Grant endorsed the idea of a national government modelled upon commissions which would be responsible to the people and Parliament only in the last resort. And Sandford Fleming, who rationalized international time-keeping, appealed to the Canadian Institute to similarly rationalize politics. "Within the present century," wrote the foremost Canadian engineer of his day, "scientific methods have made conquests over traditional methods in nearly every sphere of life."[34] Everywhere the scientific spirit marched triumphant; surely it was not beyond its capacity to devise an electoral system that would reflect the national interest more accurately than the two-party system which in effect disfranchised nearly half the population. In 1912 Leacock was a member of Fleming's Electoral Reform Committee, an association which worked in conjunction with the Proportionate Representation Society of the United Kingdom. But generally the leaders of imperialism placed more hope on education and the cultivation of independently minded men than on institutional changes.

In this they found a sympathizer in a rather strange place. Few imperialists scourged the pettiness of politicians so harshly as did Henri Bourassa, the leader of the anti-imperialist, nationalist movement in Quebec. The nationalists of Quebec, he told a Toronto meeting, believed in the party system but not in party slavery. "There is," he said, "work and scope for a strong body of enlightened men who take the broad national patriotic point of view – men who are above the narrowness of party."[35] Like his adversaries, Bourassa had his own aristocratic ideal of leadership and he maintained that party government was unstable and that it weakened the principles of authority and corrupted public morality. "We Nationalists," he admitted in 1921, "are not devotees of democracy."[36] However much they disagreed with Bourassa in other matters, the imperialists at least found in him a welcome lucidity, honesty, and the faith that ideas would win over raw appetites, drift, and materialism.

III

Out of his life-long involvement in teaching, his association with Upper Canada College, and his work as organizer of the Rhodes Scholarship Trust, George Parkin fashioned the most thorough and comprehensive

34 Sandford Fleming, *An Appeal to the Canadian Institute on the Rectification of Parliament* (Toronto, 1892), 131.
35 Henri Bourassa, "The Nationalist Movement in Quebec," *Addresses Delivered Before the Canadian Club of Toronto, Season 1906–07* (Toronto, 1907), 62.
36 Cited in M. P. O'Connell, "The Ideas of Henri Bourassa," *Canadian Journal of Economics and Political Science*, XIX (Aug. 1953), 368.

answer to the question of leadership which preoccupied all imperialists. Though in his youth he had hailed the free school movement as another manifestation of the march of enlightenment and progress, Parkin remained very conscious of the gaps which universal public education could not fill, and troubled by the feverish quest for patronage which was so pronounced a feature of political life in his native region. Scarcely anywhere else in the whole Empire, he once wrote, "have so much talent, effort, and time been spent in trying to squeeze public and private prosperity out of politics as in the Maritime Provinces of Canada."[37] From Thring he had learned that the public school was not primarily concerned with cultivating intellectuality or imparting technical expertise; the "actual teaching and knowledge part of the matter," said the Headmaster of Uppingham, was not the "main thing."[38] The underlying purpose of the school was to mould the character of the future leaders of society by instilling into them a sense of obligation and responsibility, strengthening their group spirit, and teaching them that they must learn obedience in order to receive it from others in the future. Thring was especially emphatic on the point that every boy could do something well and that through close individual attention it was the master's business to discover and develop the special talent of each pupil. He passionately believed that "education was, in a special sense, a work of God," not only because the proclaimed objective was to produce Christian gentlemen, but because the whole aim of character development through work implied the fulfilment of God's creation.[39] Parkin saw that the English public schools exerted a far-reaching and formative influence upon the entire society because youths from the "better homes" who were trained in them subsequently took up careers in the professions, universities, and in commerce and industry. To cultivate certain values in these boys at such a strategic stage in their development was in effect to shape the outlook of the ruling class. By inculcating the group spirit, especially through organized sports, social solidarity was ensured. To learn responsibilities and independence, said Thring, "to bear pain, to play games, to drop rank, and wealth, and home luxury, is a priceless boon" and herein lay the source of the manliness and adventurousness of the British people.[40] In its broad outlines there was nothing original about Thring's conception of the public

37 G. R. Parkin, *The Great Dominion: Studies of Canada* (London, 1895), 105.
38 G. R. Parkin, *Edward Thring, Headmaster of Uppingham School: Life, Diary and Letters* (London, abridged edition, 1900), 67. A succinct account of the place of the public schools in Victorian society and the guiding ideas of their headmasters is given by Asa Briggs, "Thomas Hughes and the Public Schools," in his *Victorian People* (New York, 1963), 140–67.
39 Parkin, *Thring*, 65.
40 *Ibid.*, 425–6.

school, but it was from him that Parkin received the inspiring notion of its work and influence and to him the Headmaster of Uppingham always remained the exemplar of a life devoted to this high avocation. Parkin returned to Canada determined to establish such an institution but his proposal to the senate of the University of New Brunswick that residential schools be created in the province was unsuccessful. The President of the university made it clear that he "did not think we could make those schools, which were used almost exclusively by the English nobility and gentry, our models." It was impossible, he submitted, to "take a patch of a system and apply it to another country."[41] Parkin never accepted the force of this criticism because he remained convinced that in the loosely-knit, democratic community where social fluidity was the rule, the public school as a centre of discipline and training was more and not less necessary than in Britain where the habits of authority and deference had been nurtured by centuries of history. The conservative and stabilizing influences of such schools, he believed, were required to curb equalitarianism and to subdue the social irresponsibility of self-made men. Admittedly, the assertiveness and ambition of the self-made man was a valuable national asset, but it needed some check, some counterforce, which could only be provided by the inspiration of a "worthy family history," the tempering consciousness of *noblesse oblige* and a sense of service.[42] Parkin thought that both the United States and Canada had suffered because the rich and powerful families of the past had failed to transmit their social and political influence to their descendants. The result was that we "are compelled to manufacture our leading men and our governing social forces anew each generation out of the raw material which comes from our Farms and Work-shops." "There is little conservation of that culture and personal superiority," he explained, "which gives its highest tone and greatest efficiency to old communities. The loss which Canada and the United States have suffered from the absence of those conditions which tend to conserve this culture and efficiency is incalculable."[43]

In 1895, when he was appointed headmaster of Upper Canada College, he came to an institution which had not only been established for two generations but which also operated in an environment which was slightly more congenial to his educational philosophy than the Maritimes had been. In his first address to the college, Parkin told the boys that he did not care whether they won prizes for academic excellence, became athletes, or even learned the social graces. Obviously these things were important, but the school had something still more import-

---

41 Parkin Papers, vol. 107, clipping from St John *Daily Telegraph*, June 24, 1876.
42 *Ibid.*, vol. 64, note, n.d.
43 *Ibid.*, vol. 64, MS Address delivered at the University of New Brunswick, 1899.

ant to give them – character development, the highest and fullest development of their talents and energies. Character, or, as Parkin termed it, "manliness," did not depend upon brains, physical strength, or good manners; it meant the fulfilment of the individual's qualities through work and discipline. Parkin believed that the "sheer force of surrounding conditions" in a capitalistic society made it almost impossible for the sons of the prosperous to be properly educated. How can the homes of the rich in Toronto and Montreal, he asked, with their luxury, servants, social excitements, and diversions, ever provide suitable places "for steady discipline and the simple life" which were so necessary for the cultivation of manliness? Because the residential school was itself a self-contained, artificial environment, isolated from the distracting features of modern life and embodying the stern and hard precepts, he saw it as one of the last bastions where materialization and softness could be counteracted.[44]

The essence of Parkin's educational thought was summed up by his former student, Bliss Carman, in an essay entitled "Of Breeding." All individuals, Carman explained, were endowed with a superabundance of egotism, but character was most fully developed through the resignation of small and selfish aims. "Good breeding," he said, "is scrupulous in requiring the sacrifice of our own comfort for that of others."[45] Selfishness was not merely an undesirable social trait; it was a disregard for one's own character and the nature which God had given every man to develop through service.

Parkin believed that his work for the Rhodes Trust "was on the direct line of the ideas about national unity which had filled my mind for many years."[46] It was also in line with his educational thought. It was expected that the education of students from the Dominions and the colonies at Oxford would not only promote imperial unity through mutual understanding but would also inculcate that sense of obligation and self-sacrificing service which was at the heart of the imperial ideal. "The dream that floated before his vision," Parkin said of Rhodes, was that of "an empire recognizing its enormous mission and responsibilities in the world – with wisdom and trained ability adequate to governing rightly and justly the hundreds of millions of weaker races dependent upon it ..."[47] Because these scholars were looked upon as prospective leaders of opinion and makers of history they were to be, as Rhodes put

44 *Address by Dr. Parkin to the Boys of Upper Canada College, 1895* (n.p., n.d.), 4–5; Parkin Papers, vol. 80, clipping "The Principal's Prize Day Address," Oct. 18, 1895.
45 Bliss Carman, "Of Breeding," *The Kinship of Nature* (Boston, 1903), 223–9.
46 Parkin Papers, vol. 74, note, n.d.
47 G. R. Parkin, *The Rhodes Fellowships* (Toronto, 1912), 12. See also Parkin Papers, vol. 64, MS "Oxford and the Empire," n.d.

it, "the best men for the world's fight," not bookworms.[48] "The objective Rhodes had in view," Parkin advised the registrar of McMaster University, "was not to do an act of charity, but to find strong men likely to have an influence in the future of their own countries."[49] Along with mere academic attainments, the qualities of athletic prowess, manliness, courage, chivalry, and moral force of character were to be compounded in just proportion. The comingling of British and colonial youth and the daily interchange of thought and experience, Parkin believed, would not only provide a corrective to narrow provincialism, but would also ultimately add dignity and refinement to political life. Canadians, with their commendable freedom from conventionality would acquire those graces of manner and cultured habits of an older society; British youth, bred in a conservative social system and often lacking in adaptability, would benefit from contact with men imbued with the robust spirit of the new world.

Partly because his area of administration did not include continental Europe, Parkin said little about the Pan-Teutonic aspects of the scheme or the virtues of educating Germans in Britain, but he repeatedly underlined the necessity of having American students exposed to British life in order to establish a sympathetic understanding between the United States and the Empire and he dwelt at length upon those features most relevant to Canada. Like Governor-General Grey, he emphasized the benefits of educating French Canadians at Oxford. The scholar selected by Laval University because of his orthodox ultramontane opinions, Grey informed Parkin, "has had his eyes opened at Oxford, and is now resolved to devote his energies to emancipate the people of Quebec from priestly control." The "ignorance" of that province, Grey added, was a major imperial weakness; therefore, "the more French Canadians as Rhodes scholars the better."[50] "I agree very fully with all you say," Parkin replied, "about the desirability of getting young Frenchmen under the influence of Oxford."[51] Imperialists, moreover, felt that there was a particular urgency in teaching prospective Canadian leaders to see things from the imperial point of view. In 1908 George Wrong told Parkin that within ten years "the question of possible separation from Great Britain will be regarded as entirely open, and unless we have men as leaders who have a large outlook, some turn of politics might make Canada a second United States." The whole question will

48 Cited in Lord Elton, "The Rhodes Trust," *The First Fifty Years of the Rhodes Trust and the Rhodes Scholarships 1903–1953* (Oxford, 1956), 4.
49 Rhodes Trust Records, Ontario Scholarships, Parkin to E. J. Bengough, Sept. 21, 1915.
50 Parkin Papers, Grey to Parkin, May 28, 1909.
51 Rhodes Trust Records, Quebec Scholarships, Parkin to Grey, June 10, 1909.

then depend on the political leadership of the nation; "it is of vast importance now to get hold of every man who promises leadership and educate him to think imperially." Such a man was Chester Martin, a Maritimer, and "precisely the young man that Cecil Rhodes would have delighted to see" at Oxford. "To educate a man like Martin at Oxford," Wrong wrote, "is of more importance to the British Empire and the British idea than to educate a dozen young men from the United States."[52]

There were those, of course, who could not attach the same significance as Parkin did to the presence of twenty-five Canadians at Oxford in 1906, and who could not believe that the education of a handful of university men would alter the orientation of an entire nation. Those sceptical of the scheme could perhaps scarcely repress a smile when reading one Canadian scholar's explanation of the advantages of an Oxford training. After mentioning that on first contact the English undergraduates noticed how the Rhodes scholar "uses his fork, how he brushes his hair, how he conducts himself at his Tutor's tea," he went on to say that a "man who has read the imperial and foreign columns of the *Times* for three years, who has discussed the European situation with his friends over his coffee, who has seen the Canadian navy from the point of view of imperial defence, can never settle down to his sometime provincialism."[53] But for those like Parkin whose ideal of political leadership was essentially aristocratic and who did not believe that disinterested and far-sighted leaders were magically called forth by the ordinary workings of democracy, the Rhodes scholarship plan represented the best hope for both imperial unity and the improvement of Canadian political life.

Imperialist political thought occupies an important place in the long tradition of the intellectuals' disenchantment with Canadian politics, a heritage which runs back at least to Canada First and forward to the present. With an unerring sense for the apt parallel, the historian F. H. Underhill in 1959 prefaced an appeal for a group of intellectuals to raise the level of political discussion with a reference to the ideas of G. M. Grant. Mourning the absence of an "elite society of educated people" who might have raised the intellectual standards of political debate and given leadership to the mass democracy, Underhill judged that "Canadian political activities seem unutterably dull to the more educated classes, whose abstention from politics is the very thing that

52 Rhodes Trust Records, Ontario Scholarships, Wrong to Parkin, April 3 and 27, 1908.
53 D. C. Harvey, "The Rhodes Scholar," *University Magazine*, xi (Dec. 1912), 603, 614.

keeps politics so dull."[54] The imperialists' reaction to Canadian politics was the same; so too was their remedy. Just as their impression of the United States grew out of reality as interpreted within a particular frame of reference, so too their view of party government was based upon real and not imaginary incidents of corruption and evidence of drift as seen through the eyes of men who were conservative in temperament and élitist in political philosophy. But it was also a reaction to the failure of imperialism to force its way to the centre of the stage and be debated in an atmosphere uncluttered by distracting, partizan interests. Like all passionate believers they attributed opposition to ignoble causes and thought that everyone must surely understand and support what they so clearly saw themselves. When this was not so, they found a scapegoat in parties and politicians. The most effulgent protests against partyism in Canada have always come from groups who felt their interests, either material or ideological, sacrificed by the compromises and adjustments which the nature of the country makes inescapable, and this condemnation follows a familiar pattern whether it was Bourassa condemning Laurier for bending backwards to please imperialists, Parkin charging that the French Canadians exercised an unwarranted influence on the councils of the Dominion, or a western agrarian radical declaiming upon the old parties as servants of eastern economic power.

54 F. H. Underhill, "The University and Politics," *Queen's Quarterly*, LXVI (Summer 1959), 216–25; *The Price of Being Canadian* (Toronto, 1961), 10–11.

9

Mission

One of the most distinctive features of the imperialist mind was the tendency to infuse religious emotion into secular purposes. The contention that the British Empire was a providential agency, the greatest secular instrument for good in the world, was a widely held conviction among imperialists, but in few places was the conception of Christian responsibility which underlay it more graphically presented than in the writings and experiences of G. M. Grant and G. R. Parkin. They called for a dedication of material things and human effort to spiritual ends and created an imperialist ethic which was so intense, so insistent upon self-sacrifice, that men must have wondered whether it could ever be achieved in this world.

Long before the surge of imperialism in the late nineteenth century, British North Americans had looked upon the Empire as the vehicle and embodiment of a progressive civilization which was designated by Providence to spread its culture, religion, and political institutions across the face of the earth. The citizens of British America might be colonials living on the fringes of the European world, but it was their proudest claim that they belonged to this magnificent and powerful state and that in time they would share in its world-wide work. In 1856 one clergyman spoke of Britain's "proud position to which she has been raised by a benign Providence, of being the dispenser of Gospel blessings, and liberalizing institutions in every region of the earth."[1] Another in 1867 declared that Britain had been commissioned by Providence to teach the world the noble language which contained the richest scientific and literary treasures, the principles of religious toleration, of justice, and of government. "She has been called to India," he said, "for mighty purposes ... to attend as physician to a people who were sinking into the decrepitude of a worn-out civilization."[2] Alexander Morris, writing in

1 Rev. William Blackwood, DD, *Lecture on the Eastern War, Its "Social, Religious, and Commercial Results." Delivered Before the Mercantile Library Association in Mechanics' Hall, Hamilton, Canada West, 22nd January, 1856* (Hamilton, 1856), 38.
2 *The Mission of Great Britain to the World, or Some of the Lessons Which She is Now Teaching. A Lecture delivered at Stratford by Rev. James George, D.D.* (Toronto, 1867), 8, 19.

the 1850s, dared to hope that the coming Britannic Confederation of the North would one day take up this mission to the human race.[3]

While the view of the Empire as a divine agency of progress and civilization was a traditional one, it became so firmly fused with the imperialist conception of Canadian nationality and purpose that the attainment of nationhood itself was made contingent upon the acceptance of the white man's burden. In the decades after 1880, moreover, this sense of obligation became one of the major justifications for maintaining imperial unity. No longer an object of simple pride, the idea of mission was increasingly characterized by a note of anxiety lest the British people fail to respond adequately to the duties imposed by power – fail, that is, to discharge the will of God.

I

"We have a mission on earth," said Grant in the Jubilee year of 1897, "as truly as ancient Israel had." "Our mission was to make this world the home of freedom, of justice, and of peace, and to secure these ends the British Empire was the highest secular instrument the world had even known."[4] Neither he nor Parkin regarded the wealth and territory of the Empire in a gloating, boastful way, nor did they believe that it had been built up chiefly for moral ends. To think that, said Parkin, "would be hypocrisy."[5] While admitting that commerce had figured prominently in the acquisition of overseas territory, they still believed that the very power the Empire had attained imposed duties and responsibilities. "Three hundred millions of mankind," Parkin wrote, "who do not share British blood, of various races and in various climes, acknowledge British sway, and look to it for guidance and protection; their hopes of civilization and social elevation depending upon the justice with which it is exercised, while anarchy awaits them should that rule be removed."[6] In this he saw a transcendental purpose. "I am one of those," Parkin confessed, "who believe that extended power and influence are not given to nations without some Divine purpose. I am convinced that when the moral energy of a nation does not rise to the fulfillment of that purpose the nation is

3 Alexander Morris, *Nova Britannia; or, Our New Canadian Dominion Foreshadowed. Being a Series of Lectures, Speeches and Addresses* (Toronto, 1884), 54, 56.
4 G. M. Grant, "Current Events," *Queen's Quarterly*, v (July 1897), 85; G. M. Grant Papers, vol. 25, clipping from the *Daily Times*, May 5, 1897.
5 G. R. Parkin, "True Imperialism," *United Empire: Royal Colonial Institute Journal*, new series, ii (Dec. 1911), 848.
6 G. R. Parkin, *Imperial Federation: The Problem of National Unity* (London, 1892), 46–7.

doomed to decay."[7] In every corner of the earth Britain had assumed vast responsibilities in the government of weak and alien races, and, in order to discharge this burden, she "needs to concentrate," he said, "her moral as well as her political strength for the work she has to do."[8] Warning that the removal of British power from Africa and Asia would lead to what Grant termed "chaos among the three hundred millions over whom God in His Providence has placed us," they expected that the whole force of Christian sentiment would be thrown onto the scales on the side of imperial unity.[9] The realization that imperial power was morally justifiable only in terms of the responsibility that went with it would itself constitute a powerful impulse to unity, greater even than trade advantages or defence.

This sense of mission was simple in formulation but extremely complex in its origins and ramifications. For Parkin and Grant it was predicated upon three distinct but interrelated conceptions which were fused by religious emotion. The first of these was the belief that spiritual and not material factors made a nation great and that the preponderant forces in history were the human will and ideals. They set up no dichotomy between the material and the spiritual and they did not believe in any necessary irreconcilability between the two. Their attitude was not so much an indifference to this world but rather a determination to infuse secular work with religious meaning. Because they exalted the role of ideals in human affairs, they became distressed about the predominance of the commercial spirit and money-making in their time. "What are we in this world for?" asked Grant. "Surely for something higher than to accumulate money ... we are here to think great thoughts, to do great things, to promote great ideals." In one of his last public addresses, he warned that the most dangerous threat to Canada was "the vulgar and insolent materialism of thought and life, which is eating into the heart of our people."[10] Parkin also recoiled from the "fierce race for power, for wealth, for pleasures, for material surroundings" which he compared to the "Rome of the Caesars." "We must," he believed, "fight against the temptation to lose the great moral purposes of life in the race for gain."[11] Imperialist rhetoric was replete with allusions to

---

7 Parkin, "True Imperialism," 847.
8 G. R. Parkin, "The Reorganization of the British Empire," *Century Illustrated Monthly Magazine*, XXXVII (Dec. 1888), 192.
9 G. M. Grant, *Advantages of Imperial Federation: A Lecture Delivered at a Public Meeting Held in Toronto on January 30, 1891, under the auspices of the Toronto Branch of the Imperial Federation League* (Toronto, 1891), 18.
10 *Ibid.*, 19; G. M. Grant, "Thanksgiving and Retrospect," *Queen's Quarterly*, IX (Jan. 1902), 231.
11 Sir George R. Parkin Papers, vol. 69, MS "The Christian Responsibilities of Empire," n.d.

the fate of empires in classical antiquity and permeated by a vague uneasiness and foreboding of collapse.

Personally suspicious of wealth as either an index of social status or an object of ambition, Parkin and Grant sought to re-establish the ideals of service and duty in order to check self-indulgent individualism. They were able to think that this was possible because they believed that the human will, when inspired by ideals, was the real engine of history. Both were heavily influenced by Carlyle's conception of the role of great men in the past and both rejected determinism, especially the variety presented by Goldwin Smith in his argument for continental unity. While Smith himself was not as unaffected by idealism as he sometimes pretended to be, his insistence on the economic advantages of commercial union and the geographical obstacles militating against Canadian and imperial unity appeared to all imperialists to assume a rather dispirited view of human nature. Surely "geography is not the sole or even the primary factor in the formation of nations," Grant protested. "When we are told that it is impossible to fight against geography, a little reflection assures us that all history teaches the opposite, and that each new triumph of science is simply another victory of man over nature."[12] Germany, he said, was once separated into many states; the United States was also divided into different regions. Human sentiment, intent, and resolution, not geographical inevitability, had made them great countries. Convinced that a nation, like an individual, benefitted from adversity and struggle, Grant felt that a people who built a country in defiance of natural obstacles were finer than those who had simply followed the easy and predetermined path of least resistance. He attributed the strength of nationalism in the United States to the fact that in the Civil War her people had been forced to choose between the material and the ideal, between the dollar and sentiment, and "sentiment proved the mightier." Canada had gone through no such experience; "We have not been tried in the furnace ... Few of us have had to suffer, few of our children have had to die for the nation." As a consequence our sense of nationality was weak.[13]

The trouble with those who doubted whether Canada or the Empire could be held together in face of natural and material forces, said one of Goldwin Smith's critics, was that they did not take sufficient account of the pride and faith of people. "The obstacles that beset a country," this critic wrote, "are not absolute, but relative; the only real measure of

12 *Week*, VIII (May 1 and 15, 1891), 349, 382; G. M. Grant, "Canada and the Empire: A Rejoinder to Dr. Goldwin Smith," *Canadian Magazine*, VIII (Nov. 1896), 76.
13 G. M. Grant, "Canada First," *Canadian Leaves: History, Art, Science, Literature, Commerce. A Series of New Papers read before the Canadian Club of New York* (New York, 1887), 252–4.

them is the spirit of the inhabitants."[14] "I am not such a fatalist ... ,"
added the poet Wilfred Campbell, "to believe that mere force of numbers and geographical considerations are the only forces left in the
world. It is not only a challenge to the spirit of a free people, but an in-
sult to their personality and worth to say that they are but the drift-
wood, the puppets of mere population and physical geography."[15] In
the struggle for imperial unity, wrote Parkin, the "strongest arguments,
the deepest convictions, the most strenuous moulders of public opinion,
will win." Circumstances or the course of events may favour or thwart
human effort but will and determination remained the driving forces in
the world's affairs.[16] Leacock scoffed at the misapplication of the concept of "evolution" to politics and rejected its ready-made explanation
of all things, that "whatever is, is, and whatever will be, will be." "We
cannot sit passive to watch our growth," he said. "Good or bad, straight
or crooked, we must make our fate."[17] All imperialists disdained the
notion that men, like animals, merely responded to the stimulus of nature; to them, deterministic environmentalism was a counsel of despair.
Men made history – men inspired by ideals.

The second foundation of the sense of mission was the idea of work,
a notion which was translated from the area of personal ethics to apply
to whole peoples and nations. In mid-Victorian culture work was more
than a means of achieving success or acquiring money and social position. It was a virtue in itself, a process in which character was disciplined and man's nature developed. One was to work in the correct
spirit, ever conscious that he was serving God in a secular calling.[18] The
roots of this belief ran far back into the Protestant tradition and there
was nothing unique about Grant's statement of it in two sermons in
1866. Man "is free," he said, "when he delights to follow the nature
God gave him; when he approves of the law within and gladly obeys it."
Man's character is a combination of raw appetites, passions, and de-
sires, and the "regulating principles" of self-love, the instinct of benevolence, conscience, and "a freedom of will in virtue of which he could
take one course of conduct or its opposite." Genuine freedom consists
in developing this character, in fulfilling it through work in this world.
Man was put on the earth to be a mirror of God, to complete God's

14 O. A. Howland, *The New Empire: Reflections on its Origin and Constitution
and its Relation to the Great Republic* (Toronto, 1891), viii.
15 Wilfred Campbell, "Imperialism in Canada," *Empire Club Speeches: Being
Addresses Delivered Before the Empire Club of Canada During its Session of
1904–05* (Toronto, 1906), 38.
16 Parkin, *Imperial Federation*, vi–vii.
17 Stephen Leacock, "Empire and Education," *Empire Club Speeches ... 1906–07*
(Toronto, 1907), 288.
18 Walter E. Houghton, *The Victorian Frame of Mind, 1830–1870* (New Haven,
1963), 242–62.

work. He was sent into the world, said Grant, "not as into a play ground; but as into a school, that he might be educated into likeness to Himself; and therefore it was necessary that he should work at the same kind of work that God was working at; that through experience, habits of industry, and patience, of trust in God, gratitude, wisdom might be built up in him, and all his powers and capacities be developed to all their rightful issues." Through labour men learned obedience, justice, benevolence – they learned, in short, the secret of the Lord. Progress was the evidence of man doing God's work. "Trace the course of human progress," said Grant, "the history of nations; ... the struggles for liberty, for improvement, for happiness. See how evil has been overruled for good; how the selfishness of the individual has been made to advance the interests of others." But progress was only one of the effects of work, not the end of it. The object of labour was "not to guide the ongoings of spheres and galaxies, of earth and sea," but to bring dead souls to life, "to recreate them in His own image."[19]

This conception of work was turned from a traditional article of Protestantism into an inspiring vision by Thomas Carlyle. Both Grant and Parkin venerated this prophet of earnestness and will; both had studied his works during their most impressionable years. Of Carlyle's reminiscences, Grant wrote that they were "enough to inspire one to do any work in the right spirit, no matter whether the work be 'delving or Kingdom-founding.' " In 1881 he told a friend that the "world seems poorer to me now that he is gone. What a grand spiritual force he was! As I read his writings now, I am half-crying."[20] In the biographies of Frederick the Great and Cromwell and *Sartor Resartus*, Parkin similarly discovered a view of work as the realization of divine purpose. When "special work is to be done in the world, (and all work is in one sense special work)," he wrote in his diary, "... it is not left to accident to provide the labourer fitted to perform it."[21] Carlyle's invocation to toil, his praise of labour as self-fulfilment, and the notion that in work directed in the proper spirit man was continuing the work of God, provided the taproots of the imperialistic ethic.

When the Carlylean ideal of work was extended to the sphere of imperial politics it came to mean the duty of advanced nations to work for

19 G. M. Grant, *Sermon Preached at the National Scotch Church, Saint Matthew's, Halifax, on the Morning of the First Sunday of 1866* (Halifax, 1866), 6–7; *Sermon Preached Before the Synod of Nova Scotia and Prince Edward Island, in Connection with the Church of Scotland, on June 26th, 1866* (Halifax, 1866), 4–5, 8.
20 Sir Sandford Fleming Papers, vol. 18, Grant to Fleming, n.d. and March 3, 1881; W. L. Grant and C. F. Hamilton, *Principal Grant* (Toronto, 1904), 178–9.
21 Parkin Papers, Diary, 1872, Dec. 12, 1872.

the well-being of less developed ones. The sense of imperial mission found expression in exactly the same words and phrases which had been used to describe individual work. The most important advantage of imperial unity, said Grant, was not that it was economically profitable but that it "means the development of the best that is in us and in the nation ... Christianity calls men the children of God. True progress, then, must be not so much the acquisition of more wealth or even of more rights as the better performance of duties. That is equally true of the individual and the nation."[22] The far-flung Empire presented human nature with challenges, and in dealing with these, in taking up the responsibility for the "weaker races," character was developed. "The work that the British Empire has in hand," he said in 1891, "is far grander than the comparatively parochial duties with which the [United] States are content to deal. Its problems are wider and more inspiring ... Already our sons are taking their part in introducing civilization into Africa, under the aegis of the flag, and in preserving the *Pax Brittanica* among the teeming millions of India and South-Eastern Asia." Within a generation, he predicted, when the best lands upon the North American continent were occupied and settled, "We shall take part in work that is of worldwide significance."[23] For Parkin the ultimate argument for preserving the Empire was that "it presents the most splendid and inspiring arena for noble human effort that ever yet was granted to any race or nation."[24] Nations, like men, had their calling to fulfill and their mission to discharge. In exactly the same way as individuals developed their character through service and self-denial, nations had duties imposed upon them by Providence and in the discharging of these responsibilities they realized themselves.

The third conviction which underlay the belief in national mission and which made imperialists feel that they were riding the crest of the tidal wave of history was social Darwinism, or the belief that the same ineluctable forces which impelled and guided biological evolution also worked in human affairs and world politics. Neither Parkin nor Grant experienced any crisis in accommodating Darwinian science to their religious outlooks. Grant said in a matter-of-fact way that the only thing the notion of evolution changed was that what was once thought to have taken place directly and suddenly, must now be understood to have been done indirectly and successively. Whether he spoke of church union or imperial consolidation the phrases of evolution came easily to him. The organism, he repeatedly said, must be adapted to the ever-changing environment. Parkin's interest in science had been aroused at

22 Grant, *Advantages of Imperial Federation*, 5.
23 *Ibid.*, 18–19.   24 Parkin, "True Imperialism," 846.

the University of New Brunswick and, although it was only in 1902 that he read Darwin's *Origin of Species*, he admitted that the ideas of natural selection, the struggle for existence, and the survival of the fittest had "been in a way familiar to me for years through reviews & quotations." Evolution did not change the essentials of old beliefs, he said; rather it presented "a very noble and encouraging view of the Universe and its Maker or Designer" whose thoughts were read by scientists in the book of nature.[25] Throughout the late nineteenth century the task of reconciling scripture and science proceeded apace, and an optimistic accord was ultimately achieved. The process of evolution, ran the synthesis, explained the history of life but not its origins: evolution was simply God's method, God working through nature. Once this reconciliation with Christianity was accomplished, it appeared that history was an ever upward movement towards the ultimate realization of Divine purposes. In the movement towards the integration of political communities and the reunification of the churches, these men saw God immanent in His works. In working for the unity of the Empire, they felt themselves in tune with a cosmic law of life.

The bearing of this encouraging version of evolution upon the conception of mission is obvious at every point in Parkin's geopolitics. He took "the world-view of Canada," as Bliss Carman said,[26] and no other Canadian imperialist had such a firm grasp of the realities of power, none matched his imaginative understanding of the integral character of the imperial system. His view of the Empire was undoubtedly due to his travels. "Only those who have traversed every ocean, visited every port, studied every continent," he once remarked, "can form more than a vague idea of what it means."[27] But his writings also bore the unmistakable imprint of the geopolitics of H. J. Mackinder, the imperial history of J. R. Seeley, and the naval doctrines of Alfred Mahan. He knew these men personally and eagerly devoured their books. In his presidential address to the British Geographical Association in 1912 he recalled that "one of the strongest intellectual inspirations I had came in the form of geographical study," and he singled out *Earth and Man* (1863) by the Princeton geographer, Arnold Guyot. From that book he had come to realize "how intimate was the relation between us insects who are crawling over the Earth and the great Earth itself upon which we live and move, and how the whole destiny of mankind ... has been shaped and moulded ... by the configuration of the continents, the position and character of mountains, plains, and rivers, and the

25 W. L. and Maude Grant Papers, Parkin to Maude, Nov. 22, 1902; **Parkin Papers**, Notebook, 1871, "Moses."
26 Parkin Papers, Carman to Parkin, April 10, 1895.
27 *Ibid.*, vol. 66, MS "The Duty of the Empire to the World," 1915, 7.

relation of sea and land."[28] Parkin regarded geography as the foundation of imperial education and it figured prominently in all his works. Parkin was not one of those who were so impressed by the diversity, separation, and isolation of the parts of the Empire that they could not see the unifying influences that held them together. For him, Canada was the "keystone" of the entire Empire, a point he illustrated in a map prepared with the Edinburgh cartographer, John Bartholomew, for use in schools. "I give prominence to Canada," he explained, "by showing the far East in both the right & left hand sides of the map, with the Dominion as the connecting link."[29] Canada not only fronted on the Atlantic and Pacific oceans, but abundant coal deposits, so indispensable for naval power, were located near her natural harbours on Vancouver Island and in the Maritimes. Dependent as she was for food and raw materials upon the security of the ocean, Britain's naval power, said Parkin, would fall by half if Canada were lost. Like most Canadian imperialists, he insisted upon the superiority of the Canadian Pacific Railway over the Cape of Good Hope route or the Suez Canal. That railway was remote from European attack, afforded unimpeded and rapid transit to troops, passed through a healthier climatic zone, and, above all, ran near additional coal deposits on the eastern slopes of the Rockies and on the prairies. With coal, moreover, the treeless and cold North-West could be settled and become the main source of Britain's food supply. The very contours of the St Lawrence and Great Lakes system which joined the wheat belt in the west to the Atlantic ports closest to Britain, suggested "the natural direction" of the flow of food.[30] In 1905 Parkin called upon Canadians to make plans "for a large future ... as a Pacific Power" and summarized the strategic position of the Dominion to the maintenance of the Empire: "A country which links by its railway lines the naval bases of the Empire on the Atlantic with those of the Pacific; which can furnish abundant supplies of coal to both; and which has at the same time the capacity to make the Empire almost self-contained in the most essential elements of food-supply, means much to an ocean Power which must settle the balance of naval influence on the two great oceans."[31]

Beneath Parkin's analysis of these interrelationships and his discussions of the physical basis of power, ran the clear assumption that imperial expansion had "not been abnormal, but strictly organic – the outcome of racial instincts and the fundamental necessities of national

28 Raleigh Parkin Collection, photostat of Parkin's "Presidential Address."
29 Fleming Papers, Parkin to Fleming, April 18, 1893.
30 Parkin, *Imperial Federation*, 117-24; G. R. Parkin, *The Great Dominion: Studies of Canada* (London, 1895), 73–88.
31 G. R. Parkin, "Canada and the Pacific," in C. S. Goldman, ed., *The Empire and the Century* (London, 1905), 411.

life." For one who accepted the idea of evolution as a providential process and who saw evidence of some high purpose in the unity of the imperial system, expansion appeared "as natural and organic as the force which compels the bursting of a bud, or the transformation of a chrysalis." The very complexity of the Empire was an indication that it had attained a high level of development, that it had successfully adapted to the environment. "This is a great law of nature," he wrote, "well known to apply to the material world, vegetable, mineral, and animal. But nothing is more certain than that it applies to the life of nations as well."[32] In the construction of the Canadian Pacific Railway and in laying the oceanic cable, which Sandford Fleming significantly called "the electric nervous system of the Imperial organism,"[33] men worked in harmony with irresistible national forces. The physical and geographical unity of the Empire, the wonderfully complementary character of its seemingly diverse parts, pointed to the conclusion that it was not really the outgrowth of accident but somehow the realization of Divine intent. "God, who appointed the bounds of our habitation," said Grant, "made us the natural keystone between the old world of northern Europe and the older world of China and Japan."[34] This was not a mere figure of speech, nor did such sentiments imply that men should abdicate work and struggle and simply await the outcome of events. Nature and evolution moved toward integration, but men must consciously work with them. And their work was to be inspired by the consciousness that the Empire was the physical embodiment of providential purpose.

The sense of mission, then, grew out of this conception of the immanence of God in the world: history has not accidently placed millions of the "weaker races" under the protection of the Empire, nor was the evolution toward a stronger union a fortuitous and fitful process. The main justification for imperial power was work directed toward the Christianization and civilization of these races. Such work would not only fulfil God's own purposes, but would also burn away the selfishness and pride bred by power.

II

The crux of the idea of mission was the issue of race and upon this question Grant and Parkin maintained ambivalent positions. Both believed that the Anglo-Saxon race had demonstrated a singular capacity for

32 Parkin Papers, vol. 80, MS "The Geographical Unity of the Empire," 1894, 4, 6, 16.
33 Fleming Papers, Fleming to Earl Grey, Jan. 28, 1905 (copy).
34 G. M. Grant, "Response on Behalf of Canada to Address of Welcome, at the World's Parliament of Religions," *Queen's Quarterly*, I (Oct. 1893), 158.

self-government, for creating an ordered and progressive society, and for responsibility and service. British rule in India, said Grant, "has brought order out of chaos, given peace to warring creeds and races, chained human Tigers, introduced civilization, established justice, opened wide the doors for all the forces of Christianity to enter ... India is perhaps the greatest monument of her fitness to govern races unfit for self-government; but what else could she do, we ask?"[35] By their own extensive travels both were confirmed in the belief that the "weaker races" needed external guidance and inspiration in order to develop an advanced civilization. The history of the Negro peoples in Africa and the United States, Parkin contended, demonstrated that they did not have "the power to advance on their own initiative" and that the "impulse towards any beginnings of civilization have come almost entirely from outside."[36] Though the major aim of the imperialism of mission was to uplift the backward races, these spokesmen thought it a national blessing that Canada, Australia, and New Zealand had no large numbers of coloured peoples. Neither Parkin nor Grant, however, regarded racial attributes as unalterably fixed for all time. Grant spoke of the white race as the only one which had proved its governing capacity "so far," and Parkin, in alluding to Kipling's invocation to take up the white man's burden, said that the task of the British was first to govern and then lead forward to self-government the millions of dependent peoples. True to their evolutionary outlook, they were highly conscious of racial differentiations and tended to assume that the unprogressive peoples could be improved but only over a very long period of time. It may, said Parkin, take "centuries" to bring the Africans even to the level of India in mental and spiritual culture and industrial development. Their attitude to the culture and religions of some of the "weaker races," moreover, was far from the mocking commentaries of Macaulay in the early nineteenth century. In 1920 Parkin could say that the people over whom the British ruled had "ancient civilizations, literatures and highly developed industries of their own. Many, especially in Asia have religions of a highly spiritual type, to which, in their better manifestations, we are bound to pay respect."[37] Their descriptions of these races were invariably followed by the qualification and the warning that "we have had no right to assume the industrial direction and exploitation of Africa unless we accept in full the moral responsibility for the just government and steady uplifting of the people."[38]

35 G. M. Grant, "Current Events," *ibid.*, IV (Jan. 1897), 236.
36 Parkin Papers, vol. 66, MS untitled, n.d., 2.
37 *Ibid.*, vol. 69, clipping from the *Scottish Chronicle*, Nov. 5, 1920.
38 *Ibid.*, vol. 69, notes, n.d.

Racialism could function as a block as well as a stimulant to imperialism. One of Goldwin Smith's favourite ways of heaping discredit upon imperialism was to ask whether the white races would be ultimately ruled by millions of black voters. "Is Quashee," he queried, "to vote on imperial policy?"[39] French-Canadian fears of imperial federation also dwelt upon the prospect of being dominated by what one Montreal paper called "Pagan Asiatics, Brahmins, Buddhists, Musselmen, fire-worshippers, in a word by people vomited by Satan upon the earth." Sooner than deliver ourselves to three and a half million non-Christians, it warned, "we would like better still to become Americans."[40] To those who were apprehensive over such prospects Parkin replied that no one wanted to repeat within the Empire the disastrous experiment of Reconstruction in the United States when the former slaves were suddenly enfranchised. He felt that the franchise would necessarily have to be carefully controlled and made dependent upon the attainment of a certain level of education and that for a very long time coloured voters would pose no threat to the formulation of imperial policy by whites.

To the long-range question of whether Africans and Indians would become completely self-governing Parkin had no simple answer, although he tended to regard prospects for racial improvement largely in terms of the ideas of the American Negro leader, Booker T. Washington, whom he met and admired. Washington believed that the salvation of the American Negro lay in agricultural and industrial training and not in the immediate acquisition of political rights. Frankly saying that he wanted to recruit those "who have no idea of the proper location of the various knives, forks and dishes upon the dinner table" rather than those who were principally concerned with the place of the Alps and Andes on the map, Washington's school at Tuskegee, Alabama, was designed to enable the Negro to improve himself through work and self-help, become economically necessary to society, and thereby earn political privileges.[41] During his trip to the South in 1903 Parkin was struck by the "low average of the negro type" that he saw in the streets, felt "what a mercy it is to be free from this frightful black problem," and was overwhelmed by the hopelessness of the caste system. Imagine, he told his wife, a man like Washington, acknowledged as one of the foremost philanthropic spirits in America, unable to ride home in any other than a "Jim Crow" streetcar.[42] Though he fully understood that the more educated the Negro became and the more he qualified himself for

39 Parkin, *Imperial Federation*, 190.
40 Parkin Papers, vol. 80, clipping of a letter to the editor of the *Weekly Sun* quoting the Montreal *L'Etendard*, n.d.
41 *Ibid.*, vol. 87, clipping, Booker T. Washington, "The Negro Problem From the Negro Point of View," the *World Today*, April 1904.
42 *Ibid.*, Parkin to Nan, Feb. 1, 3, and 7, 1903 (copies).

free citizenship and political equality, the stronger white resistance and race feeling grew, Parkin nevertheless concluded that in Washington's programme of industrial education lay the key to the elevation of the Negro people in Africa as well as the United States.

On the when and how of ultimate independence for these peoples Parkin remained imprecise: on the need for imperialism to serve them he was insistent and exacting. It would be difficult to establish whether the exponents of missionary imperialism were primarily concerned with the welfare of the unprogressive peoples or whether they regarded the assumption of the burden as mainly advantageous to the British people. Did they egotistically seek salvation through good works or were they moved by a desire to altruistically sacrifice themselves for the good of others? Clearly, any answer is debatable, but equally clear is that the entire notion of civilizing mission would have collapsed in futility had it been assumed that race character was intractable and unchangeable. For then they would have been summoning the Anglo-Saxon race to perform Sisyphean labour, which, however much it might exalt the character of those who performed it, would none the less be hopeless and self-defeating in the end.

In terms of this outlook the British and the American people were joint custodians of the racial mission. Significantly, those like Parkin and Grant who were foremost in investing imperial unity with religious purpose also led the way in urging that Canada help forge closer co-operation between the United States and Great Britain. The future of the world, said Grant in 1898, "depends upon a good understanding between Britain and the United States ... Their greatest interest is peace, and the thought, or rather passion, which stirs them is the welfare of humanity by the extension of liberty, the reign of law and the establishment of justice."[43] Sharing Josiah Strong's belief that the application of the social gospel within the nation was a prerequisite for extending Christianity abroad, Grant hoped that Canada would become a "living link" in the Anglo-American relationship, a kinship based upon the recognition of the common mission. As early as 1888 Parkin pointed out that the British Empire in Africa and India confronted the same challenge and discharged the same duty as the Anglo-Saxons within the United States in dealing with the immigrant and Negro problems. Throughout the 1890s he listened sympathetically to those Americans who were beginning to advocate an imperial foreign policy. Parkin knew Senator Henry Cabot Lodge of Massachusetts, said that he learned a good deal from him, and "got on sundry new lines of thought," and for the naval strategist, Mahan, he had nothing but adulation. Mahan's religious feeling, he told his wife, was akin to that of Thomas à

43 G. M. Grant, "Current Events," *Queen's Quarterly*, v (April 1898), 327.

Kempis and General Gordon: they had, he said, "a splendid discussion."[44] Parkin also met Theodore Roosevelt and though their conversation did not turn to imperial topics, he could not but feel admiration for the American whose personal ethic and nationalism were so close to his own. Whenever Parkin spoke of the "better elements" in the United States it was men like these that he had in mind and it was to them that he addressed his invitations to take up the white man's burden. Few of his speeches delivered in the United States under the auspices of the Rhodes Scholarship Trust failed to mention the parallel between the American mission in the Philippines and the British experience in India. "If only your people," he said in 1918, "could make up their minds to help us carry the 'white man's burden' in Asia and Africa, it would create a wonderful bond between us and we could learn much from each other."[45] Both peoples faced the same tasks because of the very state of civilization they had attained.

III

"The key ... to the emotionalism of imperialism," wrote one historian, "is the transposition of evangelicalism to wholly secular objects, or alternatively the translation of secular objectives to a religious level."[46] The sense of mission was gripping in its emotional power and it was the chief source of that passion and certitude so characteristic of the imperialist mentality. Appeals for imperial unity invariably dwelt upon the avocation of the race. When Nathaniel Burwash of Victoria University declared in 1904 that Kipling's poem on the white man's burden depicted a "great moral fact,"[47] he was invoking what had long before become a conventionality. The only way to convey the indescribable sensation which this idea called forth is to sample a concentrated rendering of it. At an Empire Day banquet sponsored by the Empire Club of Toronto in 1914, R. B. Bennett, a Maritimer by birth and at that time a Conservative member of Parliament for Calgary East, declared that imperial expansion into India and Egypt did not arise from any petty regard for territory. "We are there," he explained,

> because under the Providence of God we are a Christian people that have given to the subject races of the world the only kind of decent government they have ever known. (Applause.) We are the only

44 Parkin Papers, Parkin to Nan, Dec. 1897, April 14, 1900 (copies).
45 *Ibid.*, Parkin to W. R. Newbolt, Dec. 13, 1918 (copy).
46 Eric Stokes, *The English Utilitarians and India* (London, 1959), 308.
47 N. Burwash, "Imperialism and Education," *Empire Club Speeches ... 1903–04* (Toronto, 1904), 36–7.

colonizing race that has been able to colonize the great outlying portions of the world and give the people the priceless boon of self-
government, and we have educated men year after year until at last
those who were once subjects became free, and those who were free
became freer, and you and I must carry our portion of that responsibility if we are to be the true Imperialists we should be ... An Imperialist, to me, means a man who accepts gladly and bears proudly
the responsibilities of his race and breed. (Applause.) If that be so,
what a trust is ours, what a trust is ours! What a splendid trust it is,
to think that you and I are the trustees for posterity, that you and I
will one day be measured by the manner in which we have discharged
our obligations to those subject races and the millions of people that
one day must fill the great fertile fields of the west, the great plains of
Australia, that will cover the great plains of South Africa and New
Zealand. If that thought sinks into our minds, how can you and I
think of independence, how can we be concerned about an independent Canada? Eight or nine million people could not discharge the responsibilities that have come down to us; we cannot be true to the
race from which we are sprung. If, believing these things, and I know
one must believe them, if we are students of history, if we believe the
British Empire is no accident, if we believe under the Providence of
God we are given freedom, justice, equality, laws well enforced, a
proper conception of law and discipline, and all those things that go
to make a people great, we have developed character, without which
there can be no people, we have given men ideals, without which
there can be no state; if we have done these things, how can we talk
of an independent Canada? An independent Canada means this, that
we Canadians are afraid of responsibility and obligation of power,
afraid to accept the responsibilities of our race and breed; afraid to
think we are Britons, afraid to face the future in the eye.[48]

How trifling and pale must discussions of tariffs have sounded to those
who thought in this way.

Like Bennett, Parkin and Grant made the realization of Canadian
nationhood contingent upon the acceptance of racial responsibility and
fulfilment of the mission. Mission was fundamental to the manner in
which they conceived of nationality. Canada, they said, could only be
a nation if she acted and functioned like one, and, to them, this meant
that she must assume her share of the civilizing work within the Empire
and be ready to defend that agency of progress. This, they thought, was

48 *Empire Club of Canada: Addresses Delivered to the Members During the
Sessions of 1912–13 and 1913–14* (Toronto, 1915), part II, 203–5.

implicit in the Canadian character and in keeping with history. Her more humane treatment of the Indians, the presence of her missionaries in the Far East, and the extension of her commerce and investments abroad, were harbingers of the role she would soon be called upon to play. This fusion of nationalism with religion also accounts in part for the opposition to imperial unity among French Canadians. Imperialists themselves tended to see this hostility as a colonially minded fear of assuming responsibilities, as did W. L. Grant when he stated that Bourassa's notions amounted to saying that "WE are getting on very nicely in our little provincial backwater."[49] But it was not only isolationism that made imperialism suspect in Quebec; it was also another variety of mission. By the late nineteenth century the belief that French Canadians had a messianic duty to preserve the purity of Catholicism and to stand as exemplars of the true faith in North America had gained universal support among the clergy and the people.[50] A sense of patriotism which centred upon the exaltation of Catholicism could not but find dangerous and disquieting a sense of patriotism which was rooted in the Protestant mission. Yet for both the French-Canadian nationalists and the English-Canadian imperialists, history had ordained a special avocation, and nationalism was consecrated by the hand of God.

49 W. L. Grant Papers, vol. 15, MS untitled, 1910 or 1911, 16.
50 Jean-Charles Falardeau, "The Role of the Church in French Canada," in M. Rioux and Y. Martin, eds., *French-Canadian Society* (Toronto, 1964), I, 350.

10

Militarism

Imperialism, military preparedness, and militarism, or the admiration and exaltation of the martial virtues, were inextricably bound together. After the mid-1890s the Canadian imperialists were in the forefront of the movements for the reform of the militia and the establishment of cadet drill in the schools; it was they who pressed most fiercely for Canada's participation in the Boer War and who were most apprehensive over the naval scare of 1909. They urged the adoption of their defence programmes out of a genuine fear that, as Denison put it, "... our empire has not relatively the strong and predominant position that she held forty or fifty years ago" and the assumption that a militarily weak Empire implied a vulnerable Canada.[1] They were moved by a real sentiment of gratitude for the free defence that British sea power had provided Canada in the past. But for the dominance of the British navy on the high seas, said Robert Borden in 1913, "there would in fact be no Canada as we know it to-day."[2] They desired that Canada take up military responsibilities and thereby attain national stature. As long as Canadians took no steps to defend themselves and continued to be a weakness to the Empire, wrote one imperialist, "we shall live in the depressing sense that we are a dependency, ... and so our citizenship will be of an inferior grade, and our sense of nationhood will be one of uneasy self-consciousness, with its fretful and feverish side."[3]

Arguments for military and naval preparedness, however, customarily ran far beyond technical and constitutional aspects. Some imperialists rested their case for imperial defence upon a general interpretation of the role of force in international affairs; some demanded far-reaching measures of compulsory national service in order to arrest what they regarded as the decay and deterioration of the national

1 *The British Empire League in Canada. Its Officers, Committees, and Constitution, including Report of Annual Meeting held at Ottawa, February 20th, 1902* (Toronto, 1902), 21.
2 J. Castell Hopkins, *The Canadian Annual Review of Public Affairs, 1913* (Toronto, 1914), 175.
3 C. F. Hamilton, "Shall Canada Have a Navy," *University Magazine*, VIII (Oct. 1909), 397.

character. Though these men were not, strictly speaking, militarists in the European sense of looking forward to the dominance of a military class, they none the less tended to extol the martial spirit and identify it with a healthy nationalism. As a consequence of these beliefs, as well as their activities, their enemies invariably equated imperialism with militarism. Goldwin Smith called militarism an "inevitable consort" of imperialism; the French-Canadian nationalist, Olivar Asselin, believed that "the bulk of the Canadian people have come to regard and to use 'anti-Imperialism' and 'anti-Militarism' as synonymous terms";[4] and Wilfrid Laurier often said that the imperialists sought to draw Canada into the vortex of militarism.

I

While the idealization of the martial character had been central to Colonel Denison's thinking as early as the 1860s and continued to affect even his views on tariff policy right down to the First World War, and while the question of imperial defence had never been remote from the concerns of the Imperial Federation League and the British Empire League, the pronounced emphasis of imperialists on the necessity for preparedness and military training increased in scale after 1900. "Since the South African War," the historian of the Canadian militia noted in 1902,

> there has been manifested in Canada a growing disposition to recognize the importance of maintaining an efficient military spirit. The country realizes that its whole life has been stimulated, the standard of its manhood built up, the national character strengthened by the achievements of its sons in the Fenian Raids, the Red River Expedition, the Nile Campaign, the North-West Rebellion, and the South African War. True, the laurels have been moistened with the tears of Canadian mothers, but a price has to be paid for everything that is worth having. The mother of a coward does not often weep.[5]

The concern with defence was infused with urgency by the revival of American expansionism after 1898, the intensification of the European arms race, and especially by the German challenge to the primacy of the British navy.

Canadian advocates of military training were inspired by the appear-

---

4 G. Smith, *Commonwealth and Empire* (New York, 1902), 34; O. Asselin, *A Quebec View of Canadian Nationalism* (Montreal, 1909), 8.
5 Ernest J. Chambers, *The Governor-General's Body Guard* (Toronto, 1902), 121.

ance of British organizations like the Navy League, the National Service League, and the Lads Drill Association, and they borrowed a good deal of their ideology from the rapidly growing body of literature devoted to justifying preparation for war. Though they were never merely echoes of their counterparts in Britain and the United States, Canadian imperialists were very much aware of such books as Benjamin Kidd's *Social Evolution* (1894), which passed through nineteen editions in four years and popularized the idea of the ceaseless, unremitting, and necessary struggle between states, or Homer Lea's *The Valour of Ignorance* (1909), which warned of the inevitable decrepitude and downfall of those nations which neglected the military side of life for the sake of commercial greed. A great favourite with the imperialists was *The Influence of Sea Power upon History, 1660–1783* (1890) by the American navalist and historian, Alfred Thayer Mahan. "By making England understand more fully than she ever understood before what Sea power has meant in her history," wrote Parkin, "he has greatly stiffened English resolve not to surrender without a struggle the supremacy on the ocean which she has enjoyed so long."[6] Canadian appeals for strengthening naval power invariably made admiring allusions to the doctrines of Mahan. There were those as well who were familiar with the classic vindications of militarism through General von Bernhardi's *Germany and the Next War* (1911) or through the journal of the British National Service League, *Nation in Arms*. The Canadian imperialists' preoccupation with defence and the threat of war was very much a by-product and result of European, and especially British, concerns.

These Canadians, moreover, were not immune to the illusory views of modern warfare that were prevalent everywhere before 1914. Personal experience and vicarious knowledge shaped their conception of war as a rather exhilarating kind of sport in which few were killed and from which, so it was said, many desirable consequences followed. Apart from the Civil War in the United States, the actual conflicts in the second half of the nineteenth century were minor and short, and those like Denison who read assiduously in the literature of war missed the true dimensions of the American conflict partly because their attention was focused upon cavalry tactics. And even this most enthusiastic exponent of the martial spirit never killed an enemy in combat; his service during the Northwest Rebellion of 1885 was confined to guarding the telegraph station at Humboldt. What he and Mair and other veterans of that expedition remembered was the arduous march along the north

6 Sir George R. Parkin Papers, vol. 64, notes, n.d.

shore of Lake Superior, the cold and discomfort, the comradeship of the tent, the tumultuous welcome in the Toronto streets, and the general sense of purpose and accomplishment which sprang from the satisfaction that the rebellion had been put down by Canadians without any aid from Britain. This entirely typical experience did much to confirm the impression that war was more a manly triumph over the obstacles of nature than massive and indiscriminate slaughter.

Canadian experience in South Africa did nothing to change this idea. Apart altogether from the fact that journalistic depictions of casualties and carnage suffered from reticence and a lack of realism, contemporary accounts like *Canada's Sons on Kopje and Veldt* (1900) by T. G. Marquis, professor of English literature at Queen's University, stressed the incidents of individual heroism, the rescue of the guns and trials of the march, and often dwelt upon the release of tension in the sunburnt spaces. Other records concentrated upon the journey of the first Canadian contingent aboard the *Sardinian*, camplife, and, of course, the homecoming, when, as one representative had it, the whole population of Halifax turned out to witness "the war-tried sons of Canada ... with faces browned and straightened backs, with shoulders square and heads held high, down they came, the heroes of the Empire."[7] Casualty statistics also affirmed the idea of war as limited and heroic and even led some military writers to conclude that with the progress of science war would become more and more humane. "Of the total force of 7,368 that went to South Africa," the *Canadian Military Gazette* authoritatively reported, "224 died and 252 were wounded, making in all 476 casualties. The number killed was 63. Thirty-one died of wounds, 127 succumbed to disease ..."[8] Since most fatalities were due to disease, it could be reassuringly said that in modern war "the proportion of killed, wounded and sick is steadily decreasing"[9] and that the "wars of our people in ever increasing degree are becoming more humane, more restrained, more Christian."[10] When the imperialists talked of war, their insistence upon toughness and hardness, conflict and testing, were exaggerated and deceptive, for their understanding of what was involved bore a closer resemblance to the deeds chronicled by Sir Walter Scott than the realities to come.

7 *"G" Company, or Every-Day Life of the R.C.R. Being a Descriptive Account of the Typical Events in the Life of the First Canadian Contingent in South Africa by the Late Russell C. Hubly* (Montreal, 1901), 106.
8 *Canadian Military Gazette*, XVIII (Feb. 17, 1903), 7.
9 William Wood, "The ABC of the Imperial Defence," *ibid.*, XV (April 17, 1900), 5.
10 Maurice Hutton, "Militarism and Anti-Militarism," *University Magazine*, XII (April 1913), 192.

Naturally the most forceful devotees of the cause of military preparedness were found in the ranks of the militia officers. The press organ of the Canadian militia, the *Canadian Military Gazette*, which declared itself to be "nothing if it is not Imperial,"[11] sponsored all kinds of plans to increase military efficiency and opened its pages to writers who made their appeals in the broadest possible terms. The Canadian Military Institute, founded in Toronto in 1890 for "the promotion of Military Art, Science and Literature," also functioned as a centre of the martial imperialists. Primarily a social club for commissioned officers, it prided itself on the fact that most of the five hundred members in 1910 were descendants of United Empire Loyalists. The foremost political object of the institute, declared Lt. Col. William Hamilton Merritt, president between 1905 and 1914, was to cement the unity of the Empire. Merritt was undoubtedly the most active spokesman for the preparedness cause. Born in 1855, the son of the builder of the Welland Canal and trained as a mining engineer, he had served in the Governor-General's Body Guard during the western rebellion of 1885 and had succeeded Colonel Denison to the command of that unit. After service in the Boer War and a trip to Switzerland in 1905 Merritt began advocating compulsory military service for Canadians. In his speeches and writings, particularly in *Canada and National Service* (1917), which summed up his prewar ideas, he showed a ready familiarity with military thought currently popular in Europe. He was, in addition, one of the moving forces behind the creation in 1909 of the Canadian Defence League which through its journal, the *Canadian Field* (later renamed *Canadian Defence*), and through public lectures, worked for the "systematic physical and military training of all our youths."[12] The league neither enjoyed, nor did it ever claim, widespread public support, but what it lacked in numbers was made up for in both the geographical concentration and social eminence of its backers. By 1912 nearly six hundred of its eight hundred members came from Toronto and it received the support of such religious figures as Rev. Albert Carman, general superintendent of the Methodist Church in Canada, and Rev. T. Crawford Brown, minister of New St Andrew's Church; educators like Nathaniel Burwash of Victoria University, Rev. Daniel M. Gordon, principal of Queen's, and Maurice Hutton, principal of University College in the University of Toronto; and journalists like John A. Cooper,

---

11 *Canadian Military Gazette*, XVII (March 18, 1902), 10.
12 The origins of the Canadian Defence League are described in *Canadian Defence: Official Journal of the Canadian Defence League*, III (Jan. 1912), 205–7.

formerly editor of the *Canadian Magazine* and then editor of the *Canadian Courier*, and Walter J. Brown, editor of the *Weekly Globe and Canadian Farmer*. The league received endorsement and financial contributions from business leaders as well – from Edmund Walker, president of the Canadian Bank of Commerce, Featherstone Osler, president of Toronto General Trusts, Henry Pellatt, millionaire devotee of all manner of martial projects, and J. C. Eaton, son of the founder and president of the T. Eaton Company. Though these individuals were drawn to the league for a variety of reasons, their membership certainly suggests that Merritt's plans were accorded substantial support in the most imperialistic city in Canada.

Another organization which popularized the case for imperial defence was the Navy League. Both in Britain, where it was founded in 1894, and in Canada, to which it was soon extended, the league appealed for increased expenditures on the fleet, endeavoured to drive home the notion that Canada was, and always had been, dependent upon British sea power for its survival, and sought to strengthen the conception of the identity of interest in sea power between Britain and the Dominions. It drew support from individuals like George Parkin and Sandford Fleming who had earlier been associated with the Imperial Federation League, claimed the blessings of two members of the Laurier cabinet, Sydney Fisher, minister of agriculture, and Sir Frederick Borden, minister of militia between 1896 and 1911, and attracted to its branches as presidents other prominent Canadians like Charles Hibbert Tupper of Vancouver, Senator Sir George A. Drummond of Montreal, and Augustus M. Nanton of Winnipeg. None of these individuals marshalled the case for a united fleet more cogently than Lt. Col. William Wood, the secretary of the Navy League in Quebec. Wood had been educated at military schools in England and Germany, and, apparently independently wealthy, he could afford to indulge his historical curiosity about the legends and folklore of the St Lawrence region which he recorded with fidelity and obvious affection. Like Merritt, he was a convinced social Darwinist, confessing that "I took to Darwin like a duck to water."[13] Darwinism taught him to see the human kinship with the animal kingdom and led him to denounce the thoughtless slaughter of birds and beasts and to propose conservation measures. But evolutionary thought also convinced Wood that war was natural and inevitable and in his articles he drew out the implications of this view for imperial defence.

The Canadian Defence League and the Navy League were certainly

13 William Wood, "Alouette" (Part i), *University Magazine*, x (April 1911), 294–5.

not the only sources of ideas which can only be termed militaristic. The cause of military and naval preparedness, as well as the justification of compulsory military service as socially desirable, was taken up by other imperialists whose connection with these leagues was tenuous or doubtful. But whether the argument was worded in the excited and egotistical rhetoric of Sam Hughes, minister of militia in Borden's cabinet after 1911, or in terms of the educational philosophy of his brother, James Hughes, the chief inspector of Toronto schools, or in the precise and reactionary language of Andrew Macphail, who once wrote that "A nation which is good in war is good in peace; and a nation which is no good in war is good for nothing,"[14] the essence of militarism was present all the same. While not all imperialists were unabashed admirers of the martial spirit, militarism was neither peripheral nor tangential to the imperialist outlook. The way in which these men regarded war not only reinforced their predisposition to see imperial military and naval co-operation as absolutely essential, but also influenced their understanding of Canada's place in the world. Given the external stimulus of the Boer War and the European armament race, militarism emerged logically and inexorably out of the complex of assumptions and scheme of values which made up Canadian imperialism.

II

As the imperialists themselves recognized, they faced a problem in Canada which was monumental and almost hopeless. They were fully aware that "No country exhibits a greater corporate indifference to her defence than does Canada,"[15] and that in urging military preparations they were running against the massive indifference of an "unmilitary people." Their appeals consequently followed a peculiar line of attack. In order to convince the public that a determined effort had to be made to come to terms with international realities, they had first to disabuse the popular mind of what they considered dangerous delusions and misconceptions. The lack of concern with these realities, or the outright hostility to military preparations of any kind, came from many sources – from the French Canadians who said that they would defend their country but would not be dragged away to fight imperial wars, from nationalists who rejected proposals for a common defence arrangement because it might infringe upon Canadian autonomy, from those who did not believe that war was imminent, and from others like Laurier who thought the security of Canada ensured by the Monroe doctrine.

14 Andrew Macphail, "Theory and Practice," *ibid.*, xii (Oct. 1913), 390.
15 *Canadian Military Gazette*, xvii (Nov. 4, 1902), 9.

In 1909 one observer attributed the outcry against militarism to the Trades and Labour Congress, the Grange, the Society of Friends, a committee of the Toronto Methodist Conference, pacifist groups, and to Goldwin Smith's paper, the *Weekly Sun*.[16]

From whatever sources it came, however, the protest against militarism was usually phrased in the indignant language of mid-Victorian liberalism. In an ideological sense, liberalism was the most important seed-bed of anti-imperialism and anti-militarism. Canadian liberals had made many compromises and adjustments in accommodating the pure doctrines of Cobden and Bright to the environment of a new country, but one of the elements of that faith which lingered long, and, indeed, was reinvigorated in the new world, was the dislike of all things military. In its classic formation, Manchester liberalism had assumed that once artificial, mercantilistic restrictions upon trade were removed friendly economic interdependence among nations would grow apace and that war and international conflict would ultimately disappear. The democratization of domestic politics, moreover, would also promote international peace because the aristocratic dominance, which was thought to be one of the causes of war, would be ended. Nationalism itself was looked upon as a desirable and progressive force in history because self-determination and the breakdown of institutional encumbrances were expected to liberate the human spirit, galvanize creative energies, and promote international goodwill. The hope for universal peace, so effulgently celebrated at the Crystal Palace in 1851, was still a certitude with many Canadian liberals in 1914. And, in a general way, men who were liberal by conviction tended to regard the growth of armaments with dismay and express distaste for any praise of the martial spirit. By far the most astringent critic of imperialism in Canada was Goldwin Smith who retained his Manchester principles intact down to his death in 1910 and who tried to scotch the monster of militarism wherever he found it. And he found it everywhere – in the cadet corps, Canadian involvement in the Boer War, even in the inscriptions on the monuments commemorating battles of the War of 1812.

Allied to this mistrust of militarism, or anything that smacked of militarism, was an indigenous North American isolationism which focused upon the supposed differences between the old world and the new. As early as 1888, a continental unionist voiced a conviction which was to become one of the stock responses of the anti-imperialists when he said that "Nothing is more striking to the natives of this continent than the state of armed peace prevalent [in Europe]. Armaments every-

16 Hopkins, *The Canadian Annual Review of Public Affairs, 1909* (Toronto, 1910), 281.

where ... Military glory! the bane of the old world."[17] From within this frame of reference, imperial federation and military alliances were seen as a kind of contamination. F. H. Underhill noted the relevance of this sense of isolationism for liberalism when he observed that Laurier's conception of Canadian nationality "had a strong strain of North American isolationism in it, which most Canadian liberals and all French Canadians found congenial."[18] It is hardly surprising that this association of liberalism, isolationism, and the conventional liberal view of war should be detected in a man whose political philosophy was essentially a domesticated version of English liberalism.

The liberal indictment of war received reinforcement in the years after 1900 by a vigorous international pacifist movement. The signing of over one hundred and thirty arbitration treaties between states in the period 1899–1910 and the partially successful attempts at international co-operation through the Hague conferences of 1899 and 1907 strengthened the humanitarian aspiration that war was becoming obsolete and that disputes could be settled by peaceful adjudication. Pacifist optimism rested upon an economic interpretation of the causes of conflict. Most fully elaborated by Norman Angell in his popular book, *The Great Illusion* (1909), and placed within the Canadian context by such works as Christopher West's *Canada and Sea Power* (1913), this argument was founded on the belief that modern capitalism had made nations so interdependent, and that industry and commerce were so internationalized, that war could no longer be waged for profit. Related to this restatement of the traditional liberal view was the notion that wars were mainly the result of the very existence of armaments and that the armament makers, while not the sole instigators of war, were its only beneficiaries. While in substance pacifism was very much the same regardless of whether it stemmed from England or the United States, Canadian anti-imperialists discerned a special congruency between the North American experience and the peaceful settlement of disputes.

It was, significantly enough, Mackenzie King, chairman of the organizing committee of the Canadian Association for International Conciliation and a firm believer that international tensions could be settled in the same manner as labour disputes, who was one of the first to suggest that the one hundredth anniversary of peace in North America should be suitably commemorated. "In the years that have elapsed since the

17 J. N. Blake, *The True Commercial Policy for Greater Britain. An Address Delivered ... Before the Commercial Union Club at Association Hall, Toronto, April 5th, 1888* (Toronto, 1888), 26. See also *'Imperial Federation', by George Edward Fenety, Queen's Printer, Province of New Brunswick, Canada* (Fredericton, 1888), 13.
18 F. H. Underhill, *In Search of Canadian Liberalism* (Toronto, 1960), 220.

War [of 1812]," he told an audience at Harvard University, "no sword has been drawn and no shot has been fired across the four thousand miles of boundary which separates British from American territory on this continent." "We have," he said in a subsequent speech, "... between our two countries an unprotected frontier of some four thousand miles ... We have substituted for competitive arming a system of international conciliation and arbitration, as a means of settling international differences." Arbitration, which had guaranteed peace since 1814, was "the great object-lesson which we of the New World have to give to those who come to us from the Old."[19] Traversing the same ground, J. A. Macdonald, editor of the influential Toronto *Globe* and undoubtedly the most effective popularizer of the myth of one hundred years of tranquility, told the Canadian Club of Toronto in 1914 that

> The international relations between Canada and the United States and our common boundary line, unbarbarized by forts or battleships or guns, are of significance, not for these nations alone, but for all the world. That unprecedented and unparalleled fact of 4,000 miles of civilized internationalism is a message to all continents, the supreme message of North America to all the world. What has been done by these proud and ambitious Anglo-Saxon peoples ought not to be impossible in Europe or elsewhere in the civilized world.[20]

In a more extended fashion Macdonald delivered a series of lectures at Vanderbilt University during 1917, praising the unguarded frontier, the one hundred years of peace, and arbitration. The lectures were published under the revealing title of *The North American Idea.*

This consanguinity between liberal anti-imperialism and isolationism, pacifism, and anti-militarism, was of course more sharply presented in the literature of controversy than in the sphere of politics and the association suggested here is meant only to describe a tendency of thought rather than a key to explaining party politics. But whenever the indifference and opposition to the imperialists' military plans became articulate, it dwelt upon traditional liberal precepts, economic causes of wars, North American immunity and moral superiority, and the charge, invoked again and again, that almost any kind of precautionary military measures constituted "militarism," the disease of the old world. The imperialists had to dispel the illusion of security and shatter the feeling of immunity before they could get a hearing at all, and, prid-

19 W. L. M. King, *The Message of the Carillon and Other Addresses* (Toronto, 1927), 164, 148, 176.
20 J. A. Macdonald at the banquet for President Taft, Jan. 29, 1914, *Addresses Delivered Before the Canadian Club of Toronto, Season of 1913–1914* (Toronto, 1914), 119.

ing themselves upon their realism, they did not need to look very far in both contemporary affairs and history to find examples and ideas which would undermine the unlimited and unwarranted faith in human goodness and underline the necessity for self-defence.

History itself, and especially the record of the series of wars arising from national unification and colonial expansion in the second half of the nineteenth century, discredited the romantic illusion that conflicts would become less frequent and ultimately disappear with the progress of civilization. "Consider the last fifty years of the greatest and most civilized century in the world," George Foster remarked in the House of Commons in 1909, "and what are the examples? The fire that was kindled in the Crimea, the blood-red streams that ran in India, the long struggle in the United States between South and North, the Franco-Prussian war, the Spanish-American battles, the British-Boer war, and the Japan-Russian war – all these are outstanding, large examples of the fact that all the restraints of Christian morals and of ethics are impotent to curb the ambitions and the passions of nations; examples of the sad disappointments of those who believed that the era of peace, and enduring peace, had been ushered into existence."[21] It was not possible to believe, said a journalist in alluding to the role of the yellow press of Hearst, Pulitzer, and Lord Northcliffe in generating popular enthusiasm for war, "that the masses of the people do not want wars, and are dragged unwillingly by the ambitions of princes into quarrels in which they have no interest."[22] War, added the editor of the Canadian Magazine, could no longer be attributed to the pressure of financial interests alone; war was the result of "strong national feeling."[23]

The lesson that "progress" did not make warfare obsolete fell hardest upon those who had been nurtured in the certitudes of the liberal faith or those who once shared the pacifist hope but doubted that it was realizable. "I had hoped," George Ross told Colonel Denison, "that with the advance of civilization, general disarmament would take place, – that the arts of peace would be cultivated to such an extent as to exclude the warlike spirit of the human race. Great as has been the progress of the world in the last fifty years in other directions, I fear our progress in this direction has been very slow. No nation is secure that depends for its existence entirely on the good-will of its neighbours."[24] At the Columbian Exposition at Chicago in 1893, G. M. Grant acknowledged that there was something real and appealing in the hopes men placed in arbi-

21 George E. Foster, Canadian Addresses (Toronto, 1914), 138–9.
22 John Lewis, "The Future of Imperialism," Canadian Magazine, xv (July 1900), 257.
23 John A. Cooper, "Editorial Comments," ibid., xi (May 1898), 77–8.
24 G. T. Denison Papers, Ross to Denison, Feb. 5, 1901.

tration tribunals and peace congresses but he also noticed how the crowds surged around the displays of weapons, fascinated with the modern engines of war. In 1899 he confessed that "the real roots of war will remain for a long time in human nature."[25] Other imperialists sought to convince those whom James Cappon called the old-fashioned philosophical liberals that their "ideal of universal peace" could best be promoted through the "new and greater political units of our time" rather than through the breakup of empires.[26]

Like Cappon, William Grant had nothing but contempt for those fire-eating colonels who hankered for the martial exploit and he hoped, as had the American philosopher William James, that men could find some moral substitute for war, some activity which would enlist the heroism and risk-taking which made war so exciting and appealing. Yet he too felt that the foundation of the liberal philosophy had been shown to be defective in its estimation of human character and its exaltation of self-sufficient nationalism. The trouble with the Victorian liberals and their intellectual offspring in Canada, he wrote in 1912, was that they "thought too nobly of the soul, and of the power of sweet reasonableness." If history proved anything, he elaborated,

> it is the inadequacy of the nation as a permanent ideal. When we compare the hopes of Mazzini and of the German theorists of 1848 with the present situation, one knows not whether to laugh or weep ... The hope of Mazzini was that in Nationalism a people would find space to develop all that was best in it. We now know that Nationalism results in wanton truculence. Surely Providence has something better in store for Canada than to become a nasty little quarrelsome nation. From this point of view, a closer union of the British Empire, which at least makes it impossible for the component parts to fight each other, and which would probably be too strong to attack, is not a council of despair, but a very noble second-best, indeed the biggest practical step towards "the parliament of man, the federation of the world."[27]

This critique of liberal nationalism was not intended as an academic exercise: Grant described what was wanting in liberalism because he found that the anti-imperialists like Ewart and Bourassa were still prisoners of that faith. A completely independent Canada, isolated from the Empire and without need of defence, was an unattainable dream, he

25 G. M. Grant, "Current Events," *Queen's Quarterly*, I (July 1893), 73; *ibid.*, VII (July 1899), 76.
26 James Cappon, "Current Events," *ibid.*, X (Jan. 1903), 391.
27 W. L. Grant, "Current Events," *ibid.*, XX (Dec. 1912), 226–7.

told them. Within "this idea there lies a fallacy," he wrote, "and the fallacy is the belief that there is any such thing as independence. In this new world, every state is bound to every other by filaments as impalpable yet as real and as numerous as those which thrill the instruments of Marconi." Canada could never be totally independent, neither would the self-respect of her people permit her to remain a colony of Britain or become a dependent of the United States. She must, he counselled, recognize that isolationism is impossible and become "something more than a mere hermit crab, cowering in a shell we have done nothing to create."[28]

The imperialists' attempt to establish a state of mind conducive to the consideration of imperial military co-operation began, then, with a preliminary critique of the fundamental assumption beneath liberalism. The argument for military preparedness, however, did not end here. Other imperialists who were more enamoured of the military life and more cognizant of the military thought of their time stated the case for preparedness in profounder terms – in terms, that is, of social Darwinism, religion, and national health.

III

Canadians were not original in transposing the doctrines of biological evolution to account for social and political phenomenon, nor were they unique in applying such ideas to explain the place of war in international relations. According to the popularized, or rather, vulgarized, conceptions of social Darwinism prevalent at that time, war was understood to be the result of forces deeply embedded in the process of social evolution and warfare was accepted as progressive because victory through struggle attested to the adaptability and superiority of the national organism. The derivative nature of these judgments did not affect the unshakeable conviction that they were relevant to Canada. Whenever opponents of military preparedness objected that wars were caused by personal influences, ambitions, and antipathies, or that those who advocated a strong imperial navy were the paid agents of the armament manufacturers, thereby implying that the sources of conflict were superficial and controllable, they were confronted with the objection, clothed in the garb of pseudo-science, that the causes of war were ineradicably rooted in human nature and that war between states was simply the product of the fixed laws of social evolution. Appeals for

28 W. L. Grant, "The Fallacy of Nationalism," *Empire Club of Canada: Addresses Delivered to the Members During the Session of 1911–12* (Toronto, 1913), 222–8.

contributions to the imperial fleet or for a more effective militia establishment seldom left unmentioned the necessities and imperatives of social evolution.

In an address to the Faculty of Education of the University of Toronto in April 1909, Lt. Col. Merritt told the students that though war and bloodshed were horrible, they were, like death and disease, nevertheless inevitable. "Nature," he said, "seems to regulate that the world shall not be over-run with one species ... The study of both biology and history show that the weak go to the wall. It always has been and always will be the survival of the fittest."[29] One of Merritt's associates in the Canadian Defence League was a professor at the University of Toronto, J. T. Fotheringham, who succinctly stated the relevance of social Darwinism for martial training. No one can deny, he wrote, "that the condition of human progress most constantly in evidence, most far-reaching, most ineluctable, is rivalry, competition, the pitting of the strong against the strong, the survival of the fittest. From the lowest organism, up through sentient and insentient grades of life alike, to the highest forms of the organized community among the most intelligent animal as yet evolved on the earth, the principle holds true that 'he must keep who can.' "[30] "We are accustomed," wrote a student of the same university, "to hear from biologists that development towards the higher comes through the law of Natural Selection. War is the means whereby this law acts on human societies."[31] In his Ethics of Imperialism (1905), a book which attracted widespread attention and which was one of the most hairy-chested presentations of Darwinian imperialism, the chief editorial writer for the Montreal Star, Albert Carman, candidly submitted that imperialism was nothing less than the egotistical instinct for survival writ large and that international rivalry was simply the struggle for existence between great "Fighting Units." As such, imperialism was incompatible with altruistic Christianity; talk of the civilizing mission was "pharisaical chatter." In this world there can be no safety for any person or thing, said Carman, "except through the protection of brute force."[32]

The implications for the Dominion of this explanation of international tension and war were traced through most explicitly by William Wood. "The world," he wrote in 1898, "is still within that phase of

29 Canadian Military Institute, Selected Papers (Welland, Ontario, 1909), no. 17, appendix, 52.
30 J. T. Fotheringham, "Military Knowledge as a Cultural Subject," Canadian Defence, III (Jan. 1912), 208.
31 H. R. Gorden, "War," Arbor, III (Dec. 1911), 70.
32 Albert A. Carman, The Ethics of Imperialism: An Enquiry Whether Christian Ethics and Imperialism are Antagonistic (Boston, 1905), 99–100.

evolution in which war is the main determining factor." Notwithstanding the anticipations of the sponsors of the International Exhibition of 1851, all the powers have been at war, many of them several times, and the history of the last fifty years offered irrefutable confirmation that war "is an essential part of the universal struggle for existence; its first knowable cause is the necessity for fighting for survival, for life, for the fulness of growth and expansion."[33] Delay in immediate adaptation by increased naval and military expenditures, he implied, was a vain attempt to "suspend the laws of Nature and with them, the struggle for existence."[34] Since *"war is still an inevitable form of the universal struggle for existence,"* he foresaw that "some day the whole Empire, and every individual in it, will be literally at war; both those at home and those at the front; all alike. This is true of every kind of human activity, from the prayers of the churches to the fluctuations of the money markets; for nothing escapes the hand of war."[35] Wood himself was, as he said of another, a "believer in the Darwinian theory of world politics" who understood "the inevitable nature of the struggle for international existence."[36] In his *Fight for Canada* (1904), a detailed examination of the fall of New France, he fused the insights of Mahan and his own Darwinian view of conflict in order to demonstrate one of the main planks in the platform of the Navy League, that "the Command of Sea has always been the one inevitable and over-mastering factor which has determined the whole development of racial dominion in the New World." The conquest of Canada by Britain "depended at every turn, upon issues of world-wide naval strategy." The success of Wolfe's expedition, which Wood described as "nothing else but a great landing-party," was contingent upon the complete blockade of the continental French ports and the penetration of the St Lawrence. Throughout the book, Wood drew parallels between the elemental causes of the Seven Years War and the tensions of his time, and, indeed, he found that the entire conflict was "one long object-lesson in the evils of disunion in imperial defence."[37]

Wood's writings were consciously designed to arouse an awareness of the imminence of war and to develop a more responsive attitude to imperial defence. An editor grasped the point of one of his articles when

33 W. Wood, "In Case of War," *Canadian Magazine*, XI (June 1898), 93–4.
34 W. Wood, "The Empire and the War Factor," *Canadian Field: Official Journal of the Canadian Defence League*, II (April 1911), 12.
35 W. Wood, *The British Command of the Sea and What it Means to Canada* (Toronto, 1900), 8–9. Italics in original.
36 In a review of Emil Reich, *Success Among Nations* (Toronto, 1904), in *Review of Historical Publications Relating to Canada*, IX (Toronto, 1905), 2.
37 W. Wood, *The Fight for Canada: A Naval and Military Sketch from the History of the Great Imperial War* (London, 1904), 26, 43, 310.

he said that it "should do away with much of our senseless opposition to military expenditure."[38] The Darwinian conceptions which Wood and others used, and obviously believed in, were perfect instruments for this purpose, confirming as they did the belief that physical and brute force lay at the foundation of civilization and legitimizing the idea that preparation for war was the only way to avoid it. The Canadian people had to be reminded that the law of international relations is force, said one observer in 1913, because they have a tendency to talk "in rather a superior way about the 'vortex of European militarism,' and have a holier-than-thou attitude toward the peoples who still believe in the might of blood and iron." The only alternative to adjusting to this law by military preparedness was "to abdicate the glorious destiny that we have announced for ourselves and retire into decent obscurity, to become eventually a protectorate of some stronger nation, probably the United States."[39]

IV

Combined with the idea of war as an inescapable aspect of the struggle for existence between nations, was the conception of conflict as progressive because it advanced the boundaries of a superior civilization and secured peace through force. The numerous wars waged against primitive, native races or against "decadent" colonial powers like Spain made this view appear commonsensical. In an article calculated to show that in some instances war was "a highly necessary evil" and to prove that the wholesale charges of militarism were misdirected when applied to all advocates of imperial defence, the military historian and war correspondent, Charles F. Hamilton, asked people to compare the state of west Africa before and after British intervention. They would find, he wrote, that before the coming of the British human beings were sacrificed in every native village, the slave trade flourished, and life was hideously insecure. When Benin was captured, he reported,

> the place so reeked with human blood that the working parties which cleaned the town were almost constantly nauseated. The white man comes. Perhaps there is a war, a short and sharp struggle in which twelve-pounder, maxim, and rifle assert once again their superiority to the Dane gun and the poisoned arrow. Then crucifixions, fetish

38 J. A. Cooper, "Editorial Comments," *Canadian Magazine*, xi (June 1898), 173.
39 J. Macdonnell, "National Service," *Arbor*, iv (Feb. 1913), 185.

sacrifices, slave trade, tribal warfare, and other dismal horrors cease. Life and property become secure ... Industry is given an opportunity to develop ... I ask, was that war in which the shell and bullet crushed the ju-ju warriors the worst thing that could have happened [to] that negro population?[40]

Writing with the Philippine rebellion against their American liberators fresh in mind, a journalist remarked that "we have had in our mind's eye the spectacle of savages being torn and minced by machine guns and shrapnel with each morning's issue of the papers," and though one might briefly sympathize with the natives for not understanding how those "who are racking them fore and aft with grape and canister are the best friends they have," civilization in general has done the savages more good than harm. "The rule of most African chiefs," he affirmed, "is a continual carnival of fiendish cruelty, the extirpation of which would be a gain to humanity, even if whole tribes had to be blotted out in the process."[41] In a Christmas message to the readers of the *Canadian Magazine* in 1899 during the wars in South Africa and the Philippines, its editor admitted that it was "difficult to write of 'Peace on earth, good-will toward men' when both branches of the Anglo-Saxon people are engaged in subduing inferior races." But it was none the less of some comfort to know that war was frequently necessary in the interests of peace and "progressive civilization" which would presumably be secure "when the Boer and Filipino have been made to realize that the Anglo-Saxon race never errs, that it makes war only for the benefits of humanity."[42]

This view of war as salutary and beneficial in the interests of civilization was the universal explanation of the Spanish-American and South African conflicts offered by sympathetic Canadians. Seldom, however, was it stated in such ardent and intoxicated vocabulary as that employed by the *Methodist Magazine*. Though its editor, Rev. William Withrow, advised his fellow divines to "preach and write against the brute force of War," he greeted the outbreak of hostilities between the United States and Spain with unrestrained acclaim and forthwith presented the "missionary view" of that conflict. "Not since the time of the crusades," his journal announced in June 1898, "has the world ... witnessed a war declared for more unselfish ends. The American nation at great cost of

40 C. F. Hamilton, "Militarism," *University Magazine*, IX (Dec. 1910), 525.
41 J. A. Ewan, "Current Events Abroad," *Canadian Magazine*, XIII (May 1899), 85–6.
42 J. A. Cooper, "Editorial Comments," *ibid.*, XIV (Dec. 1899), 193.

treasure, and at great peril of death by yellow fever, small-pox, and the deadly wounds of modern war, seeks to rescue not the empty sepulchre of our Lord, but His living image." In the true spirit of the noblest chivalry and self-sacrifice, the United States sends forth its best to succour men of an alien and mixed blood.[43] Spain, he said, was "the lagging hindermost of civilization and Christianity," by which he meant that she had excluded Protestant missionaries from her dependencies. Protestants could therefore look upon "the coming of the American fleet to Manila as the sword of the Lord to smite the man of sin and unbar the gateway for the entrance into those tropic islands of the messengers of the Prince of Peace."[44]

This endorsement of the American cause by the magazine of Canadian Methodism hardly differed in detail from the exhortations of leading American proponents of the imperialism of righteousness which had played so large a role in bringing on the conflict in the first place, nor was it altered in substance when a few months later its sanction was brought to justify the war against the Boers. Terrible as that ordeal appeared to be, ran the answer to the question of whether this too was a righteous war, "we believe that Briton and Boer shall alike rejoice in a higher civilization in South Africa, that the black race, freed from the oppressions of the Boers, shall enjoy the blessings of the Gospel as they never enjoyed them before."[45] The growth of the "cosmopolitan spirit," the McMaster University Magazine magisterially pronounced, was one of the most impressive features of the nineteenth century. "Because of this spirit the peoples of the West have stretched forth their hands to lift the nations of the East to a higher plane of activity; because of it the Anglo-Saxon race has sought to scatter everywhere the seeds of a higher civilization; and because of it Britain is to-day dying red the African veldt with the life blood of her sons." This spirit "is in truth the essence of the teaching the Master taught some nineteen hundred years ago among the olive groves about Jerusalem, and upon the sunny vine-clad slopes of Judea."[46]

It was perhaps in the sermons delivered to military units that the Christian rationalization for war was most clearly expressed. The chaplain of the 10th Royal Grenadiers, in a sermon to the two thousand men of the Toronto garrison, took as his text Phillipians I, 12: "I would that ye should understand, brethren, that the things which have happened unto me have fallen out rather unto the furtherance of the

43 Methodist Magazine and review, XLVII (June 1898), 578.
44 Ibid., XLIX (Jan. 1899), 95.
45 Ibid., LI (Mar. 1900), 281.
46 "Editorial Notes," McMaster University Magazine, IX (Jan. 1900), 177-8.

Gospel."[47] In a sermon delivered to the men of Strathcona's Horse in St Andrew's Church, Ottawa, the Rev. W. T. Herridge suggestively revealed how the concept of war as progress, the spirit of imperialism, and Anglo-Saxon racism could fuse in the emotionalism of religious idealism. "War must now have some moral purpose," he said, "or it will fail to enlist the noblest sympathies." The moral duty was then explained:

> To the English-speaking race the Providence of God has committed no small part of the duty of advancing the civilization and Christian principle of the world. However divided by distance, by local interests, or even by varying modes of government, reason and conscience alike suggest an Anglo-Saxon federation of pure and upright hearts, a federation which is not satisfied until it has made right more easy and wrong more difficult everywhere, until it has given a new impulse to human progress, until it has subdued the demons of vice and avarice, and brought back to mankind the angel-presence which does not fear to look into the face of the Father who is in heaven.[48]

The conviction that the Anglo-Saxon race held in its hand the destiny of the world, coupled with the belief that the race was enjoined by God to disseminate the seeds of civilization, inevitably led to the conclusion that when the furtherance of "liberty," the "Gospel," and "progress" was impeded by either an inferior race or a lower civilization, the resulting conflict and war could be neither inglorious nor morally wrong. Though both the intensity and frequency of this Christian approbation of war decreased with the conclusion of the conflict in South Africa, its fundamentals remained alive until they were re-echoed a thousandfold during the First World War.

V

Beneath the strident self-confidence and certainty of pre-eminence so characteristic of imperialist thought there lurked gnawing doubts concerning the vitality of the race and its future primacy. Imperialist social thinking was grounded upon a repugnance towards capitalistic values and an abiding suspicion that the ferocious concentration upon material development and the single-minded pursuit of wealth and pleasure were

47 *Canadian Military Gazette*, xv (June 5, 1900), 24.
48 W. T. Herridge, *A Sermon preached in St. Andrew's Church, Ottawa, to "Strathcona's Horse" Previous to their Departure for Service in South Africa* (Ottawa, 1900), 11.

undermining the nation's zest for adventure, respect for authority, and spirit of service and self-sacrifice. The antipathy to materialism, the rejection of pecuniary standards for judging either character or institutions, and apocalyptic warnings of impending doom were regular features of imperialist literature and thought. In Britain, the United States, and Canada this sense of pessimism led to the glorification of the soldierly character as an antidote to the evils of contemporary social life and ended in the campaigning for universal military service.

The American imperialists like Theodore Roosevelt, Henry Cabot Lodge, and Alfred T. Mahan believed that the real enemy of a forceful foreign policy was not so much the professional pacifist or the hidebound isolationist, but rather the businessmen who identified national stature with material prosperity. Roosevelt's own contempt for the business civilization was far more than a simple instance of the soldier's hostility to the merchant: it was part and parcel of a deliberate effort to hold up a cult of military valour as a purgative to luxury and ease. In an address to the Naval College in 1897, he declared that there "are higher things in life than the soft and easy enjoyment of material comfort. It is through strife, or the readiness for strife, that a nation must win greatness ... a rich nation which is slothful, timid, or unwieldly is an easy prey for any people which still retain those most valuable qualities, the martial virtues." There are those, he said, who always wallowed in material complacency, who "are always ready to balance a temporary interruption of money-making, or a temporary financial and commercial disaster, against the self-sacrifice necessary in upholding the honor of the nation." If Americans lose "the virile, manly qualities, and sink into a nation of mere hucksters, putting gain above national honor, and subordinating everything to mere ease of life; then we shall indeed reach a condition worse than that of the ancient civilizations in the years of their decay."[49]

An identical insistence pervaded the poetry of Rudyard Kipling. There were many reasons for his popularity in Canada but for those like Denison who read everything he wrote and quoted him extensively, the attraction of Kipling lay in his ability to articulate the antipathy to the urban and atomized society with its liberal creed of self-enjoyment. To Kipling, Professor Stokes explained, the Empire "represented not simply the appointed task bequeathed by history, it represented that type of life and work which would combat deterioration

49 John P. Mallan, "Roosevelt, Brooks Adams, and Lea: The Warrior Critique of the Business Civilization," *American Quarterly*, VIII (Fall 1956), 219; William H. Harbaugh, *The Life and Times of Theodore Roosevelt* (New York, 1963), 101.

of character brought about by an excessively urbanized and intellectual civilization."⁵⁰

This disquieting and worrisome spirit and the animus against capitalistic standards runs like a red thread through imperialism. The point that the commercial spirit was incompatible with nationalism had been made by Denison long before when he asked, what is Little Englandism but "a pounds, shillings, and pence basis in considering everything?" For those who thought like him, who looked with trepidation upon the unwillingness of Englishmen and Canadians to take military precautions and who disdainfully dismissed liberal anti-imperialism as a self-destructive, hedonistic, and cowardly creed, the response of the British people to the Boer War stood out as reassuring proof that the strenuous character had not been completely undermined. It seemed even more important that the conflict provided a purgative to England's corruptions than that it marked another forward step in imperial co-operation. "We have seen men of wealth, of birth, and position leave their comfortable homes by hundreds," said Denison, "we have seen them leave all the luxury and ease of the greatest and finest and highest civilization that this world has ever seen, to undergo dangers, trials, wounds, and in many cases death, all for this cause."⁵¹ Even Charles Mair, who admitted that it was a pity that Britain was forced to fight "a race of yeomen soldiers sprung from our common stock," thought the war desirable "in order to redeem her from the gangrene of wealth and luxury and easy victories over savages, and prepare and harden her for the still larger struggle looming in the future."⁵² This refrain was a constant accompaniment of invocations for military preparations. "It is a law of nature," declared a spokesman of the Canadian Defence League, "over and over exemplified in history, that the rich, ease-loving, mammon-hunting people must go down, before the poor but military race."⁵³ C. F. Hamilton wondered whether the popular aversion to war was really due to humane feeling or whether in fact it might be attributed "to a mere desire to continue to make money?" The pursuit of wealth, he said, must be subordinated to "the moral and spiritual sides of our life" and the martial spirit must be cultivated for it "includes among its ingredients courage, discipline, duty, devotion to the service of one's country rather than one's self, a desire for glory as distinguished from

50 Eric Stokes, *The Political Ideas of English Imperialism: An Inaugural Lecture Given in the University College of Rhodesia and Nyasaland* (London, 1960), 27–35.
51 G. T. Denison, *The Struggle for Imperial Unity* (Toronto, 1909), 52, 277.
52 Denison Papers, Mair to Denison, Nov. 29, 1899.
53 J. T. Fotheringham, "The Duty of Imperial Defence," *Arbor*, II (Apr. 1911), 304.

the ambition to amass wealth."[54] For William Wood, too, the chief value of military training as well as actual combat was that both checked self-satisfaction and lethargy. Writing at a time when "most ears are deafened to everything else by the ceaseless roar of clamorous statistics" and when the "higher call is only heard at large during some rare interlude between the acts of the drama of dollars and cents," he warned a generation pampered by peace and plenty that warfare was an indispensable aspect of civilization, even an indispensable aspect of character formation, for it "is the scourge of all the skulking vices." All "the noblest qualities of individuals and nations have to prove their worth in time of war."[55]

Many imperialists believed that these qualities had to be artificially protected and nurtured. Nothing reveals their revulsion from the materialism of their time and their desire to check its debilitating influences so clearly as the campaign for cadet drill and physical exercises in the schools. This movement had originated in the mid-nineteenth century but had gathered substantial support only after the Boer War. In 1907 Lord Strathcona announced that he would contribute $250,000 to create a fund to encourage physical and military training in schools, and the militia department agreed to provide instruction for teachers during the summers, supply the schools with arms, ammunition, and other equipment, and give a bonus of between fifty and one hundred dollars per year to teachers who qualified themselves as drill instructors. In 1913 there were 759 cadet corps companies in existence, a very large number of them in the province of Quebec, with an estimated membership of over thirty thousand.[56] While the movement enlisted the support of educators, medical men, and politicians who were not primarily interested in its imperial aspects, imperialists, particularly those associated with the Canadian Defence League in Toronto, were nevertheless the most devoted proponents of drill.

The obvious purpose of military drill was to produce men for the defence of Canada and the Empire. The cadet corps, said Sam Hughes, were "the foundation of the volunteer force, and the foundation of the defence of the Empire." A lifelong supporter of school drill, Hughes

54 C. F. Hamilton, "Militarism," 527, 531–2.
55 W. Wood, *In the Heart of Old Canada* (Toronto, 1913), vii; "The ABC of Imperial Defence," 5.
56 W. H. Merritt, *Canada and National Service* (Toronto, 1917), 78. The background of the campaign for cadet drill and the legislation affecting it are given in F. F. Manly, "Drill and Physical Education," *Proceedings of the Thirty-Seventh Annual Convention of the Ontario Educational Association held in Toronto ... 1898* (Toronto, 1898), 105–11, and J. E. Hett, "The Benefits derived from Physical Training and Medical Inspection," *Proceedings of the Forty-Eighth Annual Convention of the Ontario Educational Association held in Toronto ... 1909* (Toronto, 1909), 342–8.

had entered a plea for "an Empire Militia" in 1905 saying that if he were in control "I would divide the Empire according to school divisions, and I would begin with the boys at the age of twelve ..." Such a system would be "democratic and cheap" and when the boys were older "I would have them drafted into regiments and brigades."[57] When he became minister of militia in 1911, Hughes promptly announced that forty thousand school boys would go into training that summer.[58] "In five years from now," he announced in 1912, rather prophetically as it turned out, "I want to have some hundreds of thousands of our youths trained to shoot and march."[59]

But the rationale for drill and physical exercises in schools extended beyond this simple provision of potential soldiers. Such training was justified in therapeutic terms. Believing that the herding of people into cities caused physical degeneration, a fact apparently confirmed by British army statistics, its supporters argued that drill would build up the race, ward off diseases, and avert the tendency toward physical and mental decline. Military training, wrote Professor Hutton, "is in itself a safeguard against physical degeneracy and that physical decadence which industrialism continually brings in its train."[60] The development of modern society itself seemed incompatible with the survival of military prowess. Canadians were no longer as familiar with the gun as they were half a century ago, Parkin told the British Empire League, and "the training in shooting that our pioneers had ... must be given in some other way."[61] The Canadian Boy Scout movement, which had ten thousand members in 1910, was also calculated to perpetuate qualities being lost because of "teeming cities" and "the state of over-civilization." Lt. Gen. Baden-Powell, the founder of the movement, contended that scouting was a far more effective and thorough preparation for soldiering than regimental drill. When the time came for a scout to join a defence force, he said during a Canadian tour, his experience in campaigning and woodcraft would make him "a far superior soldier than if he received merely the usual Cadet Training."[62]

The champions of drill, like James Hughes, a pioneer of physical

57 Hopkins, *The Canadian Annual Review of Public Affairs, 1911* (Toronto, 1912), 349; Sam Hughes, "The Defence of the Empire," *Empire Club Speeches: Being Addresses Delivered Before the Empire Club of Canada During its Session of 1904–05* (Toronto, 1906), 183.
58 Canada, Department of Militia and Defence, *Memorandum on Cadet Corps Training by the Minister of Militia, January 20, 1911* (n.p., n.d.), 3.
59 Hopkins, *The Canadian Annual Review of Public Affairs, 1912* (Toronto, 1913), 284.
60 Hutton, "Militarism and Anti-Militarism," 184.
61 Denison Papers, Scrapbook, 1897–1915, 73.
62 Lt. Gen. Sir R. S. S. Baden-Powell, "The Boy Scout Movement," *Empire Club Speeches ... Session of 1910–1911* (Toronto, 1911), 11–17.

culture on the playgrounds and a disciple of Pestalozzi and Froebel, claimed that drill gave a man more strength, greater agility, a better poise, bearing and dignity, a more definite step, and that it cultivated the spirit of co-operation and reverence for law.[63] Alfred E. Dunn, rector of St Paul's Cathedral in London, Ontario, endorsed the scheme because it was an unparalleled agency for moulding character and instilling proper attitudes. "Untidiness, uncleanliness, slovenliness – the great failings of boyhood – are inconsistent with a uniform. A boy in uniform feels disgraced if his hands are filthy, his neck unwashed, his hair unkempt, his boots dirty, or his clothes unbrushed." The habits of cleanliness and orderliness formed by drill "act on the moral nature of the boy, and he is improved all round." ("The science of war," he added, "cannot be wrong. God's chosen people were a nation of warriors. Christ has not forbidden war.")[64] Another enthusiast proclaimed that military exercises under a male drill instructor were needful in order to counteract the prevailing influence of female school teachers. It would present boys with an example of manly character as well as "teach them a lesson of discipline – of law and order, of obedience and regularity, of punctuality and precision ..."[65] Military training instilled "obedience," "promptitude," "subordination" – especially, subordination. Even women were invited to participate because it would teach them "taciturnity."[66] Cadet conscription, moreover, was not vulnerable to the objection so often directed at European conscription. Far from being a drain on the national resources by taking men away from useful employment for three or four years of the best part of their lives, cadet drill actually contributed to productivity and efficiency. "It turns a weedy, anaemic lad into a well-knit, upstanding young man with sound organs and well-developed limbs ... The effect in the workshop is visible at every turn. It is not too much to say that military service has been in a great measure the making of industrial Germany."[67]

Nearly all appeals for cadet training were phrased in terms of loyalty to the Empire and assumed that the martial spirit was a desirable ingredient of national feeling. In an address in 1909 to the young ladies of the normal school and the Faculty of Education of the University of Toronto, Miss Constance R. Boulton, the honorary secretary of the Imperial Order Daughters of the Empire, asserted on behalf of the

63 James L. Hughes, "National and Ethical Value of Cadet Training," *Empire Club of Canada Addresses ... Session of 1911–12* (Toronto, 1913), 104–11.
64 *Canadian Military Gazette*, XXI (March 13, 1906), 15.
65 W. R. Givens, "The Privilege of Self-Defence," *University Magazine*, VIII (Apr. 1909), 328, 330.
66 M. Hutton, "The Five Lamps of Education," *Arbor*, III (Nov. 1911), 24.
67 *Canadian Field*, II (Apr. 1911), 4.

homemakers of the Dominion that "nothing can contribute more effectively to practical patriotism than the teaching of physical training and
military drill in the schools." Our loyalty can be made practical by encouraging everyone "to be his own rifleman, and to be able to hit his
man." To the same audience, the chief inspector of Toronto schools declared that in Toronto, "where we have so many foreign lads, I am sure
the quickest and best way we can make them respect the British flag is
to march them through the streets in uniform and behind that flag."[68]
Cadet drill and physical exercises were therefore commended for national, industrial, ethical, social, as well as military, reasons.

Running through all these arguments was the feeling, as Professor
Hutton put it in summing up the case, that "military training is the training compensatory of the foibles and the weaknesses of our age and our
political system; antithetic to the virtues of our age, and therefore for
us antiseptic: antiseptic against the excesses of our own systems and our
own shibboleths." It was a compensation for an overly intellectualized,
lazy, and inactive people, "an offset to democracy and liberty," a deter-
rent to sloth. We need more of the obedience and spirit of service which
the martial spirit embodied, he said: "We want these qualities even
more against ourselves than against any possible external foe."[69] Those
associated with the Canadian Defence League, the cadet corps, and the
Boy Scouts, Andrew Macphail concurred, should stop protesting that
militarism is not their aim. "Militarism is in the heart of every boy, and
that is the spirit to which they should appeal and foster before it is
destroyed by the perverted virtue of the trader and the misapplied industry of the world."[70]

VI

Militarism was not some minor aberration in the structure of imperial
thought, nor was its function in that outlook incidental. The acceptance
of war as an ever-present reality, a necessary incident in social evolution, and a result of unchangeable forces underlay the imperialists' insistence that the problem of imperial defence was urgent and unavoid-
able. These convictions also led them to dismiss Canadian opposition to
military and naval preparedness as utopian and dangerous. Just as warfare was seen as a rather strenuous sport and an expression of national
self-assertiveness and fitness, so too the martial spirit appeared to be
synonymous with a masterful and upright manhood, order and stability,

68 Canadian Military Institute, *Selected Papers*, appendix, 41, 49.
69 Hutton, "Militarism and Anti-Militarism," 196.
70 Macphail, "Theory and Practice," 392.

a necessary aspect of vital national feeling, and an antidote to the follies of the age. Seldom did imperialists go to such lengths as Sam Hughes when he told the Board of Trade of the Eastern Townships in 1913 that history proves "that the most brilliant periods in the life of a nation follow those of war," and implied that the Augustan age of Rome, the Renaissance in France, and Elizabethan age in England, were all products of the exhilarating impact of war.[71] But in general they looked upon war as inescapable and real, and upon military training as desirable and necessary, as a preserver of certain values which modern civilization was destroying.

In their praise of the martial spirit, no less than in their hankering for an agrarian society, the imperialists betrayed the essentially reactionary character of their thought. At the turn of the century the Austrian economist, Joseph Schumpeter, studied the resurgence of imperialism among the European nations and concluded that its socialist and liberal critics were incorrect in appraising its motives in economic terms and regarding it as a logical extension of financial capitalism. Capitalism, wrote Schumpeter, was pacific: business had no vested interest in war as such. Looking at the recurrent celebrations of the martial virtues and the deliberate efforts at preserving those traditional ideals which were most antithetical to capitalism, Schumpeter pronounced imperialism a great atavism, a reaction against, not an extension of, modern society.[72] If it is necessary to place these militant Canadian imperialists into such a general framework, ignoring for the moment the large areas of disagreement among them, then the context would not be that of predatory business but rather the tradition of the opponents of unchecked industrialism and capitalism such as the agrarian protest movements.

71 Hopkins, *The Canadian Annual Review of Public Affairs, 1913*, 217. Perhaps the most extreme justification of warfare was made in Byron Nicholson, "The Ethics of War," *Canadian Magazine*, VI (Feb. 1896), 333–6.
72 J. Schumpeter, *Imperialism and Social Classes* (New York, 1961).

11

Conclusion

Imperialism was one form of Canadian nationalism.

This sense of nationality was grounded upon a definite conception of Canada's past, her national character, and her mission in the future, and at its heart was a yearning for significance and a desire to obliterate the stigma of colonialism. "I ... am an imperialist," said Stephen Leacock, "because I will not be a Colonial."[1] "There is no antagonism ... between Canadianism and imperialism," declared the premier of Ontario in 1900. "The one is but the expansion of the other."[2] Because they thought that the United Empire Loyalists had planted and protected the ideal of imperial unity in Canada when the British people had questioned and deserted it, and because they saw history as the record of the gradual steps by which Canadians had acquired the rights of British citizens, these Canadians regarded imperialism as a native product, embedded in the traditions of their country. Canadians possessed complete internal self-government and it remained only to assert their authority over the Empire as a whole through some form of imperial federation. In the later 1800s it was necessary to protect the British connection because it provided economic and military support to the new nation. What imperialists defended, however, was not so much the imperial system as it then stood but rather the hope that as Canada grew in strength and population the Empire would be transformed so as to accommodate her weight and influence. The movement for imperial unity was partly a reactionary desire to preserve; it was also expressive of what George Foster called a sense of power. In 1901 he explained that with Canada's expansion and growth, "the perception of increased power and influence, and the appreciation of future possibilities, there has arisen, first in a dim sort of way but gradually gaining clearness and strength, the sense of power to be exercised within the Empire, of responsibility to imperial duties, of attachment to imperial ideals, and

1 Stephen Leacock, "Greater Canada: An Appeal," *University Magazine*, VI (April 1907), 133.
2 Quoted in R. J. D. Page, "The Impact of the Boer War on the Canadian General Election of 1900 in Ontario" (MA thesis, Queen's University, 1964), 149.

of co-operation in the achievement of imperial destinies ..."[3] Canadian imperialism was the emotion evoked, not by the actual exercise of power, but by the anticipation of it.

One of the most arresting features of Canadian imperialist thought was how seldom praise was lavished upon England. True, imperialists extolled the British constitution and political system and gloried in the cultural and historical achievements of the English people, and there were always those who spoke of Canada as an appendage or possession of the old country. But from Canada First down to the World War the customary attitude of Canadian imperialists to England was a curious mixture of affection and anxiety, resentment and solicitude. Charges that Canadian interests had been sacrificed by British diplomacy, quick and indignant responses to manifestations of superciliousness, and apprehensive warnings that the insularity and narrowness of Englishmen were jeopardizing the Empire, ran all through imperialist thought. There was very little of the deferential spirit in the men examined in this study. While they admired many aspects of English society, they neither saw it as an unblemished model nor did they believe that Canada was a pallid transcription of it. Denison was typical of them, though in an exaggerated way, when he went to England to warn of degeneracy and collapse, not to pay homage. They valued the British connection for reasons of power as well as sentiment. Echoing the forebodings of Parkin and Denison, J. S. Willison wrote in 1910 that "Empires as powerful and as affluent have sunk into moral decay, and intellectual barrenness, and physical weakness, and if the British peoples grow careless, if they neglect their defences" and if they continue to be misled by the theories and maxims of free trade, then their own Empire "may shrink into two islands on the Atlantic mourning the power and the glory that have passed."[4] These imperialists believed that a weak or diminished Empire meant the subversion of Canadian nationalism because the imperial system was the vehicle through which she would attain nationhood.

The literature of imperialism was characterized by a profound emotional attachment to Canada. Far from denigrating Canadian things, imperialists were positively utopian in their expectations and it was exactly this overestimation of Canadian capacities which enabled them to believe that their country would become "the future centre and

3 Sir George Foster Papers, vol. 78, MS "Canada, at the Opening Century," (1901), 14.
4 "The True Seed of Britain. An address at the unveiling by Sir John French of the South African memorial shaft in Toronto, May 24th, 1910," *Partners in Peace: The Dominion, the Empire and the Republic, Addresses on Imperial and International Questions by Sir John Willison* (Toronto, 1923), 71.

dominating portion of the British Empire."[5] The only differences among them on this matter were the words and metaphors they used to express it. Stephen Leacock once compared England to an aged and feeble farmer whose sons had arrived at maturity. "The old man's got old and he don't know it," Leacock wrote, "can't kick him off the place, but I reckon that the next time we come together to talk things over, the boys have got to step right in and manage the farm."[6] In one of the most sensitive and perceptive depictions of the Canadian imperialist mentality, Sara Jeannette Duncan's novel, *The Imperialist* (1904), young Lorne Murchison conceived of Canada's future within the Empire in identical terms. Though Lorne thought of Britain as the Mecca of the race, he was repelled by her materialism and parochialism. To him, London seemed "all taken up with inventing new ways of making people more comfortable and better amused"; the city was only "a collection of traditions and great houses." He condemned England's "political concentration upon parish affairs," "cumbrous social machinery," and "problems of sluggish overpopulation." The dream that danced in his imagination was that Canada would inherit the greatness and power of Britain. "England," he said, "has outlived her body. Apart from her heart and her history, England is an area where certain trades are carried on ... In the scrolls of the future it is already written that the centre of the Empire must shift – and where, if not to Canada?"[7] No wonder that Lorne was not understood by his English friend Hesketh, or for that matter, by those Canadians whose support he sought.

The Canadian advocates of imperial unity were still imperialists, however, still attached to those conservative presuppositions which they shared with their counterparts in Great Britain and the United States. Their toryism was more than a political position; it was a total acceptance of assumptions which underlay their admiration for the British constitution and the agricultural economy, their belief that in national and individual affairs the acceptance of duties was more important than requesting privileges, and their insistence on abiding by tradition and precedent. It also affected their critique of American social and political practices, and, sometimes, their appreciation of French-Canadian life and character. From William Kirby's *The U.E.: A Tale of Upper Canada* (1859) to Andrew Macphail's denunciations of the inversion of values on the eve of the World War, the repugnance toward the business calculus and unchecked capitalism permeated the imperialist senti-

5 W. D. Lighthall, *Canada, A Modern Nation* (Montreal, 1904), 78.
6 Quoted in John S. Ewart, "A Perplexed Imperialist," *Queen's Quarterly*, xv (Oct. 1907), 90.
7 Sara Jeannette Duncan, *The Imperialist* (Toronto, 1961), 123, 125, 229.

ment. Those like Denison and Macphail, who felt out of place in a world of capitalism, had matured in a Canada that was predominantly rural and they belonged to professions remote from the business milieu. Their imperialism, particularly their praise of military training as an antidote to social atomization, often seemed little more than an attempt to recapture that society which they remembered and romanticized. The religious idealism of Grant and Parkin was not simply one among many arguments for imperial unity: it was, for them, the most fundamental aspect of imperialism because they were certain that the character of nations and individuals was shaped by obeying the Christian injunction to self-sacrifice and work.

This sense of Canadian nationalism and the commitment to conservatism which shaped it was the essence of Canadian imperialism as these men understood it. Tariff preferences, improved communications, and defence agreements were its instruments and servants, not its substance.

When Canadian imperialism is defined in this way the limitations of its appeal are obvious and its failure almost self-explanatory. It demanded too much of human nature and its conception of national interest was too far out of reach. The imperialists' antipathy to business and their conviction that moral ideals and values must transcend material considerations certainly placed them in opposition to some of the most powerful forces in the Canada of their time. When Denison campaigned against unrestricted reciprocity with the United States he was not primarily interested in safeguarding Canadian industries. He thought that commercial policy undesirable because he felt that any arrangements with the United States would only complicate and possibly delay the coming of intra-imperial free trade. Ironically, he inadvertently worked to protect the very interests which made the realization of imperial unity impossible. Canadian business enterprise was no more willing to remove tariff protection against British manufacturers than against American ones. G. M. Grant realized that Canadian manufacturers were "the most formidable opponents" of imperial free trade: they have, he truly stated, "no intention of sharing their home market, with their British competitors."[8]

Critics of imperial preference correctly saw that it would stultify Canadian industrial growth and prevent a diversification of her economy. "A country would not be great which was only one large rural district, and whose inhabitants were cut off from great intellectual

8 Sir J. S. Willison Papers, Grant to Willison, April 9, 1896; G. M. Grant "Current Events," *Queen's Quarterly*, III (July 1895), 156.

centres," said Adam Shortt in 1903. "Therefore, we could not meet the request that we should curtail our normal development and devote ourselves to supplying food or other raw materials and limit our manufacturing to primary industries."[9] While there is little reason to doubt that Denison welcomed the very prospect that Shortt feared, other imperialists who did not go this far still justified imperial unity by arguments that recognized economic considerations but did not accord priority to them. In a course of extension lectures delivered at Ottawa in 1906, Leacock stressed the "claim of Imperial Unity over purely commercial considerations,"[10] and in 1911 Parkin contemptuously repudiated "the idea that any mere trade relation is going to change our national feeling."[11] They made extensive use of economic arguments but were not themselves driven by economic motives.

However much this emphasis testified to their rectitude, it did little to broaden the support for their cause. In a review of Parkin's *Imperial Federation*, a Winnipeg paper judged that imperialism "is simply an appeal to sacrifice practical advantages in order to gratify a sentiment which does not exist except in the case of a few individuals here and there."[12] A press report described those attending a meeting sponsored by the Imperial Federation League as composed mainly of members of the "comfortable, prosperous classes," as distinct from those "to whom life is an arena of perpetual struggle and toil for the wherewithal to supply the daily wants, and who may therefore be pardoned if they are disposed to take a more intensely practical view of such questions ... "[13] And in Miss Duncan's novel, when Lorne is rejected by his party he is told: "You didn't get rid of that save-the-Empire-or-die scheme of yours soon enough. People got to think you meant something by it." Word got about "that you would not hesitate to put Canada to some material loss, or at least to postpone her development in various important directions, for the sake of the imperial connection."[14]

The very nature of the imperialist ideology ensured that those who accepted it as totally and as seriously as did G. M. Grant and Parkin would always remain a very small number. Many invoked the slogans

9 *Addresses Delivered Before the Canadian Club of Toronto, Season 1903–1904* (Toronto, n.d.), 20.
10 *May Court Club Lectures: McGill University Lectures Six Lectures on the British Empire by Stephen Leacock* (n.p., n.d.), unpaginated.
11 UT, G. M. Wrong Papers, Parkin to Wrong, March 10, 1911.
12 Sir George R. Parkin Papers, vol. 80, clipping from the Winnipeg *Tribune*, Nov. 12, 1892.
13 *Ibid.*, vol. 83, clipping from the *Week*, undated.
14 Duncan, *The Imperialist*, 262.

of imperial unity, but for few did these have such an intense personal meaning. A determined mental effort was required to grasp the inter-relationships and see the geographical reality of the Empire as Parkin did. "I sometimes think that only those who have seen can understand," he admitted, "but to see one must sail on every ocean and traverse every continent."[15] Their European education and world travels made Parkin, Grant, and Macphail very exceptional Canadians and it was with some justice that John Ewart asked, "How can Canadians love the British Empire which they have not seen, when they do not love their own country which they have seen?"[16]

Many factors limited and curtailed the appeal of imperialism: the First World War killed it. Military co-operation between the dominions and Great Britain encouraged some to hope in the early stages of that conflict that permanent means of union would soon be formalized. In 1915 Parkin was certain that "the dreams we have had of national consolidation, and the ends for which we have worked for many years seem nearer their realization than ever."[17] Such expectations quickly vanished as the early enthusiasm for participation in the war changed to disenchantment and disillusionment. By 1918 sixty thousand Canadians were dead in Europe and that fact overshadowed and domi-nated all discussions of Empire, imperialism, and Canadian nationality. It gave an enormous impetus to North American isolationism, and strengthened the suspicions of the old world and of all empires. Mem-bership in the Round Table groups in Canada dwindled in the last two years of the war and in 1920 Andrew Macphail discontinued the *Uni-versity Magazine*, partly because few found his preachments sufficiently interesting. An imperialist who was concerned that Canadians "under-stand their relation to world responsibility" admitted in 1919 that an imperialist campaign would be inopportune and unwise, and concluded that the only alternative to complete isolationism lay in working for the League of Nations.[18] But Canadian foreign policy after 1921 stressed status rather than responsibilities and guarded autonomy against any kind of imperial co-operation. In the 1920s, even the history of the movement for imperial unity came to be regarded as a struggle of sub-servience against autonomy, a conflict noteworthy only to illustrate the follies of the Victorian past and to underline the inevitability of what had come to pass.

The death of the political programme of imperialism is relatively

15 Parkin Papers, vol. 69, MS "The Church in the Empire," n.d.
16 *Report of the Canadian Club of Winnipeg together with the Inaugural Address of the First President, Mr. J. S. Ewart, K. C., 1904–1906* (n.p., n.d.), 17.
17 Parkin Papers, Parkin to Sir Samuel Way, Nov. 18, 1915 (copy).
18 *Ibid.*, A. J. Glazebrook to A. Milner, Nov. 24, 1919 (copy).

easier to date than the destruction of the ideas and sentiments which supported it. No single and decisive event marked the disintegration of the imperial ideal in Canada. Because imperialism fused so many nationalistic attitudes and because it touched upon so many of the permanent Canadian questions, many of its constituent elements survived long after the cause with which they had been allied lost its relevance. The feeling that American society was less stable and ordered than Canadian was far older than the movement for imperial unity and outlived it. The idea that Canada was to function as an interpreter between the United States and Great Britain was also refashioned and reformulated in the 1920s and 1930s. From the point of view of imperialist thought George Parkin Grant's *Lament for a Nation* (1965) appears to be only a depressing footnote. In spite of differences in vocabulary, the nation which this professor of religion mourns bears a close resemblance to the nationality conceived by his ancestors. "My lament," he wrote, "is not based on philosophy but on tradition," – "the older traditions of Canada." There is the same insistence that Canada was once a more variegated country, less "homogenized" than the United States, and the same opinion that the main threat to Canadian nationalism has always come from the south, whereas the British connection had been its source and strength. The charge that the Liberal party of Mackenzie King and the business establishment were mainly responsible for making Canada into a replica and a servant of the United States has all the characteristics of a Denisonian invention. The contention that capitalism, technological progress, and liberalism were the enemies of Canada is only a more sophisticated rendition of the idea that the standards of the counting house were incompatible with nationalism. "Capitalism," Grant explained, "is, after all, a way of life based on the principle that the most important activity is profit-making." Capitalism and liberalism made conservative values irrelevant and "the impossibility of conservatism in our era is the impossibility of Canada."[19]

Imperialism belongs to the remote past but the problems with which it grappled and the state of mind it represented are not totally unrecognizable in the present. The imperialists are excellent examples, not of men who quested for the Canadian identity, but of those who had already found it and who tried to bring reality into alignment with their vision. They are a salutary reminder that our own mental outlook, which seems so coherent and final, so free from extravagance, is unlikely to appear that way to posterity.

19 George Parkin Grant, *Lament for a Nation: The Defeat of Canadian Nationalism* (Toronto, 1965), 4–5, 33, 47, 66–8.

NOTE ON SOURCES

An indiscriminate listing of all items read in the preparation of this study would be pedantic and redundant. The most relevant primary, printed materials have been identified in the footnotes and, in some instances, in the text, but a general indication of the usefulness of certain manuscript collections, periodicals, and secondary works may be of interest to those who want to pursue the subject further.

The richest holdings for this subject in the Public Archives of Canada are the personal papers of G. M. Grant, G. T. Denison, and Sir G. R. Parkin. The last two accumulations are large in bulk and include numerous press clippings relating to the imperial movement as a whole. Allied collections of equal significance and value are the Sir Sandford Fleming, William L. Grant, W. L. and Maude Grant, and Sir John S. Willison papers. The Raleigh Parkin collection consists of one volume of additional material on G. R. Parkin assembled by his son. The Rhodes Trust records (Sir George Parkin, General; Ontario Scholarships; Quebec Scholarships), on microfilm, contain copies of some letters between Parkin and Canadian imperialists on a broader range of subjects than the titles suggest, though the bulk of the correspondence concerns the day-to-day administration of the scheme. The Henry Morgan papers are barren of information on Canada First; those of William Wood are almost exclusively devoted to his conservationist interests; and those of D'Alton McCarthy contain a few letters from G. M. Grant on the Equal Rights movement but are otherwise disappointing on imperial unity. Other accumulations at the Public Archives – the Sir Wilfrid Laurier papers, Sir George Foster papers, and Grey of Howick papers – were used selectively as were the G. M. Wrong papers at the Thomas Fisher Rare Book Library, University of Toronto. The G. M. Grant papers at the Douglas Library, Queen's University, are insignificant, but the Charles Mair papers contain a large number of intimate and revealing letters from Colonel Denison. The G. T. Denison papers in the Baldwin Room, Toronto Public Library, relate mainly to his family, his early life, and the Canada First period. A letter book containing copies of his official correspondence while emigration commissioner in Britain is held by the Province of Ontario Archives. This repository also has the William Kirby papers and William Canniff papers which are helpful for understanding two romantic historians who did so much to popularize the loyalist cult. A collection of newspaper clippings, entitled "Canada First Scrapbook," has been microfilmed by the Canadian Library Association and may be consulted at the Ontario Archives.

In general these collections of personal papers were useful chiefly for interpreting character, personal interrelationships, and intellectual influences. But the essence of the imperialist case was an appeal to popular opinion and it was in the contemporary journals that the doctrine was most readily apprehended. For the purposes of this study, detailed examination of the periodical literature was confined to the years before 1914. The dates following the names of an item indicate the time when it appeared and when publication ceased: in cases where publication continued well beyond 1914, no terminal date is given.

Those periodicals devoted exclusively to the imperial cause are naturally indispensable. These include two British publications – *Imperial Federation: The Journal of the Imperial Federation League* (1886–93), which covered the activities of the movement throughout the Empire; and the *Proceedings of the Royal Colonial Institute* (1869–1909), renamed *United Empire: The Journal of the Royal Colonial Institute*, new series (1909–), which contains many articles and reports of addresses by Canadian members of that organization. In an almost officially imperialist category, at least for the period under review, are the *Empire Club Speeches: Being Addresses Before the Empire Club of Canada* (1903–) and United Empire Loyalist Association of Ontario, *Annual Transactions* (1898–1912), which continue after 1912 under the auspices of the United Empire Loyalist Association of Canada. Of special significance for the militaristic side of imperialism are: Canadian Military Institute, *Selected Papers*, (1890–); *Canadian Military Gazette* (1892–); *Canadian Field: Official Journal of the Canadian Defence League* (1911–12), renamed *Canadian Defence: Official Journal of the Canadian Defence League* (1912–). *The Round Table: A Quarterly Review of the Politics of the British Empire* appeared in London, England, in 1909, and was of relatively minor importance for an investigation of imperial thought in the preceding half century.

Reviews and journals of discussion carried many articles, both favourable and critical, bearing on imperial unity. The most fruitful sources of these are: The *Nation* (1874–76), the *Canadian Monthly and National Review* (1872–78), renamed *Rose-Belford's Canadian Monthly and National Review* (1878–82); the *Week* (1883–96);

the *Canadian Methodist Magazine* (1875–88); renamed *Methodist Magazine and review* (1888–1906); the *Canadian Magazine of Politics, Science, Art and Literature* (1892–); *Queen's Quarterly* (1893–); the *University Magazine* (1907–20). The publications of the Canadian Clubs of Toronto and Ottawa – *Addresses Delivered Before the Canadian Club of Toronto* (1903–) and *Addresses Delivered Before the Canadian Club of Ottawa* (1903–), both of which appeared under slightly altered titles over the years – are of exceptional interest, not only for imperialism as such, but also for nearly all facets of national affairs in the period before the World War.

Aspects of Canadian imperialism which were only touched upon in this study have been dealt with in several recent works. Apart from the monograph by Penlington mentioned in the Introduction, the most relevant of these are: D. M. L. Farr, *The Colonial Office and Canada, 1867–1887* (Toronto, 1955); R. C. Brown, *Canada's National Policy, 1883–1900: A Study in Canadian-American Relations* (Princeton, 1964), chapter v; D. C. Gordon, *The Dominion Partnership in Imperial Defense, 1870–1914* (Baltimore, 1965); and R. Preston, *Canada and "Imperial Defense": A study of the origins of the British Commonwealth's defense organization, 1867–1919* (Toronto, 1967). N. Shrive, *Charles Mair: Literary Nationalist* (Toronto, 1965) describes the association of Denison and Mair at considerable length and explores the role of Canada First in the Red River insurrection in more detail than that aspect of its existence received here. G. R. MacLean, "The Imperial Federation Movement in Canada, 1884–1902" (PH.D thesis, Duke University, 1958), though completed before several crucial manuscript collections became available, is a useful factual record of the work of the League in Canada and is especially informative on the imperialists' conception of leadership. *Sir George Parkin: A Biography* (London, 1929) by Sir J. S. Willison and *Principal Grant* (Toronto, 1904) by W. L. Grant and C. F. Hamilton provided personal detail, but both books were written by men who shared the general outlook of their subjects and are generally uncritical.

Imperialism as a concept and body of thought has been subjected to many examinations, some of which were useful for comparative purposes. The discussions of British and American imperialism to which I am most indebted are: C. A. Bodelsen, *Studies in Mid-Victorian Imperialism* (London, 1924); W. L. Langer, *The Diplomacy of Imperialism* (New York, 1951), chapter III; A. P. Thornton, *The Imperial Idea and its Enemies: A Study in British Power* (London, 1959); B. Semmel, *Imperialism and Social Reform: English Social-Imperial Thought,*

1895–1914 (London, 1960); E. Stokes, *The Political Ideas of English Imperialism: An Inaugural Lecture Given in the University College of Rhodesia and Nyasaland* (London, 1960); R. Faber, *The Vision and the Need: Late Victorian Imperialist Aims* (London, 1966); R. E. Osgood, *Ideals and Self-Interest in America's Foreign Relations: The Great Transformation in the Twentieth Century* (Chicago, 1953); and R. Hofstadter, "Manifest Destiny and the Philippines," in T. P. Greene, ed., *American Imperialism in 1898* (Boston, 1955), 54–70.

Index

274INDEX

Imperialism, Canadian: definition and meaning of, 3, 12, 49, 107–8, 259–62; origins of, 3–4; support for, 5, 78, 84–9, 134, 135, 237–8, 268; interpretations of, 5–9; special character of, in Maritimes, 23–4, 154–5; weaknesses and failure of, 262–4
ideas of: view of Canadian national character as "northern," 53, 62–3, 128–33; image of French Canadians, 58–9, 131–2, 134–47; view of US as hostile, 60–1, 165–70; concept of imperial federation as alliance of nations, 60–6, 70–1; impossibility of Canadian independence outside imperial system, 60–6, 169–70; views of immigration, 66–8, 147–51; critique of party government ("partyism"), 68–9, 199–207; views of the Canadian past, 89–107, 109–19; view of imperial association as climax to development of Canadian self-government, 119–23, 127; rejection of plans for imperial federation, 123–6; idealization of agricultural life, 141–2, 177–82, 191–3; critique of American government and society, 155–62; views of American "race problems," 162–5; ideal of Anglo-American understanding and cooperation, 170–3, 229–30; social gospel of G. M. Grant, 183–6; Parkin on health of society, 186–9; social criticism, 189–98; élitist conception of leadership, 207–16; concept of imperial mission, 217–32 passim; views of war, 235–6, 239–51; justifications for military training, 251–7; see also Democracy, Determinism, Geopolitics, Population of Canada, Preferential trade, Progress, Racism, Social Darwinism, United Empire Loyalist tradition, Work
major spokesmen for: see Bourinot, Sir J. G.; Denison, G. T.; Grant, G. M.; Grant, W. L.; Leacock, S. B.; Macphail, Sir A.; Parkin, Sir, G. R.
Innis, Harold A., on Leacock's imperialism, 43
Isolationism, 240–1

Jesuit Estates Act, 134; G. M. Grant on agitation over, 136

Kidd, Benjamin, on social evolution, 187
King, W. L. M., on "undefended border," 241–2
Kingsmill, George, 59
Kipling, Rudyard, 20, 252–3
Kirby, William, 66, 95, 141; on UELs, 92–3, 99; on Indians, 163; on agricultural society, 178–9

Lampman, Archibald, on politicians, 200
Laurier, Sir Wilfrid, 5, 234; on future size of Canada's population, 114; on British sacrifices of Canadian interests, 122
Lavergne, Armand, on French-Canadian loyalty, 139
Lea, Homer, 235
Leacock, Stephen Butler, 10, 39, 42, 47, 48, 174, 221, 259, 261, 263; on Parkin, 39; life and character of, 43–4; H. A. Innis on, 43; social satire of, 44; on modern scholarship, 44–5; Lord Grey on, 46; on Macphail, 46, 47; on future size of Canadian population, 114; on responsible government and imperial unity, 120; on Canadian representation in imperial Parliament, 126; on immigrants, 151; on Monroe doctrine, 170; on business standards, 195–6; on politicians, 202–3; on democracy, 206; on university, 209
Leadership, imperialists' concept of, 207–16; see also Public school
Le Moine, Sir James, 95
Le Sueur, William; on loyalty, 83–4; on weaknesses of democracy, 205
Liberalism, as source of anti-militarism, 240–5
Liberty, progress of, in Canadian history, 115
Lighthall, William D., 196
Lindsey, Charles, 73
Little Englandism, 60
Local historical societies, and patriotic history, 96–7
Lodge, Senator Henry Cabot, 229